Outrageous
Fortune

For Frank, Miriam and Tom —
inspiration, conscience and brother

Outrageous Fortune

*What's Wrong with Hall of Fame
Voting and How to Make It
Statistically Sound*

JAMES F. VAIL

McFarland & Company, Inc., Publishers
Jefferson, North Carolina, and London

ALSO BY JAMES F. VAIL

The Road to Cooperstown:
A Critical History of Baseball's
Hall of Fame Selection Process
(McFarland, 2001)

Library of Congress Cataloguing-in-Publication Data

Vail, James F., 1948–
    Outrageous fortune : what's wrong with Hall of Fame voting
and how to make it statistically sound / James F. Vail.
        p.   cm.
    Includes bibliographical references and index.
    ISBN 0-7864-1126-0 (softcover binding : 50# alkaline paper) ∞
    1. National Baseball Hall of Fame and Museum.   2. Baseball —
United States — History.   I. Title
    GV863.A1V34   2002
    796.357'64'07474774 — dc21   2001044841

British Library cataloguing data are available

Manufactured in the United States of America

McFarland & Company, Inc., Publishers
    Box 611, Jefferson, North Carolina 28640
    www.mcfarlandpub.com

Contents

Introduction

The impetus for this book can be traced to the summer of 1960 and the publication of Fleer's first-ever set of Baseball Greats trading cards. Like many 11-year-old boys of the time, I was an avid card collector; and, after several summers of buying and trading the dominant Topps cards, which included only players active at the time, the competing Fleer version, which featured old timers I had read about but had rarely seen photos of, offered several opportunities which had not been available until then.

First, the set was a small one (only seventy-nine cards in all), which made it a lot easier — within the practical confines of my weekly allowance — to acquire them all, and alleviated the frustration of the previous year, when I had fallen about a half-dozen shy of collecting the entire 572-card Topps set (including a much-coveted Frank Robinson, #435). Second, the set included 42 of the 66 men who were elected to the baseball Hall of Fame as players through 1960, which meant that — along with Hank Aaron, Willie Mays, Ernie Banks and other current stars available among the Topps cards I'd collected — one could construct some pretty nifty all-star teams to battle it out on the bedroom floor using dice and a pre-arranged list of outcomes for each roll ("snake eyes" was a strikeout, "box cars" a homer). But, most important, the cards provided a vehicle for vital communication with my father.

Frank Raymond Vail was born on a farm near Kirksville, Missouri, on 20 December 1900, the same date that Hall-of-Fame catcher Gabby Hartnett entered life at Woonsocket, Rhode Island. His professional careers included those of heavyweight boxer, baseball pitcher, Golden Gloves coach and history teacher before he died a few weeks after I graduated from elementary school in 1962.

Like Hartnett, my father's sports career began at the start of the Roaring Twenties. But unlike Gabby, whose statistics are easily found, any record of my father's athletic career is lost, and always has been unavailable to me (or anyone else), because — in a habit common to the values of his era in the aftermath of Jim Thorpe's Olympic-medal experience of 1912 — he boxed and played baseball under assumed names in order to protect his treasured amateur status. Unfortunately, he never told me any of the pseudonyms he used; and he died long before I had acquired any research skills adequate to uncover his record, if I had known those names. So, the only evidence I have of his athletic achievements are some yellowed old photos and sketchy memories of the stories he told during my childhood.

I was told that he played baseball across the western United States, from California to Colorado; and I have a precious few photos of him in the uniforms of teams which I can't identify — no doubt the town or industrial clubs that flourished almost everywhere in America back then. I was told that he once struck out Babe Ruth — hardly an uncommon feat, but nonetheless impressive to a little boy — during one of the Bambino's barnstorming trips, but was never informed of the date, location, or what the Babe had done in his other at-bats against my dad, if there were any. I also was told that he pitched professionally for several teams, including Denver, in the then–Class–A Western League, during the early 1920s. But again, I don't know what pseudonym he used; the names I've seen of pitchers on the Denver rosters for those seasons aren't even vaguely familiar to me; and I can't prove to myself or anyone else that he ever actually played there.

Nonetheless, my father claimed that his Denver contract was purchased by the Detroit Tigers, when Ty Cobb was their manager (probably around 1923–24). Although he was almost as impressed by Willie Mays, to his dying day my dad regarded Cobb, with whom he shared a middle name, as the greatest all-around player ever — an opinion which required an amazing amount of objectivity considering what supposedly transpired next. Cobb was a notorious racist; and there are numerous documented incidents in which he verbally or physically abused Afro-Americans for no apparent reason but hate-induced sadism. On his first day in Detroit, my father said that he saw the Georgia Peach go into just such a tirade against a black man outside of then–Navin Field. In northern Missouri, my dad's Scottish-American family had sided with the Union during the Civil War, and he did not tolerate racism in any form. Unable to abide by Cobb's behavior, and apparently too idealistic (or naive) to project the likely consequence, he immediately exchanged heated words with the baseball legend. The next thing he knew, Detroit had released him and he was leaving the Motor City without ever having been given a chance to pitch, even in batting practice.

The story is somewhat traceable, as even without a name to go by, I could easily learn whether or not the Tigers acquired the contract of any Western League player during those seasons, and check on whether or not one was released or shipped back to the minors almost immediately. But the tale might also have been nothing more than some blarney concocted by a baseball never-quite-was who took to drink in his later years to self-medicate his asthma and emphysema, and who just wanted to impress his son. Either way, the story rings true of both men's personalities. And if it is a lie, I don't think I'd ever want to know.

My dad was 47 when I was born, and he was almost sixty by the time I was old enough to play kids' baseball, when his breathing problems made it difficult for him to teach me much about the game by anything but word of mouth. In that light, it's impossible to overemphasize the degree to which the initial impulse for this book formed in my eleven-year-old mind as I perused the sparse biographical and statistical details on the backs of those Fleer trading cards and then peppered my father with questions: "Who was better, Dad, Cobb or Ruth?" "Who was the best shortstop you ever saw?" "Who was the all-time best player at each position?"

He answered those questions as thoroughly as his patience (or hangover) would allow. It's impossible to know how objective his answers were, because like every baseball fan — and arguably to a greater degree, then, before basketball and football softened our devotion — his judgments about players' relative skills were shaped by his own prejudices regarding what constituted talent, the players' styles and personalities, and even the teams for which they played. But, for the brief period in which I got to ask him my questions, the method of his preferences became clear to me; and, looking back, it was remarkably consistent with the philosophy that was prevalent in baseball during the early part of this century, when my dad began to play it in earnest.

Above all else, my father valued the skills of men who could play "inside" baseball, as it was called back then: guys who could field their positions, run the basepaths, bunt, foul off pitches to work the count, hit behind the baserunners, get on base consistently, and — most important — play the game intelligently. In practical terms, this meant that he admired players with high batting averages and solid fielding skills above one-dimensional power hitters, and preferred players whose intelligence showed above raw talent. As a former boxer and long-time coach, he also was adamant about conditioning — so the only players I ever heard him disparage were ones he perceived as out of shape, or mentally or physically lazy. With the possible exception of Mays, he didn't like "showboats," because he perceived the behavior as a sign that they didn't take the game seriously. But he could also admire cockiness as a sign of self-confidence — provided that the player's performance consistently justified it. Finally, as a Missouri native, he was a Cardinals fan first, a National League fan second, and he despised the Yankees with a passion (and, predictably, so do I).

As a result of all this, it's not surprising that my father considered John McGraw, the old Baltimore third baseman, the greatest manager ever. And he always rated Cobb above Ruth — making it clear that the judgment was based on his perception that, despite Babe's pitching and slugging ability, Tyrus could perform more things with excellence on a ball field, especially run. He invariably preferred George Sisler over Lou Gehrig as the game's best first baseman, because he felt Sisler's fielding was in a class by itself; and (although he never said it) I always had the sense that Sisler was really his favorite player ever.

Like most baseball fans, my father's all-time team consisted entirely of men from his own era. But despite his prejudices, he was still objective enough to name two Yankees to a lineup that, surprisingly, featured no Cardinals whatsoever. The team included Walter Johnson and Carl Hubbell, pitchers; Bill Dickey, catcher; George Sisler, first base; Charlie Gehringer, second base; Joe Cronin, shortstop; Pie Traynor or Red Rolfe, third base; and Cobb, Tris Speaker and Paul Waner, outfield. Only one of those men is the statistical leader for his position in this book, but it's not a bad lineup, even without Babe Ruth.

This book, along with one previously published by McFarland (*The Road to Cooperstown: A Critical History of Baseball's Hall of Fame Selection Process*), is the ultimate result of those discussions. Originally, the two were conceived and written as one volume, with the historical critique of Hall-of-Fame voting making up the first half of the original manuscript and providing the logical justification for the method applied herein (the first two chapters of this work are distillations of that criticism). The resulting manuscript grew so large that two separate books were necessary.

I am grateful to my mother, Miriam, and my wife, Patti. Arguing is something I was born to, I think; but if I have any skill for setting my arguments down on paper, and without brutalizing them, it came mostly from the former. The latter has shown amazing patience during the writing of this work, and I am eternally grateful for the love and consideration she has provided during the process.

Beyond all that, I would like to thank Pete Palmer, with whom I have had the sincere pleasure to become acquainted, and Bill James, whom I have not met. Anyone who has tinkered with baseball statistics on any serious level since the late 1970s owes a debt of gratitude to both men for their roles in advancing the application of statistical science to baseball and for demonstrating that intelligent statistical commentary can find both a publisher and an audience. Thanks also to archivist Steve Gietschier and *The Sporting News* for their assistance in locating and providing the photos included in the text, and to Bruce Koon, for his generous contribution to their acquisition. Finally, I owe a note of appreciation to friends like Tom Crooks, Frank Domiano, Allen A. Gwinnell and Lawr Michaels, for helping me to keep my goal in its proper perspective, and to our cat Romeo, who always told me when I had been working far too long.

CHAPTER 1

Subjectivity versus Statistics

Through the 2000 voting, and excluding its media representatives, 249 men had been chosen for membership in the baseball Hall of Fame (HOF) at Cooperstown, New York. The roster included 185 men selected for their on-field performance as major-league players, 16 managers, 17 team or league executives, eight umpires, six pioneer contributors to the game, and 17 others chosen for their roles in the Negro leagues which gradually disbanded after Jackie Robinson joined the Brooklyn Dodgers in 1947.

For most baseball fans Cooperstown is a sacrosanct place, known to many as the "Shrine." But reverence for the institution takes two forms. Most of baseball's more casual followers perceive that election to the Hall is face-value proof of a man's stature among the true greats of the game, and they have little reason to question the legitimacy of anyone's membership. But, to the sport's most ardent and knowledgeable fans, Hall-of-Fame membership is akin to Roman Catholic sainthood. For many of these faithful, the HOF roster has been tainted over the years by the elections of men they perceive as undeserving of the honor, and by the continued omissions of other players who may be better qualified.

If errors exist in the Cooperstown roster, there is little doubt that they have resulted because the Hall-of-Fame selection process is almost entirely subjective. To date, the only measurable criteria applied to HOF election is a requirement that the candidate have at least 10 years of major-league service in the capacity for which he is elected (i.e., as player, manager, umpire, etc.), and even that proviso was waived on one occasion — the 1978 enshrinement, at the urging of commissioner Bowie Kuhn, of pitcher Addie Joss, who played in only nine big-league seasons before his premature death at age 31. Beyond that, the only other guidelines ever applied to Hall-of-Fame election have been (1) a vague dictum, enacted in 1945, equating HOF qualification with undefined terms like "playing ability," "sportsmanship" and "character," (2) a 1991 ruling that men placed on baseball's ineligible list for gambling or other indiscretions cannot be considered for membership, and (3) a series of changes in the voting rules which, over the years, have redefined a candidate's period of eligibility for election.

But the terms in the 1945 guideline do nothing to define a Hall of Famer with any specificity, and they undoubtedly hold widely different meanings for the roughly 500 members of the Baseball Writers Association of America (BBWAA) and the 15-man Veterans Committee which serve as Cooperstown's two elective bodies. Also, the 1991 ruling was enacted solely for the purpose of keeping Pete Rose, a certain electee banned from baseball for his alleged betting on ballgames, off of the writers' ballot. And, sadly, rather than inject greater fairness into the process, many of the eligibility refinements have been little more than poorly disguised efforts to assure that at least one man is elected each year (so that the Cooperstown museum, whose financial success is largely dependent on how many fans attend the annual induction ceremony, can turn a profit). As a result, except for the 10-year service requirement, the standards that define a Hall of Famer are now, and always have been, dependent entirely on the collective, but fallible "wisdom" manifest among the subjective biases of Cooperstown's individual voters.

The absence of any meaningful objective criteria for baseball's highest honor is incongruous with the game's overall fixation on its statistics. Indeed, without its statistics, baseball might not have evolved into the professional sport that Cooperstown celebrates. The game has been dominated by its numbers ever since journalist and HOF member Henry Chadwick devised the precursor to batting average and refined the rudimentary box score during the mid–1800s. Chadwick's innovations, published in newspapers, helped stimulate interest in the game and the demand for high-caliber, professional play. In turn, the first team composed entirely of paid players appeared in 1869, followed two years later by the National Association (NA), the game's first organized pro circuit and forerunner to the still-existent National League (NL)—which in 1876 became the first league recognized as having "major" status. Other short-lived circuits with equal rank followed in 1882, 1884 and 1890, before the American League (AL) became the NL's permanent competitor in 1901. Each step of that evolution brought expanded public interest in the game, increased amounts of newspaper space devoted to baseball and its numbers (league standings, box scores, and lists of statistical leaders), added attendance and higher revenues.

The availability of individual statistics met the fiscal needs of players and owners alike, for (although neither group had a truly active role in determining the form of the numbers used) both have regularly applied them as bargaining tools in contract negotiation. Eventually, the socio-cultural linkage between professional baseball's statistics, popularity and finance was cemented in 1930 when Babe Ruth publicly justified his then-unheard-of $80,000 salary (more than President Herbert Hoover was making at the time) by arguing that, with his 49 homers and 136 RBI, he'd "had a better year" than America's depression-beleaguered chief executive.

No other sport generates as many player statistics as baseball. By and large, basketball aficionados are adequately served by lists of individual leaders in points scored, assists, rebounds, blocked shots and steals per game; football fans, by the leaders in scoring, rushing, passing, receptions, interceptions and punting. But, baseball produces, and its followers demand, a multitude of categories delineating individual-performance leadership: games played, at-bats, hits, doubles, triples, home runs, total bases, runs scored, runs batted in, stolen bases, walks, batting and slugging averages for hitters; putouts, assists, errors, double plays, total chances per game and fielding average for defensive players at each position; and games pitched, games won, games lost, winning percentage, earned run average, innings pitched, hits allowed, walks allowed and strikeouts for pitchers. And those are just some of the traditional statistics in use for much of major-league history; there are many more. Baseball has generated literally dozens more measures of individual player performance than any other sport.

Finally, no other game imprints its statistics on the American consciousness as deeply as baseball does. Although Kareem Abdul-Jabbar and the late Walter Payton are the all-time scoring and rushing leaders for the National Basketball Association and National Football League, respectively, many fans of those sports would be hard-pressed to cite exactly how many points Abdul-Jabbar scored or how many yards Payton gained during their pro careers. In contrast, even before Mark McGwire and Sammy Sosa made home-run headlines in 1998, many people who were not serious baseball fans could've told you that Babe Ruth hit 714 homers in his career, Hank Aaron 755, or Roger Maris sixty-one in 1961. Along with McGwire's 70 dingers in 1998, those magic numbers have legendary identities that stand alone as revered parts of American cultural history.

Because of all that, it's predictable that no discussion about the relative skills of various baseball players — whether verbal or written, whether by Hall-of-Fame electors or two fans sitting in front of a television at a sports bar — can possibly be conducted without some reference to the statistical achievements of the men in question. And it follows that no man (not even Babe Ruth) has ever been elected to Cooperstown for his performance as a major-league player whose selection was not based on some element of his career statistics.

Despite all that, there is (and always has been) considerable resistance to adoption of any formal statistical criteria for Hall-of-Fame election. In part, that stems from a notion, rooted in the romance of baseball, that "greatness" supersedes the ability to measure it statistically, and is subjectively recognizable to anyone sufficiently knowledgeable about the game. So, individual fans and Hall-of-Fame electors alike are prideful about their evaluations of players' skills, and — although willing — willing to cite any statistic that supports their opinion about a player's ability — they are loath to acknowledge data that subverts or contradicts those impressions.

Beyond that subjective arrogance, however, there are some valid reasons to oppose any absolute numerical standards for Hall-of-Fame selection. Baseball's norms for individual performance are inevitably subject to changes in rules and playing conditions, and they do in fact vary considerably over time. A .300 career batting average, often perceived as a hallmark of excellence in any era, actually has much greater relative significance if compiled during a period when pitching dominated (e.g., the dead-ball era of 1901–19, or the 1960s) than if achieved in an era in which hitters reigned (e.g., from 1920 to 1945 when the introduction of livelier baseballs inflated batting averages across both leagues). Conversely, a dead-ball pitcher with a career earned run average of 2.50 may be run-of-the-mill for his era, while a hurler with the same stat may rank among the very best of the 1930s. As a result, the validity of using absolute numbers to compare the performance of players from different eras is negated by the variations in normal performance over time. The same ebb and flow disallows the adoption of minimum statistical standards for enshrinement, because they might eventually cheapen the honor of Cooperstown membership. In turn, any use of statistics for cross-generational comparisons must somehow account for and neutralize these differences to be valid.

But, given the importance of career statistics to a man's Hall-of-Fame credentials, and in the absence of formal numerical guidelines, the HOF selection process has inevitably become a prisoner of de facto standards for election. Every knowledgeable fan knows that 300 wins for pitchers and either 3000 hits or 500 home runs for batters have become marks that guarantee entry to Cooperstown. Yet, because of their continued insistence upon the application of subjective evaluation, neither the Hall-of-Fame trustees nor the electors publicly acknowledge that these de facto standards exist. All the same, through the 2000 voting, every player who had achieved at least one of those milestones was enshrined at Cooperstown. And, over time, their first-ballot elections by the BBWAA have become common.

Unfortunately, because they are based on the cumulative achievement, the existing de facto standards create the same problems for Hall-of-Fame selection as would the adoption of any formal, minimum statistical criteria. The possibility always exists that some player with above-average but not truly great ability will reach or surpass one of those standards by the grace of longevity and slip into Cooperstown based on accomplishments that are less significant than those of others with shorter careers. Also, by fixing the voters' attentions on one, essentially arbitrary level of career achievement, de facto standards have a detrimental impact on the selection process. In the long run, achievement of a de facto criterion overshadows any and all negative aspects of a player's candidacy. At the same time, failure to reach such a standard comparatively demeans the candidacies of other players whose (probably shorter-term) accomplishments may merit far more consideration than they receive. Overall, in a process dominated by subjective evaluation, any standard based merely on cumulative numbers (whether formal or de facto) must inevitably compromise the voters' abilities to place a player's credentials in an appropriate relative context.

The result of all this is a Cooperstown roster that includes Tommy McCarthy, Chick Hafey, Fred Lindstrom, Ted Lyons and Jesse Haines — men whom many knowledgeable fans believe unworthy of the same recognition merited by Babe Ruth, Hank Aaron and Walter Johnson. At the same time, the roster does not include many well-known players (Spud Chandler, Joe Gordon, Bobby Grich, Roger Maris, Carl Mays, Ron Santo, Ted Simmons, Vern Stephens, Maury Wills, and Darrell and Dwight Evans, for instance) and a handful of more obscure ones (e.g., Harlond Clift and Harry Stovey) whose skills and relative credentials may be superior to those of McCarthy, Hafey, Lindstrom, Lyons, Haines and others among the current Cooperstown roster.

Belief that the Hall-of-Fame roster is flawed was evident in numerous books published during the last two decades, each of which used different methods to produce either rankings of the greatest baseball players in history, or arguments why various unenshrined players should be inducted. But generally, these efforts either relied on subjective criteria, or (if they attempted any statistical analysis) were limited in scope to baseball's traditional set of statistical data. So, the most innovative of such works have been authored by practitioners of sabermetrics, a new realm of statistical analysis whose name derives from the Society for American Baseball Research (SABR, hence sabermetrics), a group founded in 1971 that now includes about 6,000 of baseball's most ardent fans. The impetus for sabermetrics was a realization among the game's most mathematically astute followers that baseball's traditional player-performance measures have failed to provide adequate data about the comparative value of various types of individual achievement, and — in that failure — have contributed to errors among Cooperstown's roster.

Some new statistics developed by sabermetricians or their pre-SABR counterparts — notably saves (SV) by relief pitchers and on-base average (OBA) for batters — have been recognized for their enhancement of the wealth of numbers already available to measure performance, and been adopted officially by Major League Baseball. Saves were created by *Chicago Sun-Times* sportswriter Jerome Holtzman (now a member of the Hall of Fame's Veterans Committee) in the late 1950s, and on-base average was first used by the team of statistician Allen Roth and big-league executive Branch Rickey during the same decade. But, recognition of these new stats has been slow coming. Saves were not officially adopted until 1969, and on-base average was not added to baseball's accepted measures until 1984. Other sabermetric tools have been even slower gaining formal acceptance, although some — like the ratio of baserunners (RAT) and the number of strikeouts-per-nine-innings (SO/9) for pitchers — have been added to the data regularly provided by some baseball periodicals such as *The Sporting News* and *USA Today*'s *Baseball Weekly*.

Generally, the most widely read and influential sabermetric works have been those written by either Bill James or the team of Pete Palmer and John Thorn. James gained attention with his series of annual *Baseball Abstracts* (1977–88), in which — among much else — he identified a difference between the value of a player's peak and career performance (e.g., the moment of Roger Maris's 1961 season, clearly the high point of his major-league tenure, was far more statistically impressive than the sum of his career achievements), and introduced a totally objective method of performance measurement, Runs Created (RC), which initially combined the incidence of a player's hits, walks, total bases and at-bats into an estimate of their overall run value. Aware of his readers' fixation on the issue of Hall-of-Fame credentials, in 1985 James also published a *Historical Baseball Abstract*, in which he provided a broad-ranging, decade-by-decade overview of major-league history that concluded with statistical analysis of the HOF credentials of about two hundred of the game's best players. A decade later he followed up with *The Politics of Glory: How Baseball's Hall of Fame Really Works*, which was less statistically oriented, and delved primarily into the human foibles that dominate the Cooperstown election process.

Palmer and Thorn's first major work, *The Hidden Game of Baseball: A Revolutionary Approach to Baseball and Its Statistics*, was published in 1984. Using a system called linear weights, the authors devised an innovative set of statistics called Batting and Pitching Runs (BR and PR, respectively), derived from calculations of the run-producing (or run-preventing) values for various batting and pitching events, that produced seasonal and career totals for each player's overall achievement, leading to an ordered, objective ranking of their performance value. By 1988, in cooperation with numerous other SABR researchers, Thorn and Palmer also had published the first edition of *Total Baseball*, an exhaustive encyclopedia of major-league history and statistics in which a related formula for Fielding Runs (FR) was added to produce a Total Player Rating (TPR) measuring complete seasonal and career values for each man who has appeared in the majors since 1876. At first, the book was a revisionist alternative to *The Baseball Encyclopedia*, published by Macmillan, which had served since 1969 as the sport's official source of seasonal and career records. By 1994, with publication of *Total Baseball*'s fifth edition, the tome had supplanted the Macmillan work as Major League Baseball's official record.

The slow recognition of sabermetric tools derives, in part, from the inherent conservatism natural to appreciation for the game's traditions. Most of the statistics familiar to baseball fans, players and Cooperstown electors have been in use for at least a century (a few since the formation of professional leagues in the 1870s), and the emergence of a large set of new data threatens many people's comfortable familiarity with some of the game's most cherished trappings.

But, the reluctance to embrace some sabermetric tools (including several that are among the best-suited for measuring relative Hall-of-Fame credentials) also stems from the fact that many of them require more conceptual thought about the run-producing relationships between various on-field events, or more understanding and application of algebraic calculation than most baseball fans or Cooperstown electors care to apply. It's easy to understand the simple relationships inherent in a batting average (hits divided by times at bat) or even a pitcher's ERA (earned runs allowed times nine, divided by innings pitched). But comprehending a stat derived from a complicated-looking equation using multiple parenthetical factors is an entirely different matter. As a result, many of these new statistics are not especially "fan friendly," despite the best efforts of their creators to keep them relatively simple and to thoroughly explain them. So, even many SABR members (far more of whom are fans than mathematicians) are confused or irritated by the complexity of a formula like that used to calculate Palmer and Thorn's Batter Runs: $BR = (.47)1B + (.78)2B + (1.09)3B + (1.40)HR + (.33)(BB + HB) - (.25)(AB - H) - (.50)OOB$. After all, they want to talk baseball, not feel as though they've time-warped back to their high school algebra class.

Although individual baseball performance has always been quantified far more than in any other sport, there are unavoidable gaps and quirks in its statistical records. Some of these occurred because of years when certain statistics were not kept (runs batted in are generally not available for the major-league American Association during the years 1882–88), and others resulted because the sport's evolution precluded any need for them prior to a specific rule change (stolen bases, for instance, were not permitted during the first decade of big-league play) or because a rule change was reversed repeatedly (the sacrifice-fly rule was adopted in 1908, discarded in 1931 and brought back in 1954). Any measure that attempts to be comprehensive must suffer from, and be further complicated by these inconsistencies — as evidenced by that fact that Bill James eventually had to devise fourteen separate formulas to calculate his Runs Created measure, each of them adapted to fit the availability of various statistics from specific periods of major-league play. So, although some sabermetric tools provide a far more accurate measure of career achievement than any of the sport's traditional statistics, their validity as all-encompassing measures is limited, and in some ways compromised by these inconsistencies in the statistical record. And because of the missing data, the creation of a single, comprehensive and definitive measure of player performance is likely to remain the sabermetricians' Holy Grail.

Despite all of these factors, the creation of valid, objective criteria for Hall-of-Fame election and membership — comprehensive, yet friendly to fans who do not possess the mathematical skills and contemplative temperament of a Bertrand Russell — is not beyond the reach of statistical science. Such a creation requires the avoidance of any emphasis on absolute standards in favor of a focus on a player's career achievements *relative* to those of all other candidates. One can then determine. (1) whether a player rates among the best players of all time; (2) whether he ranks among the best-ever players at his position; or (3) whether he was one of the very best players of his era.

The method of this comparison is a statistical tool called the Z Score, which measures the distance (in standard deviations) that a man's career performance is above or below the average of a group of players for a particular statistic. The score is calculated by subtracting the mean (i.e., average) for the group from the player's individual performance number, and then dividing the result by the standard deviation of the group as a whole. The beauty of the Z Score is that comprehension of the result requires no special fluency in statistical science — or, even any thorough understanding of that dreaded term "standard deviation." Instead, one need only recognize that the result represents a position along a number line, like the one shown below, whose center (zero) is average for the group measured, and whose positive and negative extremes reflect scores that are progressively better or worse than that average.

Positive Score		Negative Score
(+4) — (+3) — (+2) — (+1) —	(0) —	(–1) — (–2) — (–3) — (–4)
Above Average	Average	Below Average

Clearly a positive number indicates that the player's performance is above average, a negative number that it is subpar, and a score of zero that it is exactly average for the group. So, the larger the positive number, the more significant the individual performance; conversely, the larger the negative number, the less impressive the result. By mathematically comparing the player's performance to the mean for the group, the Z Score provides a measure of the value of that performance relative to the group as a whole.

The Z-Score measurement also provides a context for valid cross-generational comparisons of players' career achievements. For example, through 1994 (the last year in which a player could be active in the major leagues and still be eligible for Cooperstown election by 2000), Hall of Famers Stan Musial and Willie Stargell were tied for 16th place on the list of all-time leaders with 475 home runs each. Both men were primarily left fielders and were cited as such upon election, although each played frequently at first base during the latter years of their careers. Compared to all other Hall-of-Fame non-pitchers (+3.93) and to men who played left field (+3.42), their individual Z Scores for career home runs are identical, because their totals are compared to the same, yet separate home-run distributions in each measure. But, Musial's career (1941–63) spanned baseball's postwar era (1946–60), whereas most of Stargell's (1962–82) fell within the game's Expansion period (1961–75); and Stan's Z Score for his time (+3.69) is significantly higher than Willie's is for his era (+2.94). Musial's advantage over Stargell, then, stems from Stan's playing during a period when fewer men achieved a high number of career home runs. So, although their career totals are identical, Musial's represents a greater accomplishment in the context of his time.

The Z-Score calculation can be applied to every statistic relevant to Hall-of-Fame election — in separate subsets that compare a player's performance to those of all eligible candidates as a whole, to men who played the same position, and to men from the same era — providing measures of each player's achievement in the separate contexts of the criteria most significant to his prospects for selection. The resulting scores can then be averaged to produce a single number representing a summation of a given player's career performance compared to every other candidate, allowing for an ordered, objective ranking of each man's relative statistical credentials for Cooperstown. In the process, the distribution of the Z-Score averages also produces a bottom line, or "Cooperstown Baseline," indicative of the minimum level of relative performance needed to validate a man's election.

This book performs that process on a very large scale, identifying the most-qualified Hall-of-Fame candidates, statistically, among players from each of major-league baseball's historical eras, among players at each position, and among all eligible candidates as a whole, leading to a final ranking that represents the cumulative result of all three scales combined. In a similar fashion, it will also identify which managers and players from the Negro leagues are best-qualified for baseball's shrine. In the process, it will demonstrate that a fair and objective measurement of Hall-of-Fame credentials is not only possible, but also vital to the elimination of errors among the Cooperstown roster; and it will suggest a simple means by which those errors can be reduced in a manner that preserves the subjectivity built into the current selection process. But, before these results are provided, it's vital to understand the flaws in the current selection procedures which justify their application.

CHAPTER 2

Subjective Injustice

For most of its 65 year history, the Hall-of-Fame selection process has involved two different sets of electors, both of which vote annually. Since the second year of voting, the Baseball Writers Association of America (BBWAA) has served as Cooperstown's primary electorate, with the results of its balloting, announced every January, widely perceived as the "front-door" (or, preferred) form of admission. The "back-door" is a Veterans Committee (VC), existent since 1953, which meets to vote in Florida during spring training, usually in March. Both organs use a standard of collective wisdom in which 75 percent support is required for election. Eligibility rules for both elections have been changed many times over the years, and the current ones reflect an ongoing process of trial and error, in part the result of past confusion between the two elective organs regarding who was (or should be) eligible for each ballot.

At present, the BBWAA votes only on players, each of whom must meet the 10-year-service requirement, cannot have been active anytime during the five years prior to their first appearance on the ballot, and must be approved in advance by a screening committee whose purported function is to weed out men with insignificant credentials (it's practical mandate also limits the ballot to forty names or fewer, as the fewer on the list, the more likely that at least one will be elected). In theory, each man who passes this screening has a 15-year window of eligibility in the writers' voting. But a rule in place for the last decade or so has removed candidates immediately after failure to receive at least 5 percent support in any BBWAA election (further enhancing the prospect there will be an annual electee). Given that most men with viable Hall-of-Fame credentials play until they are almost 40, the ages of men on the writers' ballot generally range between 45 and 60.

The Veterans Committee has jurisdiction over players passed over by the BBWAA whose eligibility for the writers' voting has been expired for at least three years. The committee also considers non-players (e.g., managers, umpires, executives) and old Negro Leaguers. This imposes a 23-year wait between retirement as a player and VC eligibility; so most of the men in the panel's purview are sixty or older before the committee examines their merits. During its first three decades the VC could weigh the credentials of virtually any man overlooked by the scribes, but in recent years eligibility for the panel's ballot has been restricted. As part of the 1991 compromise in which the BBWAA agreed to keep Pete Rose off its ballot, among players whose big-league careers began after 1945, the VC is now limited to considering only those who received at least sixty percent support from the writers in at least one election, plus a short list of men who had earned 100 votes or more before the agreement and were grandfathered into this group (this proviso has severely cut the number of post–World War Two players the VC may consider).

All of this suggests that the Cooperstown selection process has been flawed from its beginning. The system was and remains broken because (1) insufficient forethought was given to details of the process at its outset, and (2) subsequent refinements have all been susceptible to the varied motives of the Hall of Fame's trustees (whose interests are primarily economic) and its separate electors (whose interests are mainly jurisdictional).

The first Hall-of-Fame election was held in 1936, when five men — Ty Cobb, Walter Johnson, Christy Mathewson, Babe Ruth and Honus Wagner — were the initial recipients of baseball's highest honor. Cobb led the voting with 222 of a possible 226 BBWAA votes, for 98.2 percent support; Ruth and Wagner had 215 votes and 95.1 percent each; Mathewson earned 205 votes for 90.7 percent; and Johnson trailed with 189 and 83.6 percent. Although there was no complaint about the selection of any of those men (and shouldn't have been), the initial voting misfired in several ways.

First, there were two different ballots in 1936. Members of the BBWAA were charged with selecting "modern" players who appeared in the majors after 1901. The five electees of 1936 all were chosen from their ballot. A second set of electors, an Old-Timers Committee (OTC) whose 78-man composition is currently unknown (but probably consisted of the elder statesmen among the BBWAA's active and retired membership of the era), was supposed to select five men who played primarily in the 19th century. But the OTC failed to anoint anyone, their ballot led by first baseman Cap Anson and catcher Buck Ewing, both of whom earned 40 votes and just 51.3 percent support. The OTC's failure left the 19th century — which comprised almost half of major-league history to that time — without representation and prompted formation of a six-man Centennial Commission (CC), headed by baseball commissioner Kenesaw Mountain Landis, which operated during 1937–38 and was intended to address the oversight, but failed to do so in any meaningful fashion. The CC and a second Old-Timers Committee (or OTC2, which functioned from 1939 to 1949) were both progenitors of the Veterans Committee; and none of these organs (at times, for simplicity, all three will be cited in the text as "veterans committees") might ever have existed if the original OTC had fulfilled its mandate.

Second, there was little forethought given to the Hall of Fame's eligibility requirements. The oversight created several problems which took years to iron out, and it's safe to say that the most recent refinement in the eligibility rules — the Pete Rose agreement noted above — will not be the last.

To begin with, it was never made clear who should be eligible for either of the 1936 ballots. As a result, eight men whose playing careers overlapped the century demarcation (Jimmy Collins, Lou Criger, Ed Delahanty, Willie Keeler, Nap Lajoie, John McGraw, Honus Wagner and Cy Young) earned votes in both elections; one OTC member voted for Jake Daubert, a first baseman whose big-league career did not begin until 1910, a decade after the Nineteenth Century had ended; and nine players (Mickey Cochrane, Jimmie Foxx, Frankie Frisch, Lou Gehrig, Lefty Grove, Rogers Hornsby, Al Simmons, Billy Terry and Pie Traynor) received support from the BBWAA electors though they had not yet retired by 1936. Some of the confusion was settled in 1937, when active players were removed from consideration, but the issue of which candidates should fall under BBWAA or veterans committee jurisdiction remained a source of dispute for at least two decades.

The Hall of Fame had been conceived, in part, as an outgrowth of a failed effort by organized baseball to obtain Congressional funding during the 1920s for a Washington, D. C., monument to honor the game's greatest players. But it was never clarified prior to the 1936 voting whether anyone would — or should — be rewarded for contributions beyond their playing careers. As a result, four men (Charles Comiskey, Connie Mack, John McGraw and Wilbert Robinson) received support in one or both versions of the first year's voting which could be attributed to their non-playing achievements. All four had been players of some note during the 19th century. But, by 1936, Comiskey was better-known as the founding owner of the American League's Chicago White Sox; Mack had served in the same capacity for the Philadelphia Athletics; and Mack, McGraw and Robinson had all enjoyed lengthy and successful careers as 20th-century managers. In turn, it remains impossible to know with certainty whether Comiskey and Robinson's support from the OTC (six votes each), Mack's lone vote from the BBWAA, or McGraw's votes on both ballots (seventeen OTC, four BBWAA) were intended to reward their roles as players, pilots or executives. Later, Comiskey was added to the Hall for his service as an executive, while the other three were chosen as managers.

The lack of forethought regarding eligibility also encouraged some electors to vote for players with relatively short big-league careers. The OTC members voted for eight different men in 1936 who played fewer than 10 seasons in the Show, including one who never appeared in an official big-league game. Seven of those men (catcher Doug Allison, second sacker Ross Barnes, shortstop George Wright, third baseman Joe Battin, outfielder Charlie Pabor, and pitchers Tommy Bond and Albert Spalding) had been stars in the National Association (NA), baseball's first professional league, for most of the period 1871–75. But, for obscure reasons, many of the game's historians have never considered the NA a true "major" circuit, and because none of the men receiving OTC votes played more than Bond's eight seasons in the National League or other recognized "majors" after 1875, the support for them was dubious — especially the lone vote for Pabor, who played only before the NL began operation and never appeared in a recognized "major-league" game. Wright and Spalding were elected to Cooperstown by the VC's progenitors in 1937 and 1939, respectively. The former compiled a .350 batting average in the association, but hit only .256 in seven NL seasons; the latter had been the NA's most successful pitcher, achieving a 204–53 won-lost record and .794 winning percentage, before going 48–12 in 1876 and 1877, his only two major-league campaigns. But Spalding earned as much or more fame later on for his sporting goods company, which supplied the National League with its baseballs, and for publishing annual guides which were forerunners to modern magazines about the sport. Upon their election, both men were cited as "pioneer contributors" to the game, not as players.

The eighth short-timer to receive votes from the OTC in 1936 was outfielder Bill Lange, whose big-league career comprised just seven seasons (1893–99). Although Lange had just one statistical title to his credit (he topped the NL with 73 stolen bases in 1897), he compiled a .330 career batting average, which was better than all but 21 of the 185 Hall of Fame players elected through 2000. Often compared to later greats like Ty Cobb and Joe Jackson, Lange probably merited HOF consideration, and might have been elected with a lengthier career. But he abruptly ended his playing days at age 28 when, after falling in love with the daughter of a San Francisco real estate baron, his future father-in-law decreed that he would never allow the girl to marry a ballplayer. Absent any clarity regarding eligibility, the six votes cast in favor of Lange (along with those given to the other NA players) set a precedent which, during the first couple decades of Hall-of-Fame balloting, encouraged many BBWAA electors to cast votes for about thirty other players with short-term careers. A few of them may have deserved consideration, but the support for some was inexplicable — notably the lone vote in 1950 for infielder Jewel Ens, whose career included only 186 big-league at-bats in four seasons and a .513 winning percentage in 344 games as a pilot. By 1960, the Hall's braintrust had concluded that short-term players don't belong on the ballot, and the 10-year service requirement was enacted to exclude them.

But, although it represents the only objective criteria for Hall-of-Fame election, the 10-year requirement is arbitrary, and has led to some absurd injustices regarding who has been eligible for Cooperstown since 1960 and who has not. Bobby Tiefenauer (a 10-year pitcher with a 9–25 career won-lost record and .265 winning percentage) and John Vukovich (six career homers and a .161 batting average) met that standard, for instance, but Don Gullett (109–50, and a .686 winning percentage) and Tony Conigliaro (166 four baggers, .264 BA) did not. In that light, the 10-year rule has done little to clarify what a Hall of Famer is or should be, and has defined only what he is not (i.e., someone who played in less than 10 big-league seasons). Beyond that, it also greatly reduced the number of players eligible for election. From the National League's inception through the 1994 season, about 14,000 men appeared in at least one major-league game. Among them were slightly fewer than 2,300 who played in 10 seasons or more, so the service requirement, reducing the number of HOF-eligible players by a factor of about six, can be interpreted as another blatant effort to insure that someone will be elected each year.

Ironically, the short-timer votes of 1936 coincided with the OTC members' failure to give any support at all to eight 19th-century players who were later enshrined by veterans committees. They included outfielder Jim O'Rourke (chosen by the OTC2 in 1945), and VC selections Pud Galvin (pitcher, 1965), Joe Kelley (outfielder, 1971), Mickey Welch (pitcher, 1973), Sam Thompson (outfielder, 1974), Roger Connor (first baseman, 1976), George Davis (shortstop, 1998) and Bid McPhee (second baseman, 2000). Davis, whose career spanned 1890–1909, also could have earned votes on the 1936 BBWAA ballot, but didn't. The merits of some of their selections are debatable, although Galvin and Welch were both 300-game winners, Connor was baseball's career home-run leader prior to Babe Ruth, and — statistically, at least — McPhee was the greatest defensive player of the 19th century. Nonetheless, their credentials suggest that they should have received support from the OTC in 1936, but didn't. Joe Kelley did receive one vote each in the BBWAA elections of 1939 and 1942. But the other seven, along with dead-ball–era pitcher Vic Willis (chosen by the VC in 1995), are the only men elected to Cooperstown as players without ever getting a vote in any BBWAA election. As a result, some of their selections — along with those of many other veterans committee choices — contributed to ongoing complaints by the writers that the back-door panels have been allowed to enshrine too many of the scribes' rejects.

Another eligibility dilemma involved the BBWAA's 1936 support for Hal Chase. At the time Chase, whose career began in 1905, was widely regarded as the slickest-fielding first sacker ever. But he had been blackballed from baseball after the 1919 season for alleged involvement in game fixing (his 402 errors at first base are almost fifty–percent more than any other man who has played that position since the start of the twentieth century, an exorbitant ratio for the "best" fielder at any position, and circumstantial evidence that Hal's slickness involved more than just his glove). All the same, Chase received eleven votes in 1936, more than future Hall-of-Fame first basemen Bill Terry and Frank Chance. The support for Chase apparently displeased the Cooperstown braintrust, as did the two votes received that same year by Joe Jackson, the most famous member of the Chicago Black Sox who threw the 1919 World Series. So by 1945 the trustees had imposed a regulation stipulating that "candidates shall be chosen on the basis of playing ability, integrity, sportsmanship, character and their contribution to the team on which they played and to baseball in general." But, beyond its obvious function as a morality clause intended to discourage future support for Chase, Jackson and others, this rule did nothing to clarify eligibility or identification of true Hall of Famers, because it left the definitions of each of its criteria to the subjective interpretations of voters. It's failure to intimidate some BBWAA electors also was evident in 1946 when, after a decade of receiving no support at all, Jackson received two more votes from the writers.

There also was minimal regulation for the 1936 voting regarding how the electors should allocate their support. Electors were allowed to list a maximum of 10 men on their ballots, but could vote for less than that number if they wished (a format applied throughout the history of BBWAA voting). Beyond that, there were no other guidelines given. Some voters might support one man from each position on the field, some might vote for 10 pitchers if they wished, and others might support only the two or three candidates they deemed best-qualified for the honor, regardless of where they played on the diamond. Table One provides a positional breakdown of the 1936 voting by both groups of electors, showing the number of men who received votes (Men w/V), the percentage of all men receiving votes who represented that position (Pos Pct), the total number of votes received by players from each position (Tot Vote), the rounded average number of votes earned by each player from each position (Avg Vote), and the equivalent support percentage which that average represented (Avg Sup). Because of their distinct Hall-of-Fame citations, Mack, McGraw and Robinson are treated as managers (Mgr) in the table, while Comiskey, Wright and Spalding are counted in the "Other" category.

Table One
1936 Hall-of-Fame Voting, BBWAA and OTC, By Position

BBWAA (Maximum 2,260 Votes Possible)						OTC (Maximum 780 Votes Possible)				
Pos	Men w/V	Pos Pct	Tot Vote	Avg Vote	Avg Sup	Pos	Men w/V	Pos Pct	Tot Vote	Avg Vote	Avg Sup
p	12	25.5	636	53	23.5	p	8	14.0	71	9	11.4
c	5	10.6	146	29	12.9	c	4	7.0	45	11	14.4
1b	6	12.8	174	29	12.8	1b	7	12.3	47	7	8.6
2b	5	10.6	321	64	28.4	2b	4	7.0	7	2	2.2
ss	2	4.3	216	108	47.8	ss	8	14.0	42	5	6.7
3b	4	8.5	76	19	8.4	3b	6	10.5	19	3	4.1
of	11	23.4	647	59	26.0	of	15	26.3	104	7	8.9
Mgr	2	4.3	5	3	1.1	Mgr	2	3.5	23	12	14.7
Other	0	0.0	0	0	0.0	Other	3	5.3	16	5	6.8
Total	47	100.0	2221	47	20.9	Total	157	99.9	374	7	8.4

It's clear from Table One that the two sets of electors in 1936 applied very different voting philosophies to their assigned task. With 2,221 of a possible 2,260 votes cast, the BBWAA members filled in over 98 percent of the maximum possible spaces on their ballots, with most of the electors voting for the 10-man maximum allowed. In contrast, the OTC members cast only 374 votes, about 48 percent of the 780 available, listing an average of fewer than five names per ballot. Combined with the OTC's wider dispersion of votes (57 men received support, compared to 10 fewer by the much larger group of BBWAA electors), the low percentage of votes cast by the Old-Timers Committee explains the group's failure to elect anyone at all. Beyond that, there was no consistency among the two groups in the treatment of players from each position. Relative to the OTC, pitchers represented almost twice the ratio of men receiving votes from the BBWAA; but the former group voted for far more shortstops than its larger counterpart; and of the two short-stops who received votes from the BBWAA, Honus Wagner got 215 and Kid Elberfeld only one — so it's incidental that the writers' organ voted for anyone from the position except the Flying Dutchman. The discrepancies in treatment of the other positions are less significant, but it's obvious that few members of either elective body cast their votes with any attempt at positional balance, and that approach has prevailed throughout the history of Cooperstown voting.

Also, although Walter Johnson (417 career victories) and Christy Mathewson (373), the two pitchers elected in 1936, ranked second and third at the time, respectively, among the career leaders for games won, neither man was anywhere close to Cy Young's 511 victories, a figure which remains the most in major-league history almost a century after Cy's retirement. Because the bottom line for a pitcher's performance is his number of games won, you'd have thought that the Cooperstown voters would've honored the all-time wins leader — especially one with such a wide advantage over everyone else — among their first group of selections. After all, Young's career victory total was no fluke: at the time of that first election, Cy's 2803 career strikeouts were second only to Johnson's 3509; and, through the 2000 Hall-of-Fame voting, Young's average of only 1.49 walks allowed per nine innings pitched has been bettered by only two other hurlers ever chosen for the Hall — 361-game winner Pud Galvin (1.13) and Addie Joss (1.41). To put Young's command of the strike zone in more recent historical perspective, among all pitchers with 10 years of big-league service since World War Two, only one — Dan Quisenberry (1.40) — allowed fewer than 1.5 walks per nine innings. Greg Maddux, considered the premier control pitcher of the 1990s, had averaged 2.03 walks per nine innings through 1999.

Young's failure to gain election in 1936 resulted, in large part, because he received votes on both ballots (his career spanned 1890–1911). Among Cy's 511 victories, 286 came before the turn of the century, as did two of his five 30-win seasons, and nine of his 15 campaigns with 20 victories or more. So Young received support from both sets of electors, but not enough from either group to be enshrined: Cy placed eighth in the BBWAA election, with 111 votes and 49.1 percent support; he was fourth on the OTC list, with thirty-two votes and 41.0 percent. And it's probable that many voters from both groups omitted his name on the premise that he belonged with the other set of eligibles and would be chosen by their electors.

But, granting the split in Young's support, his omission among the 1936 electees is still a bit mystifying when you consider that most of the BBWAA members voted for 10 men that year. Cy's ordinal rankings on both ballots are collective evidence that he was probably among the 10 best players in major-league history prior to 1936. Nonetheless, 115 of the BBWAA voters chose about nine or 10 other candidates instead; and 46 of the OTC voters left him off their ballots.

The injustice of Young's omission in 1936 was corrected when the BBWAA elected him in 1937, along with Nap Lajoie and Tris Speaker, who had placed sixth and seventh in the scribes' first year of voting. But, despite the split in his support, Cy's failure to gain election in the first year — along with the support given to dubious candidates like Hal Chase, Charlie Pabor and others — evidenced a fickleness among the HOF electors that has plagued the Cooperstown selection process throughout its 65 year history.

More recent examples of that fickleness can be traced in the voting history of the six-year span of BBWAA elections from 1979–1984. Table Two provides the rounded annual support percentages and ordinal rankings (in parenthesis) of 12 men who were leading candidates in the elections of that period. Among them, Don Drysdale, Hoyt Wilhelm, Luis Aparicio, Harmon Killebrew and Juan Marichal were elected by the writers (Wilhelm in 1985, the others in one of the years shown); four others — Nellie Fox, Red Schoendienst, Jim Bunning and Richie Ashburn — have been elected by the Veterans Committee in the period since their BBWAA eligibility expired; and three — Gil Hodges, Maury Wills and Roger Maris — were not yet in Cooperstown through the 2000 voting. The percentages and ordinals for players elected in a given year are boldfaced. Men who were not yet eligible for the ballot in a year are designated by "nye." Dashed lines indicate men who had been elected already or whose BBWAA eligibility had expired.

Table Two
BBWAA Vote Histories, Selected Players, 1979–84

Player	1979	1980	1981	1982	1983	1984
Gil Hodges	56 (4)	60 (4)	60 (3)	50 (7)	63 (7)	—
Don Drysdale	54 (5)	62 (3)	60 (3)	56 (6)	65 (6)	**79** **(3)**
Nellie Fox	40 (6)	42 (8)	42 (7)	31 (11)	46 (8)	61 (5)
Hoyt Wilhelm	39 (7)	54 (5)	59 (5)	57 (5)	65 (5)	72 (4)
Maury Wills	38 (8)	38 (9)	41 (10)	22 (14)	21 (12)	26 (12)
Red Schoendienst	37 (9)	43 (7)	41 (8)	33 (10)	39 (10)	—
Jim Bunning	34 (10)	46 (6)	41 (9)	33 (9)	37 (11)	50 (7)
Richie Ashburn	30 (11)	35 (10)	35 (11)	30 (12)	—	—
Roger Maris	29 (12)	29 (12)	23 (12)	17 (15)	18 (15)	27 (10)
Luis Aparicio	28 (13)	32 (11)	12 (18)	42 (8)	67 (4)	**85** **(1)**
Harmon Killebrew	nye	nye	60 (4)	59 (4)	72 (3)	**83** BF
Juan Marichal	nye	nye	58 (6)	74 (3)	**84** **(2)**	—

The period encompassed by Table Two included six men (not listed) who were elected in their first year eligible — Willie Mays (1979), Al Kaline (1980), Bob Gibson (1981), Hank Aaron and Frank Robinson (1982), plus Brooks Robinson (1983) — and each of them ranked either first or second in the voting for the year of their selection. The only other man elected by the scribes during this period who is not listed in the table was Duke Snider, who entered Cooperstown with Kaline in 1980, Duke's eleventh year on the ballot, after placing second in 1979.

The third-place finisher of 1979 was outfielder Enos Slaughter, whose eligibility expired after that election. Among the men listed, all but Hodges (who died in 1972) and Fox (1975) were living. Only Hodges, Schoendienst and Wills ever served as big-league managers, but Schoendienst's only service as a skipper during the period shown occurred in 1980, when he managed the Cardinals' last 37 games after Ken Boyer fell ill; and Wills was the

Mariners' field boss for just 83 games during the 1980–81 seasons. So, by and large, nothing of consequence occurred during the period shown to alter any of these men's credentials.

Among the men listed in Table Two, only one of them — Juan Marichal, who joined the ballot in 1981 and was elected two years later — saw his support percentage and ordinal ranking rise in each of the elections shown. The other 11 men's voting performances fluctuated, going up, down, or both during this six-year period. The most interesting history on the list may be that of Luis Aparicio, whose first year on the ballot was 1979, and who was elected in 1984.

Aparicio's 18-year major-league career spanned 1956–73. He was the American League's Rookie of the Year in 1956, he was a solid fielder at a key defensive position and he led the circuit in stolen bases in each of his first nine seasons. As runner-up to teammate Nellie Fox for the AL's 1959 MVP, he was instrumental in the White Sox' pennant that year (their first since 1919), and, along with Maury Wills and Lou Brock, he was regarded as one of the premier leadoff hitters of his era (despite a woeful career on-base average of only .313). Like many players at his position, Aparicio lacked power and compiled a relatively poor batting average (.262), although it was about thirteen points higher than the composite AL norm during the pitching-dominated years when he played (Rabbit Maranville, at .258, is the only HOF shortstop with a lower BA; Joe Tinker hit .262).

Nellie Fox's 19-year career spanned 1947–65. He and Aparicio were teammates in Chicago for seven seasons (1956–62), where they formed one of baseball's most-admired double play combos, and second sacker Fox usually followed the shortstop at the top of the batting order. Fox was chosen for the AL All-Star team 12 times, Aparicio 10. Luis hit more home runs (83 to 35), but neither man had notable power, and Nellie compiled higher batting (.288), on-base (.349) and slugging averages (.363 to .343). Except for their stolen bases (Aparicio led 506 to 76), their other key batting stats were similar: Aparicio had 2677 hits, 1335 runs scored, and 791 runs batted in; Fox amassed 2663 safeties, 1279 runs and 790 RBI. The shortstop won more Gold Glove trophies (nine to three), but the award did not begin until Aparicio's rookie season, and Fox won three of the first four, indicating he might've earned some others had the honor existed earlier in his career. The significant difference in their stats, if there was one, involved Most Valuable Player voting: in addition to topping Aparicio for the 1959 award, Fox compiled 815 MVP votes during his career, finishing fourth once, seventh twice, plus eighth and ninth once apiece, and received votes for the award on 10 occasions. Beyond his runner-up status in 1959, Aparicio placed among the top 10 only one other time (ninth in 1966) and collected a career-long total of 399 votes in 10 mentions. While they were teammates, Fox outpolled Aparicio 617 to 287 in MVP balloting.

Consistent with that difference, Fox earned 40 percent support for Cooperstown in 1979 (his ninth year on the ballot), while Aparicio received just 28 percent, and Nellie retained a 10 percent lead over his ex-teammate in the 1980 voting — all predictable, given that the writers who vote for Most Valuable Player are essentially the same ones who cast ballots for Cooperstown. Fox's edge increased to 30 percent in 1981 when, for unclear reasons, only 12 percent of the scribes voted for Aparicio. But somehow, the following year, Luis' support jumped to 42 percent while Nellie's fell to just 31; and, after that, although Fox's numbers rose again, Aparicio's climbed faster until he was elected in 1984. Fox's last year on the writers' ballot was 1985, when his 74.5 percent support was the closest any man has ever come without gaining election. He was selected in 1997, however, when the Veterans Committee bestowed the honor.

Maury Wills, another shortstop and leadoff hitter, didn't get to the majors until he was 26, so his 14-year career (1959–72) was four seasons shorter than Aparicio's. Like the White Sox shortstop, Wills was a base bandit, and although he led his circuit in steals only six times (compared to Aparicio's nine), he swiped more bases overall (586), and set a (since broken) record of 104 in 1962 (Aparicio's single-season high was 57), when he also was voted the National League's MVP. Having played fewer years, Wills predictably amassed fewer hits (2134), home runs (20), runs scored (1067) and RBI (458) than Aparicio; but Wills' batting (.281) and on-base/slugging averages (both .331) averages were higher. Wills won two Gold Gloves, was a five-time All-Star, and his teams won four pennants compared to Aparicio's two. Despite his shorter career, the Dodger had more MVP votes (521) than his A.L. counterpart, receiving mention on eight occasions, and — in addition to his 1962 trophy — placing third, sixth and ninth once apiece.

In the first three years Aparicio was on the ballot, Wills — whose eligibility began in 1978 — topped him by margins similar to those of Nellie Fox. But in 1982, for some reason, Wills' candidacy went into decline at the same moment that Aparicio's began to skyrocket. Given his career advantage in stolen bases and higher on-base percentage, Wills was the better leadoff hitter; Aparicio, no doubt, was the superior fielder. If projected to an 18-year career, Wills' totals for hits, homers, runs and RBI would be comparable to the numbers posted by Aparicio. Based on their records in MVP voting, Wills was held in higher regard by the writers than Aparicio, but their performances in that balloting came in separate leagues, so they may not be entirely comparable. Subjectively, there doesn't seem to have been enough difference in their skills or career numbers to justify either man's big margin over the other at any point in the Cooperstown voting.

Among the candidates in Table Two, a final comparison bears brief mention. Harmon Killebrew's Cooperstown eligibility began with 60 percent support in 1981, the same year that Aparicio's votes bottomed out at 12 percent. Killebrew was a slugger, while Aparicio was a speedy defenseman — so, skill-and-stat-wise, there was nothing comparable about the two players, except that Killebrew's career batting average (.256) was slightly worse than Aparicio's. But, when you consider Killebrew's 573 home runs, 1584 RBI and 1283 runs scored (only 52 fewer than Aparicio), it's difficult to comprehend why — in the span of just four elections — Harmon went from being 48 percent better than Aparicio in 1981 to two-percent worse in 1984, when both men were elected.

Similar comparisons could also be made among other sets of players in Table Two (e.g., Drysdale-Bunning-Marichal as contemporary pitchers, and Fox-Schoendienst as second basemen of the 1950s). But the bottom line is that the table reveals a fickleness among BBWAA voters that has been typical of the balloting in every decade since HOF voting began. The fluctuations above demonstrate that, unless a man is elected in his first year eligible, there is often no true consensus among the voting scribes about the merits of his credentials until the year of his election. And for those who are not anointed by the BBWAA, the up-and-down patterns of their annual support often demonstrate an absence of any consensus at all. So, there is little evidence that the passage of time enhances or solidifies most voters' perceptions of a given man's credentials — for, if it did, each man's scores would either rise steadily toward election (as other men are chosen ahead of him), decline toward oblivion, or remain static over his period of eligibility. Because they generally don't do that, it's dangerous to isolate any unelected man's specific-year score as indicative of his merits relative to anyone else.

That point is important because, in the last decade or so, the 5 percent support requirement to retain BBWAA eligibility has imposed a premature judgment on the elective viability of many players who were dropped from the ballot, often after their first appearance. In recent years, some notable victims of the rule have included Darrell Evans (414 home runs, 1354 RBI), Dwight Evans (382 homers, 1384 RBIs), Ted Simmons (2472 hits, more than any other man who played mostly as a catcher, and 1389 RBI, second only to Yogi Berra among the same group), Al Oliver (2743 hits, .303 batting average), Bobby Grich (224 home runs), Fred Lynn (only man to win MVP and Rookie of the Year honors in the same season), Bill Madlock (four batting titles), Graig Nettles (390 home runs, 1314 RBI), and Dave Kingman (442 homers).

But, historically, most Hall of Famers have required several ballots to gain election. Including Roberto Clemente (elected on a special ballot in 1973 shortly after his death in a plane crash), only 35 of the 93 players enshrined by the BBWAA through 2000 had been chosen in their first year eligible. As a group, the writers' 58 other inductees averaged just over 25-percent support in their first appearances on the ballot and typically required more than seven tries to gain election. So, many candidacies start slowly, some with no obvious momentum. Based on their elective histories, if the rule had been in force since 1936, 17 BBWAA electees (Luke Appling, Lou Boudreau, Joe Cronin, Joe DiMaggio, Charlie Gehringer, Hank Greenberg, Gabby Hartnett, Harry Heilmann, Ralph Kiner, Ted Lyons, Joe Medwick, Red Ruffing, Al Simmons, Bill Terry, Pie Traynor Dazzy Vance and Paul Waner), over one-fifth of the writers' selections prior to the 1990s, would've been dropped from the ballot for failure to maintain at least five percent support, all of them but Heilmann and Traynor after their first year eligible. Overall, including men chosen by veterans committees, more than seventy of the men who were Hall of Famers by 2000—about one-third of all members who were not umpires or players in the Negro leagues—received less than five percent support at least once in their early years on the ballot.

With all of that in mind, and coupled with the fickleness displayed by BBWAA voters throughout the history of Cooperstown balloting, who's to say that either of the Evanses, Simmons, Oliver, Grich, or any of the others noted above would or could not have climbed from their low-support totals in their early years on the ballot to gain election later, like Luis Aparicio after 1981? And what wisdom or fairness exists in drawing a time line which deprives men who retired after an arbitrary date (around 1985) of the same opportunities for election that were afforded to players who retired before them? Above all else, the injustices prompted by the five percent rule are ample evidence that the BBWAA portion of the Cooperstown selection process is still broken, despite 65 years of attempted repairs.

In recent decades, the 10-year service requirement and persistent application of de facto standards for cumulative achievement in games won, hits and home runs have strongly implied that Cooperstown election is intended to reward performance over the full length of a man's career. But it was not determined at the beginning of the voting—and has not been to date—whether the honor should also go to players who accomplish feats which are momentarily, or incidentally unique; and the failure to do so led to another problem with the BBWAA process. Over the years, a number of players have received votes simply because they achieved something fleetingly historic, or participated in a single, noteworthy event. The first of these was probably second baseman Bill Wambsganss, who netted thirteen Hall-of-Fame votes from 1942 to 1956. Wambsganss was a competent big-league regular for eleven seasons. But, with just seven home runs and a .259 career batting average, there was nothing particularly Cooperstown-worthy about his career, and there is no doubt that he received support solely because of his unassisted triple play in the 1920 World Series.

Wambsganss' first vote in 1942 set a precedent that encouraged support for others like Johnny Vander Meer (back-to-back no-hitters in 1938), Leon Cadore and Joe Oeschger (dueling hurlers in the 26-inning tie game of 1920, which was baseball's longest), Fred Toney (the victor over Hippo Vaughn in baseball's only double no-hitter, in 1917), Don Larsen (perfect game pitched in the 1956 World Series) and Bucky Dent (won a 1978 AL playoff game with his home run at Fenway Park), none of whose credentials are significant minus their moments in the sun. Vander Meer, whose career won-lost record was just 119–121, got the most obvious mileage from his unique achievement, receiving 700 HOF votes during the years 1945–71 (Larsen got 492 during 1974–88, but none of the others topped Wambsganss' 13 votes). There are several other men whose Cooperstown support obviously benefitted from singular feats, notably Hack Wilson (a major-league record 191 RBI in 1930), Bobby Thomson (playoff-winning home run in 1951), Harvey Haddix (12-inning perfect game in 1959) and Roger Maris (61 homers in 1961). But each of those also possessed other credentials which lent more credence to the votes they received, while — with the debatable exception of Vander Meer — it's hard to fathom the support received by the others. Except for Wilson (who was added to the HOF roster by the VC in 1979), none of the players who performed these "feats" had been enshrined through the 2000 voting.

All the same, it's arguable that the impulse for Wambsganss-type support reached its height of absurdity in the Hall-of-Fame votes received by Hub Pruett, an obscure reliever whose seven-year major-league career was spread over 11 seasons, 1922–32. Pruett compiled a 29–48 career won-lost record, lowlighted by a 7–17 ledger and 6.05 earned run average in 1927, his only campaign as a starter. But he somehow netted one vote in each of the five HOF elections from 1949 to 1953. The votes, perhaps from the same writer, were probably motivated by Pruett's ability to strike out Babe Ruth early in his career, as the lefty fanned the Bambino nine of the first dozen times he faced him in the Show (some sources claim it was 10 of the first 14). Regardless, Ruth struck out 1330 times in his career, so Pruett's feat was in no sense as rare as Wambsganss' triple play. A medical student in the off season, Pruett at least was smart enough to realize that Babe had been his big-league meal ticket: in 1948, shortly before Ruth's death, Pruett thanked him for "putting me through med school. If it wasn't for you, no one would have heard of me." Pruett's HOF support may have been a fluke, and the 10-year service rule would prevent him from getting on the ballot now, but the reliance upon subjective evaluation in the Cooperstown selection process assures that — like Bucky Dent, the most recent Wambsganss beneficiary — other poorly qualified candidates will receive similar votes in the future.

Its frequency may be incidental, but — because the BBWAA voters are limited to supporting a maximum of 10 candidates per ballot — votes for players like Pruett or even Wambsganss, inevitably deprive better-qualified men of the support they deserve. After all, symbolically, the results of BBWAA voting represent a numerical dialogue on each man's credentials for the Hall of Fame. If that dialogue is thoughtful and even-handed, then each man worthy of serious consideration should receive adequate "discussion" (i.e., votes) during his eligibility to evidence a defensible conclusion regarding the merits of his candidacy; and failure to gain election should be ample proof, within the scope of the writers' presumed collective wisdom, that a player doesn't belong in Cooperstown.

But throughout the history of the writers' voting, coupled with the 10-man-per-ballot restriction (and, abetted in recent years by the 5 percent-support rule), the subjective nature of the BBWAA process has denied adequate consideration to many relatively qualified players, including some who never received a vote at all. Proof of that is evident from the ongoing need for veterans committees and their selection, to date, of eight players who were totally ignored in the front-door voting. Those eight are just the tip of an iceberg that includes, but is not limited to, infielders Harlond Clift, Cecil Cooper, Del Pratt, Al Rosen and Vern Stephens, plus outfielders Pete Browning and Jimmy Ryan, none of whom ever received a single vote. Some may not belong in Cooperstown, but each of them possesses statistical credentials superior to a lot of players who received votes from the writers, and perhaps some Hall of Famers at their respective positions. Whether or not they belong, their credentials should have been sufficient to assure that a few attentive writers (at least) had cast a vote for them at some point.

The same is true of numerous pitchers. Through the 2000 voting, there were 58 hurlers on the Cooperstown roster, and another 184 had received BBWAA votes without being elected. Combined, those groups averaged 173 career wins per man, with a median victory total of just 166. At the same time, only 95 pitchers in history had won 200 games or more, yet — among the 91 eligible for Cooperstown by 2001 (excluding only Roger Clemens, Greg Maddux, Orel Hershiser and Dennis Martinez) — 14 of them had never received a single Hall-of-Fame vote. But, all told, 165 pitchers with fewer than 200 victories had received support, including 104 with fewer than 150 wins and 39 with fewer than 100. There isn't much justice in a system where Hub Pruett's 29 wins attract five votes, Dickie Kerr's 53 victories convince the electors to vote for him 75 times, and yet Tony Mullane's 284 wins and Frank Tanana's 240 go totally unrewarded.

Typical of such injustices, Table Three provides comparisons of the Hall-of-Fame vote histories and key career statistics of four pairs of contemporaries from various eras. In each instance, the two men involved played the same position. The table indicates the time span of each man's career (Years), his primary position (Pos), and the total number of votes he received in Hall-of-Fame elections (Vote); it also includes his career numbers for hits (H), home runs (HR), total bases (TB), runs scored (R), runs batted in (RBI), batting (BA), slugging (SA) and on-base (OBA) averages. At the top, in italics, the table also gives the mean career numbers for each category among all non-pitchers who had received Hall-of-Fame support through the 2000 voting. Names of men who were elected by the writers or veterans committees are followed, respectively, by the designations "HW" or "HV." Within the confines of each comparison, the higher career total for each statistic is bold-faced. The table is not intended as evidence for or against any of the men's candidacies, but merely to demonstrate that both sets of Hall-of-Fame electors have often failed to do their homework regarding the relative merits of analogous contemporaries.

Table Three
Typical Injustices in BBWAA Voting

Player	Years	Pos	Vote	H	HR	TB	R	RBI	BA	SA	OBA
All Men with Votes				*1719*	*131*	*2544*	*898*	*816*	*.282*	*.414*	*.352*
Wally Schang	13–31	c	22	**1506**	5	**2127**	**769**	**720**	**.284**	**.401**	**.393**
Ray Schalk HV	12–29	c	659	1345	**11**	1675	579	594	.253	.316	.340
Bob L. Johnson	33–45	lf	2	2051	**288**	3501	**1239**	1283	.296	**.506**	**.393**
Joe Medwick HW	32–48	lf	1279	**2471**	205	**3852**	1198	**1383**	**.324**	.505	.362
Vern Stephens	41–56	ss	0	**1859**	247	**2991**	**1001**	**1174**	**.286**	**.460**	**.355**
Phil Rizzuto HV	41–56	ss	1154	1588	38	2065	877	563	.273	.355	.351
Ted Simmons	68–88	c	17	**2472**	**248**	**3793**	**1074**	**1389**	.285	**.437**	**.352**
Thurman Munson	69–78	c	489	1558	113	2190	696	701	**.292**	.410	.350

Table Three includes examples from virtually every period of Cooperstown voting. All four comparisons involve players whose eligibility has expired, and whose vote histories are now complete. In one instance, left fielder Joe Medwick received a total of 1,279 Cooperstown votes spread over 11 ballots and was elected by the writers (in 1968), while his contemporary Bob Johnson — whose career stats were certainly comparable, and easily exceed the averages posted by all men with votes to date — received just one vote each in two elections (1948 and 1956). In two other instances, catcher Ray Schalk and shortstop Phil Rizzuto both received significantly more support from the BBWAA than their contemporaries Wally Schang and Vern Stephens, and were eventually anointed by the Veterans Committee (in 1955 and 1994, respectively). But, in both cases, the career stats posted by the unelected players were clearly superior to the two enshrined. In the final, most recent example, although neither man has been (or now can be) elected, Thurman Munson received far more support than contemporary catcher Ted Simmons, yet the latter's career stats are superior than Munson's in all but one category. In each instance given, and based on their stats, it is difficult to justify the wide disparity of Hall-of-Fame support for the two men. There are dozens of similar injustices from throughout the history of Cooperstown voting which could also be cited.

Over 65 years, the number of participating HOF electors has ranged from the 78 members of the 1936 OTC to the 499 who voted in the BBWAA election of 2000, with an average of 324 per ballot. Each of those voters has applied his own set of biases which, because no effort has ever been made to curb them, manifest in extremes ranging from the absurd vote for Jewel Ens in 1950 to the equally ridiculous fact that 11 writers in 1936 chose not to vote for Babe Ruth. Four of those men voted for Ty Cobb, who may have been a better candidate to many voters in 1936; but most of them who omitted Ruth's name also found eight or nine other men to list on their ballots instead. Such foolishness was not an aberration of the 1930s, and often is not limited to a small set of voters: eight of the 1982 voters concluded, for some reasons, that Hank Aaron did not belong in Cooperstown; and Joe DiMaggio was omitted from 252 of the 767 ballots cast during 1953–55 (including 28 when he was elected in the latter year).

Men who can find eight players in baseball history better than Babe Ruth cannot be expected to accurately weigh the subtle, comparative differences in the credentials of Ray Schalk and Wally Schang. And voters who can convince themselves that Hank Aaron is not a Hall of Famer, cannot possibly distinguish the relative merits of Luis Aparicio, Nellie Fox and Maury Wills with any accuracy and fairness. It's obvious, then that a subjective system which cannot adequately differentiate the merits of its lesser candidates must inevitably make errors of selection and omission among the players most-deserving of election.

Of course, responsibility for errors of selection and omission does not belong to the BBWAA alone. Among the 185 players chosen for Cooperstown through 2000, ninety-two of them had been added by veterans committees. As indicated earlier, these panels have often been blamed (by the writers and knowledgeable fans, alike) for what many perceive as a gradual slide toward mediocrity among the Hall-of-Fame roster, and the shrine's most debatable members — players like Tommy McCarthy, Elmer Flick, Johnny Evers, Joe Tinker, George Kelly, Chick Hafey, Fred Lindstrom, Jesse Haines and Rick Ferrell — were veterans committee selections.

The veterans committees also have been a source of controversy for other reasons. As indicated above, the six-man Centennial Commission of 1937–38, which was intended to redress the omission of 19th-century players during the first year's voting, failed its mandate by choosing instead to honor seven men (Morgan Bulkeley, Alexander Cartwright, Henry Chadwick, Ban Johnson, Connie Mack, John McGraw and George Wright) for non-playing achievements, thereby leaving the 19th-century players without representation and unilaterally expanding the Hall's original concept to honor only players. In 1939 the CC's successor, the OTC2, followed suit: it did enshrine three 19th-century players (Cap Anson, Buck Ewing and Charles Radbourn), but three other of its selections (Charles Comiskey, Candy Cummings and Albert Spalding) were cited for non-playing roles. One of those non-player selections (Cummings, another National Association player whose National League pitching record was just 21–22) probably represented Cooperstown's first true error of selection, because his election was justified largely on an unproven legend that he invented the curveball sometime before 1871. In the mid–1940s, after commissioner Kenesaw Mountain Landis had died, the OTC2 — which functioned as the Hall's trustees at the time — also engendered conflict with the BBWAA by ignoring its own guidelines regarding who was eligible for its selection process, thereby encroaching on the writers' jurisdiction; and the panel stirred up more trouble in 1945–46 when, amid several failures by the BBWAA to elect anyone at all, it effectively doubled the size of the Hall's roster, adding 21 men, several of whom are often cited among the worst selections ever (legend even has it that one of them, catcher Roger Bresnahan, was chosen — in part — on the erroneous belief that he was the first big-league backstop to wear shin guards).

Unfortunately, the controversies did not end when the OTC2 was replaced by the Veterans Committee in 1953. With formation of the VC, Hall-of-Fame players were added to the panel, ostensibly to provide their unique, on-field insights regarding the merits of its candidates (its predecessors had included only sportswriters and baseball executives). It was a good idea, in theory, but the practical result was that the panel's selection process has often resembled a bunch of ex-players arguing for, and eventually electing, their best friends or cronies. Among 19 former players who had served on the VC through the 2000 voting, only four of them — Monte Irvin, Billy Herman, Pee Wee Reese and Hank Aaron (who was appointed to the group in 2000) — had somehow avoided electing at least one of their former teammates during their time on the panel. Without doubt, these crony selections reached their nadir during the VC tenures of Hall of Famers Frankie Frisch (a committee member from 1967 to 1972), Waite Hoyt and Bill Terry (the latter both served 1971–76). Among the 23 players chosen during the decade 1967–76, eight of them had been former teammates of one or more VC member. Six of the selections from the period — Dave Bancroft, Chick Hafey, Jesse Haines, George Kelly, Fred Lindstrom and Ross Youngs — are widely perceived among the worst Cooperstown choices ever; another electee — 307-game winner Mickey Welch, enshrined in 1973 — may have been the Hall's first de facto qualifier to be an error of selection; and Frisch, at least, spent much of his time on the panel scuttling the candidacies of contemporaries he personally disliked (notably Hack Wilson).

In turn, in the years since 1976 the VC process has become increasingly infected by rampant politicking for and against various candidates, among the media and VC members alike. Phil Rizzuto, another debatable selection, was chosen in 1994, following a massive campaign for him among the New York media, and only after two other men — former Yankee teammate Yogi Berra and ex-broadcast partner Bill White — were added to the panel. It's also widely rumored that the VC candidacy of Gil Hodges (whose 3,010 BBWAA votes from 1969 to 1983 represent the most ever for a man not elected by the scribes) has been successfully blocked to date by the adamant opposition of at least one panel member.

In addition to that politicking, the VC and its predecessors have always been subject to an impulse to honor living candidates ahead of the dead, as many panelists have obviously felt that men should be rewarded before they expire. As well intended as that may seem, the habit is also driven by economic pressures (the presence of each additional, breathing recipient enhances attendance at the induction ceremony) and imposes a misguided and unnecessary delay of justice upon the families of long-dead players who are also deserving of recognition.

Over time, the VC has tended to conduct itself like a secret politburo immune to any form of oversight. Unlike the BBWAA, the full vote tallies of the panel's elections are never made public, and its members are notoriously reluctant to share the content of its elective deliberations. As a result, beyond the announcement of the men chosen, little solid information ever leaks out about the VC's actions and discussion, and much of the awareness of its processes that is available unavoidably derives from rumor. The secrecy may be motivated by defensiveness about the frequency in which the panel, like the OTC2 of the 1940s, ignores its own regulations. For most of the 1990s, the committee regularly ignored a rule that members could serve no more than two three-year terms on the panel. Also the 1998 election of outfielder Larry Doby (whose major-league career began in 1947, and never received more than 3.4 percent support in any BBWAA election) violated the stipulation that VC eligibility for players whose big-league careers began after 1945 was limited to men with at least 60 percent support from the scribes.

But to the VC's credit, although it violated regulations, the election of Doby (subjectively justifiable by his role as the first African American ever to play in the American League) also may have evidenced a well-founded resistance to the 60 percent requirement. That proviso, imposed on the panel as part of the Pete Rose compromise of 1991, currently rates with the BBWAA's requirement for 5 percent support to remain on its ballot as the biggest impediment to long-term justice among all of the eligibility rules governing either elective organ.

Through the Cooperstown voting of 2000, only eight players (Jim Bunning, Orlando Cepeda, Frank Chance, Johnny Evers, Nellie Fox, Gil Hodges, Enos Slaughter and Rube Waddell), and one manager (Miller Huggins) ever received as much as 60 percent support in a BBWAA election without subsequently being enshrined by the writers. Among that group, only Bunning, Cepeda and Fox began their big-league careers after 1945. And of the eight, all but Hodges had been added to the Hall-of-Fame roster by the VC or its predecessors. So, as of 2001, there were no post–1945 candidates who met the 60 percent requirement for VC eligibility; and the only postwar players the panel could consider were nine men — Ken Boyer, Harvey Kuenn, Mickey Lolich, Roger Maris, Bill Mazeroski, Tony Oliva, Ron Santo, Maury Wills and Luis Tiant (the latter still on the BBWAA ballot through 2002) — who had earned at least 100 votes in some election prior to 1991 and were grandfathered into the eligible group as part of the Rose compromise. Every other player whose career began after 1945 and was not elected before his BBWAA eligibility expired is no longer eligible for VC (i.e., any future Hall-of-Fame) consideration.

That leaves a lot of good players outside, looking in: one-time MVPs Dick Allen, Don Baylor, George Bell, Vida Blue, Jeff Burroughs, George Foster, Dick Groat, Willie Hernandez, Elston Howard, Jackie Jensen, Fred Lynn, Denny McLain, Thurman Munson, Don Newcombe, Boog Powell, Al Rosen, Bobby Shantz, Joe Torre and Zoilo Versalles; plus Cy Young Award winners Dean Chance, Mike Cuellar, John Denny, Mike Flanagan, Randy Jones, Vernon Law, Jim Lonborg, Sparky Lyle, Mike Marshall, Mike McCormick, Jim Perry, Mike Scott, Steve Stone, Rick Sutcliffe, Bob Turley, Pete Vuckovich and Bob Welch; and a host of others that is not limited to Buddy Bell, Bobby Bonds, Bob Boone, Bill Buckner, Lew Burdette, Bert Campaneris, Cesar Cedeño, Ron Cey, Jack Clark, Rocky Colavito, Alvin Dark, Darrell Evans, Dwight Evans, Elroy Face, Curt Flood, Bobby Grich, Frank Howard, Dave Kingman, Ted Kluszewski, Bill Madlock, Minnie Miñoso, Graig Nettles, Al Oliver, Lance Parrish, Billy Pierce, Vada Pinson, Vic Raschi, Jeff Reardon, Roy Sievers, Ted Simmons, Rusty Staub, Jim Sundberg, Frank Tanana, Kent Tekulve, Gene Tenace, Lou Whitaker and Frank White. Many of those men were dropped from the BBWAA ballot for failure to receive five percent support after their first or second year of eligibility. Under the present regulations, none can ever again be considered for Cooperstown membership.

Most of those men are not legitimate Hall of Famers. But a few of them might be, and what makes the termination of their eligibility even more unjust is the fact that under the terms of the Rose compromise, the VC may continue to consider any 10 year player whose major-league career began before 1946, regardless of his BBWAA vote history. So, technically, Johnny Vander

One of several victims of the Hall of Fame's current elegibility requirements, Darrell Evans hit more home runs than all but 19 of the men elected to Cooperstown through 2000. Under the current rules, he can never again be considered for induction by the voting writers of the Veterans Committee (*The Sporting News*).

Meer (119 victories) may still be considered, but Frank Tanana (240), Charlie Hough (216), Rick Reuschel (214), Billy Pierce (211), Vida Blue (209), Milt Pappas (209) and Lew Burdette (203) may not.

Compounding that injustice, the Hall of Fame is already loaded with players from baseball's live-ball era (1920–45), the last historical period before the end of World War Two. Including men who met the 10-year service requirement and the handful of short-timers who received votes before the rule was enacted, there had been 2,295 Cooperstown-eligible players through 1994. Among them, 458 (or 20 percent of the total) had a majority of their big-league at-bats or innings pitched during the live-ball period, of which sixty-two of them had been elected. So an era which represents about one-fifth of major-league history to date has produced roughly one-third of the Hall's 185 players, including many of those often cited as the most obvious errors of selection. In comparison, the postwar (1946–60), expansion (1961–75) and free-agent (1976–present) eras combined account for almost 45 percent of major-league history and 1,373 HOF-eligible players (about 60 percent of the overall total), but their 64 electees through 2000 comprised just 34.6 percent of the Cooperstown roster.

The prospects that any future candidate(s) will meet the 60 percent-support requirement without gaining election are also dimmed by the sharp decline in the number of men supported by the scribes. During the period 1936–60, and mimicking the writers' behavior in the first year's election, BBWAA members voted for about nine candidates per ballot. In the years since 1960, the average has dropped to around seven names per ballot, and fell to six in the decade 1991–2000. If that trend persists, the decreasing number of men listed reduces the likelihood that any given player might receive a high support percentage, and it virtually assures that any borderline candidates will have no chance at front-door election.

In that light, even if the Veterans Committee elects all nine of the post–1945 players it may currently consider (a very unlikely prospect), the 60 percent eligibility requirement greatly reduces any chances that the Hall-of-Fame roster's composition can or ever will reflect anything close to relative proportionality by era. So, it's clear that the regulation — which the BBWAA demanded as a means to halt the VC's continued election of its "rejects" and was imposed upon the panel as the price of expedience in the denial of Rose's eligibility — must be liberalized or rescinded before such balance can be achieved.

All the same, whether or not one endorses most of the veterans committees' selections over the years, the fact that virtually half of the 185 men elected to Cooperstown as players have been added to the roster to atone for real or imagined oversights by the writers offers ample evidence of flaws in the BBWAA's voting performance. Regardless of their most flagrant errors, the committees' choices have also included many men — notably Cap Anson, Dan Brouthers, Roger Connor, Sam Crawford, George Davis, Ed Delahanty, Buck Ewing, Pud Galvin, Billy Hamilton, Tim Keefe and Sam Thompson — who merited election on almost any scale imaginable, subjective or statistical. So deserving candidates can and do slip through the front-door process unnoticed; and the criticism aimed at the veterans panels over the years has unfairly overlooked the writers' culpability in their initial omissions.

With that in mind, it's evident that the first step toward improved justice in the Hall-of-Fame selection process would and should be adoption of some system that reduces the power of subjective bias in the BBWAA process. The most relevant, natural and obvious counterbalance to that bias is an application of objective measurement to a man's career statistical credentials (i.e., his actual, major-league performance).

Lies, Damn Lies and Z Scores

Most people harbor a resentment for the "science" of statistics. To begin with, it involves mathematics, which many of us learn to dislike early in life, in part because we feel deceived by it. We're taught in elementary school that every number has an absolute value — there's nothing vague about "four" — it's one more than three, one less than five, and not equal to 3.99. But, then we get to high school and are confronted with algebra and the notion that x and y are numbers too, although their values are unstated and entirely dependent upon the other information in an equation which may also include parentheses and brackets and which — except for the operators it contains — looks nothing like any math problem we've previously seen or ever imagined, even in our worst nightmares. This experience is far more traumatic than learning that Santa Claus is not real, because we keep receiving presents after we know that St. Nick's a fake, but with algebra all we get is very tedious, confusing homework — usually at a time in our lives when we'd rather be exploring our hormonal urges or (if we're a little slow to develop) playing catch. So, by age 15 or so, most folks have come to resent advanced mathematics sufficiently that, later on, they do not hunt up their freshman algebra teacher and ask him to sign their senior yearbooks.

Things get worse. Most of us don't take a statistics class in college, so — as adults — our practical knowledge of statistical science is limited to what we read in the papers or hear on television about opinion polls and double-blind, random drug testing. But, as things often seem to happen, the white-coat technicians will test a drug for years, decide it's safe for consumption, praise it as the miracle cure of the ages, and then — only after it's on the market — discover that it causes people to grow an extra nose on their foreheads, a fact which makes headlines and prompts us to forget about all the drugs that don't make us look like radiation mutants. Our faith in random testing is also shaken by the pollsters, because the political ones are right so often and the others frequently burn us. Many people dislike being told who's won an election, and why, before the votes are counted; and we've all known the loss of a favorite television show — like the original *Star Trek*, *Taxi* or *Homicide*— that resulted from poor viewer ratings. If we like Mr. Spock, Reverend Jim Ignatowski or detective Frank Pembleton, we resent having them taken away from us. So most folks feel they've been manipulated, deceived or ripped-off by the Gallups, Ropers and Nielsens of our culture. As a result, they are often wary or downright distrustful about the use of numbers to prove almost anything; and they have come to believe the cliche that there really are "lies, damn lies, and statistics," in that specific order of increasing infamy.

Finally, the few of us who do take statistics in college usually don't want to, but find out it's a requirement for our particular degree. Most students go into it dreading the math, which if they don't bomb out of the class before they actually get to do some isn't that difficult. But a lot of them drop the course by mid-semester and enroll in something easier — like elementary particle physics — instead, because they are unprepared for the fact that taking statistics is a lot like learning ancient Sanskrit or Minoan Linear A, two very old languages which the archaeologists haven't deciphered yet. The first few weeks of any statistics course are usually spent trying to comprehend a lot of terms which, at first, seem like gibberish (e.g., "curve-fitting"), medical terminology ('kurtosis," which is not a skin disease) or sexual euphemisms contrived by the very repressed ("covariance," "central tendencies," and that most dreaded and mysterious of all, the 'standard deviation," which many of us initially believe refers to something mild, like a foot fetish, as opposed to anything we might experience with a dominatrix). Even worse, many of these terms have an assigned symbol, a few of which are weird, squiggly things that, when several are contained in a statistical equation, make the problem look like a cross between a doctor's prescription notation and the score of a symphony written by some blind composer. So the statistical learning process can be traumatic, and many students who planned to be social scientists become paramedics instead — because, for them, assisting the maimed and bleeding is preferable to solving a "t-test" calculation.

All the same, statistical science is not as difficult or stressful as neurosurgery (although it requires a similar attention to detail), nor as vague and mystical as quantum theory. But it can be pretty imprecise, because what most people misunderstand, forget or never realize, is that it's inherently inexact. Although most statisticians can (and do) count accurately, their results are primarily based on the mathematics of probability, which by its very nature implies educated prediction about the tendencies of things that haven't occurred yet, based on similar events which have. So the results of most statistical analyses are really nothing more than reasonably informed guesses.

In turn, statistical probability is based on the theory of the normal curve, which hypothesizes that a sufficient number of similar but random events that occur in human behavior or the natural world as a whole should — if measured on a two-dimensional scale in which the vertical axis describes frequency, and the horizontal one variations of type — form a bell shape in which the most common of these occurrences will cluster near the central, deepest part of the bell, while the most unusual or extreme cases will lie near the thinner, curled lip along its lower edges, on either side of the middle. Bell curves assume lots of shapes, ranging from relatively flat ones whose central bulge is short and whose edges trail off gradually on both sides, to ones whose center is tall and narrow and whose sides descend steeply. Flatter curves exhibit more variety (i.e., dispersion of value) among the events measured, while tall, narrow ones indicate that a large majority of the events are more alike — perhaps almost equal — in whatever units are counted. A perfect bell curve — called a "normal distribution" — is symmetrical on both sides, but the graphs of real data often are not. Regardless of shape, theory imposes that the average (*mean*) occurrence among all the data collected will reside at the horizontal center of the bell, or very close to it if the curve is not symmetrical.

The same theory predicts that among all the data measured on the graph, about two-thirds of it will reside within one standard deviation — usually symbolized by a lower-case *s* on either side of the mean (and, for those of you who get hives or suffer minor seizures at the sight of the term, the next couple paragraphs are the only place where it will be imposed with any technical depth). So, if you've measured 30 events, the mean numerical value for them is five of whatever units you're counting, and the standard deviation is two of those units, then about twenty of the events should have a value of somewhere between three and seven (i.e., five, plus or minus an *s* of two), while the other ten will have values that are either less than three or more than seven. Generally, standard deviations that are close to zero indicate the taller, narrow bells, while increasingly larger values for *s* imply ever-flatter curves. The value for *s* is derived from an equation whose tedium, given a large body of data, makes everyone who performs it grateful for computers or scientific calculators. Its presentation here is essentially irrelevant to this discussion.

The theory also makes predictions about other portions of the normal curve. About 95 percent of all the events measured are expected to reside within two standard deviations on either side of the mean (i.e., somewhere between a value of one and nine in the example cited above); and a distance of three standard deviations from the average should encompass just over 99 percent of the data. Also, any value that lies within one standard deviation of the mean is considered "normal" for the group being measured.

As a result of all this, each separate item of data has two identities: its intrinsic numerical value and a value relative to the mean. To determine the second one, statisticians use a tool called the *Z Score*, which measures the distance, in standard deviations, that an individual event resides left or right of the mean. The Z-Score calculation is very simple: Z = (Indvidual Value – Mean)/Standard Deviation (i.e., take the numerical value of the item, subtract the mean value of all your data from it, and divide the result by the standard deviation). For the example cited above, an item with a numerical value of eight would have a Z Score of +1.5 (i.e., eight minus five equals three, divided by two, equals 1.5) — so a value of eight is one and one-half standard deviations above (or, larger than) the mean for that thirty-item collection of data. Similarly, a value of two would produce a Z Score of -1.5 (two minus five equals negative three, divided by two), indicating that it's one and one-half standard deviations below (smaller than) the mean.

These Z Scores have a practical limit of ±3.99 (or, a rounded ±4.00). That's because statistical theory also imposes that, in a "normal" distribution, all of the data should reside within four standard deviations of the mean. But, occasionally, a Z-Score calculation produces a result with a larger positive or negative value. When that occurs, statisticians say that the specific item of data involved is an "outlier," because it resides outside of, or beyond the results predicted by theory, and represents an event that is truly unusual for the body of data as a whole. As practical examples, among all of the HOF-eligible batters measured in this book, Hank Aaron's Z Score for career home runs is +6.77, Babe Ruth's is +6.35, and for that particular stat, they are outliers in the extreme.

So, by comparing a player's performance to the mean for a group, the Z Score provides a measure of the value of that performance relative to the group as a whole; and its elegance derives from the fact that its comprehension requires no more fluency in statisticalese than what you've been told above. In turn, its value can be represented and understood on the simple linear scale depicted near the end of chapter one, where the center (zero) is average, and the positive and negative extremes reflect scores that are progressively better or worse than average.

In fact, even the number line from chapter one is unnecessary. The Cooperstown credentials of everyone measured by this study will all be presented as scores that fall within a range of ±4.00. Just keep in mind that increasingly larger positive scores indicate (i.e., those that approach plus four) progressively above-average performance, a score near zero is run-of-the-mill for whatever the group, and increasingly negative scores (i.e., those that approach minus four) represent less-impressive results. In reality, a Z Score of +2.00 or better is very good, and relatively few of the scores posted in later chapters will exceed that amount.

With all that said, one other part of statistical theory is relevant to the marriage of Z Scores and baseball performance. A specific body of data is called a *sample* by statisticians, because it normally represents a portion of a larger set of events (termed a *population*) that — in theory — are too numerous to measure in their entirety. The theoretical assumption is that a sample of sufficient size will exhibit the same characteristics as the population as a whole, provided that the sample has been randomly collected. But, unlike its use in common language, there is nothing haphazard about "randomness" as it's defined in statisticalese. For a statistician's sample to be truly random, it must be acquired in a careful manner which maximizes the likelihood that all possible subsets of the population are represented proportionally, and which minimizes any probability of bias among the data collected. The appropriate size of a sample depends upon the overall size of the population being studied: for relatively small populations, a sample of 30 is often sufficient. For large populations, such as those of interest to political pollsters, much larger samples are taken — say, 800–1500 people to represent the nation's electorate.

In addition, and as noted above, the graphs of sample data often take shapes that do not represent normal distributions. At other times, data may only appear to have a normal distribution. For instance, while graphs of data for some baseball statistics appear to represent normal distributions, in truth they don't. That's because the men who play at the major-league level represent the extreme upper echelon of all the human talent available, and as such they are not a valid statistical sample, *per se*. Over their careers in the majors, Ty Cobb batted .366, John Vukovich hit .161, and they represent the opposite extremes of batting average among all non-pitchers who met the criteria for inclusion in this study — almost all of whom played in the Show for ten seasons or more. But, even Vukovich was a better hitter at the big-league level than a lot of guys who didn't stick that long — better than a lot of minor leaguers who never made it to the majors would've been — and his career average was at least 160 points higher than the performance likely from many of us. Even some minor-leaguers might have never hit a loud foul ball off of a Bert Blyleven curve, and most of us were never destined to make the Show, because we never possessed the requisite skills.

Because of all that, some sabermetricians repudiate the validity of applying bell-curve theory to major-league statistics. Some do not. Regardless, any such application mandates reasonable skepticism.

But, as much as the accuracy of the data collected, the validity of any statistical outcome also depends upon whether the research design poses the appropriate question in the first place. Very broad questions are more difficult — often impossible — to answer. As noted in chapter 1, the search for a definitive, all-inclusive statistical method to determine the best ball-player(s) ever is a quest for something as unobtainable as the Holy Grail. And, given the unavoidable subjectivity inherent to such a determination, any claim that the lists in later chapters represent an ordered ranking by "greatness" should be immediately dismissed by anyone who reads them, and no doubt would be by everyone who disagrees with them (i.e., anyone who reads this book).

All the same, because much of Cooperstown election is dependent upon individual statistics, it is appropriate to ask which players among all those eligible are the *most statistically qualified* for membership. And that's the only question this book attempts to answer. The application of bell-curve theory in general and the use of Z Scores specifically offers a means to settle the issue that is certainly more objective than your average sports-bar argument, or even the Hall-of-Fame selection process itself. No doubt, your own acceptance of the results will depend on whether you find the method used to be fair and valid and whether the results agree — at least, somewhat — with your preconceived notions about the relative credentials of the players measured. So, if you're favorite player does well here, you may like the results; if he doesn't, you'll probably think they stink and that the whole process is another attempt at statistical manipulation.

As for the group measured, among players only, the data for this book covers the period 1876–1994, including — with one exception — every man who either (1) had met the Hall of Fame's 10-year eligibility requirement by the end of the 1994 season or (2) had received Cooperstown votes for a career of shorter duration before the 10-year minimum was imposed. The sole exception is Charlie Pabor, who earned a lone HOF vote in 1936, but was not included in the database because he played only in the National Association of 1871–75 and, therefore, never appeared in what is now recognized as an official big-league game. Poor Charlie will get no score here because his stats are not considered major-league.

There are two reasons for the 1994 cutoff. First and most important, under the Hall of Fame's current selection rules, no player eligible by the year 2000 can have been active in the majors after 1994. So, although men active since that season are included in the database as players of the free-agent era (provided they had already appeared in ten major-league seasons by the end of that year), their performances after 1994 are ignored — to be consistent with that deadline. Second, the 1995 season probably marked the first in a new era of major-league history. The "Mega-Bucks" age of 1995 and beyond (or, whatever else we may eventually come to call it) is not given separate status here because it hasn't lasted long enough yet to produce either a ten-year generation of Cooperstown-eligible candidates all its own or a database large enough to have anything approaching the statistical significance of those from previous eras.

The practical results are twofold. Players like Mark McGwire and Ken Griffey, Jr., were not included in the data set because they had not appeared in 10 major-league seasons by the end of 1994 (although the scores of players with less than ten-years experience through 1994 will be reported in later chapters, if they are high enough to rank among the listed leaders). Also, because the stats included in the database involve career totals — many of which are cumulative — players active after 1994 earn lower Z-Score ratings than they would if their entire careers were included, and the disparity increases for every season played after that date (e.g., because he played in only three seasons after 1994, Eddie Murray's Z Scores will be closer to his final, career values than those of Cal Ripken, Jr., who played in all five seasons, and whose career was ongoing even in 2001).

In strict statistical terms, the database is not a random sample. Instead, it represents the full population of major-league players who have been considered for the Hall of Fame, provided that Cooperstown's 10-year eligibility requirement is applied retroactively to the beginning of HOF balloting for all men who have never received votes. Retroactive application was necessary because the 10-year standard was not adopted until about 1960 — so the inclusion of all the short-term players who were technically eligible before then would've bloated the size of the database to a cumbersome total of about 7,000 most of whose stats have no HOF significance.

The 1994 season marked the 119th year of major-league baseball. During that time, about 14,000 men appeared in at least one big-league game. Among them, 2,295 had met one of the two criteria for inclusion in the data set. So, as defined by a minimum of 10-year longevity or the receipt of Hall-of-Fame votes for shorter careers, the data set includes, roughly, the top 16 percent of all major leaguers in history. A couple of tables in later chapters give a total of 2,297 eligible players. The discrepancy occurred because Dave Foutz and Bob Caruthers, two 19th-century players, spent relatively equal portions of most of their seasons at both pitcher and another position. In thirteen seasons, Foutz played 595 games at first base, 320 in the outfield and pitched in 251; in his 10-year career, Caruthers spent 366 games in the outfield and 340 on the mound. Although this should have resulted in both men's being defined only as non-pitchers, their HOF credentials as hurlers are stronger than at any other position. As a result, their stats were included in the data for both subsets. Two other men from that era, Jack Stivetts and Hall of Famer Monte Ward could've been treated the same way. But Ward is cited on the Cooperstown roster as a shortstop, and he pitched in only the first seven of his seventeen seasons, so his stats were not included among the pitchers' data set. In contrast, Stivetts had 388 games as a pitcher — compared to just 173 at other positions — so only his pitching stats were used.

According to bell-curve theory, the top 16 percent of a normal distribution represents a Z-Score equivalent of about +1.40. A random sampling of 300 players listed in the register section of *Total Baseball* also indicates that, in rounded terms, the average major-league career lasts about five years, with a standard deviation of 4.5. That would give every man who played at least 10 years in the Show a minimum longevity Z Score of +1.11 (i.e., 10 − 5, divided by 4.5). But, because baseball statistics do not represent normal distributions, it may be fair to argue only that, on average — and excepting short-term players like Jewel Ens — the worst players who qualified for the data set are, by longevity alone, about one standard deviation more qualified for Cooperstown than the average major leaguer in baseball history (although, obviously, a man who played 10 seasons would not be a full standard deviation above one who appeared in eight or nine). As you will see in the final chapter, where a suggestion is made for applying the Z-Score, or Cooperstown Baseline, method to the Hall-of-Fame selection process, whether or not to grant that +1.00 "head start" to every player on the ballot has a major impact on his prospects for election.

But, the Cooperstown Baseline measures much more than just longevity, which is relevant to Hall-of-Fame credentials because the current selection rules (specifically, the 10-year service requirement) make it so, and because players with longer careers usually produce higher totals in the cumulative statistics (like hits and home runs by batters, and games won by pitchers) that impress HOF electors. Instead, the Z Scores earned by men in the data set provide a rating of their career performance in each of the statistics measured, combined, which — unlike the Hall's de facto standards — do not represent any absolute, minimum-entry, numerical achievement for any specific stat. So, the fact that Dave Winfield collected 3088 hits through 1994 (on his way to 3110 for his career), the equivalent of a +2.84 Z Score for that statistic, will not be enough, on its own, to justify his HOF membership under the Cooperstown Baseline system. For Winfield to merit selection, his overall statistical performance will need to reflect a Z-Score average that is significantly above the mean for all players in the data set. And the Z-Score average required for that will not be an arbitrary number — like a de facto minimum — but will be determined, instead, by both the level of performance typical among all players measured, and the distribution of their individual scores. So the Cooperstown Baseline is a relative standard which measures the average of a man's career performance against the average among all eligible players, combined.

Because of the different statistics they produce, the players who qualified for this study were first divided into two separate data sets, one for pitchers and the other for batters (i.e., all the non-pitchers, regardless of position). The former included 813 hurlers, the latter 1,484 players from the other eight positions, combined (with Foutz and Caruthers included among each). Men elected to the Hall of Fame for non-playing capacities (notably, managers and former Negro-leaguers) were included in these subsets, at the appropriate position, only if— like everyone else — they also played 10 seasons in the majors or received votes at some time from the BBWAA electors. So, Connie Mack and John McGraw (who meet both criteria), as well as Satchel Paige (who meets only the latter) are in the database, while fellow Hall of Famers Walter Alston (who appeared in only one big-league game and never received any BBWAA votes), Joe McCarthy (who got votes, but never played in the majors), and Monte Irvin (who didn't appear in 10 seasons and got no votes) are not. But, because they were not elected for their careers as major-league players, none of those men's individual statistics are included in any summations of HOF-player averages. Also, player performance was not included among the criteria for the managerial ratings that appear in chapter 12 (the standards for those ratings are explained at that point in the text).

Hall-of-Fame election seems to be intended as a career honor, so only career statistics — some of them cumulative totals, others averages — were used in the measurements; and, as a result, Roger Maris gets no extra credit for his single-season home-run feat of 1961. Unless otherwise specified later in the text, and except for several new statistics devised especially for this study, all career stats were taken or calculated from the numbers provided in Palmer and Thorn's *Total Baseball* (Sixth Edition, 1999), the publication now recognized as the official major-league record.

Player performance was measured on three separate scales: (1) compared to pitchers or non-pitchers of the same historical era; (2) compared to men who played the same position, regardless of era; and (3) compared to all pitchers or non-pitchers as a whole. As noted in chapter one, those three comparisons comprise the basis upon which most subjective arguments are made to promote a player's HOF candidacy (i.e., he was one of the top players of his time, among the best at his position, or one of the greatest players ever). As you will see, many Hall of Famers rank among the most-qualified players in each criteria, some rate near the top of only one or two of the scales, and several — Cooperstown's true errors of selection — rank nowhere near the leaders in any of them.

Although the Hall of Fame ostensibly honors the greatest players of all time, no attempt was made to prioritize the results of each scale to fit that context — because to do so would have inevitably involved making subjective judgments about how to weight the value of overall career achievement against the statistical variations imposed by time and different positions. After all, each measurement is clearly integral to a player's HOF credentials. As an example, the long-term rigors of the position assure that the very best catchers will always achieve less as batters than the best, or even many above-average first basemen; and, because of the variations in periodic norms, the best dead-ball era catchers could not avoid having weaker offensive credentials for Cooperstown than many run-of-the-mill live-ball backstops. If each of the scales do not apply relatively equally in the voting — even on the subjective level that currently rules HOF selection — then no dead-ball catcher would have ever been chosen for the Hall, and it's possible that the Cooperstown roster would be absolutely bloated with live-ball first sackers.

But, the use of three separate scales does provide a minimal context, albeit imperfect, for comparison of players across time. As noted in chapter one, the average performance in a specific statistic will vary in different eras, and as a result, cross-generational comparisons are always tenuous, at best, even for consecutive periods. For example, Ty Cobb (.366) and Rogers Hornsby (.358) own the highest career batting averages among the non-pitchers measured. Cobb (who played in the years 1905–28) earns a Z Score of +3.47 for that variable, measured solely against his dead-ball contemporaries, whereas Hornsby (1915–37) gets only a +2.84 score against players of the live-ball era, when the mean batting average among men in the database was much higher (.285, compared to .269 for the earlier period). So, Cobb's achievement was not only better numerically, but also more impressive than Hornsby's in the context of their respective eras. But, on the other hand, both men's careers also overlapped for almost a decade: Cobb's average was inflated by Live-Ball conditions at a point in his career when most players' statistics are on the decline; Hornsby's average was boosted by the same conditions while he was at the youthful peak of his performance. It's difficult to ascertain which man accrued the most benefit or disadvantage — if any — from the difference in their ages.

Similarly, Tony Gwynn, who began his career in 1982 and was still active in 2001, had a .333 batting average through 1994 which, in the context of the free-agent era's .265 norm, earns a Z Score of +3.65. So, in absolute terms, Gwynn's BA is nowhere near to Cobb's, but it is plausibly superior, relative to the norms of their separate times. But, although the Z-Score system lends credence to such comparisons, they should not be used to make any sweeping judgments about the players' relative credentials when applied to just one statistic, like batting average.

One of the three scales, the measurement of performance by era (chapters 6 and 7), involves only men who were relative contemporaries. So, by definition, it includes no periodic bias, because dead-ball-era players, for example, all of whom performed under the same rules and relative conditions, are compared only to each other, not to men from other times. But, in their simplest forms, the results of the other two scales — the positional and overall measurements (chapters 8 and 10) — each would reflect an inherent bias, among both the pitcher and non-pitcher subsets, imposed by the variations in normal performance for different times (e.g., hurlers from the pitching-dominated dead-ball era would earn relatively higher scores than mounds-men from any other period, while batters from the live-ball era would also benefit unfairly — relative to everyone else — from that period's above-average offensive production). As a result, the individual Z-Score averages for the positional and overall scales had to be normalized to remove the effects of periodic bias.

For fielding statistics, too, the norms vary greatly from one position to another. When compared only to men at the same position, these differences are meaningless (although some bias sneaks in on a player-by-player basis, because some men play multiple positions and others do not). But, overall, the disparities in the number and difficulty of plays at each position skew any cross-positional comparisons of fielding performance in a manner that is not statistically valid. So, the fielding Z Scores for both the era and overall scales also had to be standardized for these variations in positional norms. The methods used to normalize for both periodic and positional variances are explained at the end of this chapter.

No effort was made to control or normalize any career statistics based on relative "park factors" (i.e., any advantages accrued by players because of the various home stadiums they played in during their careers). It has long been known that some ballparks (e.g., Wrigley Field and Fulton County Stadium) are or were more conducive to high run-scoring or home-run totals than others where pitchers have an advantage (Oakland-Alameda County Stadium, or the old Comiskey Park, for instance), and normalizing for these park factors is much in vogue among many sabermetricians. But, because of the reserve clause, no major-leaguer ever had much choice regarding which park he played in before the era of free-agency. And although control for park factors has some statistical validity, it is unfair for Hall-of-Fame purposes to reward or penalize men for conditions which — through most of big-league history — they could not control.

By necessity, the research design uses different sets of data for pitchers and non-pitchers and, as a result, does not allow for any meaningful comparison of the two. So, although Rogers Hornsby (among several others) earns a higher final Z Score for his career than every pitcher who was measured, that does not mean that he was a better ballplayer than Cy Young, Lefty Grove or Sandy Koufax, or that he is more qualified for Cooperstown — statistically — than they are. All it really says is that, in the context of the different statistics used, Hornsby's credentials surpass those of the average non-pitcher in the database by slightly more than the very best hurlers exceed the mean among men who threw strikes for a living.

The pitchers' database also was divided into two subgroups — one for starters and another for relievers — without which there could have been no scale for hurlers comparable to the separate positional scores derived for non-pitchers. In most instances, this assignment was clearcut, and based strictly on whether an individual moundsman appeared in more career games as a starter or reliever. But, the placement also required considerable subjective license, because — until at least the 1950s — pitchers often began their careers as starters, then moved to the bullpen later on; and it was sometimes difficult to ascertain in which role specific hurlers enjoyed the most important or successful parts of their careers. In all instances, final placement was intended to maximize whatever HOF credentials may have been most evident in the pitcher's career performance; and for most men from before the expansion era, this led to placement among the starters' subset.

Non-pitchers were assigned to the defensive position at which they played the most major-league games. For some players, this represented a majority of their games played, for others a mere plurality. As a result, Hall of Famers Rod Carew and Ernie Banks both were treated as first basemen, rather than as a second sacker and shortstop, respectively; and — except where otherwise noted — their career totals were counted among those for first base, rather than the other two positions. But they were the only two HOF members whose positional statistics produced so distinct an anomaly, and their scores relative to men at their HOF-cited positions will also be reported at the appropriate point in the text.

Where specific outfield positions (i.e., left, center and right) are designated, the assignments of players were made according to the following criteria: (1) using the "Teams and Their Players" section of the Macmillan *Baseball Encyclopedia* (Tenth Edition, 1996), players were credited with one full season as a left, center or right fielder for each year in which Macmillan listed them as the starter at that position; (2) where players were listed as either the first substitute outfielder or first utility man (provided they played a plurality of their games in the outfield that season), they were credited with a half season at whatever spot at which the listed starter had the fewest at-bats among all three of the outfield regulars that year (on the premise that the first reserve outfielder was likely to have played more games that season at that specific position); (3) the final assignment was then based solely on whichever position the player had accumulated the highest total of full and half seasons, combined. This procedure produced two minor anomalies with the positional citations among the HOF roster: Hugh Duffy, listed as a center fielder at Cooperstown, had a higher total as left fielder under this system; and Jim O'Rourke, cited as a left fielder at the Hall, had more full and half seasons in center field. Both men were assigned to the position where they earned the higher score.

Designated hitters were not given a separate positional status, but were assigned instead to the defensive position at which they played the most career games. This was done because the non-pitchers' database included several fielding statistics which have no application for designated hitters, and because no Hall-of-Fame member has yet been elected or cited as a DH. As a result, free-agent-era players like Don Baylor and Andre Thornton — both of whom appeared in more career games as a DH than at any defensive spot — were assigned to other positions (in their cases, left field and first base, respectively).

Assignment of each non-pitcher to a single position ignores individual defensive versatility; and Chapter 8 will show that an ability to play multiple positions has no positive impact on a player's Hall-of-Fame prospects. But versatility complicated the assignment process in a manner that produced at least one instance — Pete Rose treated as a right fielder — that will contradict many readers' senses of history. Positionally, Rose may be best-remembered as a Rookie of the Year second baseman and as the third sacker on Cincinnati's dominant teams of the mid–1970s. Pete played the first four of his 24 seasons at second base (1963–66), followed by eight split evenly between left and right field (1967–74), the next four as a third sacker (1975–78), and then his final eight as a full- or part-time first baseman (1979–86). Overall, he played 1327 games in the outfield, 939 at first, 634 at third and 628 at second. Unfortunately, neither of the competing encyclopedias provide totals for games played at specific outfield positions. And although it's obvious that Rose played more games at first base than either in left or right field (specifically), consistency of method dictated his categorization as an outfielder. In fairness, his assignment to left or right could've gone either way: Pete won a batting title and MVP Award playing left field in 1973; he won his other two hitting crowns as a right fielder in 1968–69. The choice of either position, then, would have had a negligible impact on his Z Scores. Right field was chosen because he played that position at the ages (27 through 30) that normally represent the prime seasons of most men's careers.

Assignment of players to historical eras was based on just one criterion for each of the two main data sets. Generally, batters were assigned to the era in which they had the most major-league at-bats, and hurlers to the period in which they had the most innings pitched. Again, however, some leeway was required, especially when players' careers spanned almost equal portions of consecutive eras. In some rare instances, the era assignments contradicted that rule if the substance of a player's HOF credentials gave compelling reasons to do so. A notable example is catcher Ted Simmons, who was assigned to the expansion era although 64 percent of his at-bats occurred during the free-agent period. Simmons played in 21 seasons, 16 of them as a catcher (split evenly between the expansion and free-agent eras), and the last five as a combination DH and reserve first baseman — so the years he played at his primary position were equal in both eras. But, he entered the majors in 1968, a year behind Hall of Famer Johnny Bench (whose assignment to the expansion era is more clear-cut), and for most of Ted's career as a catcher, he played in Bench's shadow — constantly compared to him. Because most of Simmons' Hall-of-Fame prospects were tied to that comparison, his era assignment contradicted his career at-bat totals.

Four of the six measurements taken — all three for batters, and the positional one for pitchers — included 30 separate career statistics (variables) relevant to Hall-of-Fame election, while the other two pitching scales (overall and by era) included 26 stats. The smaller number of statistics used for the latter two measurements resulted because starting and relief pitchers are judged, in part, by different standards. For example, career complete games and shutouts have no meaningful application to a relief hurler's overall performance; and the number of games pitched or won in relief tell us nothing very useful about a starter's career. So among the 30 measures of performance by starters were five variables (games started, complete games and shutouts, plus both complete games and shutouts as a percentage of starts) which were replaced in the measurement of relievers by five others more relevant to their role (games in relief, relief wins, saves, wins-plus-saves as a percentage of relief appearances, and a "relief efficiency rating" which is explained below). Because the two groups were combined in both the overall and era measurements, all five of those variables for starters, and all but saves for relievers were dropped from those scales, leaving 26 variables instead of 30. Saves were included in the era and overall scales because of the importance they have acquired as a measure of relief performance; and they were applied for all pitchers in both scales, because in the early years of big-league play, a team's most frequently used relief hurler was usually one of its best starting pitchers.

In turn, each measurement generated either 30 or 26 separate Z Scores for every player in a respective group. Those scores were then averaged to produce each man's final Z Score for that subset; and these results, presented in chapters 6 through 11, required more than 400,000 separate calculations. The final Z Scores presented in chapter 11 represent the cumulative averages for all of the scores achieved by each player, in each of his three separate measures, and produce an ordered, objective ranking of each man's relative statistical credentials for Cooperstown.

As will be shown in chapter 5, some statistics are far more important than others to a player's chances for Hall-of-Fame election (e.g., career games won count much more than a pitcher's fielding average). But, the value of each stat was not weighted in the database to reflect those differences, because that would've imposed the subjective biases applied by the Hall-of-Fame electors onto the system of measurement, subverting the method's objectivity.

No other type of weighting was used either, as that would've applied the writer's bias in some form. As a result, career games won and home runs allowed per-nine-innings by pitchers, and career batting average, stolen bases and defensive assists-per-game by non-pitchers all carry equal value in each scale. But, for those who find that approach unrealistic, an alternative measure called the "Core Z" (explained in Chapter 5) is also provided, which focuses only on some of the stats most valued by HOF voters.

Among the career variables used to measure pitchers, the scales were relatively balanced between cumulative totals and averages. The former included years played (YRS), games pitched (GP), games won (GW), Fibonacci Wins (FW), innings pitched (IP), strikeouts (SO), saves (SV), Pitching Runs (PR), Fielding Runs (FR), the career number of times a player led the league in various pitching categories (TLP), the number of pennants (PW) and World Series won (WSW) as a player (treated as separate scores), and a career total for Cy Young Award-voting point equivalents (CY PTS, a new statistic devised specifically for this study, which is explained in the next chapter)—a total of 13 in all—along with games started (GS), complete games (CG) and shutouts (ShO) for starters only, or games in relief (GR), relief wins (RW) and saves (SV) for relievers. The pitching averages used included winning percentage (PCT), earned run average (ERA), the strikeouts-to-walks ratio (SO/BB), fielding average (FA), assists per game (A/G), range factor (RF), the opponents' batting (OAVG) and on-base averages (OOBA) against the pitcher, and separate, per-nine-inning averages for strikeouts (SO/9), hits (H/9), walks (BB/9), baserunners (RAT, or Ratio) and home runs allowed (HR/9)—also a total of 13—in addition to the complete-game (CG%) and shutout percentages (ShO%) for starters, or wins-plus-saves percentage (WSP) and efficiency rating (RER) for relievers.

For hits, walks and home runs allowed, the choice of per-game averages instead of the more familiar career totals places each pitcher's performance into an equal context that is more meaningful for comparative purposes than the cumulative totals would be. But, it also has an impact on the resultant Z Scores as, by reducing the number of cumulative statistics in the scales, it lessens the impact of longevity and (especially) makes relievers—who pitch far fewer innings, and whose career totals for those categories are commensurately much smaller than those of starters—more competitive than they otherwise would be in the two cross-positional measurements of pitchers by era and at-large. As a result, the final Z Scores earned by some relief pitchers will allow them to rank as much better Hall-of-Fame candidates than their cumulative numbers might indicate, even ahead of many starters who pitched far more innings. The effect has little impact on Z Scores for men from before the expansion era, simply because very few hurlers from before 1960 could be legitimately classified as career relief pitchers. But, for the last two historical periods, the effect is more pronounced. Although some readers may reject the results, they do reflect — more fairly — the increased emphasis placed on relief pitching after 1960.

Pitchers' career batting statistics were ignored. Since the advent of the designated hitter in 1973, half of major-league hurlers never see an at-bat in any given year. So, to include batting prowess as a measure of a pitcher's HOF credentials would unfairly penalize every hurler that pitched in the American League during the last two decades of the survey. Also, over the history of Hall-of-Fame voting, there have only been a half-dozen or so pitchers — Wes Ferrell being the prime example — about whom it has ever been argued that their batting skill was a significant reason to support their enshrinements. But to date, unless you consider Babe Ruth a pitcher, no hurler, not even Ferrell, has ever been elected for his batting feats; and it is obvious that — with regard to their Cooperstown credentials — good hitting is not a prerequisite for pitching immortality.

Among the thirty career statistics used to measure non-pitchers, there was less balance between cumulative stats and averages than occurred in the hurlers' scales, and as a result, the non-pitcher measurements favor longevity more than those for moundsmen. This was unavoidable because many of the most HOF-significant statistics for batters are cumulative and, unlike those for pitchers, represent numbers that are far more meaningful than per-game averages (e.g., hits-per-game).

The twenty-one cumulative variables used for non-pitchers included years (YRS) and games played (G), hits (H), doubles (2B), triples (3B), home runs (HR), total bases (TB), runs scored (R), runs batted in (RBI), walks (BB), stolen bases (SB), runs produced (RP), Runs Created (RC), Batting Runs (BR), Fielding Runs (FR), the career number of times led league in various batting (TLB) and fielding (TLF) categories, (again, separately) the number of pennants and World Series won as a player, and career totals for MVP-and Gold Glove-voting point equivalents (BABE PTS and GLOVE PTS, also explained in the next chapter). The nine averages used included home-run frequency (i.e., at-bats per home run, HRF), separate batting (BA), slugging (SA) and on-base percentages (OBA), on-base average-plus-isolated power (OBIP), fielding average (FA), and per-game averages for assists (A/G), double plays (DP/G) and range factor (RF).

Negative batting-performance statistics like strikeouts, grounding into double plays and times caught stealing were ignored. When Babe Ruth was elected to Cooperstown in 1936, he ranked as the all-time leader in career strikeouts by a batter, with 1330. It did not prevent him from being chosen in that first year of voting, with unambivalent, 95.1-percent support. Since then, Ruth has been surpassed on that list by more than forty-five modern players. But, the three career leaders through 1994 — Reggie Jackson, Willie

Stargell and Mike Schmidt — also were elected to the Hall in their first years of eligibility; and it is obvious that strikeouts and other negative statistics have a negligible impact on, or application to Cooperstown election.

The number of separate hitting and fielding stats used to measure batters favored offense by a ratio of three-to-one (21 variables to seven, with the defensive ones including fielding average, assists and double plays per game, range factor, Fielding Runs, number of times the player led the league in fielding and the Gold Glove-points equivalent). Generally, batting statistics have a far more obvious impact than fielding on a player's HOF chances. But, because the election process is subjective, the impact of defense is difficult to gauge on anything but a player-by-player basis. With 30 variables used overall (including the two for pennant and World Series success), the ratio was chosen — albeit subjectively — because fielding ability arguably accounts for less than one-fourth of the statistical justification for any non-pitcher's election, and it was reasoned that a three-to-one ratio also would offer the prospect that (given weak offensive stats) the very best defensive players might still be somewhat competitive within the overall system. Measures of a pitcher's fielding ability — fielding average, assists per game, range factor and Fielding Runs — were included because a hurler's individual defensive skills have some direct, if minimal impact on almost every HOF-relevant aspect of his performance (except strikeouts, walks, home runs allowed, and their related stats). But the number of fielding variables used was smaller for pitchers (four) than for batters (seven), because it is likely that defense plays an even smaller role in the Cooperstown election of hurlers than it does for players at the other positions. For batters and pitchers alike, preference was given to per-game fielding averages, as opposed to cumulative totals (like putouts and assists), because they are far more descriptive of a player's true defensive performance.

Many of the statistics used are familiar to even the most casual baseball fan. But a few of them — especially those developed by sabermetrics — require further explanation.

• Home run frequency (HRF) is most often treated in the competing baseball encyclopedias as a "home-run percentage" (i.e., the number of home runs per every 100 at-bats). But, this method is not especially fan-friendly, because — in the form they are usually given — numbers which would be better presented in three-decimals, like a batting average, are depicted (for example) as 1.2 or 0.3 percent. This is done, by necessity, because so many players from before 1920 have home-run percentages that must be carried to the third decimal in order to register at all. The number of at-bats per home run, an analogous measure, was chosen instead because its form is easier to understand and, as it was used frequently by the media during the home-run exploits of 1998, is currently more familiar to casual fans. Keep in mind that at-bats per home run is analogous to a pitcher's earned run average, the lower the number the more frequent the homers, and the better the performance.

• Runs produced (RP) is a simple, cumulative measure intended to isolate the actual number of runs scored during a player's batting and base-running performance. It is equal to the sum of runs scored and runs batted in by the player, minus his total of home runs.

• On-base-plus-isolated power (OBIP) combines — by addition — a batter's on-base average (the frequency at which he reaches base) and the frequency of his extra bases attained (any bases, beyond first, accrued by doubles, triples and home runs, combined). It was chosen as an alternative to on-base-plus-slugging (OPS, also known as Production), which is currently much in vogue among sabermetricians and the more statistically adept sportswriters. Both of OPS's components — on-base and slugging average — include batting average within their separate calculations, and as a result, players with higher batting averages benefit disproportionately from having that counted twice. Because OBIP's second component (isolated power) is defined as the subtracted difference between batting and slugging average, it eliminates that redundancy and provides a sum of a player's hitting frequencies that is not biased in favor of batting average.

• Runs Created (RC) is a sabermetric estimate of the run contribution by a batter. Devised by Bill James, the calculation (in its simplest form) is hits-plus-walks, times total bases, divided by the sum of at-bats plus walks.

• Batting (BR), Fielding (FR) and Pitching Runs (PR) are the separate linear-weights estimates of offensive, defensive and pitching performance devised by the sabermetric team of Pete Palmer and John Thorn. The formula for Batting Runs is BR = (.47)1B + (.78)2B + (1.09)3B + (1.40)HR + (.33)(BB + HB) — (.25) — (AB — H) — (.50)OOB, where the first four components represent multiples of a batter's singles, doubles, triples and home runs, the fifth one a multiple of walks-plus-hit-by-pitch, the sixth a multiple of the difference between at-bats and hits, and the last a multiple of outs on base. The multiplicative factors are based on the historical run-scoring or run-preventing values of each offensive incident. Fielding Runs is the linear-weights equivalent for defense, or as Palmer and Thorn explain it, "runs saved beyond what a league-average player at that position might have saved, defined as zero." Explanation of the calculation requires more space than available here. The definition of Pitching Runs is similar — "runs saved beyond what a league-average pitcher or team might have saved, defined as zero" — but the calculation is simple: PR = Innings Pitched x (League ERA/9) - Earned Runs Allowed. Those interested in more thorough explanations of these items should consult the "Glossary of Statistical Terms" provided in *Total Baseball.*

• Range factor (RF) is a simple expression of the number of successful defensive plays performed per game, defined as putouts-plus-assists divided by games played — or, the equivalent of the per-game rates of total chances-minus-errors. Ironically, the highest range factors among all positions are always produced at first base, the easiest position to play — because of the large number of putouts made there per-game after ground-ball assists. Because left-handed batters are a minority, right fielders tend to have the lowest range factor of any position, which explains why the worst fielder on kids' teams almost always gets stuck in right field.

• Career totals for the times-led-league variables were based on seasonal leadership. A total of 16 categories were used for batting and pitching leadership: games played, at-bats, hits, doubles, triples, home runs, home-run frequency, total bases, runs scored, runs batted in, walks, stolen bases, batting average, slugging average, on-base average, and on-base-plus-isolated power for batters (TLB); and games won, winning percentage, earned run average, games pitched, games started, complete games, innings pitched, shutouts, saves, strikeouts, (separately) hits-, walks-, baserunners, and strikeouts-per-nine-innings, and opponents' batting and on-base averages for pitchers (TLP). The career fielding-leadership totals (TLF) included putouts, assists, total chances, double plays, fielding average, total chances-per-game and errors at each non-pitcher position. Some might dispute the use of seasonal leadership in errors as a positive reflection of fielding. But, at some of the more difficult defensive positions, seasonal leadership in errors can be as indicative of superior range as it is of any ham-handedness.

• The number of pennants (PW) and World Series won (WSW), the variables measuring individual postseason success, were treated in a manner intended to liberalize credit for participation on championship teams. In instances when a player performed for more than one club during a season, he was credited with having played for a pennant winner — even if he was only there for the last month or less of a season — if it was the last team he was on the roster of that year. But, because divisional play did not begin until 1969, divisional winners were not credited with pennants, as that would have unfairly penalized players from before the expansion era. Whereas participation in World Series play is dependent on injuries and managerial choices, a player was credited as a World Series winner even if he was not on the postseason roster or did not actually appear in the Series, provided that he was with the club at the end of the regular season. And although the World Series as we know it did not begin until 1903, "world series" credit was given to winning members of teams that won 19th-century postseason playoffs between the National League and American Association champions (1882 and 1884–90), as well the NL split-season series (1892) and the Temple Cup playoffs (1894–97), thereby giving players from that century a chance to earn credit analogous to their modern counterparts.

• Fibonacci Wins (FW) is named after a 13th-century Italian, also known as Leonardo of Pisa, who was probably the greatest mathematician of the middle ages. The statistic was devised by Bill James specifically to gauge the relative values of pitchers' won-lost records. The stat is derived by multiplying career games won times career winning percentage, and then adding the number of career wins above .500. The result combines games won and winning percentage into a single context that facilitates comparisons of long- and short-term careers. Its use is also applicable to the career records of managers, and would be for non-pitchers too, if it were not for the fact that because of injuries, trades and managerial lineup decisions — it would take a lifetime of research to determine every non-pitcher's precise career won-lost record. On the whole, Fibonacci Wins is an extremely meaningful statistic; and anyone who wishes to devote their life to measuring the career totals for non-pitchers is encouraged to get started as soon as possible, as many sabermetricians would be delighted to possess the results. A more thorough analysis of the statistic is provided in James's *The Politics of Glory*.

• As its name implies, the baserunners-per-nine-innings statistic (also known as Ratio, or RAT) is a simple expression of the total number of men on base allowed by each pitcher on a per-game basis. A thorough form of the statistic would include — at minimum — all men who reach first by hits, walks and hit-by-pitch. But, for ease of calculation, the form used in this study was simply the estimate derived by combining the per-nine-inning ratios of hits and walks allowed.

• Two of the stats used specifically for relief pitchers Wins-plus-Saves Percentage (WSP) and the Relief Efficiency Rating (RER) are essentially analogous. The former measures only positive relief-pitching performance and is calculated by adding career games won in relief to career saves, and then dividing the total by career relief appearances. The latter uses almost the same formula, but includes negative performance, as well, by subtracting the total of career games lost in relief from the numerator, before the division process is applied. Both stats produce a three-place decimal figure similar in appearance to a batting average. The relief won-lost records used were taken from the data provided in Macmillan.

As noted earlier, the variations in norms for both positional and periodic performance impose an inherent bias among the raw Z Scores in some of the measurements. To maximize fairness, that bias had to be removed from any scales involving multiple positions or eras. Of course, many candidates played at more than one position, had careers that overlapped two historical eras, or both; and, because each man was assigned to just one position and era for measurement purposes, the elimination of absolutely all of these biases, on a player-by-player, statistic-by-statistic basis would have proven unbearably tedious and no doubt doubled (if not tripled) the number of calculations required to produce the rankings. So for simplicity, the bias was removed — in a process called "normalization" of data — by separate methods that each produced estimates of the amount of bias present. And neither procedure was either perfect or the only method available.

Both estimates were derived from the fact that statistical theory imposes that the mean of all Z Scores for any sample must be virtually zero (i.e., the average Z Score must be average, represented by zero). As a result, any variation from zero in the Z-Score mean for all members of a positional or periodic subset should reflect the amount of bias accrued in favor or to the detriment of the members of that subset. The bias, then must be removed by subtracting that variation from each of the players' raw scores. The net result is to lower the Z Scores of men from subsets whose means are above the average for the scale as a whole and to raise the scores for men from subsets with below-average means, moving almost everyone's score closer to zero.

For defensive statistics, the process was applied separately to each of the seven fielding categories common to both the era and overall measures. Such a statistic-by-statistic application was necessary because each defensive position produces very different performance norms for each of the statistics used. But even this careful adjustment, which was applied to both the era and overall scales for non-pitchers, could not negate all of the advantages accrued as a result of various fielding inequities, especially by men who played multiple positions. All the same, the removal of positional bias more accurately reflects the relative difficulty of playing shortstop as opposed to a much easier position like first base.

A rigorous, statistic-by-statistic adjustment for periodic bias might have proved more accurate, but normalizing the number of statistics involved — 30 per scale — would also certainly have taken far more time than the standardization of the seven fielding scores in each measure. As a result, the amount of periodic bias in both the positional and overall scales was estimated by using the variation between the mean Z-Score average for all statistics, combined; (for all players from a specific era within a scale) and the mean Z-Score average for all stats, combined; (for all players in the scale as a whole). Although this method was less precise, stat-by-stat tests on small subsets from each scale indicated that the error involved was, on average, less than three percent per man. But because the method was applied identically to all men in each relevant scale, any error applied equally to each of them, and the net effect on each man's Z-Score average was identical to that of the fielding adjustment.

The net result of both normalizations is to negate, as much as possible, any positional and periodic advantages in a manner that allows for accurate comparisons of performance across position and time. But, although the periodic and fielding normalizations removed two of the most obvious biases from the Z-Score scales, other, more subtle statistical advantages remain in each measurement. As noted earlier, no effort was made to remove any bias for park factors, and there was no attempt to normalize for any advantages accrued to batters as a result of their normal defensive position(s). In addition, there are no doubt biases that result from whether a batter or pitcher is right- or left-handed, whether a player performed mostly in day or night games, whether his team traveled mainly by rail or air, and whether a batter played during the early eras when starting pitchers were commonly expected to complete their games, or during modern times when several relief pitchers were used in each game. Some of those biases are objectively measurable, others are not. There is simply no way to thoroughly remove all bias from every scale.

The list of variables used for this study is certainly not all-inclusive, but it does feature almost every batting-, pitching- and fielding-performance statistic likely to be cited as relevant to Hall-of-Fame election. All the same, it's impossible to discuss HOF credentials without also examining a player's record in voting for postseason awards.

Postseason Honors

Baseball has numerous postseason honors for players, each with varying relevance to a man's Hall-of-Fame credentials. The Most Valuable Player Award (MVP) is the oldest and most prestigious, dating to 1911 (the Chalmers autos), 1922 (the league awards), or 1931 (the ongoing BBWAA honor), depending on how you define it. Except for the American League version of the 1920s (when previous winners were ineligible to repeat), the number of MVPs earned by a man has become an important aspect of his HOF merits. Thirteen out of 20 winners of the first two variants, and all but two of the 20 winners in the first decade of the current version have been enshrined at Cooperstown. Through 2000, only two multiple winners (Roger Maris and Dale Murphy) had missed election to the Hall.

The Rookie of the Year Award (ROY) is the next oldest, having first been given in 1947. The first couple of decades of ROYs included 10 players who have since been chosen for Cooperstown (seven of whom were elected in their first year on the ballot) and several later winners are certain to be enshrined when they become eligible (e.g., Eddie Murray and Cal Ripken, Jr.). On the whole, most of the recipients have enjoyed substantial major-league careers. But there have also been some notable duds among the selections, like Earl Williams (1971) and Joe Charboneau (1980), who never repeated their rookie performances, and several others (e.g., Herb Score, Ken Hubbs and Mark Fidrych) whose careers were shortened by injury or tragedy. So it's a hit-and-miss honor that also involves a specific moment in time, which — unlike the MVP — cannot be repeated later. As a result, there's minimal value to using the honor as a measure of HOF credentials.

The Cy Young Award (CYA) and Gold Glove trophies (GG) both date to the mid–1950s. Like the MVP, both of these awards have been around long enough to acquire a separate tradition and prestige of their own. And because they also may be won on multiple occasions, the number of either accrued by a player also has meaningful impact on a man's Hall-of-Fame prospects.

There are other awards, notably the Rolaids Relief Man/Fireman of the Year and the Silver Slugger trophies, but neither has much significance to HOF election. The relief-pitching honor has only been around since the 1970s, and the Silver Sluggers (presented by *The Sporting News*) were not given before 1980. So, although the latter may one day achieve a status for batters similar to what Gold Gloves imply about positional fielding, neither trophy has yet had time to earn much notice. Also, with only two identifiable, career relief pitchers elected to the Hall to date (Hoyt Wilhelm and Rollie Fingers), there is no reason at present to cite the Rolaids/Fireman award as a significant credential.

Over time, the MVP, Cy Young and Gold Glove honors have become relatively integral to discussion of any player's Hall-of-Fame prospects. In part that's because, of late the trio reward the three main aspects of the game — batting, pitching and fielding. The Cy Young and Gold Glove are obviously linked to pitching and defensive prowess, and, although supposedly available to men of every position, the MVP has in recent decades (and due mainly to the existence of the Cy Young trophy) become almost exclusively the property of batsmen.

But regardless of who they honor or what those awards measure, the biggest problem they pose for anyone trying determine their impact as Hall-of-Fame credentials is the fact that there are so many years in which the awards did not exist. There are no official MVP honors for any of the 19th-century major leagues (the National League of 1876–1900, the American Association of 1882–91, the Union Association of 1884 and the Players League of 1890), none for either the National or American circuits during the years 1901–10, 1915–21 and 1930, none for the Federal League of 1914–15, and none for the NL of 1922–23 or the junior circuit of 1929 — a total of 78 separate league seasons — or over one-third of the 227 league seasons in major-league history through 1994. There are no Cy Young Awards for any circuit before 1956, (a total of 141 league seasons) and no Gold Gloves until 1957 (143 missing league seasons) leaving more than half the seasons of big-league history through the last year of this book's database without player recipients. How, then, can anyone determine whether the accomplishments of Barry Bonds, Yogi Berra, Roy Campanella, Joe DiMaggio, Jimmie Foxx, Mickey Mantle, Stan Musial and Mike Schmidt (the only three-time MVPs through 1999), Roger Clemens (the only five-time CYA winner), and Brooks Robinson (sixteen-time Gold Glove recipient) are equal or superior to what would have been accomplished by Honus Wagner, Christy Mathewson or any 19th-century player, if the awards had existed earlier? Would Cy Young actually have won the award named for him more often than any other pitcher?

Since the advent of sabermetrics, there have been many attempts to fashion retroactive lists of probable award winners for the years in which the major postseason honors did not exist. The most authoritative of these, no doubt, was compiled by Bill Deane, a former senior research associate for the National Baseball Library and Archive at the Hall of Fame, whose lists and record of real award voting — including Hall-of-Fame elections — comprise roughly forty pages in each edition of *Total Baseball*. To date, Deane has not included Gold Gloves among his retroactive honors. But he has made choices for all of the missing years of MVP and CYA voting since 1901.

Although Deane's selections probably come as close as possible to an accurate estimate of the winners of the missing awards, his method poses problems. First, he has omitted the 19th century, so his list of hypothetical winners is still incomplete. Second, he has only selected winners, so the work cannot provide an estimate of the complete, career voting histories of men who might have finished second, third or anywhere lower in the balloting for these nonexistent awards; and to use his list as a source for Z-Score data requires giving each man credit only for the real or hypothetical honors he received. That would impose a black-and-white misreading of history, and it would underestimate the full careers of already-enshrined players like Lou Gehrig, who, although he won the American League MVPs of 1927 and 1936, also finished second twice (1931-32), fourth once, and fifth on three occasions. Third, as Deane readily admits, his choices inevitably utilize subjective criteria (his own opinions, plus those of various SABR retroactive-award surveys). All of the missing awards would have inevitably involved subjective judgment by the contemporary voters as well, but there is no way to assure that Deane's opinions, or those of other SABR members, accurately reflect the subjective values that would have been applied by voters at the times in question. If anything, given Deane's expertise and thoroughness, his own opinions may over-emphasize any apparent biases prevalent during the missing years (notably, the early MVP weight placed on winning the league batting title). But the same is unlikely of the SABR voters as a whole, the majority of whose subjective criteria is as likely as not to be influenced by modern hindsight and stats generated by sabermetric tools. Finally, Deane also used Pete Palmer's linear-weights system in his selections. But the linear-weights method was not published until the mid–1980s, and should not serve as a means by which to predict awards from a time when the statistic did not exist — because the voters of the past could not possibly have been influenced by it.

To resolve these problems, three new statistics have been developed specifically for this book that estimate the overall MVP — Cy Young — and Gold-Glove Award values of the full careers of each of the 2,295 men in the database. None of them is perfect, and one is a much better predictor of the winners than the other two. But, despite their flaws, they do accomplish one thing that all the other retroactive award lists don't — they provide an award-equivalent numerical value for every player's full career.

Consistent with the naming of the Cy Young trophy, the MVP-value estimate is called "Babe Ruth Points" (or simply, "Babe Points"), because it turns out — predictably — that Ruth is the all-time leader among this batters-only statistic. For sake of consistency with what it purports to measure, the CYA-value equivalent is called "Cy Young Points" (or "Cy Points," for short), although baseball's all-time wins leader did not achieve the highest career score for this pitchers-only variable (Walter Johnson did). Similarly, the Gold Glove statistic is called "Gold Glove Points" (or, just "Glove Points"), although it could also be named for the all-time leader in this category, Bid McPhee, a 19th-century second baseman who was arguably the greatest individual fielder of all time.

Much like the exit polling done at election time, the three award-points stats are based on voting trends historically demonstrable among balloting for the real MVP, Cy Young and Gold Glove honors. Each of them utilizes only traditional batting, pitching and fielding statistics which, even if they were not in use during all of the missing years in question, at least were available to electors throughout the history of the actual voting for each award. In their predictive format, they also take into account any relative predilection among the voters for these honors to reward players from first-place teams — as a reflection of such bias is a necessary component of accuracy in the projections.

The formats of the Babe- and Cy-Points estimates follow those used by the respective MVP and CYA elections. The former assigns points to each of the top 10 batters in a league among a group of traditional offensive statistics which are relevant to MVP election, on a basis that is identical to the 14 points which MVP candidates currently receive for a first-place vote, nine for second, eight for third, and so on, through one point for tenth place. The latter follows a similar process, but rewards only the top three pitchers in various CYA-relevant statistical categories, because the Cy Young voting format awards five points for first place, three for second, and one for third.

Because of the inconsistent number of electors involved in the Gold-Glove voting (19 electors in 1957, 400 or so over the next seven seasons when players voted for the honor, and then a number of managers and coaches that changed slightly every year beginning in 1965), the format for Glove Points had to be contrived. So, for simplicity, Glove Points were estimated using a form identical to that of the Cy Young process, by rewarding the top three players in each statistic used, on the basis of the CYA's five-three-one point assignment, separately for each defensive position. Outfielders were treated as a whole rather than grouped separately as left, center and right fielders because the Gold Glove voting has followed that process during most of its history. Although Gold Gloves are also awarded to pitchers, their fielding has a minimal impact on their Hall-of-Fame prospects, so Glove-Points estimates were not calculated for that position.

All three estimates are based on the frequencies at which players who led their league in various statistical categories also have won the MVP, Cy Young and Gold Glove Awards. Because the real award-voting formats assign a specific point value for each ordinal position on the ballot (i.e., first, second, third, and so forth) and require electors to prioritize their choices accordingly, once the frequencies are known, it is possible to calculate a point-share equivalent for each statistic, assigning values for each ordinal position among that category's leaders which also diminish proportional to the points awarded in the actual voting. This process is the same for all three estimates — although the point shares assigned vary for each version and statistic, depending upon the number of electors and votes possible in each election, and on the number of ordinal places allowed in the balloting for each award. Among the three systems, the calculation of Cy Young Points is the simplest and easiest to follow, so the process is described here in detail as a model for the other two.

There have been eight primary pitching statistics available, in common use and relevant to positive performance, through most of the history of baseball; and all of them have been readily available to Cy Young electors from the beginning of the award in 1956. They include games won (GW), innings pitched (IP), complete games (CG), earned run average (ERA), winning percentage (PCT), shutouts (ShO), strikeouts (SO) and games pitched (GP). Allowing for that, Table Four displays the number of times that the pitcher who led his league in each of these categories (separately) also won the CYA in the years 1956–94, and provides the resulting frequencies at which the leaders for each statistic can justifiably have been expected to win the award during the years 1876–1955. The variables are listed, left-to-right, according to their descending frequencies.

So, among the traditional statistics listed, league leadership in games won is clearly the best predictor of the actual Cy Young voting results during 1956–94. The league leader in pitching wins was chosen as the CYA winner about 68 percent of the time. The leader in innings pitched won about 34

Table Four
Frequency of Cy Young Awards by Statistical Leadership, 1956–94

League Leader In	GW	IP	CG	ERA	Pct	ShO	SO	GP	Total
Won CYA this many times	46	23	21	19	18	17	15	3	162
For a frequency of	.676	.338	.309	.279	.265	.250	.221	.044	2.382

percent of the time, and, on the opposite end of the frequencies, the leader in games pitched won only about four percent of the awards.

But, obviously, there were more league leaders in those eight categories than Cy Young Awards given during the 1956–94 period, and as a result, the frequencies noted in Table Four add up to over 238 percent. Because of this, the data requires a simple adjustment before it can be used to predict any hypothetical CYA voting for the missing seasons. Dividing the raw numbers by the total of occurrences (162, on the right end of Table Four) redefines their value as a percentage of all incidents, and places them in a context where they represent the percentage of overall points possible, or "point share," that is likely to be awarded for leadership in a given statistic. For example, the league leader in pitching victories has won the award 46 times, or the equivalent of 28.4 percent of the 162 occurrences noted. From that figure, you can infer that, on average, leadership in games won equates to a point share of about 28 percent of the overall points possible in a given CYA election.

Another variable also has a direct bearing on who wins the Cy Young Award. Twenty-eight of the CYA winners in the 1956–94 period have been members of the team with a league's best winning percentage for the season, and although team standing is not necessarily an indicator of a given pitcher's individual performance in a season, the frequency for this variable (.412) is higher than those for all but one of the stats listed in Table Four. So, any system that attempts to retroactively predict the results of hypothetical CYA voting prior to 1956 must — in order to reflect the voters' historical bias favoring first-place teams — give team standing the same consideration.

To do that, the point shares were recalculated, combining team standing with the eight performance variables, producing a total of 190 occurrences (the 28 CYA winners whose teams had the highest winning percentage, plus the other 162 incidents noted above). The results provide the true frequencies at which pitchers receive shares of the CYA voting points for each of the nine variables. Table Five gives the percentages of the overall point total that are predictable shares for the leadership in each category (with team standing listed as "TS").

In the real Cy Young balloting, the number of electors has varied from two per each team — that is, two sportswriters who covered each club in a circuit — for the 1956–69 seasons, to three per team in the years that followed.

Table Five
CYA Frequencies, Adjusted for Team Standing, 1956–94

Leader In	GW	TS	IP	CG	ERA	Pct	ShO	SO	GP	Total
Won this many times	46	28	23	21	19	18	17	15	3	190
Point-Share Equivalent	.242	.147	.121	.111	.100	.095	.089	.079	.016	1.000

Because the Cy Points system is intended to reflect the years before 1956, the method uses the initial, two-voter format. During most of the period 1876–1955, there were two eight-team leagues in operation each season, meaning that if the original procedure had always been followed, there normally would've been 16 electors in the voting for each league's award. As a result, each election would have a maximum of 144 points available, provided each elector voted and filled in all three spaces on the ballot (i.e., 16 voters times the total of nine points available in a five points-for-first, three-for-second and one-for-third-place format). This equates to a total of 80 points shared among pitchers who ranked first in the nine categories (i.e., 16 electors times the five first-place points allotted), 48 points split among pitchers who ranked second (16 times the three second-place points), and 16 points in all for the third-place pitchers.

The final element of the calculation allows for assignment of point shares to each of the top three pitchers in the league in each of the nine variables. The shares are calculated by multiplying the point-share equivalents provided in Table Five by the total number of points available for each ordinal ranking. The result is the point-share matrix provided in Table Six, which shows the number of points likely to be received, on average, by the first-, second- and third-place pitchers in each of the nine variables for an eight-team league.

Table Six
Point-Share Matrix for Hypothetical CYAs, Eight-Team League

Pitcher Rank	GW	TS	IP	CG	ERA	Pct	ShO	SO	GP	Total
First	19.36	11.76	9.68	8.88	8.00	7.60	7.12	6.32	1.28	80.00
Second	11.62	7.06	5.81	5.33	4.80	4.56	4.27	3.79	0.77	48.01
Third	3.87	2.35	1.94	1.78	1.60	1.52	1.42	1.26	0.26	15.99

The point shares in Table Six are then assigned to each pitcher who ranked among the top three in the league in each of the statistical categories. Where ties occur, the points are divided equally among all pitchers who share that ordinal position (e.g., if two men tie for third place in games won, they split the 3.87 value between them; if four men are tied for first in that category, the total number of points allotted for games won is shared equally, four ways).

The National League of 1884 provides a simple example of how the system is applied to real seasonal performance. That year, a total of only five pitchers placed either first, second, or third in each of the variables measured. Their individual, ordinal rankings in each category are shown in Table Seven.

Table Seven
Pitchers' Ordinal Rankings, By Statistic, NL of 1884

Pitcher	GW	TS	IP	CG	ERA	Pct	ShO	SO	GP
Charlie Buffinton, Boston	2	3	3	3	—	2	3	2	3
Pud Galvin, Buffalo	3	—	2	2	—	—	1	3	2
Charlie Getzein, Detroit	—	—	—	—	3	—	—	—	—
Hoss Radbourn, Providence	1	t1	1	1	1	1	2	1	1
Charlie Sweeney, Providence	—	t1	—	—	2	3	—	—	—

Hoss Radbourn led the league in every category except shutouts, and his Providence club also topped the league standings. So, he gets all the first-place point shares in seven categories and splits the first-and second-place shares for team standing with teammate Charlie Sweeney, who also was second in ERA and third in winning percentage. Pud Galvin led the circuit in strikeouts, while he and Boston's Charlie Buffinton were second or third in most of the other rankings. Buffinton gets the third-place points for team standing, because Boston finished in second place in the league, the highest finish among the non–Providence pitchers on the list. Sweeney and Charlie Getzein pick up a handful of points for their positions in the other categories. Commensurately, these rankings produce the final point-share matrix and totals shown in Table Eight.

Table Eight
Hypothetical CYA Points Total, NL of 1884

Pitcher	GW	TS	IP	CG	ERA	Pct	ShO	SO	GP	Total
Radbourn	19.36	9.41	9.68	8.88	8.00	7.60	4.27	6.32	1.27	74.80
Buffinton	11.62	2.35	1.94	1.78	0.00	4.56	1.42	3.79	0.26	27.72
Galvin	3.87	0.00	5.81	5.33	0.00	0.00	7.12	1.26	0.77	24.16
Sweeney	0.00	9.41	0.00	0.00	4.80	1.52	0.00	0.00	0.00	15.73
Getzein	0.00	0.00	0.00	0.00	1.60	0.00	0.00	0.00	0.00	1.60
Totals	34.85	21.17	17.43	15.99	14.40	13.68	12.81	11.37	2.31	144.01

So, the method predicts Radbourn as the 1884 Cy Young winner in a lopsided vote in which he would have earned about half of the 144 total points available in the balloting. Buffinton would have placed second in the voting, ahead of Galvin by slightly more than the advantage he received from his team's higher finish in the standings (Galvin's Buffalo club placed third that year).

Radbourn's 74.8 Cy Young Points for 1884 can then be added to his point totals for the other years in his career to produce an overall CYA-equivalent

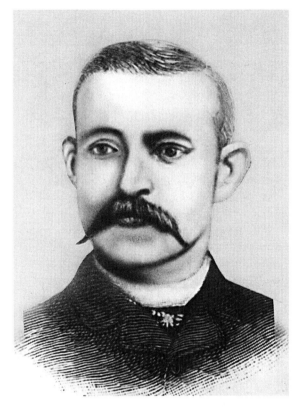

Charles "Old Hoss" Radbourn, a 300-game winner and 1939 inductee, surely would have won the Cy Young Award, if there had been one in 1884 (*The Sporting News*).

value for his combined major-league performance. The method can be applied, in the same fashion, to the statistical leaders for each season in baseball history (including those in which real Cy Young voting occurred) to produce an objective prediction for any such voting that might have taken place, and to create a series of points for each pitcher which, when totaled, give a CYA-equivalent value to his full career. Pitchers who never placed among their league's top three in any of these categories earn a career value of zero.

The validity of this statistical method depends in part upon its accuracy at predicting the winners of the real Cy Young Awards presented since 1956. Among the 68 winners during the years 1956–94, this system correctly predicts 42 of them, for a reliability rate of .618 — which does not meet the normal statistical-science standard of .667 required for a valid predictor. But there are some factors which indicate that its accuracy for the years 1876–1955 may be higher.

Ballots for both the Cy Young and MVP awards are collected by the last day of the regular season, to prevent the voters from being influenced by postseason performance. So prior to 1969, when the two major leagues initiated divisional play and its multi-tiered playoff system, unless a playoff was required, the electors knew which teams had won the pennant when they cast their ballots. But, since 1969, they have voted knowing only the identity of the league's divisional winners, and of the team with the circuit's best overall record. This change in format has altered the predictability of a voting system that initially favored players from pennant-winning teams. Of the 15

Cy Young winners in the years 1956–68, 12 of them (80 percent) pitched for pennant-winning clubs. But, only 18 of the 53 subsequent winners through 1994 (about 34 percent) played for clubs that won their league playoffs and advanced to the World Series. So, because the CYA electors have been uncertain since 1969 of which team would actually win the league pennant, they have shown a greater willingness to reward pitchers solely for individual performance rather than for their team's overall success. All the same, these circumstances would not apply to the seasons before 1956: the impact of playing for the known pennant winner would be more clear-cut, and the standards which applied during 1956–68 would have been likely to prevail.

An increased emphasis on relief pitching also has altered the predictability of the Cy Young voting process. In 1974, the Dodgers' Mike Marshall was the first reliever to win a CYA, and a total of eight bullpen specialists were voted the honor between 1974 and 1994. The Cy Points system allows no real possibility that a relief pitcher would win a hypothetical CYA prior to 1956 because they are simply not competitive in seven of the nine variables used (all but games pitched and team standing). So while reliever Jim Konstanty was the National League MVP in 1950 (there was no Cy Young trophy then), the system cannot predict a CYA for him that year because the points he accumulated for games pitched and being a member of the pennant-winning Phillies are insufficient to overcome the advantage earned by starting pitchers in the other seven stats. As a result, the method projects — no doubt, inaccurately — Boston's Warren Spahn as the NL's CYA recipient that season.

But the Cy Points system is intended to reflect conditions under which CYA honors would've been given in the distant past, and scant attention was paid to relief pitching in the early years of the award. Among 43 men who received votes for the honor in the first 14 years of Cy Young balloting (1956–69), only one of them was a relief pitcher. Ironically, it was not Elroy Face, who got zero CYA votes in 1959, despite his 18–1 record and .947 winning percentage. Instead, the only reliever ever recognized in the balloting prior to 1970 was the Cardinals' Lindy McDaniel, who received just one vote in 1960. A decade passed before any other relief hurler received CYA support, but Dave Giusti, Wayne Granger and Ron Perranoski all got votes in 1970, and a total of eight other relief performances earned votes during the other three seasons that preceded Mike Marshall's 1974 trophy. So any CYA emphasis on bullpen specialists did not manifest before 1970.

Given that history, the best test of the Cy Points system's validity for the years 1876–1955 is its predictive success for the first 13 years of voting (1956–68), when, like most of the major-league seasons that preceded them, there was little emphasis on relief pitching, the leagues were not split into separate divisions, and the electors usually knew who had won the pennant at the time they cast their ballots. The two lefthand columns of Table Nine list the actual CYA winners for those seasons or, for the years in which only one award was given (1956–66), the pitcher ranked highest in the balloting from the league opposite the winner. The two righthand columns give the league winners projected by the Cy Points system. Men who won the award are listed in boldface; incidents of agreement between the real and predicted awards are italicized; errors in the Cy Points predictions are underlined.

Of the 15 Cy Young awards given during the period covered by Table Nine, the Cy Points accurately predict 13 of the recipients as the CYA winner in their respective leagues, a success rate of .867. The two errors involve the National League predictions of Ernie Broglio over Vernon Law in 1960 and Jim Bunning instead of Mike McCormick in 1967. During 1956–67 there were five instances where the projected league winners could not be compared to actual CYA runners-up — Sandy Koufax's three unanimous awards (1963, and 1965–66, when no one else received votes), and the CYAs for 1960 and 1962 (when no American League hurlers received support). Among the remaining six opportunities, the Cy Points system accurately projects three of the non-winners who were also the highest-ranked hurlers in the voting from the league opposite the actual recipient (Warren Spahn in 1958 and 1961, and Larry Jackson in 1964). So, assuming that these men would have won any CYA for their respective leagues, the method correctly predicts 16 out of twenty-one possible winners overall, a success rate of .762, which is well above the normal standard for a valid statistical predictor. Also, although the Cy Points' league-oriented format implies that scores from separate circuits are not competitively analogous, the five highest, single-season Cy Points totals among this group were earned by each of the five unanimous CYA winners during this period — Koufax, for each of his awards, plus Denny McLain and Bob Gibson in 1968. All of this indicates that the Cy Points method is a valid, although certainly not perfect, means to predict retroactive Cy Young honors for the seasons prior to 1956.

The Babe and Glove Points methods both follow the same basic procedure as Cy-Points to derive their separate estimates of career batting and fielding accomplishments. Both use traditional (i.e., non-sabermetric) statistics which have been available to MVP and Gold Glove electors throughout the history of the awards, and both also reflect the relative predilections of voters for each honor to reward players from first-place teams.

Like its Cy Young counterpart, the Babe Points system uses nine separate variables to predict MVP winners for the missing years. In order of their relative importance to election, they include team standing (TS), plus seasonal leadership for runs batted in (RBI), slugging average (SA), total bases (TB), home runs (HR), runs scored (R), batting average (BA), hits (H) and stolen bases (SB). Three other stats — on-base average, doubles and triples —

<table>
<tr><td colspan="5" align="center">Table Nine
CYA Winners v. Cy-Points Leaders, 1956–68</td></tr>
</table>

| | CYA Winner, Or Highest in Voting | | League Leaders, Cy Points | |
Year	American	National	American	National
1956	Ford (3rd)	**Newcombe**	<u>Lary</u>	***Newcombe***
1957	Donovan (2nd)	**Spahn**	<u>Bunning</u>	***Spahn***
1958	**Turley**	Spahn (2nd)	***Turley***	*Spahn*
1959	**Wynn**	S. Jones (2nd)	***Wynn***	<u>Spahn</u>
1960	none	**Law**	J. Perry	<u>Broglio</u>
1961	**Ford**	Spahn (2nd)	***Ford***	*Spahn*
1962	none	**Drysdale**	Terry	***Drysdale***
1963	none	**Koufax**	Ford	***Koufax***
1964	**Chance**	L. Jackson (2nd)	***Chance***	*L. Jackson*
1965	none	**Koufax**	Grant	***Koufax***
1966	none	**Koufax**	Kaat	***Koufax***
1967	**Lonborg**	McCormick	***Lonborg***	<u>Bunning</u>
1968	**McLain**	**Gibson**	***McLain***	***Gibson***

were also considered, each of which had a higher predictive frequency for MVP success than at least one of the statistics that was used. But, although on-base average was a better MVP predictor than either hits, doubles, triples or stolen bases, it was rejected as a variable because its was not devised until the 1950s and not recognized as an official statistic until the mid–1980s. Doubles and triples were both better predictors than stolen bases, but they also were rejected, because in combination with runs scored, hits and batting average, stolen bases offered a better (if slim) chance that base-stealing specialists near the top of the batting order might be relatively competitive with power hitters on this scale.

Unlike the other two measures, Glove Points utilizes only eight variables to predict the likely winners of that award. In order of their impact on Gold Glove honors, they include total chances (TC), putouts (PO), team standing (TS), assists (A), fielding average (FA), total chances per game (TC/G), double plays (DP) and errors (E). No other statistics were considered, as these represent the ones most readily available in the encyclopedias and have been available to Gold-Glove electors throughout the history of voting for the award. Leadership in errors was included, (again) because it can be as much a measure of range as of poor fielding. Although the predictive frequencies for each variable differ for each separate defensive position, the point-share equivalents used reflect all Gold-Glove voting as a whole, because that method provided a larger database as a source for the estimates.

Table Ten lists the leadership frequencies and final point-share equivalents, rounded to three decimal places, that accrued for both the Babe and Glove-Points systems. This data corresponds to the Cy Young leadership frequencies provided in Table Four, and to the point-share equivalents in Table Five.

Table Ten
MVP (1911–94), Gold-Glove (1957–94)
Leadership Frequencies and Point Shares

Babe Points	TS	RBI	SA	TB	HR	R	BA	H	SB	Total
Leadership Frequency	82	55	47	45	36	35	29	19	7	355
Point-Share Equivalent	.231	.155	.132	.127	.101	.099	.082	.054	.020	1.001

Glove Points		TC	PO	TS	A	FA	TC/G	DP	E	Total
Leadership Frequency		169	151	150	140	129	128	123	31	1021
Point-Share Equivalent		.166	.148	.147	.137	.126	.125	.121	.030	1.000

Although they represent MVP-value estimates, Babe Ruth Points measure only the career credentials of batters; pitching statistics were omitted from consideration in the statistic. Although this mirrors the recent trend excluding hurlers from serious consideration for the MVP awards, it also has a negative impact on the Babe-Points system's success as a predictor of those laurels. Among the 150 actual MVPs awarded during the years 1911–94, 23 of them were given to pitchers. The Babe Points method cannot predict any of them.

Two other factors also negatively impact the Babe Points' predictive accuracy. First, because of the physical demands of the position, catchers tend to have significantly lower batting statistics than players at almost every other position. So, because of Babe Points' emphasis on offensive performance, catchers also fare poorly in the method. The history of MVP voting includes 15 awards given to catchers through 1994, none of which are accurately predicted by the system. Second, the method includes no controls for years in which players were excluded from MVP election because they had previously won the award (these include 1912, when 1911 winners Ty Cobb and Wildfire Schulte withdrew from consideration in the Chalmers awards, plus the American League awards of 1923–28, when previous winners were ineligible). Among these years, there were two instances (1924 and 1928) when the AL winner projected by the system — Babe Ruth in both instances — was not eligible for the actual balloting.

Overall, the Babe-Points method accurately predicts just 53 of the 127 non-pitcher MVPs awarded from 1911 to 1994, a success rate of .417. There also were eight instances in which the batter projected as MVP by the system was the highest-scoring non-pitcher in the MVP balloting, and, among the fifteen MVPs awarded to catchers, there were five occasions when the Babe-Points winner was runner-up in the actual voting. Although there was no official award for the American League in 1929, the winner predicted by the system, Al Simmons, did receive one of two unofficial

MVPs presented that year. Combined with the two instances when Babe Ruth might have won, if he were eligible, and allowing for a one-half credit in the unofficial 1929 voting, these circumstances give the method a maximum predictive success of 68.5 out of 151 chances, for a rate of just .457. So the Babe-Points system is, unavoidably, a less-accurate tool for predicting the MVP winners than the Cy-Points method is for its comparable award.

For the period 1956–94, the Glove-Points method accurately predicts 234 out of 526 Gold Gloves awarded to non-pitchers, a success rate of .445. Positionally, the range of predictive success varies between a high of .493 (37 out of 75) for catchers, to a low of .320 (24 of 75) for shortstops. There were also 41 instances — about 8 percent of all the awards — in which players who had never previously won a Gold Glove were projected as winners by the system in a given year, did not receive the real honor, but then won it in the next. This may lend credence to an ongoing criticism of the Gold-Glove process: because voting is done before a season's official defensive statistics are published, the electors tend to vote based on the previous year's performance, rather than the season at hand. But if that is true in some cases, then the voters are not focusing solely on fielding average — as some suggest in another critique of the process — because that particular defensive statistic has only the fifth-best predictive rate among the variables listed in Table Ten. If one argues that those 41 instances were injustices fostered by the subjective flaws in the real Gold-Glove process, that would push the predictive success of the Glove-Points method to a maximum of .523 (275 out of 526).

The predictive success of the Babe and Glove-Points systems also may be hindered by their reliance on the most familiar, traditional statistics. As noted earlier, on-base average is a better predictor of MVP selection than two of the variables used in the Babe-Points calculations; and it may be that other measures of defensive skill — like the per-game averages of assists and double plays used in the database as a whole — would prove better predictors of the Gold Glove awards than the traditional stats that were utilized instead.

But, again, the Cy-, Babe-, and Gold Glove-Points methods are intended only as estimates of the award support likely to have accrued during any player's career. So, despite their relative flaws at predicting winners, they are applied to every major-league season on a consistent, objective basis, and do completely fill the gaps in an incomplete historical record whose missing data requires that any other attempt to do so must be equally hypothetical. They also offer a more comprehensive estimate of the relative award value of pitching, batting and fielding achievement among the large group of players in the database than a reliance upon other, more subjective methods which focus only on award winners.

Table Eleven provides listings of the career leaders in all three of the award-value measures included among the variables used to derive the overall ratings for this book, with individual totals rounded to the nearest whole number. The Babe-and Cy-Points lists include the top ten career values accrued by players in the database, while the Glove-Points section presents the career leader at each position (including the top three outfielders). Below that, the table also provides the career leaders in the number of individual awards predicted by each system. On both sets of lists, the names of men elected to the Hall of Fame through 2000 are boldfaced.

Some other calculations not yet mentioned were required to produce the final career-point values displayed in Table Eleven. First, as noted earlier, each of the award-value estimates is based, in part, on the number of electors who were likely to have participated in the balloting for any given season, and — therefore — the number of points possible in a particular election. But, as noted above, the number of electors in Cy-Young and Gold-Glove voting has fluctuated over the years, and so has the number of voters who participate in MVP balloting. When the BBWAA took over the MVP voting in 1931, there was only one elector per league team. The number of voters was expanded to three per team in 1938, and it was then reduced to two per club in 1961. In 1938, the process also switched from awarding just 10 points for first-place votes, to 14 thereafter, and the latter system has remained in use ever since. Each of these changes altered the maximum number of points possible in the MVP election. For simplicity, the Babe-Points system utilizes a two-voter-per-team, and 14-for-first-place point matrix for every year measured.

But, the number of teams in a league has also varied over time, and each of the expansions since 1961 has increased the number of award electors. As a result, a separate point-share matrix (like the one in Table Six), reflecting the appropriate number of teams and voters, and with different first-, second-, and third-place shares is required for any season in which the number of a league's teams was greater or less than eight. These seasons include the National League of 1877–78 and American Association of 1882 (six teams each), the American and Union Associations of 1884 (13 teams started the former's season and twelve began the latter's, but only eleven clubs finished the AA season, and just five played all, or nearly all of the UA schedule; the matrices used reflected the smaller number in each case), the National League of 1889 and 1892–99, the American League of 1969–76, and the NL of 1969–92 (12 teams each), the AL of 1961–68 and NL of 1962–68 (10 teams), the AL of 1977–94 and the NL of 1993–94 (14 teams). Inclusion of each of these matrices would require more space than practical here, and the point-share values for each are calculable from the other information already given.

Table Eleven
Career-Total and Individual Award
Leaders, Babe-, Cy- and Glove-Points

Rank	Babe Points	Total	Cy Points	Total	Glove Points	Total
1	Babe Ruth	2847	Walter Johnson	742	G. Hartnett (c)	724
2	Ty Cobb	2751	Warren Spahn	657	Cap Anson (1b)	799
3	Hank Aaron	2542	Grover Alexander	586	Bid McPhee (2b)	1071
4	Honus Wagner	2390	C. Mathewson	502	Ozzie Smith (ss)	899
5	Stan Musial	2368	Lefty Grove	472	B. Robinson (3b)	834
6	Rogers Hornsby	2289	Cy Young	465	Tris Speaker (of)	697
7	Ted Williams	2266	Bob Feller	444	Max Carey (of)	645
8	Lou Gehrig	2208	Steve Carlton	413	R. Ashburn (of)	613
9	Willie Mays	2090	Robin Roberts	355		
10	Sam Crawford	1885	Tom Seaver	346		

Rank	Predicted MVPs	Total	Predicted CYAs	Total	Predicted GGs	Total
1	Honus Wagner	8	Grover Alexander	6	Gary Carter (c)	9
2	Ty Cobb	7	Walter Johnson	6	Bill Terry (1b)	7
3	Rogers Hornsby	7	Bob Feller	6	Bid McPhee (2b)	11
4	Babe Ruth	7	Warren Spahn	6	Ozzie Smith (ss)	7
5	Ted Williams	7	C. Mathewson	4	Ron Santo (3b)	8
6	Stan Musial	6	Lefty Grove	4	Willie Mays (of)	11
7	Hank Aaron	5	Robin Roberts	4	Tris Speaker (of)	11
8	Lou Gehrig	5	14 tied with	3	Max Carey (of)	10
9	Mike Schmidt	5				
10	3 tied with	4				

Because variations in league size dictate changes in the number of participating voters and the number of points possible in a given election, the point estimates for each of these systems are inevitably inflated during years when there were a relatively large number of teams in a league, and deflated for those when there were not. To correct for this, the point-share estimates accrued by players in each situation were normalized. Since eight-team leagues were the norm through most of major-league history, that standard would have been preferable. But, the factors required proved mathematically cumbersome. So, for simplicity of calculation, this was done by multiplying each of them by whatever factor — a decimal figure greater or less than one — equalized the shares to the amount that would've accrued had the season involved a ten-team league.

Beyond all that, for the purposes of the database — which already includes two separate variables measuring regular- and post-season success — each of the point-value systems described in this chapter are intended to focus on the degree to which a player's specific batting, pitching or fielding performance contributed to his award prospects during his career. In that light, although the final season's standing of a given player's team obviously impacts his chances for MVP, Cy Young or Gold Glove recognition in a particular year, its relevance to career measurements is negligible — beyond the degree to which relative team success enhances or diminishes individual statistics. So, although the points accrued for team standing are important to each system's award-predictive accuracy, they have been removed from the individual totals in Table Eleven, and were not included in the career values used for the database as a whole. But, rather than merely subtract the team-standing points from each man's career total, the removal was accomplished by recalculating point shares based on the performance variables, alone, and then applying the results to whatever matrix was appropriate in a given season for the player's league.

In addition to the MVP, Cy Young and Gold Glove awards, one other baseball honor clearly has an impact on a player's Hall-of-Fame prospects: selection for the All-Star Game. Although not directly analogous to the postseason awards, the All-Star tradition, begun by Chicago *Tribune* sportswriter Arch Ward in 1933, is almost as old as the MVPs. It has acquired its own prestige, and a large number of All-Star appearances by a player is indicative that he was held in high esteem during his career.

All-Star appearances are like the other awards in another aspect, because there are 105 missing league seasons in which no All-Star Game was played (all major-league seasons before 1933, plus the AL and NL seasons of 1945, when the contest was not held because of wartime travel restrictions). As a result, 565 of the 2,295 men in the database — including 66 Hall of Fame players — were gone from the majors before the All-Star tradition began: To be fair to candidates whose careers ended before 1933, measurement of the All-Star credentials of every man in the database would also require a system to project retroactive all stars for those missing years.

Compared to balloting for the other main awards, the methods of choosing all stars have varied greatly over time, bouncing back and forth between selection by big-league managers and election by the fans — the former method appearing to reward players' skills or timely performance, the latter mainly popularity. Because the game is played at mid-summer, a time for which player statistics are not available in the encyclopedias, it is also difficult to measure whether selection patterns are ruled by performance during the first half of the given season, a man's accomplishments from the year before, or by his overall career achievement. And, no doubt, dominance by any one of those factors has been transient over time, depending on who made the selections. As a result, any numerical system to project retroactive all stars would be doomed to mimic postseason All-Star teams, like the ones chosen annually by *The Sporting News*, rather than the midseason choices that were really made; and it is likely that its predictive success would be even worse than that of either the Babe-or Glove-Points systems. So, All-Star appearances were not included among the variables measured in the database, but, where relevant to his HOF credentials, the number of times each man was selected will be noted in the player comments in later chapters.

Finally, although they have flaws as predictors of the actual award winners, the individual career totals for Cy-, Babe-, and Glove-Points are relatively effective as measures of Hall-of-Fame credentials. As the next chapter will show, career Cy Young Points are a better predictor of HOF election than all but two of the variables included in the overall database for pitchers; career totals for Babe Ruth Points are the eighth-best predictor of Cooperstown membership among the 30 statistics applied for non-pitchers, and, although Gold Glove Points rank only 18th among the non-pitcher variables used, they are nonetheless better predictors of HOF selection than any of the other defensive statistics utilized in the overall Z-Score calculations.

CHAPTER 5

Cooperstown Standards

Six decades of Hall-of-Fame selections constitute a substantial precedent from which some identifiable statistical standards — beyond the de facto minimums for hits, home runs and games won — must have evolved, if only by default. But, the number of electors has varied over the years, so the subjective preferences of each voter assure that there have been anywhere from 78 to 499 different standards applied in any given election through 2000. The skills of ballplayers also vary greatly, so, unlike Ty Cobb or Walter Johnson, most HOF members do not rank among the career leaders in almost every statistical category. As a result, clear-cut standards for most statistics are difficult to identify.

If any standards exist, a clue to their identities should be evident in the relative degrees to which various statistics predict Hall-of-Fame membership. Some stats are certain to be better forecasters than others, and, although the predictive rates for each are dependent upon the biases historically operative among the electors, they should be useful to understanding which statistical performances dominate Cooperstown election. Table Twelve provides the HOF-predictive rates for each of the 30 non-pitcher variables in the database, and for the 26 statistics shared among all three Z-Score measurements of relative pitching performance, with the defensive variables italicized. Sabermetric measures (designated by an S, and broadly defined as statistics which have come into use during the last three decades) are also differentiated from the older, traditional (T) stats. There were 127 non-pitchers and 58 hurlers enshrined through 2000; the rates below are based on the number of those players who ranked among the top 100 career leaders for the non-pitcher variables, or the top 50 for pitching (including ties for the last spot on both lists) through 1994, the last year of the database.

Table Twelve
Hall-of-Fame Predictive Rates for Z-Score Variables

Rank	Non-Pitcher Variables	Rate	Rank	Pitcher Variables	Rate
1	Runs Created (S)	.760	1	Pitching Runs (S)	.820
2	Runs Produced (S)	.740	2	**Games Won** (T)	.780
3	**Hits** (T)	.693	3	Cy Young Points (S)	.740
4	Total Bases (T)	.690	4	Fibonacci wins (S)	.720
	Runs Scored (T)	.690	5	Led League, Pitching (T)	.692
6	**Runs Batted In** (T)	.670	6	**Innings Pitched** (T)	.680
7	Batter Runs (S)	.630	7	**Strikeouts** (T)	.620
8	Babe Ruth Points (S)	.620	8	Ratio (S)	.420
9	Doubles (T)	.604	9	Years Played (T)	.418
10	**Batting Average** (T)	.567	10	Opps' On-Base Avg (S)	.407
11	Games Played (T)	.564	11	**Winning Percentage** (T)	.333
	Triples (T)	.564	12	**Earned Run Average** (T)	.308
13	Led League, Bat (T)	.551		SO-to-BB Ratio (S)	.308
14	Years Played (T)	.482	14	Games Pitched (T)	.255
15	Slugging Average (T)	.467	15	Opps' Batting Avg (S)	.250
16	On-Base Average (S)	.446	16	Pennants Won (T)	.227
17	Walks (T)	.440	17	HR-per-9 Innings (S)	.220
18	*Gold Glove Points* (S)	.410		BB-per-9 Innings (S)	.220
19	On-Base+Is. Power (S)	.408	19	Hits-per-9 Innings (S)	.216
20	*Led League, Field* (T)	.370		*Assists-per-Game* (T)	.216
21	**Home Runs** (T)	.363	21	*Range Factor* (S)	.196
22	Stolen Bases (T)	.333		*Fielding Runs* (S)	.196
23	Pennants Won (T)	.321	23	World Series Won (T)	.149
24	Home Run Frequency (S)	.290	24	SO-per-9 Innings (S)	.100
25	*Fielding Runs* (S)	.252	25	*Fielding Average* (T)	.052
26	World Series Won (T)	.202	26	Saves (S)	.040
27	*DP-per-Game* (T)	.140			
28	*Assists-per-Game* (T)	.137			
29	*Range Factor* (S)	.120			
30	*Fielding Average* (T)	.030			

Two of the pitcher variables — Pitching Runs and games won — are better predictors than the best among the non-pitcher subset (Runs Created). But only seven of the 26 pitching statistics forecast Hall-of-Fame membership at a .500 rate or better, and just 13 of the 30 non-pitcher categories exceed that percentage. Even worse, the two-thirds standard for a valid predictor (.667) is surpassed by only 12 of the 56 stats, combined. Also, among the three statistics that involve the obvious de facto criteria for hits, home runs and games won, only two meet the two-thirds standard. Career home runs, perhaps the glamour stat in all of baseball history, is a poor predictor of HOF membership, with a rate of just .363.

It's also clear from Table Twelve that fielding statistics have a negligible impact on Hall-of-Fame election. No defensive stat ranks better than 18th out of the 30 non-pitcher variables (Gold Glove Points, at .410), and four of the seven fielding categories land at the bottom of that list. Among the four defensive stats used for the pitcher measurements, the best forecaster is tied for 19th out of 26 variables (assists-per-game, at just .216), and the other three rank no higher than 21st. Combined, the 11 fielding statistics from both lists have a mean predictive rate of just .193, and except for the presence of relief-pitching saves, fielding average — probably the most familiar measure of defense — would be the worst predictor on both lists. None of that is particularly surprising, given the voters' obvious emphasis on batting performance. But the poor predictive scores for the fielding variables contradict the prevailing notion that most Hall of Famers are chosen for their all-around performance.

Among the five variables used only to measure starting pitchers (which are not listed in Table Twelve), career shutouts is the best predictor, scoring at a .686 rate, followed by career games started at .600. The two rank sixth and ninth, respectively, among all the pitching statistics used. But the other three variables exclusive to starters — career complete games (a predictive rate of .460), shutouts as a percentage of starts (.260) and complete games as a percentage of starts (.200) — are all relatively poor forecasters of Cooperstown election for hurlers. With only two relief pitchers currently in the Hall, the four variables exclusive to their measurement — games in relief, relief wins, wins-plus-saves percentage and the relief efficiency rating — have no better than a 3- or 4-percent success rate, just like saves. In turn, they have no value as predictors at present, and until many more relievers are added to the roster, their predictive rates cannot improve much.

Among the batting statistics measured, the sabermetric tools are marginally better predictors than the traditional stats. The 10 modern measures among the non-pitcher subset have an average predictive rate of .468, compared to .444 for the 20 traditional statistics. But, on average, the 12 older stats among the 26 common pitching variables outscore their 14 sabermetric counterparts .394 to .347, and the margin of their relative superiority (.047) is larger than the advantage enjoyed by sabermetric measures among the non-pitcher variables (.024). Combining both data sets, the 32 traditional statistics used have an average predictive rate of .425, while the two-dozen Sabermetric measures score at .397. The predictive edge enjoyed by the traditional statistics is not surprising, because most sabermetric measures were not available for use by Cooperstown electors until very recently, so they cannot have played a significant role over the 65-year evolution of any Hall-of-Fame statistical standards that are tied to trends in voting.

But most of the variables in Table Twelve leave something to be desired — in many cases, quite a bit — as tools to forecast Cooperstown election. As a group, the 30 non-pitcher statistics predict Hall-of-Fame membership at only a .452 clip, while the 26 pitcher categories have an overall success ratio of just .369. The 56 variables, combined, forecast at a mean rate of only .413, yet the entire list includes almost every batting or pitching stat (or a facsimile, in the cases of the OBIP-for-OPS, and MVP-, Cy Young-and Gold Glove-Points substitutions) likely to be cited by someone as a justification for a man's election. So, more than anything else, the data in Table Twelve demonstrates that there is no strong consensus among Cooperstown electors regarding which statistics are the most valid measures of Hall-of-Fame credentials. That's to be expected, given the subjective foundation of the selection process.

All the same, both lists in Table Twelve also include five statistics in bold-face: hits, runs scored, runs batted in, batting average and home runs for non-pitchers; games won, innings pitched, strikeouts, winning percentage and earned run average for hurlers. Each of these stats has been around since the beginning of the Cooperstown selection process, is regularly provided by news-papers and magazines in a form that requires no additional calculation, and is meaningfully applicable to every batter or pitcher in the database (unlike shutouts or complete games). So, arguably, they comprise the career stats which are the most readily available and comfortably familiar to most people (including the electors). As a result, they are likely to make up the core of any subjective discussion of a player's Hall-of-Fame credentials. Throughout the rest of this text, the player rankings will include two separate Z Scores, one for mean performance among the appropriate pitcher or non-pitcher variables as a whole, and another for the average score among either set of five statistics only, hereafter referred to as the "Core Z" (or, simply, Core). This second Z Score is provided as an alternative career-value estimate for those who might argue that the overall study includes too many stats of minor significance. But note that there may be considerable variation between the two scores for any given player, and the Core-Z average will generally be much higher than the Total-Z for high-profile Hall of Famers like Hank Aaron or Babe Ruth. Regardless, in all instances the overall rankings for any measurement will be based only on the Total-Z average among all the variables, as a whole.

If only by familiarity, the Core-Z variables include the traditional stats which have dominated the Hall-of-Fame selection process for most of its history. Among them, the five statistics for non-pitchers have an average HOF predictive rate of .597, and the ones for pitchers forecast at a .544 clip. Despite the weak scores posted by home runs, winning percentage and earned run average, the mean success ratio for all ten Core stats, combined, is .570.

Another way to identify Cooperstown's statistical standards involves the average performance levels among Hall-of-Fame players for the statistics in the database. Table Thirteen lists the means and standard deviations among all players inducted through 2000 for each of the 56 common variables, and— on the pitchers' side, separated by lines — for each of the stats exclusive to the starters' or relievers' subsets. The data for the Core variables is boldfaced again.

Table Thirteen
HOF Means and Standard Deviations, All Variables, Through 2000

Batter	Mean	s	Pitcher	Mean	s
Years Played	17.7	3.4	Years Played	17.1	4.1
Games Played	2103.3	482.5	**Games Won**	**265.0**	**72.7**
Hits	**2373.4**	**583.0**	**Winning Percentage**	**.5912**	**.0448**
Doubles	404.6	120.7	Fibonacci Wins	237.3	84.8
Triples	116.2	57.1	**Earned Run Average**	**2.941**	**.4499**
Home Runs	**202.0**	**179.2**	Games Pitched	593.0	154.7
Home-Run Frequency	90.1	92.2	**Innings Pitched**	**3980.9**	**1108.0**
Total Bases	3615.9	1015.0	Opps' Batting Avg	.2436	.0168
Runs Scored	**1316.9**	**351.4**	Opps' On-Base Avg	.2995	.0173
Runs Batted In	**1207.4**	**397.5**	Hits-per-9 Innings	8.284	0.729
Runs Produced	2322.4	588.7	BB-per-9 Innings	2.528	0.725
Walks	883.0	377.2	Ratio	10.812	0.863
Stolen Bases	222.5	204.4	**Strikeouts**	**2127.7**	**900.7**
Batting Average	**.3047**	**.0246**	SO-per-9 Innings	4.871	1.588
Slugging Average	.4634	.0682	SO-to-BB Ratio	2.005	0.630
On-Base Average	.3793	.0306	HR-per-9 Innings	0.438	0.269
On-Base+Is. Power	.5379	.0788	Pitching Runs	286.9	141.2
Runs Created	1458.4	454.2	Saves	26.3	52.0
Batter Runs	336.9	274.3	Cy Young Points	243.1	150.0
Babe Ruth Points	796.2	653.1	Led Lg, Pitching	23.3	17.0
Led Lg, Batting	14.1	17.3	Fielding Average	.9517	.0260
Fielding Average	.9668	.0220	Assists-per-Game	1.426	0.570
Assists-per-Game	1.118	1.165	Range Factor	1.771	0.626
DP-per-Game	.2763	.2671	Fielding Runs	3.9	28.5
Range Factor	4.478	2.362	Pennants Won	3.1	2.4
Fielding Runs	42.2	91.9	World Series Won	1.6	1.8
Led Lg, Fielding	13.1	11.3	Games Started	495.8	136.6
Gold-Glove Points	316.2	246.0	Complete Games	304.3	131.0
Pennants Won	3.3	2.7	CG Percentage	.6244	.2032
World Series Won	1.6	2.0	Shutouts	46.1	16.5
			ShO Percentage	.0955	.0303
			Games in Relief	962.5	78.5
			Relief Wins	115.5	12.0
			W+Sv Percentage	.4195	.1054
			Relief Eff. Rating	.3135	.0983

The career of a typical Hall-of-Fame position player lasts almost 18 years in which the batter compiles a total of about 2372 hits, 202 home runs, 3616 total bases, 1317 runs scored and 1207 RBI to go with a batting average of .305. On average, HOF pitchers spend about 17 years in the majors, win 265 games for a .591 winning percentage, compile a 2.94 earned run average in about 3981 innings, and strike out 2128 batters. Starting pitchers also average 496 career starts, 304 complete games, 46 shutouts, a complete-game percentage of .624, and a shutout percentage of .096. Between them, the

Hall's two relief pitchers — Hoyt Wilhelm and Rollie Fingers — average 963 games in relief, 116 relief wins, 284 saves (the relievers' averages are not listed separately, above), a wins-plus-saves percentage of .420 and have a Relief Efficiency Rating of .314. Subsequent chapters will reveal that these averages are a cut above those compiled by all the HOF-eligible players as a whole.

Of course, because they are averages, the career stats of every Hall of Famer do not meet or exceed the means for each statistic listed in Table Thirteen. In fact, none of the Cooperstown members chosen through 2000 meets or exceeds all of them. Overall, 27 of the 58 moundsmen in the Hall through 2000 equal or surpass the Hall-of-Fame means in at least half of the 26 pitching variables, and 54 of the 127 position players do the same for their statistics. Among hurlers, Walter Johnson and Christy Mathewson score the best — their career stats are equal to or better than the 2000 HOF average in 23 (or 88.5 percent) of the 26 pitching variables. They are followed by Grover Alexander and Tim Keefe, both of whose stats meet or exceed the means for 21 of the pitching measures (80.8 percent). The leader among non-pitchers is 19th-century first baseman Roger Connor, the career home-run leader prior to Babe Ruth, who scores 26 out of 30, for 86.7 percent. Connor is followed closely by Stan Musial, Tris Speaker and Honus Wagner, with 25 variables each, for 83.3 percent.

But, the upper echelon of any of those measurements has no relevance to the Hall's operative statistical standards, because players at that end of the spectrum are all high-end outliers in the given variable measured, among both Cooperstown members and the database as a whole. On average per man, the 127 position players in the Hall meet or exceed the HOF mean in 13.7 (or about 46 percent) of the 30 non-pitcher variables (with a standard deviation of 6.0), while the 58 Cooperstown hurlers typically equal or surpass the average in 12.3 (47 percent) of the 26 statistics common to all of their measurements (posting a s value of 4.4).

As noted in Chapter Three, statistical theory postulates that any number within one standard deviation of the mean is normal for a group. So the s values for the number of variables in which the already-enshrined batters and pitchers meet or exceed the Hall-of-Fame means can be subtracted from the averages for the same to obtain an estimate of the minimum number of all the statistics used in which a viable candidate should equal or surpass the HOF means to provide a useful starting point for the objective identification of Cooperstown's true errors of selection and omission. The result — a minimum of about eight variables for batters and pitchers, alike (the equivalents of a .267 success rate for batters, and .308 ratio for hurlers) — can then be used to argue that there should be extremely compelling reasons why anyone who does not meet that eight-variable criterion should ever be elected.

Through 2000, there were five pitchers and 18 position players enshrined at Cooperstown whose career stats did not meet or exceed the Hall-of-Fame average in at least eight of the database variables. Based on that standard, the least-qualified pitchers in the Hall were dead-ball era Giant Rube Marquard, who equals or surpasses the current HOF average in only four of the variables (a .154 success rate), and Jesse Haines, who scores only slightly better at five (for .192). They are followed by Dazzy Vance (six variables, .231), plus Red Ruffing and Early Wynn (seven stats and .269, each). Among the HOF position players, the lowest scores are earned by catcher Roger Bresnahan and outfielder Tommy McCarthy, who both equal or surpass the Cooperstown average in just two of the 30 non-pitcher variables (for a success rate of .067), followed closely by Ernie Lombardi and Fred Lindstrom at three variables each (.100). Other Hall of Famers who fail to meet the eight-stat standard include Ross Youngs (four variables, .133), Jimmy Collins (five, .167), Earle Combs, Larry Doby, Rick Ferrell, Elmer Flick, George Kell, Edd Roush, Ray Schalk and Hack Wilson (six variables, .200), and Frank Chance, Chick Hafey, Mike 'King' Kelly and Lloyd Waner (seven, .233).

In comparison, among the unenshrined men who qualified for the database, there were 66 pitchers and 88 position players whose career stats met the eight-variable minimum standard through 2000. Beyond that, there were 267 other unenshrined hurlers among the 813 in the overall pitcher subset that scored as good or better than Rube Marquard; and 1,116 additional unenshrined position players among the total of 1,484 in that subgroup that equaled the success rates of Bresnahan and McCarthy. Those numbers subvert the argument that any of the Hall of Famers near the bottom of this scale are statistically qualified for Cooperstown.

There are, however, only 12 unenshrined men among the database — nine position players and three pitchers — who meet or exceed the 2000 Cooperstown means for as many as half of the variables measured, and a handful of others who come relatively close to that ratio. Table Fourteen lists the highest success-rate scores achieved by non-Hall of Famers in the database, based on career stats through 1994. The ranks shown indicate the man's ordinal position among the non-pitcher or pitcher subsets as a whole, with a lower-case "t" indicating ties. Players active after the 1994 season are italicized.

The non-pitcher side of Table Fourteen is dominated by recent players: four of them (Rose, Darrell Evans, Garvey and Staub) retired in the 1980s; four others (Andre Dawson, Dwight Evans, Dale Murphy and Dave Parker) were active into the early 1990s; and six more (all italicized) were still playing after 1994, and not yet eligible for Hall-of-Fame consideration by the 2000 voting. Given that each of the non-pitchers listed compiled career stats (through 1994, at minimum) that meet the HOF average in at least 13 of the 30 variables measured, their scores are strong evidence that — statistically, at least — each of them is well-qualified for Cooperstown. In that light, there is

Table Fourteen
Unenshrined Players with Highest
Success Rates Meeting 2000 HOF Means

Rank	Non-Pitchers	Rate	Rank	Pitchers	Rate
t16	*Eddie Murray*	.700	t17	Hooks Wiltse	.538
t22	Pete Rose	.667		Smoky Joe Wood	.538
t35	Bill Dahlen	.600	t23	*Roger Clemens*	.500
t44	Darrell Evans	.567	t31	Bob Caruthers	.462
	Dwight Evans	.567		Jim McCormick	.462
	Dave Winfield	.567		Ed Reulbach	.462
t51	*Andre Dawson*	.533		Doc White	.462
t58	Mickey Vernon	.500	t39	Bert Blyleven	.423
t63	Steve Garvey	.467		Spud Chandler	.423
	Gil Hodges	.467		Dave Foutz	.423
	Paul Molitor	.467		Sam Leever	.423
t70	*Wade Boggs*	.433		Carl Mays	.423
	Joe Gordon	.433		Gary Nolan	.423
	Rickey Henderson	.433		Deacon Phillippe	.423
	Dale Murphy	.433		Bruce Sutter	.423
	Graig Nettles	.433	t49	Eight tied with	.385
	Dave Parker	.433			
	Rusty Staub	.433			

no doubt that, absent his alleged gambling problems, Pete Rose, baseball's all-time hits leader, would be there already; and there is little reason to question whether de facto qualifiers Eddie Murray (504 home runs, 3255 hits), Dave Winfield (3110 hits), Paul Molitor (3319 safeties) and Wade Boggs (3010) will be elected soon after they become eligible.

In contrast, the pitchers' section of Table Fourteen is loaded up with hurlers from bygone eras: only five of the 15 men listed played in the majors after World War Two (one of those, Spud Chandler, barely did that, having retired after the 1947 season); most of the rest are 19th-century and/or dead-ball-era hurlers. Only Roger Clemens is not yet eligible for the Cooperstown ballot. All of the pitchers listed compiled career stats that equal or surpass the current Hall-of-Fame average in at least 11 of the 26 categories measured, again strong evidence that their statistical credentials are better than those of Rube Marquard and several other hurlers chosen for the Hall. Clemens reached his 38th birthday during the 2000 season, and with 247 wins through 1999, his chances of reaching the 300-win de facto standard were marginal. But, coupled with his rare-for-a-modern-pitcher MVP trophy and record five Cy Young awards, his Table Fourteen score demonstrates that he will be an easy first-year selection when he becomes eligible for the Hall.

Among the recent players in Table Fourteen, five of them — Garvey, Murphy, Parker, Bert Blyleven and Bruce Sutter — were on the BBWAA ballot in

2000. But the chances that any of them might be elected by the scribes are fair at best. Garvey's eligibility began in 1993, when he received 41.6-percent support from the writers, but that was his best-ever showing on eight BBWAA ballots. His average annual support had dropped to 36.8 percent after the 2000 voting. Sutter joined the ballot in 1994, and in his first seven tries he averaged only 29.2-percent support, with a high of 38.5 percent in 2000. Parker became eligible in 1997, and his four-ballot vote history included a high of 24.5-percent support in 1999 and an average of only 19.7 percent. Blyleven joined them in 1998, but his high-support level of 17.5 percent that year, and his three-ballot average support of 16.3 percent offer little hope for his election. Murphy's name first appeared on the ballot in 1999, and in his two appearances through 2000, his highest support level was just 23.2 percent.

Five of the other men listed in Table Fourteen were on the BBWAA ballot in recent years. Pitcher Gary Nolan retired after the 1977 season and became eligible for Cooperstown in 1983, but he never received a vote from the writers. Graig Nettles became eligible in 1994, but received an average of only 6.8-percent support over four elections before he was dropped from the ballot for failure to meet the 5-percent minimum required for retention. The same fate befell Rusty Staub and both Darrell and Dwight Evans, each of whom was on the ballot for one or more years during the 1990s but was dropped when his support fell below 5 percent. Under the Veterans Committee's current guidelines, none of those five can ever be considered by that panel. Table Fourteen indicates that their denial of any future eligibility is a definite injustice.

Because each of them played in at least 10 big-league seasons and all of their careers began before 1946, the other men in Table Fourteen are technically eligible for VC consideration. Six of them — pitchers Bob Caruthers, Dave Foutz, Jim McCormick, Ed Reulbach, Doc White and Hooks Wiltse — never received a vote from the BBWAA or the 1936 Old-Timers Committee (Reulbach, the most recent, last played in 1917). The unsuccessful vote histories of the other nine are varied: Gil Hodges netted 3,010 votes on 15 ballots without ever being elected; Mickey Vernon received a 16-ballot high of 96 votes and 24.9-percent support in 1980; Joe Gordon's best showing in 14 elections was 97 votes and 28.4-percent support in 1969; and, among nine ballots, Smoky Joe Wood topped out with 29 votes (18.0-percent support) in 1947. None of the rest ever received more than six votes in a single election, (Sam Leever fared the poorest, getting just one tally in 1937.) Bill Dahlen was a shortstop whose career spanned 1891–1911, and for part or much of that time he was a contemporary of six other Hall of Famers at his position — Monte Ward (1878–94), George Davis (1890–1909), Hughie Jennings (1891–1912), Bobby Wallace (1894–1918), Honus Wagner (1897–1917) and Joe Tinker (1902–16). Dahlen's score in Table

Fourteen (.600) is better than those posted by four of them, Jennings (.367), Tinker and Wallace (.300) and Ward (.267); but Dahlen got just one vote in the 1936 OTC balloting and another lone tally in the BBWAA election of 1938. Except for Hodges and Gordon, both of whom reportedly received support in the 2000 VC balloting, the Cooperstown prospects of all these men are now slim.

The lists in Table Fourteen clarify that, in the absence of absolute statistical standards for the variables relevant to Cooperstown election, the performance of every player can be measured against the Hall-of-Fame norms for those statistics, to produce an estimate of each man's HOF credentials. But ranking players solely by the standards in that table leaves many men tied at each level of relative qualification. Those deadlocks can be resolved by applying the Z-Score process — that is, measuring the distance of every man's career performance for each statistic from the numerical HOF means, providing each with a career score relative to the Cooperstown norms. Table Fifteen lists both the top (in descending rank) and the bottom 10 Z Scores (in ascending order) earned among Hall-of-Fame members through 2000, based on the Total Z-Score average accrued for all the variables common to their appropriate pitcher or non-pitcher subset, along with the 15 best scores earned by players not yet enshrined through 1999 (by descending rank, again), with players active after 1994 in italics. The Core-Z averages are included for each player, although they may or may not represent a score that would have qualified for a similar listing based only on that data. Keep in mind that a Z Score of zero represents one that is exactly on-par with the Hall-of-Fame average, so that men with positive scores are (or would be) above-average Hall of Famers and those with negative tallies are below the norm.

Table Fifteen provides an objective measure of the best-and-least-qualified Hall of Famers, based on their performance versus the Cooperstown means, and unenshrined players who (if not yet eligible for the Hall) are virtually assured of election, or (if already eligible) may have been unfairly overlooked in the selection process. Among the list of lowest-scoring HOF members are five of the OTC2 selections of 1945–46 (Roger Bresnahan, Frank Chance, Johnny Evers, Tommy McCarthy and Joe Tinker), along with three of the Frankie Frisch-Bill Terry-Waite Hoyt VC cronies of the 1970s (Fred Lindstrom, Chick Hafey and Ross Youngs). All of the non-pitchers on that list are Veterans Committee selections. But, surprisingly, four of the hurlers — Ted Lyons, Dizzy Dean, Bob Lemon and Early Wynn — are BBWAA inductees, the latter of them a 300-game winner.

Among the unenshrined players with the best Total Z Scores compared to Hall-of-Fame means, most of the men listed also scored well in Table Fourteen. So, again, the non-pitchers are dominated by recent players, while most

Table Fifteen
Best and Worst Z Scores v. HOF Means

Top HOF Non-Pitchers	Total Z Avg	Core Z Avg	Top HOF Pitchers	Total Z Avg	Core Z Avg
Babe Ruth	1.51	2.04	Walter Johnson	1.09	1.45
Ty Cobb	1.32	1.92	Christy Mathewson	1.04	1.21
Lou Gehrig	1.21	1.45	Cy Young	1.03	1.69
Stan Musial	1.20	1.68	Grover Alexander	0.77	0.93
Hank Aaron	1.05	2.14	Ed Walsh	0.67	0.11
Tris Speaker	1.03	1.11	Tom Seaver	0.43	0.70
Willie Mays	0.97	1.58	Warren Spahn	0.36	0.56
Jimmie Foxx	0.93	1.24	Eddie Plank	0.35	0.71
Honus Wagner	0.91	0.93	Tim Keefe	0.34	0.69
Eddie Collins	0.89	0.71	Mordecai Brown	0.32	0.26

Bottom HOF NPs	Total Z Avg	Core Z Avg	Bottom HOF Pitchers	Total Z Avg	Core Z Avg
Ray Schalk	-0.97	-1.71	Jesse Haines	-0.74	-0.95
Tommy McCarthy	-0.95	-0.99	Ted Lyons	-0.61	-0.81
Roger Bresnahan	-0.88	-1.49	Rube Marquard	-0.53	-0.74
Ross Youngs	-0.77	-0.94	Waite Hoyt	-0.46	-0.72
Rick Ferrell	-0.76	-1.22	Early Wynn	-0.40	-0.20
Johnny Evers	-0.75	-1.30	Dizzy Dean	-0.39	-0.69
Fred Lindstrom	-0.73	-0.73	Eppa Rixey	-0.38	-0.51
Ernie Lombardi	-0.64	-0.72	Red Faber	-0.38	-0.46
Frank Chance	-0.64	-1.25	Bob Lemon	-0.37	-0.56
Joe Tinker	-0.64	-1.30	Jim Bunning	-0.35	-0.33

Top Unenshrined NPs	Total Z Avg	Core Z Avg	Top Unenshrined Ps	Total Z Avg	Core Z Avg
Pete Rose	0.71	1.12	Smoky Joe Wood	0.07	-0.36
Eddie Murray	0.47	0.70	Tommy Bond	0.05	-0.23
Dave Winfield	0.22	0.88	Bert Blyleven	0.00	0.17
Bill Dahlen	0.12	-0.20	Jim McCormick	-0.01	0.02
Keith Hernandez	0.11	-0.36	Carl Mays	-0.01	-0.47
Mickey Vernon	0.10	-0.16	*Roger Clemens*	-0.04	-0.26
Rickey Henderson	0.09	-0.17	Ed Reulbach	-0.09	-0.22
Darrell Evans	0.06	-0.19	Eddie Cicotte	-0.11	-0.25
Gil Hodges	0.04	-0.31	*Dennis Eckersley*	-0.12	-0.76
Dwight Evans	0.02	0.14	Doc White	-0.13	-0.49
Paul Molitor	-0.02	0.08	Bob Caruthers	-0.15	-0.13
Steve Garvey	-0.02	0.02	Tommy John	-0.18	-0.12
Ron Santo	-0.03	-0.15	Babe Adams	-0.18	-0.58
Andre Dawson	-0.04	0.34	Will White	-0.21	-0.18
Dave Parker	-0.05	0.27	Spud Chandler	-0.21	-0.61

of the hurlers are from the distant past. But, among the non-pitchers are two additions, Keith Hernandez and Ron Santo, and the list of moundsmen features a half-dozen men who did not rate among the leaders in Table Fourteen — Tommy Bond, Eddie Cicotte, Dennis Eckersley, Tommy John, Babe Adams and Will White.

The National League's 1979 co–MVP, Keith Hernandez became eligible for the BBWAA elections in 1996, and was still on the ballot in 2000. But, to date, his prospects of selection for Cooperstown by the writers are dim. In his first five elections Hernandez averaged just 8.5-percent support, receiving a high of 10.8 percent in 1998; and he came close to losing any further eligibility with a 6.8-percent showing in 1999. Tommy John was also on the 2000 ballot, and fared somewhat better; but his long-term chances of election also appear slim. In six HOF elections the 288-game winner averaged 22.7-percent support through the 2000 election, with a high of 27.3 percent in 1998. Ron Santo appeared on 15 BBWAA ballots during the period 1980–98, averaging 26.1-percent support per try. The five-time Gold Glove winner never received as much as 60-percent support from the scribes (his best showing was 43.1 percent in his last year eligible), but, because he earned 108 votes in 1988, he can still be considered by the Veterans Committee, beginning in 2002. Babe Adams won 194 games in a career that spanned 1906–26, and he also received votes on 15 ballots (1937–55). But his support-percentage high (13.7 in 1947) and average (5.1 percent) indicate that his candidacy never generated much enthusiasm among the scribes of that era. Tommy Bond won 193 games and posted a .627 winning percentage in an eight-season career (1876–84). He got one vote from the 1936 OTC, despite his failure to appear in 10 big-league seasons (he also was 41–48 in the National Association of 1874–75). Like Bond, Will White was a 19th-century hurler who went 229–166 (.580), with two 40-win seasons, during the years 1877–86. But White never received a Hall-of-Fame vote. Neither did deadball hurler Eddie Cicotte, whose 209–148 (.585) record would have merited some support, absent his key role in the Black Sox fix; and it's safe to say that, because of his participation in that scandal, his Hall-of-Fame prospects are nil. Dennis Eckersley retired after the 1998 season and will not become eligible for election until 2004.

Although useful to a preliminary search for errors of selection and omission, the scores in Table Fifteen also unavoidably reflect statistical inequities — both offensive and defensive — inherent among the various non-pitching positions. The lists of Hall of Famers and unenshrined players with the best Z-Score averages relative to the Cooperstown norms are dominated by outfielders and first basemen; and, in contrast, six of the 10 HOF members who fare worst on that scale are catchers or middle infielders (backstops Ray Schalk, Roger Bresnahan, Rick Ferrell and Ernie Lombardi, plus second baseman Johnny Evers and shortstop Joe Tinker). Those results are caused, in large part, by the effects of the defensive spectrum, a linear estimate of the relative difficulty inherent to each different fielding position. That spectrum is commonly represented by the line diagram below, which reflects the signal importance of up-the-middle defense (i.e., catcher, the two middle-infield positions, and center field), and in which it's axiomatic that the relative degree of difficulty declines (at an uneven rate) from left to right.

C — SS — 2B — CF — 3B — RF — LF — 1B

The propriety of placing catcher at the far left of this spectrum is debatable, as the position requires nowhere near the agility, grace or speed of hand and foot required of shortstops or second basemen. But placement of the position at the far left of the scale can be justified because as a group catchers compile the poorest offensive statistics of any position; and a corollary to the spectrum's left-to-right decline in fielding difficulty is the fact that, in general, individual offensive production increases toward the right end of the scale. There are two reasons for that inverse relationship: (1) the rigors of the middle-of-the-diamond positions take a natural toll on offensive output; (2) those positions (except for catcher) require more foot speed, and the men who play them tend to be smaller, thinner, jackrabbit types who are far more likely to physically resemble Pee Wee Herman than Mark McGwire. Hall-of-Fame first baseman Johnny Mize may have been called the "Big Cat," but no one was going to confuse his speed with second sacker Felix "The Cat" Mantilla's, and although you might find some first sackers called "Jumbo" in the encyclopedias, no one at the position was ever nicknamed "Scooter."

As a result of all this, the batting statistics of non-pitchers differ from one position to another, dependent largely upon the performance variations imposed by the defensive spectrum. Table Sixteen provides the positional averages for nine key offensive statistics among all of the Hall of Famers elected through 2000, including career hits (H), home runs (HR), total bases (TB), runs scored (R), runs batted in (RBI), stolen bases (SB), batting (BA), slugging (SA) and on-base (OBA) averages. It shows the number of men elected at each position (Tot); the highest positional average for each statistic is boldfaced; the low averages are italicized; and, at the bottom, the table also gives the overall averages for all members as a whole. Top-to-bottom, the positions are listed in the same order as the defensive spectrum shown above.

Although the career data used to derive the averages in Table Sixteen belong to Hall of Famers, the relative increase in offensive production from catcher through first base is nonetheless evident in these numbers. As a group, the dozen Cooperstown catchers have the lowest career average in six of the nine statistics shown; shortstops are last, or next-to-last in eight of the stats;

	Table Sixteen								
	Average Career Batting Statistics, By								
	Position, HOF Players Through 2000								
Position	*Tot*	*H*	*HR*	*TB*	*R*	*RBI*	*SB*	*BA*	*SA*	*OBA*
Catcher	12	*1746*	187	*2739*	*890*	*995*	97	.287	.445	.365
Shortstop	19	2283	*101*	3193	1203	1041	263	.288	*.401*	*.357*
Second Base	15	2503	123	3534	1372	1076	295	.305	.434	.381
Center Field	16	2444	208	3727	1449	1161	**313**	**.317**	.485	**.396**
Third Base	9	2290	227	3564	1192	1210	133	.294	.453	.361
Right Field	21	2548	249	3980	**1464**	1318	235	.312	.480	.388
Left Field	18	**2598**	244	**4056**	1450	1349	223	.315	.493	.387
First Base	17	2320	**273**	3787	1317	**1415**	149	.310	**.506**	.388
Overall	*127*	*2372*	*202*	*3616*	*1317*	*1207*	*223*	*.305*	*.463*	*.379*

and first basemen, who reside at the opposite end of the spectrum, own the highest average for three of the statistics and are near the leadership in all but stolen bases.

Because of all this, it necessarily follows that — with or without con-scious intent — the Cooperstown electors apply a different set of statistical standards for players at each position. Any fair measure of a player's HOF credentials, then, must also apply the Z-Score process to the HOF positional averages, creating a separate ranking that rates each player against the means accrued by Cooperstown players at his specific position. Those means and their standard deviations are numerous and too cumbersome to present in the text, but Table Seventeen provides the Total-Z Scores (only) achieved versus the positional means by the top (descending order) and bottom three (ascending order) Hall-of-Fame members at each position, along with the scores of the three highest-ranked unenshrined players (descending order, again) at that position after the 2000 voting. Cooperstown members were rated at the position of their HOF citations; and, once again, players active after 1994 are italicized (keep in mind that their scores below do not reflect performance after that date). Pitchers are not included, as there is no point in making a positional distinction for this purpose with just two relievers in the Hall.

Comparing the results in tables Fifteen and Seventeen leads to prelim-inary lists of the position players who are the least-statistically qualified among Hall-of-Fame members (i.e., are probable errors of selection), and of those who — overlooked to date — represent the most likely errors of omission. The HOF members who meet both criteria as errors of selection include catchers Schalk, Bresnahan and Ferrell, infielders Chance, Evers, Tinker and Lind-strom, and outfielders McCarthy and Youngs. With negative Z Scores more than half of a standard deviation below the norm, the three lowest-ranked

Table Seventeen
Z Scores v. HOF Positional Means

Pos Top Three	Total Z Avg	Bottom Three	Total Z Avg	Best Unenshrined	Total Z Avg
C Yogi Berra	0.57	Ray Schalk	-0.77	Joe Torre	0.61
C Johnny Bench	0.44	Roger Bresnahan	-0.46	Ted Simmons	0.36
C Carlton Fisk	0.43	Rick Ferrell	-0.46	Gary Carter	0.21
1B Lou Gehrig	1.07	Frank Chance	-1.05	*Eddie Murray*	0.36
1B Jimmie Foxx	0.79	George Kelly	-0.54	Keith Hernandez	-0.04
1B Cap Anson	0.47	Orlando Cepeda	-0.35	Mickey Vernon	-0.10
2B Rogers Hornsby	0.85	Johnny Evers	-1.00	*Lou Whitaker*	-0.24
2B Eddie Collins	0.77	Jackie Robinson	-0.54	*Ryne Sandberg*	-0.31
2B Nap Lajoie	0.56	R. Schoendienst	-0.42	Bobby Grich	-0.33
SS Honus Wagner	1.22	Monte Ward	-0.61	Bill Dahlen	0.32
SS Ernie Banks	0.61	Joe Tinker	-0.56	*Cal Ripken, Jr.*	0.19
SS Joe Cronin	0.35	Phil Rizzuto	-0.43	*Ozzie Smith*	0.04
3B George Brett	0.78	Fred Lindstrom	-0.86	*Paul Molitor*	0.40
3B Mike Schmidt	0.77	George Kell	-0.55	Darrell Evans	0.28
3B Eddie Mathews	0.31	Jimmy Collins	-0.39	Ron Santo	0.05
LF Stan Musial	1.40	Chick Hafey	-0.79	*Rickey Henderson*	0.00
LF C. Yastrzemski	0.81	Ralph Kiner	-0.61	Bob L. Johnson	-0.30
LF Ted Williams	0.73	Heinie Manush	-0.50	Jim Rice	-0.33
CF Ty Cobb	1.11	Lloyd Waner	-0.63	Al Oliver	0.38
CF Tris Speaker	0.95	Larry Doby	-0.55	Tommy Leach	0.02
CF Willie Mays	0.85	Earle Combs	-0.54	Dale Murphy	-0.17
RF Babe Ruth	1.31	Tommy McCarthy	-0.87	Pete Rose	1.17
RF Hank Aaron	0.96	Ross Youngs	-0.73	Jack Clark	0.09
RF Frank Robinson	0.55	Elmer Flick	-0.71	Rusty Staub	0.07

Cooperstown pitchers from Table Fifteen — Haines, Lyons and Marquard — can be safely included on the list. The possible errors of omission include the top three unenshrined hurlers from Table Fifteen — Wood, Bond and Blyleven — each of whom would currently rate as a statistically average or better HOF pitcher, along with infielders Dahlen, Hernandez, Vernon, Santo and Darrell Evans, the only position players eligible through 2000 to make both lists.

If the Hall-of-Fame selection process was objective, one could stop here, reasonably confident that the primary errors among the Cooperstown roster had been identified. Of course, if the process was objective, the inevitable complaints about any errors among Hall-of-Fame membership would be based on something other than they currently are, and this work would either be very different in approach or nonexistent. But even the lists in Tables Fifteen and Seventeen are biased, because comparison of player statistics to the means among current HOF members unavoidably imposes the subjective prejudices of Cooperstown's electors upon the measurement. The only way to avoid that bias is to start from scratch, applying the Z-Score process in a manner that allows the career stats of all the players in the database to establish their own level of HOF qualification — and that standard, whatever it may be, is the true Cooperstown Baseline. (Note that, at this level, Z-Score measurement of performance against the Hall-of-Fame norms for each historical era has little meaning because, theoretically, there are no equally distinct differences in the HOF standards for different eras.)

Before that process is applied, one other Hall-of-Fame standard requires discussion. In 65 years of voting, 185 of the roughly 14,000 men who appeared in a big-league game during the period 1876–1994 have been elected to Cooperstown for their performance as major-league players. That total represents about 1.3 percent of all men who had appeared in the Show, and an average — equal to the historical rate of election — of around 1.5 new Hall of Famers entering the majors each year. Those who believe that the Hall is already overstocked and tainted by mediocrity would no doubt prefer a Cooperstown membership of around 140, which would approximate one percent of all players in history and equate with the 99th percentile that is the highest, traditional measure of bell-curve excellence. Others, who feel that too many deserving players have been overlooked in the selection process, might favor as much as a two-percent standard instead, which would boost the Hall of Fame's current roster to 280 players.

But no one in authority is about to agree to tossing out 40 or more current HOF members for the sake of statistical perfection; for better or worse, the men already enshrined at Cooperstown must be accepted as *fait accompli*. Similarly, the most finicky of Hall-of-Fame critics would never abide the increased mediocrity inherent in a 2-percent standard, and the constraints of the selection process assure that its adoption is virtually impossible.

In that light, and given that many of the most persnickety critics also agree that there have been errors of omission, the adoption of a 1.5-percent standard would be an appropriate compromise. Such a standard would require players to rank at or above the 98.5 percentile, which — according to the theory of normal distribution — is equal to a Z Score of about +2.44 when compared to every man who has ever played in the majors. It also would produce a 210-player HOF roster that might satisfy all but the pickiest of Cooperstown purists. Assuming that the current members are inviolate, that means there is currently room in the Hall for 25 players who have not yet been enshrined. So what follows represents an effort to identify the men who are most-qualified for that list.

CHAPTER 6

Simply Era-sistible

Although separated by at least three generations of players, Sam Crawford and Hank Aaron have several things in common. Both are Hall-of-Fame right fielders who enjoyed long careers — Crawford played 19 seasons, Aaron 23. Crawford had a total of 2961 hits and a .309 batting average, with an on-base percentage of .362, and led his league in runs batted in three times. Hank hit safely 3771 times and batted .305, with an OBA of .377, and led his circuit in RBIs on four occasions. At that surface level their stats are similar, except for the big gap in their career-hits totals, and one might think that so were there batting skills.

Reinforcing that impression, Crawford and Aaron also hold the separate major-league records which were the definitive measure of a power hitter in their disparate times. And both rank at about the same ordinal spot, with almost identical totals, among the career leaders from their respective eras in the category owned by the other man. Crawford is the all-time leader in triples (309), and Aaron hit more home runs than anyone but Sadaharu Oh (and maybe Josh Gibson). Sam's 97 home runs rank seventh among the non-pitchers of the dead-ball era; Aaron's 98 triples represent the eighth-best total among batters from the Expansion period.

Home runs were rare during Crawford's era. Because of its composition, manufacture, and the physical laws applicable as a result, the "dead" ball didn't stay aloft too long. So the ultimate test of a man's power at the time was his ability to drive the ball hard enough into an outfield gap that it would roll to the fence and allow him to hustle to third base. In Sam's time, the men who did that most often were the era's equivalents of Mark McGwire; and, although 19th-century first sacker Roger Connor was the career home-run leader, with 138, prior to Babe Ruth, there is no doubt that Crawford was one of baseball's true studs of swat before the Bambino became its first Sultan — as Sam's career total of 406 triples and homers, combined, was even better than Connor's 371.

In Aaron's era things were reversed. Thanks to the revolution that Ruth built, the core and construction of the baseball were more conducive to sustained flight (or, maybe, the ever-more-polluted air held the ball up better, or the growing hole in the ozone layer had a magnetic effect on horsehide). As a result, four-baggers were the true test of a player's power, and triples became an endangered species, the sole property of little men who could bounce the ball hard on artificial turf and then scoot like a roadrunner to the hot corner.

The Crawford-Aaron comparison demonstrates that every player's statistical performance is shaped by circumstances unique to his time, and which — except for Babe Ruth (and perhaps Amos Rusie) — have been beyond the ability of his individual skills to alter. So the context of his era can have as much, or more, impact on a man's career stats as will his positional placement along the defensive spectrum. As a result, comparisons of career statistics of players from different eras have minimal validity; and a man's performance relative to the norms of his time is, or should be, just as important to his Hall-of-Fame credentials as his achievement relative to those from the same position, or to everyone who played, regardless of era.

This and the next chapter present the Total-Z rankings of players from each of baseball's six historical eras — with pre–World War Two players covered in this one, the modern ones in the next. Space considerations prohibit listing the career-performance means from each historical period for all of the data set's 56 variables. But Table Eighteen does provide the rounded career norms for several key stats for each era among all players who qualified for the data set — enough to outline major changes in statistical performance over time. Although the 2,295 players measured do not represent all of baseball's statistical history, they do include the men from each period with the most longevity and, therefore, the highest cumulative totals among major leaguers of their times — so the relative averages are clearly representative of each period. The column abbreviations for the 19th century, dead-ball, live-ball, postwar, expansion and free-agent eras are self-explanatory. Norms for the five Core stats among each subset are once again boldfaced.

Above all else, Table Eighteen reveals the historical role of home runs. Compared to later eras, and as reflected by the career norms for homers and their frequency (the number of at-bats-per-dinger by batters and circuit clouts allowed per-nine-innings by pitchers), the number of homers was relatively constant during the first two historical periods, then more than doubled during live-ball times. The home-rune rate has been fairly stable since the end of World War Two, but they occurred even more frequently in each of the

Table Eighteen
Historical-Era Individual Career Means for Selected Key Variables

Non-Pitcher Variables	NC	DB	LB	PW	EX	FA
Number of Players	160	185	290	193	286	370
Hits	1319	1308	1329	1167	1180	1192
Home Runs	35	29	78	108	118	113
Runs	811	642	672	596	570	586
Runs Batted In	568	530	628	552	539	552
Batting Average	.274	.269	.285	.268	.256	.263
Slugging Average	.368	.356	.405	.402	.381	.392
On-Base Average	.330	.333	.351	.344	.325	.332
Triples	79	76	61	40	33	32
Total Bases	1781	1742	1921	1761	1786	1800
Home-Run Frequency	254	331	159	79	86	96
Stolen Bases	225	190	71	44	73	106
Fielding Average	.918	.957	.970	.976	.978	.978
Range Factor	4.65	4.49	4.31	3.90	4.02	3.81

Pitcher Variables	NC	DB	LB	PW	EX	FA
Number of Players	39	82	168	108	172	244
Games Won	208	151	126	109	105	98
Winning Percentage	.557	.536	.518	.522	.509	.506
Earned Run Average	3.39	2.78	3.83	3.75	3.50	3.69
Innings Pitched	3271	2441	2092	1800	1775	1673
Strikeouts	1190	1039	772	882	1095	1029
Games Pitched	404	359	389	390	452	444
Opponents' Bat Avg	.259	.251	.271	.257	.249	.255
Opponents' On-Base Avg	.313	.308	.333	.326	.317	.323
BB-per-9-Innings	2.6	2.5	3.1	3.4	3.1	3.2
Ratio	11.9	10.9	12.5	12.2	11.6	11.9
SO-per-9 Innings	3.13	3.79	3.31	4.34	5.56	5.59
HR-per-9 Innings	0.23	0.17	0.47	0.76	0.77	0.75
SO-to-BB Ratio	1.53	1.57	1.12	1.36	1.82	1.78
Saves	4	12	20	24	38	45
Complete Game Pct	.900	.694	.500	.384	.276	.193
Shutout Percentage	.055	.100	.065	.073	.066	.048

eras since then than they did during Babe Ruth's time — because the proportion of sluggers among the major-league population as a whole was larger than it was when Ruth, Jimmie Foxx and a half-dozen other guys were the main long-ball threats around. Since the beginning of the postwar era, as ever more batters swung for the fences, the rate of strikeouts-per-nine-innings increased and batting averages declined. Batting averages, in fact, were lower, among non-pitchers, in each of the eras since World War Two than they were even in dead-ball times.

The rise in home runs also changed the role of speed on the basepaths and altered defense. The number of triples since the dead-ball period has declined more steadily than the rate of home runs has increased. But, the number of career stolen bases fell more dramatically, and although it has climbed again in the two most recent eras (because of the influence of guys like Maury Wills, Lou Brock and Rickey Henderson), it is still nowhere near the norms for baseball's first two historical periods. Defensively, range factors (which are strongly impacted by the number of assists) declined marginally during the live-ball era, dropped even more after World War Two, and have remained well below those of baseball's first two periods ever since — with more batters striking out and hitting flyouts, rather than grounding out to someone in the infield, where an assist is required. Because strikeouts and fly balls produce relatively easier putouts than grounders, fielding averages increased too — although it's likely that modern improvements in gloves and turf maintenance had a larger, more beneficial impact on fielding averages.

But Table Eighteen also includes data distinct to specific periods. Note that batting and on-base averages — both those compiled by hitters and those allowed by pitchers — were significantly higher in the live-ball era than at any time before or since (probably as result of the balls in use) and that the number of walks allowed by hurlers increased with the number of live-ball homers, but were relatively stable thereafter. In turn, the live-ball hitters appear more selective than those of later eras, perhaps because there were fewer legitimate long-ball threats during that era and most batters still had to work the pitch count to get on base, like the men from earlier times (an approach which, subjectively, seems a lost art today). Note also that the average number of career runs scored was much higher during the 19th century than at any time since. Without question, the scoring decline since 1900 resulted from the overall improvement in defense. For part of baseball's first historical era fielders didn't wear gloves at all, and when they came along, they were little more than mittens or stiff pancakes, in no way as efficient as those in use since about the 1930s. As a result, fielding errors were far more frequent during the 19th century (as, no doubt, were broken fingers), and they led to a lot of runs. So when defense reached its modern norm, the number of errors and runs scored both decreased.

The format for the rest of this (and the next) chapter includes separate sections for each of baseball's historical eras. They begin with a brief commentary on HOF-relevant aspects of the period itself, or important relationships among the Z Scores reported. That is followed by a paragraph about the era's Hall-of-Fame demographics — including the number of players (overall, plus non-pitchers and pitchers) from the period who qualified for the database, the percentages of those respective totals (2,295 players overall, 1,484 non-pitchers, 813 hurlers) represented by each figure, the number and percentage of Hall-of-Fame players (185 through 2000) who were from that

era, their names, and those of any other HOF members elected in other capacities who also played during that era and qualified for the data set (but, keeping the players distinct from other Cooperstown members, the latter are not
included in the totals cited before them). Each paragraph ends with lists of
men from that era who are often cited as errors of selection and omission.

The separate Z-Score rankings for non-pitchers and pitchers from each
era follow. Keep in mind that, for this and chapter 6, the non-pitchers' scores
have been adjusted to remove any bias caused by variations in the positional
norms for the seven fielding statistics included in the scale, but that no era
adjustments were made for any other scores because every Z-Score average
involves comparison only to each man's relative contemporaries. Although
each of the six historical eras produced between 197 and 614 Hall-of-Fame
eligibles, space considerations prohibit listing any more than (about) the top
30 position players and top 20 pitchers for each era. But the lists vary slightly
in length because they do include every player from each period elected to
Cooperstown through 2000, and a more complete list for each period can be
derived from the scores provided in the Appendix. In each list, the names of
men elected to Cooperstown solely for their playing careers are boldfaced.
Among those listed who were not in the Hall through the 2000 voting, men
who never received any HOF votes at all are italicized. The tables also provide the ordinal rank for each of the players listed and each man's primary
position, along with the separate, cumulative Z-Score averages accrued by each
for all of the statistics measured as a whole (30 stats for non-pitchers, 26 for
hurlers), and for the five Core variables appropriate to their pitcher or non-
pitcher subset. The descending rankings are based solely on the first, or Total-
Z, average reported in the list. Where any Total-Z ties occur, men are listed
in the descending order of their Core-Z averages, on the premise that because
of the voting significance of those statistics, a higher Core mean indicates
they are likely to be perceived as the better-qualified candidate. Also, where
a break in the consecutive rankings has been required to list low-rated HOF
members, a horizontal line designates that discontinuity; and, if the player is
tied with other unlisted men for an ordinal position below that line, his ranking is preceded by a lower-case "t." Note again that there may be a considerable discrepancy between the Total-and Core-Z averages reported and that
the difference is likely to be greater among Hall-of-Fame members than those
who are not (in most cases, the Core-Z for relief pitchers is also much smaller
than their mean for all variables, as they are disadvantaged in the measurement by comparatively low career-innings-pitched and strikeout totals).

Accompanying each ranking is commentary on selected players from the
era. Because the statistical credentials of many Hall of Famers are never chal-
lenged (e.g., Babe Ruth and Ty Cobb), there is no point in discussing their
scores. In this chapter and the next, much (but not all) of the commentary

focuses on players often cited as errors of omission but whose final scores for all three scales, combined, will be insufficient to support their inclusion among the final Cooperstown roster proposed. Some of those final scores will be cited here but are not included in later lists because they are too low to make the cutoff for the tables which give those rankings (but they can be found in the Appendix).

Finally, remember that the rankings are not estimates of any man's degree of "greatness," as they only attempt to objectively measure each player's overall statistical credentials for Cooperstown, relative to other men from his era. In some instances, more so for non-pitchers than hurlers, the rankings are strongly impacted by longevity (which the predictive rates for years and games played in chapter Five, Table Twelve demonstrate is integral to Cooperstown election), and some players who enjoyed lengthy careers will score better than others who may have been "greater" subjectively.

The 19th Century (1876–1900)

The problem with judging the statistical credentials of players from this era — both subjectively and objectively — is the fact that the rules of the game changed radically and often from the beginning of the National League in 1876 until the mid–1890s. Pitchers were not allowed to deliver the ball overhand until 1884, and prior to 1887, the batter could request pitches that were above or below the waist. Stolen bases were disallowed until 1886, and the number of balls pitched out of the strike zone required to earn a walk steadily declined from nine in 1879 to the since-used four a decade later. But the most influential changes involved the distance from which the pitcher threw the ball — 45 feet in 1876, 50 feet by 1881, and the current 60-feet, 6-inches was not applied until 1893. Predictably, offense increased coincident with that final change: the NL — the only circuit in existence at the time — batted just .245 in 1892; the league average jumped to .280 the year the current distance was adopted, rising to .309 in 1894, and then hovering in the .280s for the rest of the Gay Nineties.

As a result, many knowledgeable fans argue, with some merit, that the modern game did not exist before 1893, and that — relative to everything done since — the statistics achieved by players before that date are suspect. For those who buy that reasoning, the list of 19th-century Z-Score leaders below includes pound signs next to the names of men who played the majority of their careers prior to 1893.

The 19th-century Z-Score lists for batters and pitchers look much like those that follow in this and later chapters. A group of Hall of Famers are clustered near the top of both, with some stragglers trailing out behind, and unelected players filling in the gaps. Note also that, partly because of the failure of the 1936 OTC, Cy Young is the only Cooperstown member from this period ever elected by the BBWAA, with the others all having been tabbed by veterans committees.

There are 197 19th-century players in the database, or 8.6 percent of the overall total. (The 160 non-pitchers are equal to 10.8 percent of that subset; the 39 pitchers equate to 4.8 percent of the hurlers measured. Bob Caruthers and Dave Foutz are included in both subsets.) The era includes 26 HOF players, or 14.1 percent of the 185 in Cooperstown through 2000. They include 18 non-pitchers — Cap Anson, Jake Beckley, Dan Brouthers, Jesse Burkett, Roger Connor, George Davis, Ed Delahanty, Hugh Duffy, Buck Ewing, Billy Hamilton, Hughie Jennings, Joe Kelley, Mike "King" Kelly, Tommy McCarthy, Bid McPhee, Jim O'Rourke, Sam Thompson and Monte Ward; eight pitchers — John Clarkson, Pud Galvin, Tim Keefe, Kid Nichols, Charles "Old Hoss" Radbourn, Amos Rusie, Mickey Welch and Cy Young; four managers — Ned Hanlon, Connie Mack, John McGraw and Wilbert Robinson; plus three men elected in other capacities — Charles Comiskey, Clark Griffith and George Wright. Often-cited errors of selection: Clarkson, Galvin, Jennings, Keefe, McCarthy, Radbourn and Welch. Often-cited errors of omission: Pete Browning, Bob Caruthers, Lave Cross, Bill Dahlen, Dave Foutz, Herman Long, Tony Mullane, Jimmy Ryan, Harry Stovey and George Van Haltren.

Until Bid McPhee's election by the VC in 2000, one problem with Hall-of-Fame membership from the 19th century was the absence of a legitimate representative from anything but the National League. The Union Association (UA, 1884) and Players League (PL, 1890) both lasted just one season, so a rep from each of them would be token at best, and difficult to identify. But the American Association (AA, 1882–91) survived for a decade, and it's absurd to credit the circuit as a "major" for historical purposes while Cooperstown's doors seem closed to its best players. Unless one counts Charlie Comiskey (player-manager of the AA's St. Louis Browns for most of their history, but whose election was justified by his later career as an executive), prior to McPhee's induction outfielder Tommy McCarthy was the only Hall of Famer who could arguably be cited as an AA player. But McCarthy spent just four of his 13 big-league seasons in the association, and as the scores indicate, statistically he was a lousy choice to represent any circuit from the era. McPhee spent eight seasons with the AA's club in Cincinnati, and the numbers in Table Eighteen imply that he is a legitimate Hall of Famer, overlooked for far too long by the Cooperstown selection process. Beyond McCarthy and McPhee, Pud Galvin is the only other HOF member who spent as many as three seasons in any 19th-century circuit except the National; and most of the others who played elsewhere were defectors to the Players League in 1890.

Table Nineteen
Nineteenth-Century Z-Score Leaders

Rank	Non-Pitchers	Pos	Total Z Avg	Core Z Avg	Rank	Non-Pitchers	Pos	Total Z Avg	Core Z Avg
1	#Cap Anson	1b	1.93	2.51	17	#King Kelly	rf	0.84	1.09
2	#Dan Brouthers	1b	1.73	2.00	18	Lave Cross	3b	0.82	1.33
3	#Roger Connor	1b	1.70	2.17	19	#Jim O'Rourke	cf	0.80	1.21
4	Ed Delahanty	lf	1.56	2.22	20	#Mike Tiernan	rf	0.79	1.29
5	#Jake Beckley	1b	1.32	2.04	21	Herman Long	ss	0.77	1.25
6	George Davis	ss	1.29	1.68	22	#Buck Ewing	c	0.71	0.86
7	Bill Dahlen	ss	1.24	1.45		#Fred Pfeffer	2b	0.71	0.79
8	#Bid McPhee	2b	1.20	0.91	24	Hughie Jennings	ss	0.60	0.43
9	Jesse Burkett	lf	1.17	1.84	25	#Jack Glassock	ss	0.57	0.60
10	Joe Kelley	lf	1.15	1.43	26	#Mike Griffin	cf	0.55	0.65
11	Hugh Duffy	lf	1.10	1.90	27	#Billy Nash	3b	0.54	0.63
12	#Sam Thompson	rf	1.06	1.84	28	Dummy Hoy	cf	0.53	0.74
13	#Harry Stovey	lf	1.05	1.14		#Paul Hines	cf	0.53	0.73
14	Billy Hamilton	cf	1.04	1.28	30	#George Gore	cf	0.51	0.62
15	Jimmy Ryan	cf	1.03	1.86	33	#Monte Ward	ss	0.47	0.66
16	G. Van Haltren	cf	0.88	1.55	t51	#Tommy McCarthy	rf	0.22	0.41

Rank	Pitchers	Pos	Total Z Avg	Core Z Avg	Rank	Pitchers	Pos	Total Z Avg	Core Z Avg
1	Cy Young	sp	1.91	2.21	11	#Tony Mullane	sp	0.42	0.67
2	#Tim Keefe	sp	1.05	1.36	12	#Dave Foutz	sp	0.40	0.12
3	Kid Nichols	sp	0.88	1.19	13	#Charlie Buffinton	sp	0.37	0.51
4	#John Clarkson	sp	0.80	1.16	14	#Will White	sp	0.26	0.42
5	#Hoss Radbourn	sp	0.65	1.00	15	#Mickey Welch	sp	0.22	0.97
6	#Jim McCormick	sp	0.58	0.70	16	#Jim Whitney	sp	0.20	0.01
	#Tommy Bond	sp	0.58	0.33	17	Clark Griffith	sp	0.18	0.23
8	#Pud Galvin	sp	0.54	1.03	18	#Silver King	sp	0.13	0.10
9	Amos Rusie	sp	0.48	0.58	19	#George Bradley	sp	0.03	-0.32
	#Bob Caruthers	sp	0.48	0.43	20	#Matt Kilroy	sp	-0.02	-0.43

Beyond Comiskey and McPhee, the association produced at least a half-dozen players with plausible Hall-of-Fame credentials — outfielders Pete Browning and Harry Stovey, along with pitchers Tony Mullane, Bob Caruthers, Dave Foutz and perhaps Will White (whose tenure in the circuit lasted only five seasons, but won 136 games during that span). Among them, only Stovey (six votes in the 1936 OTC balloting) has ever received any Hall-of-Fame support.

Browning, who spent eight seasons with the AA's Louisville club, is its best-known and most-popular candidate. His .341 career batting average is tied for 11th-best ever, the highest of any unenshrined player except Shoeless Joe Jackson. Many people are mystified that anyone who hit so well and didn't help to fix a World Series is absent from the Hall and never got a vote. He won two AA batting and slugging titles, topped the circuit in hits and on-base average once apiece and also led the Players League in hitting and doubles in its only season. He batted .402 in 1887, but lost the AA crown to outfielder Tip O'Neill's .435. Browning hit .336 or better on seven occasions and was the namesake for Louisville Slugger bats, so he has a subjective credential that is important in baseball lore.

But although Browning played a difficult position for most of his career (center field), he is regarded as one of the worst fielders ever. That reputation resulted, no doubt, because the available evidence suggests he played inebriated (or, hungover) much of the time — so it must've been difficult for him to decide which of the balls he saw coming toward him to swat at a .341 clip. Compared to all center fielders, his average Z Score for the seven fielding variables is -0.39, which puts him in 127th place among the 173 men measured at his position. But, because of the preponderance of ground-ball outs in his era, most 19th-century flychasers score poorly against their modern counterparts, and several of Browning's positional contemporaries fare even worse, including Hall of Famers Jim O'Rourke (-0.45) and Billy Hamilton (-0.52).

Given all of that, Browning's inclusion at Cooperstown may be subjectively defensible, and it would certainly add one of the game's most colorful legends to the Hall's roster. But, his Total-Z average is only +0.39, good enough for just 39th place among his non-pitcher contemporaries, and his Total-Z for all variables in all three scales (+0.31) rates no better than 373rd place in the final rankings for non-pitchers. Unfortunately, and despite his lofty batting average, those scores are insufficient to justify his inclusion on purely statistical grounds.

Like Browning, pitchers Tony Mullane, Bob Caruthers, Dave Foutz and Will White never received a Hall-of-Fame vote. Until Tommy John (288 wins) and Bert Blyleven (287) retired, Mullane's career victory total was the highest of any unenshrined pitcher (he was 284–220, for a .563 winning percentage). Caruthers was 218–99 as a hurler, including two 40-win seasons;

his .688 winning percentage is topped among the official list of career leaders only by Foutz and Whitey Ford (.690 each); and, including his time as an outfielder, he batted .282 for his career, with consecutive seasons of .334 and .357 (the latter fifth-best in the AA in 1887). Foutz was 147–66, including 41 wins in 1886, and the part-time first baseman batted .276 for his career, with two seasons above .300. In 10 big-league seasons White was 229–166 (.580), winning 40 games or more three times.

But, among their pitching contemporaries, none of the four ranks higher than Caruthers (tied with Amos Rusie for ninth place at +0.48, above). All of their careers as hurlers were essentially over before the mound was moved to its present distance in 1893: White retired after 1886, Caruthers did not pitch after 1892, Foutz pitched seven games with no decisions after that date, and Mullane posted a 25–33 record in his last two seasons, 1893-94. So, with 58 pitchers in the Hall through 2000, including eight from this era, it's difficult to justify any of their inclusions for proportional reasons. Beyond that, Caruthers rates no better than 128th (a Total-Z of +0.49) in the final rankings, and Mullane (+0.46, 136th), White (+0.41, 154th) and Foutz (+0.33, 188th) all fare worse, indicating that there are many pitchers from other eras with better overall credentials.

Thirteen Hall-of-Fame players defected to the Players League in 1890, so that circuit is more than amply represented, if only by accident. But a worthy Union Association rep is hard to find, especially one that was a star in the circuit. Second sacker Fred Dunlap led the UA in almost every offensive category in 1884, but his career stats are only good enough to tie with Tommy McCarthy for 51st among the 19th-century non-pitchers above (Total-Z of +0.22), and his final ranking (+0.22, 437th) is not worthy of the Hall. The best candidates are pitchers Jim McCormick and Tommy Bond, who tied for sixth (+0.58) in the periodic rankings above. McCormick played in only half of the UA's lone season, but posted a 21–3 record for Cincinnati that featured the circuit's top winning percentage, and he was 265–214 (.553) for his career. Bond was 13–9 in the UA, and 193–115 (.627) overall; Both men have better scores for their era than three Hall of Famers.

As indicated in the previous chapter, Bond and McCormick both score well against the current Cooperstown norms, and if added to the Hall, both pitchers would rate as average among the hurlers on the roster. Their final scores in chapter 11 (+0.71, and tied for 75th, for McCormick; +0.70, tied for 78th, for Bond) are almost identical; and both come very near to meeting the Cooperstown Baseline for pitchers. But they fall just below it, and the high representation for hurlers from their era makes it difficult — in a marginal call — to support either's addition to the roster.

Like Caruthers and Foutz, George Van Haltren was a pitcher and position player, but the latter's career was spent mainly as an outfielder, and his mound duty was limited to 93 games (a 40–31 record) in nine of his 17 seasons.

An all-around threat, he batted .316, with 2532 hits, 1639 runs scored, 1014 RBI and 583 stolen bases, and his score in Table Nineteen (+0.88) is better than a half-dozen Hall-of-Fame non-pitchers from his era. But though his final Total-Z of +0.78 is above the eventual Cooperstown Baseline, it isn't quite good enough from his amply represented era to merit his inclusion among the 25 players suggested as additions to the current roster.

A similar fate befalls shortstop Herman Long, one of a quartet of early N.L. shortstops (the others were Hall of Famers George Davis and Hughie Jennings and Bill Dahlen) who were the Alex Rodriguez, Nomar Garciaparra, Derek Jeter and Omar Vizquel of the 1890s. Long had four great seasons, 1894–97, in which he batted a combined .327 and topped the circuit in runs scored and homers once apiece. His score in Table Nineteen also evidences that, on the whole, his career stats were marginally better than those of Jennings, despite the latter's possession of some flashier numbers (including a .401 BA in 1896). But, like Van Haltren, his final Total-Z of +0.75 isn't high enough to justify his inclusion from this period.

Five of the hurlers from this era—John Clarkson, Pud Galvin, Tim Keefe, Hoss Radbourn and Mickey Welch—played all or most of their careers before 1893, so their achievement of Cooperstown's de facto-wins standard is suspect to some. Galvin (361–308, .540), Radbourn (309–195, .613) and Welch (307–210, .594) were all gone from the majors by the end of 1892. Keefe (342–225, .603) pitched through 1893, going 10–7 in his last campaign, and Clarkson (328–178, .648) quit after 1894, with a combined record of 24–27 in his last two seasons. But most players' performances decline in their last couple seasons, and all of these men also spent the first part of their careers tossing underhand to locations requested by the hitters, which — for all we know — may have counterbalanced any advantage inherent in the shorter pitching distance they enjoyed. Beyond that, the scores above do little to sully any of their credentials, except for Welch, whose Total-Z is less than half as far above average for the time as that of Rusie, the next-lowest HOF hurler on the list.

The Dead-Ball Era (1901–19)

Because of the dead-ball era's reputation for strong pitching and weak offense, you might expect that—both for this period alone, and relative to other eras—the dead-ball Z Scores below would be much higher for pitchers and lower for batters than those of other times. But it doesn't work that way. Keep in mind that these scores are derived from the means and distributions for this era only, so the chances of anyone's earning a very large Z in either group are no greater or less than those in any of the other period scales.

The first two sets of era rankings are also representative of the offensive advantages enjoyed by outfielders and first basemen and the handicap suffered by catchers. The top five non-pitchers from the 19th century and six of the top 10 for the dead-ball era were flychasers or first sackers, and only one catcher (Buck Ewing) ranks among the Z-Score leaders for either group.

Given his association with the Baltimore Orioles of the 1890s, some may quibble over the assignment of Willie Keeler as a dead-baller, rather than 19th-century player. But Keeler had more at-bats (4477) from 1901 to 1910 than he did from 1892 to 1900 (4114). Like George Davis, Bill Dahlen, Jake Beckley and some others from the previous subset, Willie's era assignment would be simplified if the dead-ball period could be dated from the year the pitching rubber was moved to sixty feet (i.e., 1893–1919), rather than the turn of the century. But that would leave too few players from the years 1876–92 to make up a separate data set with a size and statistical significance comparable to baseball's other periods, and the increased offense that accompanied moving the pitcher's mound would seem to nullify this period's primary characteristic.

The 267 dead-ballers in the database account for 11.6 percent of all players in history (185 non-pitchers, 12.5 percent; 82 pitchers, 10.1 percent). The 33 Hall-of-Famers from the era — who make up 17.8 percent of the entire HOF roster — include: 20 non-pitchers: Frank Baker, Roger Bresnahan, Max Carey, Frank Chance, Fred Clarke, Ty Cobb, Eddie Collins, Jimmy Collins, Sam Crawford, Johnny Evers, Elmer Flick, Harry Hooper, Willie Keeler, Nap Lajoie, Ray Schalk, Tris Speaker, Joe Tinker, Honus Wagner, Bobby Wallace and Zach Wheat. Thirteen pitchers also make the cut: Grover Alexander, Charles "Chief" Bender, Mordecai "Three Finger" Brown, Jack Chesbro, Walter Johnson, Addie Joss, Rube Marquard, Christy Mathewson, Joe "Iron Man" McGinnity, Eddie Plank, Rube Waddell, Ed Walsh and Vic Willis. Three managers join the list, too: Miller Huggins, Bill McKechnie and Casey Stengel. Often-cited errors of selection include Bresnahan, Chance, Chesbro, Evers, Flick, Joss, Marquard, Schalk, Tinker, Waddell, Wallace, Walsh and Willis. The most commonly cited errors of omission include Babe Adams, Gavvy Cravath, Jake Daubert, Mike Donlin, Larry Doyle, "Shoeless" Joe Jackson, Ed Konetchy, Deacon Phillippe, Ed Reulbach, and Smoky Joe Wood.

Among unenshrined dead-ball players, Gavvy Cravath's candidacy merits special consideration because he played a key role in popularizing the home-run hitter in the seasons before Babe Ruth was switched from the mound to the outfield. Cravath topped the NL in homers six times in the years 1913–19 (with a high of 24 in 1915), and he led the circuit in various batting stats on nine other occasions. When he retired after 1920, his 119 career homers were the fourth-most ever.

Cravath's home-run total is unimpressive compared with later sluggers, and he received just nine Cooperstown votes spread over five elections (1937–47). But his isolated Z Score for four-baggers versus his contemporaries

Table Twenty
Dead-Ball Z-Score Leaders

Rank	Non-Pitchers	Pos	Total Z Avg	Core Z Avg	Rank	Non-Pitchers	Pos	Total Z Avg	Core Z Avg
1	Ty Cobb	cf	2.69	3.94	19	Del Pratt	2b	0.72	0.86
2	Tris Speaker	cf	2.41	3.13	20	Jimmy Collins	3b	0.71	1.15
3	Honus Wagner	ss	2.15	2.91		Jake Daubert	1b	0.71	1.12
4	Eddie Collins	2b	2.08	2.30	22	Bobby Veach	lf	0.70	1.34
5	Nap Lajoie	2b	1.92	2.60	23	Heinie Groh	3b	0.68	0.45
6	Sam Crawford	rf	1.37	2.30	24	George J. Burns	lf	0.64	0.79
7	Max Carey	cf	1.24	1.47	25	Fred Tenney	1b	0.63	0.84
8	Fred Clarke	lf	1.09	1.82	26	John Anderson	lf	0.61	0.86
9	Zach Wheat	lf	1.06	2.36	27	Harry Davis	1b	0.58	1.01
10	Frank Baker	3b	0.98	1.34		Elmer Flick	rf	0.58	0.89
11	Sherry Magee	lf	0.97	1.47	29	Larry Gardner	3b	0.52	0.69
12	Harry Hooper	rf	0.96	1.36	30	Larry Doyle	2b	0.50	0.99
13	Ed Konetchy	1b	0.90	1.14	31	Bobby Wallace	ss	0.48	0.92
14	Willie Keeler	rf	0.88	1.78	32	Gavvy Cravath	rf	0.45	0.82
15	Joe Jackson	rf	0.87	1.23		Joe Tinker	ss	0.45	0.31
16	Jimmy Sheckard	lf	0.86	0.99	40	Johnny Evers	2b	0.30	0.14
17	Tommy Leach	cf	0.81	1.05	t53	Frank Chance	1b	0.23	0.24
18	Stuffy McInnis	1b	0.77	0.99	67	Ray Schalk	c	0.13	-0.23
					t82	Roger Bresnahan	c	-0.04	0.06

Rank	Pitchers	Pos	Total Z Avg	Core Z Avg	Rank	Pitchers	Pos	Total Z Avg	Core Z Avg
1	Walter Johnson	sp	2.02	2.83	12	Ed Reulbach	sp	0.55	0.67
2	Christy Mathewson	sp	1.89	2.31	13	Doc White	sp	0.51	0.58
3	Grover Alexander	sp	1.54	2.01	14	Vic Willis	sp	0.49	0.92
4	Ed Walsh	sp	1.53	1.14	15	Red Ames	sp	0.44	0.53
5	Eddie Plank	sp	1.15	1.81	16	Babe Adams	sp	0.43	0.37
6	Mordecai Brown	sp	1.12	1.18	17	Joe McGinnity	sp	0.42	0.82
7	Charley Bender	sp	0.85	0.94	18	Deacon Phillippe	sp	0.40	0.47
	Addie Joss	sp	0.85	0.63	19	Sam Leever	sp	0.34	0.59
9	Smoky Joe Wood	sp	0.80	0.42	20	Hooks Wiltse	sp	0.31	0.22
10	Rube Waddell	sp	0.74	1.10	21	Jack Chesbro	sp	0.30	0.54
11	Eddie Cicotte	sp	0.56	0.77	34	Rube Marquard	sp	0.04	0.37

(+3.29) is topped by only one man from his era (Zach Wheat, at +3.76, whose career overlapped the live-ball period, and who hit only 51 of his 132 homers before 1920). Beyond that, only 17 other men who played during the years 1920–94 post higher scores than Cravath for homers versus their own contemporaries, and all of them but Stan Musial (475 circuit clouts) and Dave Winfield (465) poked five-hundred dingers or more.

Gavvy's Total-Z for his era (+0.45) is as good as or better than those of five contemporary Hall of Famers, and his addition to the Cooperstown roster would not demean it. But, all the same, his final Total-Z (+0.33) is good enough only to tie for 359th place among all the eligible non-pitchers — so it's hard to support his inclusion.

Another oft-cited error of omission is left fielder Mike Donlin, who at .333 is the only unenshrined dead-ball hitter besides Joe Jackson with a career batting average above .330. But Donlin, who played for six different major-league clubs during the years 1899–1914, mostly in the NL, led his league in an offensive category just once during those seasons, topping the senior circuit with 124 runs scored for the Giants of 1905. His Total-Z versus his contemporaries (+0.24) is only 52nd-best among dead-ball non-pitchers; his final Total-Z (+0.16) ranks 475th.

Among the era's first baseman, only Frank Chance has been elected to the Hall (954 BBWAA votes spread over eight ballots, and enshrined by the OTC2 in 1946), and there is little doubt that his selection stemmed in part from the fame he received — along with Joe Tinker and Johnny Evers — as subject of Franklin Pierce Adams' 1908 poem "*Baseball's Sad Lexicon*," which extolled the trio's virtues as a double-play combo (ironically, in the years that Tinkers-to-Evers-to-Chance was a unit, they never once led their circuit in twin killings). But nine other first sackers from the period have career stats that are better than Chance's in this scale, including five with scores good enough to rank among the dead-ball leaders. Of those, Ed Konetchy — the top-ranked first sacker of the era — never got a single HOF vote, while Stuffy McInnis, Jake Daubert, Fred Tenney and Harry Davis shared a combined total of only 55 votes over the years they were on the ballot.

Neither Konetchy, McInnis, Daubert, Tenney nor Davis ever benefited from a poem that celebrated their double-play skills, but their relative lack of attention from the electors cannot be blamed solely on Adams and the New York *Globe*. None of them hit more than 75 homers in their careers, or more than twelve in a season. By the time HOF voting began in 1936, the home-run exploits of Jimmie Foxx, Lou Gehrig and Hank Greenberg had created a new standard for power at the position which, because of the realities of the dead-ball era, none of its first sackers could have possibly met. Given the scores above, it's likely that — absent poetry and Chance's service as a successful manager — any or all of them would be better choices for Cooperstown. But, the

Hall is already proportionately overstocked with first basemen; and Konetchy, the best of the five in the final ratings, ranks 163rd among all non-pitchers (Total-Z of +0.74), making all of them a tough sell. By the way, all five men had more twin killings in their careers than Chance did, and two of them — Konetchy and McInnis — had more than twice as many.

There are no unenshrined shortstops ahead of Joe Tinker above, but it's possible that — relative to Johnny Evers, second basemen Larry Doyle and Del Pratt were also disadvantaged by the Adams poem. Doyle was a National League contemporary of Evers during 1907–17. He won the Chalmers Award (i.e., MVP) in 1912, after finishing second the previous season. Evers won it in 1914, for his leadership with the miracle Boston Braves, but was no better than 10th in any other year of that balloting. Evers had 1659 hits, 919 runs, 538 RBI, and ended his career at .270. Doyle's career marks were 1887 hits, 960 runs, 793 RBIs, and .290. Larry also led the NL in hits twice, doubles and triples once each, and won the batting title in 1915. Doyle topped .300 five times, Evers twice. Playing in the junior circuit, Pratt batted above .300 six times and led the league in RBI for 1916. Pratt's top finish in Chalmers voting was just 10th-best in 1914, but his best seasons came after the award was discontinued, and he had 1996 hits, 856 runs and 968 RBIs en route to a career BA of .292. But in the final rankings, Pratt fares no better than 204th (+0.61), and Doyle rates 306th (+0.41), although both men also participated in more career double plays than Evers.

The average Hall-of-Fame career lasts 17 seasons, and many of its members sustained a high level of performance for most of their big-league tenures. So by Cooperstown standards, any man whose peak performance lasted for less than a decade had a meteoric career. Among 20th century players in the Hall, there are a dozen or so who fit that description. A majority of those men were hurlers (Dizzy Dean and Sandy Koufax being prominent examples), and several of the Shrine's most short-lived pitching stardoms occurred during the dead-ball era — notably Jack Chesbro, Addie Joss, Rube Waddell and Ed Walsh. But they were not atypical for their time, as — unlike Walter Johnson, Christy Mathewson and Grover Alexander (who had 10 or more wins in 49 of their 58 seasons, combined) — half the pitchers on the list in Table Twenty had double-digit victory totals in fewer than ten campaigns, and many rapidly used up their arms.

Also, three-fifths of the Core-Z statistics for pitchers are cumulative (games won, innings pitched and strikeouts), so short-term hurlers are somewhat disadvantaged in that score. But, among all of the pitching variables, the balance between cumulative totals and career averages allows short-career hurlers like Joss (nine years) and Smoky Joe Wood (seven as a full-time hurler) to score competitively on their Total-Z, better even than several men — like Ed Reulbach, Babe Adams and Deacon Phillippe — with longer, perhaps more substantial careers. Joss is in the Hall, thanks to Bowie Kuhn's intervention with the VC. Although there's no doubt that Reulbach, Adams and Phillippe are better-qualified than at least one of the HOF pitchers from their time, the biggest problem with any of their candidacies is that the era's hurlers are anything but under-represented at Cooperstown. Also, with the statistical advantages of pitching in the dead-ball era removed from the other two scales by normalization, none of their final scores merits their inclusion: Reulbach is 117th in the final rankings (+0.53); Adams is 154th (+0.41); and Phillippe is 166th (+0.37).

The Live-Ball Era (1920–45)

The live-ball era has so many Hall of Famers (62 in all) and oft-cited errors of omission (they are virtually legion) that what follows cannot do justice for most of them. But, if nothing else, Table Twenty-One visually portrays this era's domination of baseball's Shrine. The names of all but two men among the non-pitcher leaders are boldfaced (i.e., already on the Cooperstown roster), and 40 of the top 55 Total-Z averages among the era's position players belong to Hall of Famers. Whether all of that represents justice or the gross over-glorification of this particular period in baseball history is debatable.

The 458 players in the database represent 20.0 percent of all eligible players in history (290 non-pitchers, 19.5 percent; 168 pitchers, 20.7 percent), the 62 Hall of Famers account for a whopping 33.5 percent of all players enshrined. Forty-eight non-pitchers made Cooperstown, including Luke Appling, Earl Averill, Dave Bancroft, Jim Bottomley, Lou Boudreau, Mickey Cochrane, Earle Combs, Joe Cronin, Kiki Cuyler, Bill Dickey, Joe DiMaggio, Bobby Doerr, Rick Ferrell, Jimmie Foxx, Frankie Frisch, Charlie Gehringer, Lou Gehrig, Goose Goslin, Hank Greenberg, Chick Hafey, Gabby Hartnett, Harry Heilmann, Billy Herman, Rogers Hornsby, Travis Jackson, George Kelly, Chuck Klein, Tony Lazzeri, Fred Lindstrom, Ernie Lombardi, Heinie Manush, Rabbit Maranville, Joe Medwick, Johnny Mize, Mel Ott, Sam Rice, Edd Roush, Babe Ruth, Joe Sewell, Al Simmons, George Sisler, Bill Terry, Pie Traynor, Arky Vaughan, Lloyd Waner, Paul Waner, Hack Wilson and Ross Youngs. Fourteen pitchers also made the grade: Stan Coveleski, Dizzy Dean, Red Faber, Lefty Gomez, Burleigh Grimes, Lefty Grove, Jesse Haines, Waite Hoyt, Carl Hubbell, Ted Lyons, Herb Pennock, Eppa Rixey, Red Ruffing, and Dazzy Vance. Two managers, Leo Durocher and Bucky Harris, have plaques of their own. Often-cited errors of selection include: Bancroft, Combs, Ferrell, Hafey, Haines, Jackson, Kelly, Klein, Lindstrom, Lyons, Lombardi, Rice, L. Waner, Wilson and Youngs. Dick Bartell, Wally Berger, Dolph Camilli, Spud Chandler, Harlond Clift, Doc Cramer, Paul Derringer, Wes Ferrell, Joe Gordon, Charlie Grimm, Stan Hack, Mel Harder, Babe Herman, Robert L. "Indian Bob" Johnson, Willie Kamm, Ken Keltner, Dolf Luque, Firpo Marberry, Marty Marion, Carl Mays, Frank McCormick,

Table Twenty-One
Live-Ball Z-Score Leaders

Rank	Non-Pitchers	Pos	Total Z Avg	Core Z Avg	Rank	Non-Pitchers	Pos	Total Z Avg	Core Z Avg
1	Babe Ruth	rf	3.02	3.94	26	Jim Bottomley	1b	0.89	1.50
2	Lou Gehrig	1b	2.31	3.13	27	Pie Traynor	3b	0.85	1.18
3	Rogers Hornsby	2b	2.03	2.54	28	Rabbit Maranville	ss	0.84	0.53
4	Jimmie Foxx	1b	1.96	2.97	29	Bob L. Johnson	lf	0.82	1.42
5	Mel Ott	rf	1.80	2.85	30	Joe Judge	1b	0.76	0.89
6	Charlie Gehringer	2b	1.62	1.98		Mickey Cochrane	c	0.76	0.77
7	Joe DiMaggio	cf	1.51	2.06		Billy Herman	2b	0.76	0.77
8	Al Simmons	lf	1.43	2.46	33	Earl Averill	cf	0.74	1.40
9	Frankie Frisch	2b	1.35	1.57	34	Edd Roush	cf	0.73	1.02
10	Paul Waner	rf	1.30	1.88	35	Heinie Manush	lf	0.72	1.41
11	Goose Goslin	lf	1.29	2.00	37	Arky Vaughan	ss	0.71	0.96
12	Johnny Mize	1b	1.23	1.65	40	Joe Sewell	ss	0.65	0.90
13	Harry Heilmann	rf	1.13	1.90	41	Tony Lazzeri	2b	0.63	0.90
	George Sisler	1b	1.13	1.56	48	Lou Boudreau	ss	0.56	0.38
15	Sam Rice	rf	1.05	1.39	t51	Dave Bancroft	ss	0.53	0.25
	Bill Dickey	c	1.05	1.13	t54	Earle Combs	cf	0.51	0.71
17	Bill Terry	1b	1.03	1.35		George Kelly	1b	0.51	0.67
18	Joe Cronin	ss	1.01	1.34	t60	Hack Wilson	cf	0.47	0.92
19	Hank Greenberg	1b	1.00	1.41	t66	Travis Jackson	ss	0.42	0.55
20	Joe Medwick	lf	0.97	1.62	t69	Lloyd Waner	cf	0.41	0.75
21	Luke Appling	ss	0.96	1.17	t78	Chick Hafey	lf	0.36	0.64
22	Bobby Doerr	2b	0.93	1.11	t87	Ross Youngs	rf	0.26	0.32
23	Chuck Klein	rf	0.92	1.55	t91	Ernie Lombardi	c	0.23	0.71
	Kiki Cuyler	rf	0.92	1.25	t95	Fred Lindstrom	3b	0.19	0.59
	Gabby Hartnett	c	0.92	1.02	t97	Rick Ferrell	c	0.18	0.04

Rank	Pitchers	Pos	Total Z Avg	Core Z Avg	Rank	Pitchers	Pos	Total Z Avg	Core Z Avg
1	Lefty Grove	sp	1.96	2.59	12	Red Faber	sp	1.02	1.62
2	Carl Hubbell	sp	1.69	1.92	13	Dizzy Dean	sp	0.99	0.97
3	Carl Mays	sp	1.45	1.23	14	Eppa Rixey	sp	0.98	1.60
4	Dazzy Vance	sp	1.41	1.54	15	Dolf Luque	sp	0.89	0.93
5	Burleigh Grimes	sp	1.13	1.60	16	Waite Hoyt	sp	0.87	1.23
6	Herb Pennock	sp	1.12	1.29		Bob Shawkey	sp	0.87	1.19
7	Jack Quinn	sp	1.09	1.38	18	Paul Derringer	sp	0.86	1.21
8	Red Ruffing	sp	1.07	1.74	19	Bucky Walters	sp	0.82	0.98
9	Spud Chandler	sp	1.06	0.73	20	Fred Fitzsimmons	sp	0.80	0.99
10	Lefty Gomez	sp	1.04	1.26	27	Ted Lyons	sp	0.69	1.19
11	Stan Coveleski	sp	1.03	1.28	39	Jesse Haines	sp	0.42	0.89

Buddy Myer, Bobo Newsom, Lefty O'Doul, Jack Quinn, Wally Schang, Bob Shawkey, Riggs Stephenson, Johnny Vander Meer, Bucky Walters, Cy Williams and Ken Williams are among those whose fitness for the Hall is still hotly argued.

The era's abundant representation at Cooperstown makes it difficult to argue for the inclusion of anyone else from this period. But some often-cited errors of omission — catcher Wally Schang, second baseman Joe Gordon, third sackers Stan Hack and Harlond Clift, outfielders Indian Bob Johnson, Cy and Ken Williams, and pitchers Carl Mays, Spud Chandler, Jack Quinn, Firpo Marberry, Dolf Luque, Bob Shawkey, Bucky Walters and Paul Derringer — post scores in later chapters that merit further consideration.

Eight live-ball first basemen are already enshrined, leaving several out in the cold. Among them, Charlie Grimm, Dolph Camilli and Frank McCormick are the most popular candidates. Grimm was a player, coach and manager for 43 seasons, but longevity is his only real credential. For each of his 20 seasons as a player Grimm averaged only 115 hits, four homers, 45 runs scored and 54 RBI to go with a .290 BA, none of which is impressive, especially for his time. Charlie's Total-Z (+0.47) is tied with Hack Wilson for 60th-best among this era, but he fares no better than 369th place in the final rankings (+0.32). Camilli won the MVP in 1941, and he is tied for 49th in the era ratings (+0.54), but Dolf's final score (+0.43) ranks only 290th. McCormick's MVP came in 1940, but his score for the era (+0.42, tied for 66th) and final rankings (+0.31, 373rd) are even lower than Camilli's. Beyond them, Joe Judge, the highest-ranked unenshrined first baseman on this list, received only 32 HOF votes spread over seven ballots, and is rarely mentioned by anyone as an error of omission. His rank here is attributable mainly to longevity (20 seasons in the bigs, 16 as a regular); and, although he also fares better than the era's other unenshrined first sackers in the final ratings, his final Total-Z (+0.60) is good enough for only 212th place.

Second baseman Buddy Myer won an AL batting title in 1935, and hit .303 over a 17-year career spent mostly with the Senators. As recently as 1997, he was mentioned as a possible Veterans Committee selection. But the fact that there are already a half-dozen live-ball second sackers in Cooperstown doesn't enliven his candidacy, nor do his Z Scores — a rank of 59th for the era (+0.48), and 237th in the final ratings (+0.53).

Although he played until 1953 and was more contemporaneous with Postwar-era shortstops like Pee Wee Reese, Phil Rizzuto and Vern Stephens, a majority of Marty Marion's at-bats came before 1946 (as did his 1944 MVP trophy), so he gets cited as a live-baller. Marion's batting average (.263) would not be the worst among Hall-of-Fame shortstops, if he were inducted, but his credentials rely on his reputation as the most graceful fielder of his era, and are plausible only if you agree that Dave Bancroft, a defensive wiz from an earlier portion of the live-ball period, is a legitimate Hall of Famer. Unlike

Bancroft's, Marion's fielding stats do not rank among those of the 10 most-qualified players at his position (see chapter 9), and Marty's final score (+0.05) is tied for 577th, marking him as little better than statistically average among all the non-pitchers measured.

Willie Kamm may have been baseball's greatest defensive third baseman prior to Brooks Robinson. He topped the AL in fielding eight times, putouts seven, chances-per-game six, assists four, and double plays twice in a 13-year career with the White Sox and Indians. But Kamm's offense was below-average for his time, as he batted over .300 just once, and averaged only 62 runs scored and 64 RBI per year. He's tied for 69th-best among the era (+0.41), and his final score ranks only 341st (+0.36). Ken Keltner took over the hot corner for Cleveland a couple seasons after Kamm left and brought some power to the position (163 career homers) that was atypical for the time. But, Keltner really had just two big seasons a decade apart (1938 and 1948); his stats rank 83rd for the era (+0.32), and his final score (+0.30, 382nd) is even lower than Kamm's.

Five live-ball outfielders, Doc Cramer, Wally Berger, Riggs Stephenson, Babe Herman and Lefty O'Doul, also fail to pass initial muster. Among them, Cramer ranks highest among the era leaders (+0.53, tied for 51st), and Doc is also the only one to rate among the top 30 at his position (center field). Cramer's best HOF credential is his total of 2705 hits — through the 2000 voting, there were only five eligible players ahead of him among the career-hits leaders who had not been enshrined. But Doc's final score (+0.53) rates no better than 237th. Berger was the NL's starting center fielder in each of the first three All-Star Games (1933–35), and he led the circuit in home runs and RBI in the last of those years, on his way to 242 homers and a .300 batting average for his career. But Wally ranks 80th (+0.34) in the era ratings, and 346th in the final ledger (+0.35). Stephenson's biggest HOF assets are his .336 career batting average, and an OBA of .407. But, despite his potent bat, poor defense and a weak arm kept him from being a lineup fixture, as he topped 100 games played in only five of his 14 seasons. Stephenson ranks 94th among the non-pitchers from the era (+0.21), and his final score puts him in just 457th place (+0.19).

Babe Herman and Lefty O'Doul get more attention because both were colorful characters whose exploits are ingrained in baseball folklore. They also had high batting averages (Herman's was .324, O'Doul's even better at .349), but their other credentials are different, and neither man's are that impressive. Herman sustained above-average performance for most of his 13 seasons but never led the National League in anything but doubles, doing that only once, and he was nowhere near the statistical equal of contemporary right fielders Paul Waner and Mel Ott, from the same league. In contrast, O'Doul began his career as a pitcher, and counted just six of his 11 big-league seasons as an outfield regular. He had one great year, 1929, when he set a National League record for hits (254, tied the next season by Bill Terry) and led the circuit with a .398 average, then won another batting crown in 1932. His stats are impressive for the six years he was a regular, but they came at a point in baseball history when offense was more inflated than ever before or since, and his peak performance was too short-lived. Herman is tied for 56th among the era (+0.50), and his final score (+0.43) ranks 290th. O'Doul fares worse in both scales, 108th among Live-Ball non-pitchers (+0.09) and 585th in the final scores (+0.04). Along with Cramer's, Berger's and Stephenson's, both men's candidacies are nothing more than if-then arguments, palpable only if you think guys like Chick Hafey and Ross Youngs really belong in Cooperstown. O'Doul merits extra credit for his pivotal role introducing baseball in Japan, and with that in mind, his credentials seem more viable as a contributor of some sort.

Among live-ball pitchers, Bobo Newsom's candidacy is similar to those of Herman and O'Doul, because much of his support is based on the colorful legend surrounding one of baseball's most-often-traded players. Newsom pitched in 20 seasons for ten different teams, most of them regular denizens of the second division. As a result, he is one of the few often-cited errors of omission with a losing record as a big-league hurler (211–222, for a .487 winning percentage). He won 20 or more games three times (1938–40) and topped his circuit in complete games twice, and innings and strikeouts once each. Bobo ranks 42nd among the live-ball hurlers (+0.40), but stands no better than 188th place in the pitchers' final ratings (+0.33).

Three other pitching favorites, Wes Ferrell, Mel Harder and Johnny Vander Meer, fare no better than Newsom. Ferrell's hitting prowess was substantial (38 career homers and a .280 BA in 1176 at-bats). He won 20 games or more on six occasions and finished his career with a 193–128 ledger and .601 winning percentage. Despite that formidable record, he ranks no better than 50th among the hurlers of his era (+0.35) and is tied with Mel Harder for 197th in the final pitcher ratings (+0.31). Harder won 30 more games than Ferrell (223) but also lost 186, finishing with a .545 percentage; he won twenty or more games just twice. Despite Vander Meer's 700 HOF votes — more than Ferrell (18) and Harder (215) combined — his primary Cooperstown credential is his back-to-back no-hit feat of 1938, although he also led the NL in strikeouts for three straight years (1941–43). He never won more than 18 games in a season, and he ended with a 119–121 ledger. His stats rate just 57th among the live-ball hurlers (+0.23) and are 252nd in the final rankings (+0.19).

Among men often tabbed as the era's likely errors of selection, the lists above do little to exonerate any of them, except Sam Rice and Chuck Klein. Before the sabermetric researchers cut Cap Anson's career-hits total from 3041 to 2995, Rice's career figure (2987) was the closest to the 3000 standard. Those missing safeties didn't stop the VC from electing him in 1963, but many think his spot on the roster would be better filled by someone else, because his power was not comparable to the great outfielders of his time. But the 103 live-ball flychasers measured here averaged 101 homers and 702 ribbies during their careers. Sam hit only 34 dingers, but he plated 1078 baserunners over his 20 seasons, and his score above indicates that his overall stats were better than those of several men with much more power.

The dual rap against Klein's membership is that he benefited from playing in a park (Philadelphia's Baker Bowl) with a short right field that was tailored to his left-handed power and that he had only five great seasons in the majors (1929–33). The first argument is absurd and unfair. Given the reserve clause, Klein never had a choice regarding which ballpark he played in, and should not be penalized for the Baker Bowl's configuration any more than Babe Ruth should be for the cozy, right-field contours he enjoyed at Yankee Stadium. But the other contention has merit. Traded to the Cubs in 1934, after winning the NL triple crown the previous season, Klein's stats fell from an average of 36 homers and 139 ribbies over his five good years to just 18 dingers and 75 RBI over the next half decade. And after 1938, he spent his last six seasons as a part-timer. Klein is comparable to Hack Wilson, who had just six good seasons out of a dozen in the bigs, and only one after Hack was traded from Chicago (Wilson was just as upset about the deal as was David Wells when dealt from the Yankees in 1999). But, Klein's career totals surpassed Wilson's in all of the Core-Z variables: he amassed 2076 hits, 300 homers, 1168 runs scored and 1201 RBI to go with a .320 average. Hack's totals were 1461 hits, 244 round-trippers, 884 runs, 1062 RBIs and a .307 BA. Whether or not either man belongs in Cooperstown, the scores above indicate that, statistically, Klein was a better choice — although Wilson was inducted a year earlier (1979).

CHAPTER 7

Doin' the Time Warp Again

Differences in the periodic norms for various statistics can make players from one era appear less qualified for Cooperstown than those of another — even when they're not. In turn, the Hall-of-Fame roster as constituted through the 2000 voting included ratios of men from various eras that were disproportional to the number of eligible players from each time period. Table Twenty-Two examines the number of eligibles produced by each era (with the abbreviation "El Plyrs," standing for the total of all men who have received HOF votes plus those who met the 10-year-service requirement but failed to get any), each era's percentage of all eligible players as a whole (Era Pct), the number from each era who were elected through 2000 (HOF Total) and the percentage of all Cooperstown players that total represents (HOF Pct). It also gives the number of players (Ideal Total) and the plus-or-minus variation (Era Var) from that total which would have been in Cooperstown if the representation for each era was proportional to the number of eligibles it produced. Keep in mind that, because of the time lags built into selection process (the five-year wait for BBWAA eligibility and the 23-year delay for the VC process), portions of the variations for the expansion and (especially) the free-agent eras are unavoidable.

Regardless of the time lags involved, some portion of each era variation in Table Twenty-Two is impossible to justify, mainly because of the over-representation of the live-ball era, which had claimed one-third of the Cooperstown roster through 2000. The live-ball and expansion periods both produced the same number of HOF eligibles (458). So, unless you believe that the quality of big-league play during the earlier era (when the majors were a whites-only country club) was twice as good as that during the integrated expansion years, then it's hard to justify — relative to the variations for

Table Twenty-Two
HOF-Eligible Players by Era, Number Elected, and Era Variation

Era	Era Years	El Plyrs	Era Pct	HOF Total	HOF Pct	Ideal Total	Era Var
19th Century	1876–00	197	8.6	26	14.1	16	+10
Dead-Ball	1901–19	267	11.6	33	17.8	21	+12
Live-Ball	**1920–45**	**458**	**20.0**	**62**	**33.5**	**37**	**+25**
Postwar	1946–60	301	13.1	24	13.0	24	—
Expansion	1961–75	458	20.0	29	15.7	37	-8
Free-Agent	1976–94	614	26.8	11	5.9	50	-39
Totals		2295	100.1	185	100.0	185	0

other eras — the live-ball period's 13.5-percent representational advantage over the ratio of HOF-eligible players it produced, and its more than two-to-one edge in Cooperstown membership over the expansion period. Is Billy Herman (who is tied for 30th among the live-ball non-pitcher rankings in chapter 6) twice as qualified as Ron Santo (who, discounting Pete Rose, may have the best statistical credentials among expansion players not enshrined to date)?

The creation and continued existence of veterans committees are evidence that proportional representation at Cooperstown has been, and remains a desirable goal — at least to the Hall's trustees. So, time lags or not, the Hall-of-Fame roster should, in theory, reflect a greater degree of proportional balance by era than evidenced by Table Twenty-Two.

Unfortunately, even relative proportionality may be impossible to accomplish under the current regulations governing the Cooperstown selection process. As noted in previous chapters, the 5-percent support needed to remain on the BBWAA ballot and the 60-percent minimum necessary for post–World War Two players to gain VC eligibility both work strongly against the prospects that the postwar, expansion and free-agent eras might ever achieve proportional representation; and the recent trend among the voting scribes to fill in ever fewer names on their ballots also exacerbates the problem. As a result, it's likely that few of the unenshrined players who rank high among the lists in this chapter will ever be elected. Many of them among the Z-Score leaders for the expansion and free-agent eras are no longer eligible for consideration.

The Postwar Era (1946–60)

The postwar rankings reveal the impact of longevity. Predictably, Ted Williams and Stan Musial are one-two among the non-pitcher scores. But Stan was a big-leaguer for 22 years, a full-time player in all but one of them, and — after 47 rookie at-bats in 1941 — he never went to the plate less than 331 times in a season. Williams played 19 seasons, but two were interrupted by Korean-War service, producing just 101 at-bats, combined. Coupled with the different lengths of their World War Two service (Williams missed three seasons, Musial just one), that gave Stan 3266 more at-bats in the majors, enough to qualify for five more batting titles than Ted did, and equivalent to a good career for many players (447 of the 1484 non-pitchers in the data set — about 30 percent — had fewer than 3266 at-bats in entire their careers). The weight of Stan's production in those extra times at the plate raises Musial's scores well above those of Williams for the era.

Other longevity advantages are evident in the rankings of second basemen Nellie Fox and Red Schoendienst (19 seasons each) above Jackie Robinson (just 10) and in Yogi Berra's (19 years) wide margin over relative short-timer Roy Campanella (10 seasons). But before you decide the system is flawed because of these contradictions to subjective truth, remember that it doesn't measure "greatness" — whatever that may be — or even what might or should have been without segregation, auto accidents or military service. Instead, the system measures only the relative, unweighted value of each man's statistics as a whole; and, on that objective level, the numbers don't lie.

The database contains the stats of 301 men, or 13.1 percent of all players in history (193 non-pitchers, 12.9 percent; 108 pitchers, 13.3 percent). Twenty-four of those men made it to Cooperstown, putting the era's representation mark at 13.0 percent. The enshrinees include 17 non-pitchers: Richie Ashburn, Yogi Berra, Roy Campanella, Larry Doby, Nellie Fox, George Kell, Ralph Kiner, Mickey Mantle, Eddie Mathews, Stan Musial, Pee Wee Reese, Phil Rizzuto, Jackie Robinson, Red Schoendienst, Enos Slaughter, Duke Snider and Ted Williams. Eight pitchers added to the era's tally: Bob Feller, Whitey Ford, Bob Lemon, Hal Newhouser, Robin Roberts, Warren Spahn, Early Wynn and Satchel Paige. Kell, Rizzuto and Schoendienst are often cited as errors of selections. Lew Burdette, Walker Cooper, Dom DiMaggio, Elroy Face, Carl Furillo, Gil Hodges, Ted Kluszewski, Harvey Kuenn, Eddie Lopat, Minnie Miñoso, Don Newcombe, Johnny Pesky, Billy Pierce, Vic Raschi, Pete Reiser, Allie Reynolds, Al Rosen, Vern Stephens, Bobby Thomson and Mickey Vernon are among those thought by some to have been unjustly passed over.

Although three-time MVPs Yogi Berra and Roy Campanella were the dominant backstops of the postwar period, the era produced some other good catchers whose subjective credentials were eclipsed by Yogi and Roy. Among them, the one most often mentioned as a Cooperstown error of omission is Walker Cooper, an eight-time All-Star for the Cardinals, Giants and Braves who batted above .300 in five of his 10 seasons as a regular and merits recognition for his handling of the great St. Louis pitching staffs of the early 1940s.

Table Twenty-Three
Postwar Z-Score Leaders

Rank	Non-Pitchers	Pos	Total Z Avg	Core Z Avg	Rank	Non-Pitchers	Pos	Total Z Avg	Core Z Avg
1	Stan Musial	lf	3.17	3.85	16	Jackie Robinson	2b	0.81	0.91
2	Ted Williams	lf	2.48	3.57	17	Ralph Kiner	lf	0.79	1.23
3	Mickey Mantle	cf	2.33	2.81	18	Bob Elliott	3b	0.71	1.30
4	Yogi Berra	c	1.63	1.89	19	Vern Stephens	ss	0.68	1.31
5	Eddie Mathews	3b	1.48	2.34		Phil Rizzuto	ss	0.68	0.23
6	Duke Snider	cf	1.30	2.06	21	Del Ennis	lf	0.63	1.50
	Mickey Vernon	1b	1.30	1.58		Ted Kluszewski	1b	0.63	1.27
8	Enos Slaughter	rf	1.28	1.69		Eddie Yost	3b	0.63	0.62
9	Richie Ashburn	cf	1.23	1.16	24	Carl Furillo	rf	0.62	1.21
10	Gil Hodges	1b	1.18	1.58		George Kell	3b	0.62	0.97
11	Nellie Fox	2b	1.10	1.12	26	Joe Adcock	1b	0.61	1.26
12	Pee Wee Reese	ss	0.98	1.04		Harvey Kuenn	rf	0.61	0.89
13	Minnie Miñoso	lf	0.94	1.33	28	Larry Doby	cf	0.60	1.03
14	Vic Wertz	rf	0.91	1.13	29	Roy Campanella	c	0.59	0.55
	R. Schoendienst	2b	0.91	1.11	30	Gene Woodling	lf	0.55	0.68

Rank	Pitchers	Pos	Total Z Avg	Core Z Avg	Rank	Pitchers	Pos	Total Z Avg	Core Z Avg
1	Warren Spahn	sp	2.01	2.92		Bobby Shantz	sp	0.67	0.41
2	Whitey Ford	sp	1.80	2.22	12	Lew Burdette	sp	0.66	0.93
3	Bob Feller	sp	1.43	2.25	13	Eddie Lopat	sp	0.61	0.85
4	Robin Roberts	sp	1.22	2.09	14	Virgil Trucks	sp	0.58	1.02
	Hal Newhouser	sp	1.22	1.52	15	Elroy Face	rp	0.54	0.03
6	Bob Lemon	sp	1.08	1.30	16	Don Newcombe	sp	0.51	0.73
7	Early Wynn	sp	0.96	2.07	17	Bob Friend	sp	0.50	0.96
8	Billy Pierce	sp	0.87	1.50		Vic Raschi	sp	0.50	0.58
9	Harry Brecheen	sp	0.78	0.76	19	Mike Garcia	sp	0.47	0.77
10	Allie Reynolds	sp	0.67	1.20		Harvey Haddix	sp	0.47	0.61

Cooper received 168 HOF votes spread over 11 ballots, but his Total Z (+0.18) ranks just 66th among the position players of his era, trailing fellow backstops Sherm Lollar (+0.28, although he never received a Hall-of-Fame vote) and Del Crandall (+0.24, 38 votes). Walker's final score (+0.38) is good enough only to tie for 327th place (Lollar finishes 312th, Crandall 359th). Jim Hegan, another catcher from the 1950s who was widely considered the era's best defensive backstop, is tied for 475th in the final ratings (+0.16).

The postwar era also produced four first basemen with viable credentials (Mickey Vernon, Gil Hodges, Ted Kluszewski and Joe Adcock), but unlike the catchers — unless you count Stan Musial's 1016 games at first base — none of the era's first sackers have been elected to date. In that light, and subjectively, it's a shame to dismiss Kluszewski so early in the ratings, because — at six-foot-two and 225 pounds, with no real foot speed — it's likely that none of his 1766 big-league safeties resulted from infield cheapies, and the sight of his pale biceps bulging beneath the cutoff sleeves of his Cincinnati uniform was an enduring symbol of American masculinity among 1950s iconography. Big Klu batted over .300 seven times during his 15-year career, and led the NL in home runs, RBI and hits once apiece. In his four best years (1953–56) Ted averaged 179 hits, 43 homers, 102 runs scored, 116 RBI and batted .315 per season, compared to Hodges' norms of 159 safeties, 33 dingers, 92 runs, 115 RBI and .292 during that span. But Gil (3,010 votes) and Vernon (539) both outpolled Kluszewski (446) among the BBWAA voters because the former pair each had about twice as many productive seasons as Ted's half-dozen. So, although Klu's stats place 21st among his contemporary non-pitchers and are better than three HOF position players from the era, his final Total Z (+0.51) ranks just 252nd, insufficient to justify his addition as yet another HOF first sacker. Hodges and Vernon, both of whose careers began before 1946, are both eligible for VC election, but Kluszewski never received more than 58 votes on a single ballot and, under the current rules, can never again be considered. The same is true of Joe Adcock, whose 336 career homers were completely ignored by the BBWAA. Although Adcock ranks 26th among his non-pitcher contemporaries (+0.61), he fares no better than a tie for 259th in the final ratings (+0.50).

Two of the other postwar infielders often cited as errors of omission can also be dismissed at this point. Johnny Pesky led the American League with more than 200 hits in each of his first three seasons in the Show, and his career on-base (.394) and batting (.307) averages are the third-and eighth-best figures among all shortstops who were HOF-eligible through the 2000 voting. Third baseman Al Rosen was a two-time AL home-run and RBI champ who also topped the circuit once apiece in runs scored and slugging percentage and won the league's MVP in 1953. Despite all that, Pesky received just one Cooperstown vote; Rosen never got any. Both men played in just 10 big-league seasons (Pesky lost three to World War Two, while Rosen retired prematurely at age 32): Johnny was a regular in eight campaigns, Rosen in only seven. Their scores, then, are hurt by the relative brevity of their careers. Pesky ranks 65th among his contemporaries (+0.19), and 427th in the final ratings (+0.23). Rosen fares a little better, but not enough — he ranks 53rd for the postwar era (+0.30), and 359th on the final list (+0.33).

According to the media reports, Dom DiMaggio received support in the Veterans Committee elections of 1999 and 2000. If he is elected at a later date, it will be a statistical injustice to postwar outfielders, notably Minnie Miñoso, Vic Wertz, Del Ennis and Carl Furillo, who rank ahead of him in Table Twenty-Three but are ineligible for further consideration because of the panel's post–1945, 60-percent-support requirement. DiMaggio ranks 32nd among the postwar position players (+0.52) and is tied for 306th in the final ratings (+0.41). All four men rank ahead of Joltin' Joe's younger brother in the final ratings: Wertz is tied for 144th (+0.80); Miñoso is deadlocked at 156h (+0.76); Furillo is among three men at 216th (+0.59); and Ennis rates with three others at 232nd (+0.55). Other contemporary flychasers ahead of DiMaggio in the final ratings are Harvey Kuenn (+0.57, 223rd), who is eligible for VC consideration, plus Gene Woodling (+0.53, 237th) and Jackie Jensen (+0.49, 266th), who are not. Except for Wertz and Miñoso, however, none of these men boost scores good enough to merit further notice, given the abundance of outfielders already in the Hall. Neither Bobby Thomson (+0.42 and thirty-eighth place in the Postwar ratings, +0.28 and 393rd in the final), nor Pete Reiser (-0.18, and 820th in the final) merit further consideration, either.

The postwar pitcher ranking is the only one for any era in which all of the current Cooperstown hurlers score above everyone else who qualified, giving the impression that the selection process has not overlooked any deserving pitchers from the era. But several Postwar moundsmen are borderline candidates worthy of note, particularly starters Billy Pierce (211–169, .555), Lew Burdette (203–144, .585), Allie Reynolds (182–107, .630), Eddie Lopat (166–112, .597), Don Newcombe (149–90, .623), Harry Brecheen (133–92, .591), Vic Raschi (132–66, .667) and Bobby Shantz (119–99, .546), plus reliever Elroy Face (104–95, .523, 193 career saves). Only Pierce (+0.78, and tied for 62nd place), Face (+0.67, 88th), Brecheen (+0.66, t89th) and Reynolds (+0.63, t98th) rank among the top 100 in the hurlers' final ratings, however, and only they merit further consideration. Burdette (+0.60, t104th) and Lopat (+0.57, 109th) just miss that group, and the others trail off behind them, going as low as Newcombe (+0.46, t136th).

The Expansion Era (1961–75)

Discounting the glaring but (at present) moot omission of Pete Rose, the expansion-era rankings are evidence that the BBWAA electors of recent years have done a reasonably good job sorting the very best Hall-of-Fame candidates from the pretenders of this period. But, as noted earlier, the era also produced exactly the same number of players eligible for the database as did live-ball times, and any honest attempt at proportional representation will eventually require somewhere between 37 and 60 HOF members from the later period, both numbers considerably larger than the 29 expansion members elected thus far.

But even token proportionality will be virtually impossible to achieve. The BBWAA eligibility of most expansion players has already expired, and after the 2000 voting, only two of the era leaders listed below were still on the writers' ballot — pitchers Jim Kaat and Luis Tiant. Tiant's eligibility expires after the 2002 voting, Kaat's the following year; neither man is likely to be elected by the scribes or to achieve the 60-percent support needed to qualify for future VC ballots (through 2000, Kaat had averaged 22.1-percent support per election, Tiant just 13.0). Also, because of the 60-percent requirement, only seven other men among the period's statistical leaders — Ken Boyer, Mickey Lolich, Roger Maris, Bill Mazeroski, Tony Oliva, Ron Santo and Maury Wills — can ever be eligible for back-door consideration. Even worse, at least one prominent candidate with good credentials on both scales — Ted Simmons (+0.85 Total, +1.51 Core) — is no longer eligible for consideration by either elective organ because of the 5-percent-support rule (reliever Sparky Lyle has suffered the same fate). How all of this sorts itself out remains to be seen. But, under the present restrictions, this era is destined to be proportionately short-changed on the Cooperstown roster.

The expansion era is represented by 458 players in the database fully 20 percent (286 non-pitchers, 19.3 percent; 172 pitchers, 21.2 percent). of all players. Twenty-nine or 15.7 percent, are in the Hall, including 19 non-pitchers — Hank Aaron, Luis Aparicio, Ernie Banks, Johnny Bench, Lou Brock, Rod Carew, Orlando Cepeda, Roberto Clemente, Al Kaline, Harmon Killebrew, Willie Mays, Willie McCovey, Joe Morgan, Tony Perez, Brooks Robinson, Frank Robinson, Willie Stargell, Billy Williams and Carl Yastrzemski; plus 10 pitchers — Jim Bunning, Don Drysdale, Bob Gibson, Catfish Hunter, Ferguson Jenkins, Sandy Koufax, Juan Marichal, Jim Palmer, Gaylord Perry and Hoyt Wilhelm. Aparicio and Drysdale are, on occasion, mentioned as errors of selection; Dick Allen, Ken Boyer, Rocky Colavito, Curt Flood, Mickey Lolich, Roger Maris, Thurman Munson, Bill Mazeroski, Tony Oliva, Vada Pinson, Pete Rose, Ron Santo, Ted Simmons, Mel Stottlemyre, Joe Torre and Maury Wills are most often cited as errors of omission.

Among the unenshrined expansion-era pitchers, starters Kaat (+0.81, and tied for 59th), Tiant (+0.68, t83rd) and Mike Cuellar (+0.62, 100th, but who never received a Hall-of-Fame vote), plus relievers Lindy McDaniel (+0.65, t91st) and Stu Miller (+0.63, t98th) are the only ones who rank among the top one-hundred in the final pitcher ratings. That eliminates starters Andy Messersmith (final score of +0.61, t101st), Mel Stottlemyre (+0.55, t112th), Mickey Lolich (+0.54, 116th) and Dave McNally (+0.52, t119th), plus reliever Sparky Lyle (whose final Total-Z and ranking are identical to Stottlemyre's) from further discussion.

Expansion-era catchers Joe Torre, Ted Simmons and Thurman Munson are often cited as errors of omission, and Bill Freehan, another of the period's

Table Twenty-Four
Expansion Z-Score Leaders

Rank	Non-Pitchers	Pos	Total Z Avg	Core Z Avg	Rank	Non-Pitchers	Pos	Total Z Avg	Core Z Avg
1	Willie Mays	cf	2.66	3.33	17	Lou Brock	lf	1.26	1.60
2	Hank Aaron	rf	2.65	3.91	18	Rusty Staub	rf	1.16	1.70
3	Pete Rose	rf	2.47	2.54	19	Luis Aparicio	ss	1.11	0.93
4	Carl Yastrzemski	lf	2.27	2.72	20	Harmon Killebrew	1b	1.06	1.90
5	Frank Robinson	rf	2.12	2.88		Vada Pinson	cf	1.06	1.65
6	Joe Morgan	2b	1.70	1.60	22	Reggie Smith	rf	1.03	1.39
7	Al Kaline	rf	1.56	2.39	23	Norm Cash	1b	1.02	1.26
	Ernie Banks	1b	1.56	2.13	24	Joe Torre	c	1.00	1.44
9	Brooks Robinson	3b	1.44	1.56		Bill Mazeroski	2b	1.00	0.56
10	Willie Stargell	lf	1.43	1.93	26	Orlando Cepeda	1b	0.99	1.81
11	Tony Perez	1b	1.34	1.98	27	Johnny Bench	c	0.96	1.47
	Rod Carew	1b	1.34	1.78	28	Ken Boyer	3b	0.89	1.38
13	Roberto Clemente	rf	1.31	2.06		Willie Davis	cf	0.89	1.28
14	Ron Santo	3b	1.30	1.54	30	Dick Allen	1b	0.88	1.44
15	Billy Williams	lf	1.27	2.13	31	Amos Otis	cf	0.86	1.04
	Willie McCovey	1b	1.27	1.92	32	Ted Simmons	c	0.85	1.51

Rank	Pitchers	Pos	Total Z Avg	Core Z Avg	Rank	Pitchers	Pos	Total Z Avg	Core Z Avg
1	Sandy Koufax	sp	1.80	1.68	11	Jim Bunning	sp	0.82	1.73
2	Jim Palmer	sp	1.68	2.24	12	A. Messersmith	sp	0.78	0.92
3	Gaylord Perry	sp	1.60	2.71	13	Luis Tiant	sp	0.74	1.59
4	Juan Marichal	sp	1.53	2.04	14	Mike Cuellar	sp	0.72	1.16
5	Don Drysdale	sp	1.46	1.68	15	Mel Stottlemyre	sp	0.69	0.87
6	Bob Gibson	sp	1.41	2.28	16	Dave McNally	sp	0.61	1.11
7	Fergie Jenkins	sp	1.39	2.21	17	Mickey Lolich	sp	0.58	1.51
8	Hoyt Wilhelm	rp	1.22	1.06	18	Gary Nolan	sp	0.57	0.55
9	Catfish Hunter	sp	1.01	1.46	19	Wilbur Wood	sp	0.55	0.68
10	Jim Kaat	sp	0.91	1.86	20	Larry Jackson	sp	0.54	0.94

backstops, ranks among the top 200 players in the final non-pitcher rankings. As will be evident in the next two chapters, the Hall of Fame is proportionally short on catchers, so, among those four, only Munson can be dismissed at this point in the discussion. Thurman played 11 seasons for the Yankees, winning the MVP in 1976 and earning a deserved reputation as one of the best clutch hitters of his time before his 1979 death in the crash of his private plane. Given four or five more years like the ones he put up, Munson may have deserved election by the BBWAA. But, statistically, the sum of his career as it was cannot justify his inclusion, as he ranks just 77th in the expansion-era ratings (+0.29) and 271st in the final rankings (+0.47).

Maury Wills was instrumental in reviving the stolen base as part of baseball's offensive arsenal. He led the National League in swipes for each of his first six years as a big-league regular (1960–65), and broke Ty Cobb's single-season record with 104 thefts in 1962, en route to the MVP trophy. But Wills was not the sole cause of that revival: Luis Aparicio, who preceded Wills by almost half a decade, was the AL's top base bandit in each of his first nine seasons (1956–64), and by 1966, if not sooner, Wills was surpassed as a leadoff force in his own circuit by Hall of Famer Lou Brock — who sustained a dominance of their specialty for a longer period of time, later broke Maury's single-season record, and ultimately stole more bases than anyone else before him. Aparicio was also a better shortstop than Wills, too. The long-time Dodger led his league in a defensive category only four times in his career, while Aparicio did it on 31 occasions. Also, compared to the means for all shortstops in the database, Wills' Z-Score average for the fielding variables alone is just +0.02, while Aparicio's is +1.10. Similarly, left fielder Brock was a better leadoff man, batting .293, with an on-base average of .344; Maury hit .281, with an OBA of .331. And Brock had the added dimension of long-ball power (149 homers), which Wills lacked completely (just 20 dingers in his career). Maury's Z-Score averages — tied for 57th in his era (+0.46) and 232nd in the final rankings (+0.55) — trail shortstop contemporary Bert Campaneris (final score of +0.74, t163rd), who also stole more bases than Wills (649 to 586). Although there doesn't seem to have been enough difference between Wills and Aparicio, subjectively, to justify the latter's big edge in HOF voting noted in chapter 2, the overall statistical evidence is sufficient to justify Maury's omission at one of Cooperstown's most over-stocked positions.

Rocky Colavito and Tony Oliva were popular players during their careers, and each has many advocates claiming he is an error of omission. Colavito smacked 374 homers and drove in 1159 runs during his 14-year career. The one-time AL leader in four-baggers, RBI and slugging percentage was a six-time All-Star and possessed a rifle arm that would've gotten more recognition if he hadn't been a contemporary of Roberto Clemente. In 15 seasons Oliva won three AL batting titles, topped the circuit in hits five times, doubles four, and runs scored and slugging once each. He was chosen for eight All-Star teams but missed two of the games with injuries. Reportedly, Tony also received support in the 2000 VC balloting, his first year eligible for that panel's consideration. Despite all that, several less-heralded outfielders of their period score from much to marginally better in both the era and final rankings, including Rusty Staub, Reggie Smith, Willie Davis, Amos Otis, Bobby

Bonds, Frank Howard and Jimmy Wynn; and neither man's final scores merit Cooperstown inclusion — Colavito rates 216th (+0.59) and Oliva is 244th (+0.52).

Curt Flood ranks 55th among expansion non-pitchers. A center fielder, Flood played his entire career in the shadow of Hall of Famer Willie Mays. Curt didn't have Willie's power, but neither did anyone else except Hank Aaron and Babe Ruth. Flood put up good numbers over the 15 seasons he played, highlighted by a .293 career batting average (including six seasons above .300) that was 37 points above the norm for his era. Curt's forte was defense: he won seven Gold Gloves (Mays got 12); he led NL flychasers in various fielding categories on 13 occasions (Mays did it nine times); and, among all center fielders, his isolated defensive-Z average is +0.63, the 14th-best ever among players at his position (Mays scored at +0.99 to rank ninth). All the same, none of those stats provides a convincing argument that Flood should be in the Hall, and his scores in the final rankings land him no higher than 280th (+0.46). The foundation of his candidacy rests with whether you believe subjectively that his historic role in bringing down the reserve clause constitutes sufficient reason for enshrinement. Flood paid a steep price for his principles, both professionally and in life as a whole. And it may be argued, his long-term impact on the game as a whole may someday prove greater than anyone's but those of Babe Ruth and Jackie Robinson. But, barring the VC's being packed by the governing board of the Major-League Players Association, his stats indicate that — like Lefty O'Doul — his best argument for election is as a contributor of some sort.

Finally, there is Roger Maris, who also paid a personal toll for the achievement that made him famous. Roger's career numbers (+0.52, tied for 52nd) are barely one-half of a standard deviation above the norm for his era. As such, they are less substantial than many of his outfield contemporaries, and on the whole, his stats — just 320th-best among the final rankings (+0.39), even lower than Flood's — cannot justify his selection. The merit of Roger's candidacy depends on whether you think his accomplishments — 61 homers and back-to-back MVPs — deserve Cooperstown recognition in their own right. There are legitimate arguments on both sides.

The Free-Agent Era (1976–94)

Due to the time lag built into the selection process, the Cooperstown roster included only 11 free-agent-era players through 2000, and most of them had careers which began in and spanned a substantial portion of the expansion period. As a result, many of the best free-agent candidates were either still active in the majors, not yet on the BBWAA ballot or had been eligible for a very short time by 2000. Nine of the free-agent Hall of Famers — all but catcher Carlton Fisk and relief pitcher Rollie Fingers — also meet at least one of Cooperstown's de facto standards. So, with the exception of some men who've been shafted by effects of the 5-percent-support rule, it's too early to confidently identify errors of selection or omission.

Because of its large number of teams and big-league jobs available, the era produced 614 Hall-of-Fame eligibles (370 non-pitchers, 24.9 percent; 244 pitchers, 30.0 percent) through 1994 — one-fourth (26.7 percent) of the data set as a whole, and one-third more than those of any other historical era. So, as noted in Table Twenty-Two, relative proportionality for this era will eventually require at least 50 free-agent Hall of Famers. But, unless things change, the 5- and 60-percent-support requirements and the BBWAA voters' recent penchant listing ever fewer men on their ballots will prevent that from ever happening. This period appears destined to be the most short-changed of all among the Cooperstown roster.

The 11 Hall of Famers from the era (through 2000) account for 5.9 percent of all men enshrined, and they include five non-pitchers — George Brett, Carlton Fisk, Reggie Jackson, Mike Schmidt and Robin Yount; plus six pitchers — Steve Carlton, Rollie Fingers, Phil Niekro, Nolan Ryan, Tom Seaver and Don Sutton. Vida Blue, Cecil Cooper, Darrell Evans, Dwight Evans, Bobby Grich, Graig Nettles and Al Oliver — all having fallen below 5-percent support and barred from future consideration — are sometimes mentioned as errors of omission.

The free-agent rankings include eight players not yet eligible as of 2000 (Wade Boggs, Roger Clemens, Tony Gwynn, Rickey Henderson, Paul Molitor, Eddie Murray, Cal Ripken, Jr. and Dave Winfield) whose elections by the BBWAA are virtually guaranteed by statistical precedent, and four others whose selection by the writers are probable given their reputations from the era (Andre Dawson, Dennis Eckersley, Ryne Sandberg and Ozzie Smith). By the end of the 1999 season there were also eight men active in the majors who, although they had not completed 10 big-league seasons through 1994 (and were not included in the data set), had done so by the later date, were synonymous with the free-agent period and appeared on track for certain election by the scribes (Barry Bonds, Jose Canseco, Tom Glavine, Ken Griffey, Jr., Randy Johnson, Greg Maddux, Mark McGwire and Frank Thomas). When added to the 11 free-agent players already in Cooperstown, that would make a total of 31 members from the era, slightly more than half the amount required for proportionality.

But Table Twenty-Five also includes 16 players — non-pitchers Don Baylor, Buddy Bell, Bill Buckner, Cesar Cedeño, Jack Clark, Darrell Evans, Dwight Evans, George Foster, Bobby Grich, Graig Nettles, Al Oliver and Willie Randolph, plus hurlers Vida Blue, Charlie Hough, Rick Reuschel and

Bob Welch—who have been dropped from the BBWAA ballot after receiving less than 5-percent support in a given election, plus two others (Cecil Cooper and Frank Tanana) who never got a vote from the scribes. Beyond them, there are 25 others—Dusty Baker, John Candelaria, Ron Cey, Jose Cruz, Brian Downing, Ken Griffey, Sr., Toby Harrah, Kent Hrbek, Dave Kingman, Jerry Koosman, Chet Lemon, Greg Luzinski, Fred Lynn, Joe Niekro, Dan Quisenberry, J. R. Richard, Kent Tekulve, Gene Tenace, John Tudor and Willie Wilson (who were also dropped for 5-percent failures), plus Chris Chambliss, George Hendrick, Hal McRae, Steve Rogers and Ken Singleton (who never received a vote)—who suffered the same fates, but who rank among the era's top 60 position players or 40 best-qualified hurlers in this measure. Combined, these men make up 43 percent of the period's most-qualified candidates, statistically—and, under the current rules, none of them may ever again be given Hall-of-Fame consideration. When you add to that list other men who have arguable HOF credentials (e.g., four-time batting champ Bill Madlock and six-time Gold Glove winner Jim Sundberg, both of whom were dropped after five-percent failures), it is evident that the current eligibility limitations governing Cooperstown's elective processes will make it impossible for the free-agent era ever to achieve proportional representation in the Hall—at least with its best-qualified players.

Among men already on the writers' ballot by 2000, that leaves only 13 players—Keith Hernandez, Dave Parker, Jim Rice, Steve Garvey, Gary Carter, Dale Murphy, Bert Blyleven, Tommy John, Ron Guidry, Jack Morris and Goose Gossage (who are on the lists above), plus Dave Concepcion and Bruce Sutter (the only other two who rank among that top 100 in these ratings)—whose candidacies were still alive after the 2000 voting. Along with the first 31 men noted, their elections would push the number of free-agent Hall of Famers to 44. But, barring dramatic improvements in each of their BBWAA support, their elections are problematic at best, as only Rice seemed—as of 2000—to have a chance of ever receiving the 60-percent support required to pass his candidacy to the Veterans Committee.

All of this leaves just 12 others from the lists above (Dwight Gooden, Tom Henke, Orel Hershiser, Jimmy Key, Dennis Martinez, Don Mattingly, Kirby Puckett, Tim Raines, Bret Saberhagen, Dave Stieb, Fernando Valenzuela and Lou Whitaker), none of whom was eligible by 2000, as the most-qualified players available to fill the era's representational deficit. Some of them rank high in Table Twenty-Five, but on the whole, and especially among the non-pitchers, their statistical credentials are no better than many of the men no longer eligible for the Hall.

Among free-agent-era players active after 1994 but with less than 10 years major-league service through that date, only two men had Total-Z averages—based on their career stats through 1994—that were good enough to rank

Table Twenty-Five
Free-Agent Z-Score Leaders

Rank	Non-Pitchers	Pos	Total Z Avg	Core Z Avg	Rank	Non-Pitchers	Pos	Total Z Avg	Core Z Avg
1	**Mike Schmidt**	3b	2.41	2.38	20	*Ozzie Smith	ss	1.26	0.69
2	**George Brett**	3b	2.14	2.66	21	Gary Carter	c	1.20	1.34
3	**Reggie Jackson**	rf	1.95	2.55	22	Graig Nettles	3b	1.19	1.52
4	*Eddie Murray	1b	1.91	2.71	23	Dale Murphy	cf	1.17	1.65
5	*Rickey Henderson	lf	1.75	1.60	24	**Carlton Fisk**	c	1.14	1.81
6	*Dave Winfield	rf	1.65	2.89	25	*Ryne Sandberg	2b	1.13	1.39
7	Keith Hernandez	1b	1.58	1.38		*Tim Raines	lf	1.13	1.23
8	Dwight Evans	rf	1.51	2.03	27	*Kirby Puckett	cf	1.07	1.50
	*Paul Molitor	3b	1.51	1.86	28	Bobby Grich	2b	1.06	0.90
10	Darrell Evans	3b	1.50	1.68	29	Don Baylor	lf	1.02	1.52
11	Dave Parker	rf	1.45	2.16		*Lou Whitaker	2b	1.02	1.45
12	**Robin Yount**	ss	1.43	2.24	31	George Foster	lf	1.01	1.44
13	Al Oliver	cf	1.42	1.93	32	*Cecil Cooper*	1b	1.00	1.52
14	*Andre Dawson	rf	1.39	2.29	33	Willie Randolph	2b	0.98	0.81
15	*Cal Ripken, Jr.	ss	1.37	1.59	34	Cesar Cedeño	cf	0.96	1.23
16	Jim Rice	lf	1.33	2.21	35	*Don Mattingly	1b	0.95	1.45
17	*Wade Boggs	3b	1.30	1.62	36	Bill Buckner	1b	0.93	1.55
18	Steve Garvey	1b	1.29	1.85		Buddy Bell	3b	0.93	1.42
	Jack Clark	rf	1.29	1.37	38	*Tony Gwynn	rf	0.91	1.32

Rank	Pitchers	Pos	Total Z Avg	Core Z Avg	Rank	Pitchers	Pos	Total Z Avg	Core Z Avg
1	**Tom Seaver**	sp	2.18	2.81	14	Jack Morris	sp	0.98	1.51
2	**Steve Carlton**	sp	1.91	2.83	15	Vida Blue	sp	0.92	1.44
3	**Nolan Ryan**	sp	1.81	3.15	16	*Dennis Martinez	sp	0.83	1.26
4	**Don Sutton**	sp	1.50	2.59		*Dave Stieb	sp	0.83	1.00
5	Bert Bleleven	sp	1.48	2.34		*F. Valenzuela	sp	0.83	0.82
6	*Roger Clemens	sp	1.40	1.58	19	Bob Welch	sp	0.82	1.33
7	**Phil Niekro**	sp	1.38	2.41	20	*Orel Hershiser	sp	0.80	0.88
8	Tommy John	sp	1.24	1.93	21	*Tom Henke	rp	0.78	-0.03
9	Ron Guidry	sp	1.18	1.29	22	*Frank Tanana*	sp	0.77	1.49
10	*D. Eckersley	rp	1.06	1.20	23	Rick Reuschel	sp	0.76	1.27
11	*Dwight Gooden	sp	1.04	1.31	24	Charlie Hough	sp	0.75	1.16
12	**Rollie Fingers**	rp	1.03	0.46	25	*Jimmy Key	sp	0.73	0.88
13	*Bret Saberhagen	sp	1.02	0.83		Goose Gossage	rp	0.73	0.68

among the era leaders shown in Table Twenty-Five. They were first basemen Will Clark (with a Total-Z of +0.91) and pitcher Greg Maddux (+0.99).

There are a couple of surprises in the free-agent rankings, notably the high position of Keith Hernandez (above even Steve Garvey) and the low score earned by certain Hall of Famer Tony Gwynn. But the causes for both of those outcomes will be clarified later, as will the credentials of many other players.

CHAPTER 8

Just Doing Their Jobs

Since the advent of free agency, ballplayers are more strongly identified with their position than with the team for which they play. But that wasn't always true. In earlier eras, when the reserve clause bound players to their clubs for as long as a team chose to keep them, unless they were trade bait like Bobo Newsom or Suitcase Simpson, their identities were strongly linked to their franchise. Very good players often spent their entire careers with one club. When someone mentions Joe DiMaggio, the Yankees come to mind quicker than visions of the Clipper roaming center field. Similarly, Stan Musial's name conjures up Cardinals long before left field; and Ernie Banks is far more synonymous with Cubs than shortstop or first base. Occasionally, whole lineups stayed together. Three different Dodger managers penciled in Gil Hodges, Jackie Robinson, Pee Wee Reese, Duke Snider, Carl Furillo and Roy Campanella on their lineup cards almost every day for eight straight seasons, 1949–56. But since the mid–1970s, with many players hopping from team to team faster than Cool Papa Bell could dart from home to third on a liner into the right field corner, all of that has changed; and, with a few exceptions like Cal Ripken, Jr., we now think of players as catchers or shortstops first, rather than as Expos or Twins.

A player's position is also integral to his Hall-of-Fame credentials. Usually, when someone makes an argument favoring the inclusion of an unenshrined player at Cooperstown, rather than saying that "so-and-so was one of the greatest players ever," they will state instead the he "was one of the best (fill in any position) of all time." On one level that statement is a hedge, because all of the absolutely greatest players ever — except for Pete Rose, Joe Jackson and the handful that are still playing or not yet eligible — have already been elected to the Hall. Anyone with an iota of knowledge about baseball is aware of that, and only a person whose friends call him "Jingles" would argue that Luis Tiant, Gil Hodges or Lefty O'Doul were as good, subjectively or statistically, as Walter Johnson, Lou Gehrig or Ted Williams. But despite that, baseball cognoscenti are also aware that, because of the effects of the defensive spectrum, stats that might take a catcher from Cincinnati to Cooperstown — like those of Ernie Lombardi — should not get a first sacker any closer to the museum than Syracuse or Utica, if that far.

Until recently, the competing encyclopedias didn't differentiate games played by outfielders in left, center or right, lumping them together instead. Within that limitation, men who have played more than one position in the majors with any real frequency are relatively rare, at least among the players in the data set. The 1,484 non-pitchers averaged 86.7 percent of their games at one position. Among them, 261 (17.6 percent of the total) made all of their big-league defensive appearances at one post (81 of those, the plurality, were catchers). Beyond that, 902 of the survey's batters played at least 90 percent of their games at one spot on the diamond; 1,235 played two-thirds or more of their games at the same position; and 1,406 (all but about 5 percent of men in the non-pitcher data set) played at least half of their games at one post. So, about 250 of those players were truly versatile, and the rest of them were by-and-large positional specialists.

Although every manager would no doubt tell his players the opposite, positional versatility is not likely to get a man into Cooperstown. The 127 non-pitchers in the Hall through 2000 averaged 87.3 percent of their games at one position, slightly more than the non-pitcher subset as a whole. Only 14 Hall of Famers — Ernie Banks, Rod Carew, George Davis, Buck Ewing, King Kelly, Harmon Killebrew, Fred Lindstrom, Stan Musial, Tony Perez, Jackie Robinson, Joe Sewell, Willie Stargell, Monte Ward and Robin Yount — played less than two-thirds of their big-league games at any one post. Among them, based on the lowest percentage at his primary position, the most "versatile" man enshrined to date was muscle-bound Harmon Killebrew, who played 969 of his defensive games (43 percent) at first base, 792 at third, 470 in the outfield and eleven as a second sacker. He was truly a man without a position — a guy whose bat dictated his presence in the lineup somewhere, anywhere, regardless of his defensive impact. He also was a designated hitter 158 times; and the figure might have been higher, but the DH didn't exist until a couple seasons before he retired.

But Killebrew would not hold that honor if Pete Rose were eligible for the Shrine. No defensive liability at any position, Rose was truly versatile, came to the park to play, and no doubt would have sold hot dogs between innings had Sparky Anderson said it would get Pete in the lineup more often. Rose played 1327 games in the outfield (38 percent of his defensive appearances),

939 at first base, 634 at third and 628 at second. The books don't tell how many games, if any, he spent at the OTB site nearest to Riverfront Stadium.

Some players change positions permanently during their careers, and these moves are usually dictated by advancing age. A primary law of the defensive spectrum is that, as players get older, no one ever shifts along the line from an easier position to a more difficult one. The reasons for that are obvious, as no manager would want a 36 year old who had lost a couple steps as his shortstop, if he had a younger, quicker guy good enough defensively to take his place. That's why Cal Ripken, Jr., was moved to third base by the Orioles in 1997; and the shift was a transfer to an easier position.

Because many positional changes are dictated by age, a player's fame is often linked to the spot he occupied first in his career, during his prime, rather than the one where he saw the most duty. Ernie Banks and Rod Carew are listed on the HOF roster as a shortstop and second baseman, their initial big-league positions, although both men played more games at first base later in their careers. But their shifts had less to do with age (both men were 31) than they did with the fact that their bats were too important to their teams to continue risking their injury at the more physically demanding spot. So age is not the only motive for switching a good player from one position to another. All the same, Bank and Carew both shifted from difficult positions to a much easier one.

The position where a man enjoyed his greatest success is not always obvious. Monte Ward, listed as a shortstop by the Hall, played 21 seasons in the Show, with 826 games at that position, 491 at second base, 215 in the outfield and 291 as a pitcher. But although Ward ranked 33rd among his era's non-pitchers listed in chapter 6, his Z Score as a hurler (+0.52) was good enough for ninth place among the period's moundsmen, had he pitched in 10 seasons; and, because he only did so in seven, he wasn't included among the era's list of pitchers.

With all of that in mind, this chapter and the next report players' career Z-Score averages relative to men at the same position, with all of the scores normalized to remove any bias caused by variations in periodic norms. The format is the same as the previous two chapters — a general overview followed by a paragraph about the data-set and HOF demography for each position, then the tables and commentary about specific players. Except for the pitchers, the tables again will be limited to about the top 30 guys at each position, but will — as before — include every man in Cooperstown through 2000, with a line designating any ordinal discontinuity, names of Hall of Famers bold-faced, men without votes in italics, players active after 1994 denoted by an asterisk, and men who played a majority of their careers before 1893 noted by a pound sign. Since every game begins with a pitcher holding the ball, the scores for starting and relief hurlers are the first ones reported.

Among the non-pitchers, some of the commentary will focus on defense, with frequent reference to players' isolated Z-Score averages for fielding (i.e., the seven defensive variables in the non-pitcher measurement, treated as a unit), although those averages are not given in the tables. There is no correlate to the Core-Z average devised for defense because fielding has a minimal impact on election and the most appropriate stats would vary for each position. When fielding is discussed, these scores have not been normalized for variations in positional norms because each man is being compared only to players from the same spot on the diamond. But each man's career totals include his defensive performance at all of the positions he played, not just the one in question — so there's still some bias present, on a case-by-case basis. That's especially important among the outfielders, because some of them, like Stan Musial and Carl Yastrzemski, earned higher defensive scores than they might have because they spent substantial portions of their careers at other positions where they made more plays than most flychasers usually do (first base, in both of their cases).

Space considerations once again prohibit including the separate starter- and relief-pitcher means for every variable in the database, so Table Twenty-Six provides the positional averages for some key statistics. These are rounded, wherever possible, but all are given in the form that best emphasizes any significant differences between the means for the two subsets. Where a stat is applicable to only one group, the space for the mean is left blank in the other's column. The column abbreviations for starters and relievers are self-explanatory.

The positional variations among much of the data in Table Twenty-Six are predictable given the differences in the pitchers' jobs. On average, men who are starters for most of their careers are bound to accumulate more innings and strikeouts, get more decisions (hence, pitching and Fibonacci wins), and compile higher range factors with better fielding averages (because their larger innings-pitched totals allow for more defensive plays, and more comfort at making them), while relievers (the modern ones, at least) will accumulate more games pitched overall. The small variations in opponents' batting average and the strikeouts-to-walks ratio probably resulted, much as anything, from random chance. From this data, it's impossible to tell (and irrelevant to their separate Hall-of-Fame credentials, anyway) whether or not, or just how much, the starters' advantages in winning percentage, ERA, opponents' on-base average, Ratio and home runs-per-nine innings may be the product of the stresses inherent to relief pitching, or of the fact that until recent times many relievers were failed starters who had high averages for those stats before they were shifted to the bullpen. Finally, it also seems likely that the relief hurlers' advantage in strikeouts-per-nine innings occurred because starters before the Postwar era had significantly lower averages for that statistic, and modern relief strategies often tend to favor flame throwers like Goose Gossage and Lee Smith.

Table Twenty-Six
Pitcher Means for Selected Key Variables

Pitcher Variable	sp	rp	Pitcher Variable	sp	rp
Games Pitched	395	475	SO-to-BB Ratio	1.55	1.61
Games Won	139	60	HR-per-9 Innings	0.58	0.69
Winning Pct	.525	.495	Fielding Average	.953	.941
Fibonacci Wins	93	30	Range Factor	1.44	0.52
Earned Run Average	3.56	3.65	Complete Games	129	—
Innings Pitched	2300	1038	CG Percentage	.424	—
Opponents' BA	.258	.255	Shutouts	20	—
Opponents' OBA	.320	.328	ShO Percentage	.066	—
Ratio	11.82	12.17	Relief Wins	—	40
Strikeouts	1118	613	Saves	—	78
SO-per-9 Innings	4.36	5.40	Relief Eff. Rating	—	.177

Starting Pitchers

Even with the periodic bias removed, the list below confirms the statistical dominance of Walter Johnson, Cy Young, Christy Mathewson and Grover Alexander, the first four pitchers chosen for Cooperstown by the BBWAA in 1936–38. Only the postwar era's Warren Spahn, who would be listed at number six without the periodic normalization, prevents those pitching stalwarts from claiming a sweep of the top four spots in the rankings

There are 589 starting pitchers in database, or 25.6 percent of the overall total (72.4 percent of all men in the pitcher subset). The position includes 56 Hall of Famers, or 30.3 percent of the 185 players in Cooperstown through 2000 (96.6 percent of Cooperstown pitchers). They include Grover Alexander, Charley Bender, Mordecai Brown, Jim Bunning, Steve Carlton, Jack Chesbro, John Clarkson, Stan Coveleski, Dizzy Dean, Don Drysdale, Red Faber, Bob Feller, Whitey Ford, Pud Galvin, Bob Gibson, Burleigh Grimes, Lefty Grove, Jesse Haines, Waite Hoyt, Carl Hubbell, Catfish Hunter, Ferguson Jenkins, Walter Johnson, Addie Joss, Tim Keefe, Sandy Koufax, Bob Lemon, Ted Lyons, Juan Marichal, Rube Marquard, Christy Mathewson, Joe McGinnity, Hal Newhouser, Kid Nichols, Phil Niekro, Jim Palmer, Herb Pennock, Gaylord Perry, Eddie Plank, Hoss Radbourn, Eppa Rixey, Robin Roberts, Red Ruffing, Amos Rusie, Nolan Ryan, Tom Seaver, Warren Spahn, Don Sutton, Dazzy Vance, Rube Waddell, Ed Walsh, Mickey Welch, Vic Willis, Early Wynn and Cy Young; plus Clark Griffith, elected as an executive. Often-cited errors of selection include Chesbro, Clarkson, Drysdale, Galvin, Haines, Keefe, Lyons, Marquard, Radbourn, Waddell, Walsh, Welch and Willis. Often-cited as errors of omission are Babe Adams, Lew Burdette,

Table Twenty-Seven
Starting Pitcher Z-Score Leaders

Rank	Starter	Era	Total Z Avg	Core Z Avg	Rank	Starter	Era	Total Z Avg	Core Z Avg
1	Walter Johnson	DB	2.29	2.79	41	#Hoss Radbourn	NC	0.88	1.24
2	Cy Young	NC	2.26	2.80		Addie Joss	DB	0.88	0.59
3	Christy Mathewson	DB	2.03	2.32	43	Catfish Hunter	EX	0.86	1.06
4	Warren Spahn	PW	1.84	2.39	44	Lefty Gomez	LB	0.85	1.00
5	Grover Alexander	DB	1.83	2.07	45	Stan Coveleski	LB	0.84	1.05
6	Tom Seaver	FA	1.80	2.45	46	Eppa Rixey	LB	0.83	1.24
7	Nolan Ryan	FA	1.63	2.91	47	Bob Lemon	PW	0.81	1.00
8	Steve Carlton	FA	1.61	2.52	48	Red Faber	LB	0.80	1.26
9	Whitey Ford	PW	1.51	1.80		Jack Quinn	LB	0.80	1.06
10	Lefty Grove	LB	1.47	2.11		Ron Guidry	FA	0.80	0.90
11	Ed Walsh	DB	1.45	1.07	51	#Jim McCormick	NC	0.78	0.90
12	Don Sutton	FA	1.38	2.27	52	Rube Waddell	DB	0.77	1.02
13	Bert Blyleven	FA	1.36	2.04	53	Bucky Walters	LB	0.76	0.73
14	Gaylord Perry	EX	1.35	2.19	54	Jim Kaat	EX	0.75	1.45
15	Jim Palmer	EX	1.33	1.73		Vida Blue	FA	0.75	1.08
16	Carl Hubbell	LB	1.31	1.54		#Tommy Bond	NC	0.75	0.41
17	Sandy Koufax	EX	1.30	1.23	57	Jack Morris	FA	0.74	1.22
18	#Tim Keefe	NC	1.24	1.67	58	Billy Pierce	PW	0.72	1.12
19	Bob Feller	PW	1.23	1.82	59	*Dwight Gooden	FA	0.71	0.91
	Juan Marichal	EX	1.23	1.56		Bob Shawkey	LB	0.71	0.90
21	Phil Niekro	FA	1.22	2.10	61	Luis Tiant	EX	0.69	1.19
22	Bob Gibson	EX	1.20	1.79		Dizzy Dean	LB	0.69	0.77
23	Carl Mays	LB	1.18	1.03	63	Jim Bunning	EX	0.68	1.32
24	Eddie Plank	DB	1.17	1.83		Charley Bender	DB	0.68	0.95
25	Fergie Jenkins	EX	1.16	1.77		Fred Fitzsimmons	LB	0.68	0.81
26	Don Drysdale	EX	1.13	1.23		Dolf Luque	LB	0.68	0.67
27	Robin Roberts	PW	1.11	1.66	67	Frank Tanana	FA	0.67	1.20
28	Tommy John	FA	1.08	1.57		Waite Hoyt	LB	0.67	0.96
29	Kid Nichols	NC	1.06	1.49		Paul Derringer	LB	0.67	0.86
30	*Roger Clemens	FA	1.05	1.18	70	Vic Willis	DB	0.64	0.93
31	Red Ruffing	LB	1.04	1.31	71	Ted Lyons	LB	0.63	0.92
32	Mordecai Brown	DB	1.03	1.18		Art Nehf	LB	0.63	0.73
33	Dazzy Vance	LB	1.01	1.14		*Bret Saberhagen	FA	0.63	0.44
34	#John Clarkson	NC	1.00	1.41	74	Smoky Joe Wood	DB	0.62	0.40
35	Herb Pennock	LB	0.99	1.03	t100	Joe McGinnity	DB	0.49	0.88
36	Burleigh Grimes	LB	0.96	1.25		Amos Rusie	NC	0.49	0.68
37	Hal Newhouser	PW	0.95	1.14	t109	#Mickey Welch	NC	0.45	1.22
38	#Pud Galvin	NC	0.94	1.36	t125	Jesse Haines	LB	0.39	0.68
39	Early Wynn	PW	0.91	1.66	t132	Jack Chesbro	DB	0.35	0.57
	Spud Chandler	LB	0.91	0.67	t249	Rube Marquard	DB	0.01	0.40

Bob Caruthers, Spud Chandler, Paul Derringer, Wes Ferrell, Dave Foutz, Mel Harder, Mickey Lolich, Eddie Lopat, Dolf Luque, Carl Mays, Tony Mullane, Don Newcombe, Bobo Newsom, Deacon Phillippe, Billy Pierce, Jack Quinn, Vic Raschi, Ed Reulbach, Allie Reynolds, Bob Shawkey, Mel Stottlemyre, Johnny Vander Meer, Bucky Walters and Smoky Joe Wood.

There were 56 starting pitchers in the Hall through 2000, and all but 12 of them are among the top 56 on this list, with the highest-rated unenshrined hurler (Bert Blyleven) ranked 13th. Although they represent only two of the three scales in the complete measurement and it would be premature to draw a final conclusion from these early results, the combination of Blyleven's high score among the free-agent pitchers in chapter 6 and his rating here begins to build a positive case for his Hall-of-Fame credentials. The same is true for Carl Mays (23rd), Tommy John (28th), Roger Clemens (30th) and Spud Chandler (39th). (Given Clemens's performance since 1994, his election was a formality by 2000.)

At the bottom of the rankings, and coupled with their poor showings in chapter 5, the low scores posted by Hall of Famers Joe McGinnity, Mickey Welch, Jesse Haines, Jack Chesbro and Rube Marquard send a signal that they may be clear-cut errors of selection. The same may apply to Amos Rusie, who barely made the top 100 above, although Rusie is the only man among these six who ranks among his era's top 10.

It's premature to postulate any conclusions regarding the relative merits of the other men in this table — either the six Hall of Famers between Dizzy Dean (61st) and Ted Lyons (71st), or any of the other unenshrined pitchers on the list. Less than one-fifth of a standard deviation (0.18) separates Jack Quinn, Ron Guidry and HOF member Red Faber (tied at 48th) from Smoky Joe Wood (74th), and other hurlers who did not make the cutoff for this table may improve their scores in the overall and/or final ratings.

Although defense accounts for less than one-fourth of the variables in this measure and has little impact on a pitcher's HOF prospects, the list of leaders among starting hurlers in adjusted isolated fielding is dominated by moundsmen from the first half of this century. Topping the chart are dead-ball Hall of Famer Ed Walsh (+2.40) and Carl Mays (+2.28), whose career overlapped the dead- and live-ball eras. Four more dead-ballers follow — Harry Howell (+1.92), Nick Altrock (+1.81), Christy Mathewson (+1.80) and Addie Joss (+1.79). live-ball starter Fred Fitzsimmons and the postwar era's Bob Lemon are tied for seventh (+1.75); in ninth place is Mel Stottlemyre (+1.65), the only hurler since the beginning of the expansion era to make the top 10; and the list is rounded out by live-baller Burleigh Grimes (+1.59), the fourth HOF member in the group. The only pitchers from baseball's recent history to make the top 20 were Tommy John (+1.35, 11th) and Rick Reuschel (+1.21, tied for 14th). The absence of any 19th-century hurlers from the list is no surprise, given the relatively poor fielding norms of the era, and the preponderance of dead-and live-ball pitchers is also predictable, because assists-per-game and range factor — half of the fielding variables used for pitchers — are strongly impacted by the number of innings pitched. With the advent of modern relief strategies, starters from recent historical eras have averaged fewer innings per game than their counterparts from the first two periods of this century.

Relief Pitchers

The election of only two relievers to the Hall through 2000 is insufficient to have set any meaningful statistical standards, no matter how inadvertent, for the future selection of others. As a result, the table lists only the top 20 Z-Score averages for members of the relief corps, and, predictably, most of the leaders played during the expansion and free-agent eras. Nonetheless, three of the true pioneers of the craft — dead-baller Doc Crandall and live-ball successors Firpo Marberry and Johnny Murphy — also made the listing.

There are 224 relievers in the data set, and they account for 9.8 percent of all players considered (27.6 percent of the pitcher subset). Rollie Fingers and Hoyt Wilhelm, the two Hall of Fame relievers, represent 1.1 percent of players enshrined. There are no often-cited errors of selection; Elroy Face and Firpo Marberry are cited as errors of omission by some.

You rarely hear it said, but Hoyt Wilhelm was one hell of a pitcher, despite not being certain where each of his knuckleballs was going, and not

Table Twenty-Eight
Relief Pitcher Z-Score Leaders

Rank	Reliever	Era	Total Z Avg	Core Z Avg	Rank	Reliever	Era	Total Z Avg	Core Z Avg
1	**Hoyt Wilhelm**	EX	1.81	2.28	11	Lindy McDaniel	EX	0.96	1.67
2	*Dennis Eckersley	FA	1.77	3.38		*Tom Henke	FA	0.96	0.29
3	**Rollie Fingers**	FA	1.58	1.56	13	Doc Crandall	DB	0.95	1.38
4	Firpo Marberry	LB	1.39	1.85	14	*Stu Miller*	EX	0.94	1.03
5	Goose Gossage	FA	1.30	1.92	15	Dan Quisenberry	FA	0.93	0.40
6	*Johnny Murphy*	LB	1.00	0.73	16	*Gerry Staley*	PW	0.82	1.27
7	Kent Tekulve	FA	0.99	1.00	17	Sparky Lyle	EX	0.78	0.96
	Bruce Sutter	FA	0.99	0.62	18	Don McMahon	EX	0.75	0.93
9	Elroy Face	PW	0.98	0.88	19	Jeff Reardon	FA	0.73	0.57
10	*Lee Smith	FA	0.97	0.73	20	*Gene Garber*	FA	0.72	0.81

just because he stayed in the bigs until he was 48. Before Jesse Orosco surpassed them in 1999, Hoyt and Dennis Eckersley were the all-time leaders in games pitched (Dennis passed Hoyt by one game before the former retired after 1998). But Eckersley spent the first half of his career as a starter (361 of his 1071 games), while Wilhelm was in the rotation for only 52 of his 1070 appearances. As a result, Eckersley's 3286 innings were 1032 more than Hoyt had in his big-league tenure. Although the relief-pitcher scale does not include starter-specific variables like complete games and shutouts, one might guess that the huge innings advantage would have been sufficient — at least among the cumulative variables — for Eckersley to easily top Wilhelm on this list. Instead, he ranks just behind the knuckler, adding credence to Wilhelm's status as the first reliever chosen for the Hall.

Rollie Fingers, the other Cooperstown closer, ranks third behind Eckersley, a testament to both men's credentials. But the status of Firpo Marberry at number four, ahead of Goose Gossage and several other better-known relievers of the past four decades, begins to make a case that his election by the VC would be more than a token gesture to honor the relievers' craft. Marberry's scores here are boosted somewhat by his intermittent stints in the rotation, as he started 186 of his 551 career appearances. But, if his scores hold up through the final ratings (his +0.58 for the era scale ranked 32nd among the live-ball hurlers), he would be a justifiable addition to the HOF roster, despite the abundant representation from his era.

Marberry's fellow live-baller Johnny Murphy is also high on this list. Murphy entered the majors nine years after Firpo and pitched all but forty of his 415 appearances in relief during the years 1932–47. He was 20–9 as a starter and 73–42 out of the bullpen, with 107 career saves. He ranks 43rd (+0.39) among the live-ball pitchers measured in chapter 6. He may be almost as deserving of consideration as Marberry, but — even if his high scores persist — the addition of two live-ball relievers is hard to justify.

As for the others on this list, the merits of their relative credentials depend on how many relief pitchers are appropriate for the Hall at this time — or, hypothetically, within the next decade. As a group, relievers make up almost 28 percent of all pitchers included in the data set. But with 58 hurlers in Cooperstown through 2000, any number proportional to that total (say, about 16) is too many — because the role's importance has emerged only over the last half century, or for about 40 percent of major-league history. Forty percent of 16 could allow for a total of six or seven Hall-of-Fame relievers chosen by 2010, meaning four or five vacancies.

Eckersley, Marberry and Gossage have an obvious edge, evidenced by the wide gap between Goose's Total-Z average (+1.30) and the rest of the list. The other one or two are arguable among the closely bunched group from Murphy through Dan Quisenberry at number 15. Because of the modern

In 1933 Firpo Marberry became the first pitcher to record 100 career saves — long before the statistic had been invented or relief pitching was even in vogue. His Total-Z average of +1.39 is the fourth-best score among all relievers who qualified for the data set (*The Sporting News*).

emphasis placed on saves, Lee Smith — the career leader through 1999 — may have an advantage over the others among the BBWAA, but the numbers above indicate that Murphy, Kent Tekulve, Bruce Sutter and Elroy Face are better qualified; and, subjectively, both Sutter and Face had more historical impact.

Table Twenty-Nine provides the positional means for selected variables representing about half of those included in the non-pitcher data set. The top positional score for each variable is boldfaced. As with the pitcher means in Table Twenty-Six, the averages shown are all less impressive than those for Hall-of-Fame players reported in chapter 5 (Table Thirteen). But, note also that — with a few variations — the relative differences between the positional means are consistent with those provided in chapter 5 (Table Sixteen) as exemplary effects of the defensive spectrum.

Table Twenty-Nine Non-Pitcher Positional Means for Selected Key Variables								
Non-Pitcher	*c*	*1b*	*2b*	*ss*	*3b*	*lf*	*cf*	*rf*
Games Played	983	**1493**	1359	1380	1362	1379	1420	1421
Hits	777	**1469**	1299	1236	1285	1350	1396	1389
Home Runs	53	**139**	55	47	91	114	93	128
HR Frequency	176	**78**	190	267	165	90	137	87
Total Bases	1111	**2249**	1773	1669	1865	2035	2022	2124
Runs Scored	332	742	669	612	658	714	**764**	734
Runs Batted In	372	**766**	509	489	587	643	582	671
Stolen Bases	31	92	132	119	101	134	**172**	115
Batting Average	.252	.279	.266	.257	.265	**.281**	.279	.279
Slugging Average	.354	**.425**	.361	.344	.380	.421	.401	.422
On-Base Average	.319	.349	.333	.319	.331	**.350**	.346	.349
Fielding Average	.977	**.986**	.964	.955	.946	.967	.970	.967
DP-per-Game	0.09	**0.61**	0.51	0.48	0.21	0.06	0.04	0.06
Range Factor	5.12	**8.36**	4.80	4.52	3.32	2.36	2.49	2.31

As a group, the most difficult defensive positions — catcher, shortstop and second base — have the three lowest career averages for games played, home runs, home-run frequency, total bases, runs batted in and slugging average. First base, the easiest, has the best average for games, hits, home runs, home-run frequency, total bases, runs scored, RBI and slugging average. Clearly, the means in Table Twenty-Nine confirm the relationship between offensive output and the degree of difficulty along the defensive spectrum.

Catchers

Because catchers compile such weak offensive numbers, their career stats are not usually competitive with those of players from most other positions, including many shortstops and second basemen. Some backstops have power, and a few hit for high average, but they rarely do both. Until Mike Piazza came along in the 1990s, only one catcher in history — Bill Dickey — had as many as two-hundred homers and a career batting average above .300. In that light, the positional rankings for catchers probably provide the most reliable measure of their HOF statistical credentials.

There are 271 catchers in the database, or 11.8 percent (18.3 percent of the non-pitcher subset) of all men considered. Twelve catchers have earned Hall of Fame recognition, accounting for 6.5 percent of players in the Hall (or 9.4 percent of Cooperstown non-pitchers). They include Johnny Bench, Yogi Berra, Roger Bresnahan, Roy Campanella, Mickey Cochrane, Bill Dickey, Buck Ewing, Rick Ferrell, Carlton Fisk, Gabby Hartnett, Ernie Lombardi and Ray Schalk; plus Al Lopez, Connie Mack and Wilbert Robinson (elected as managers). Often-cited errors of selection include Bresnahan, Ferrell, Lombardi and Schalk. Walker Cooper, Thurman Munson, Wally Schang and Joe Torre have been called errors of omission.

Table Thirty
Catcher Z-Score Leaders

Rank	Non-Pitchers	Era	Total Z Avg	Core Z Avg	Rank	Non-Pitchers	Era	Total Z Avg	Core Z Avg
1	**Yogi Berra**	PW	2.58	3.27	16	*Lance Parrish	FA	1.07	2.10
2	**Johnny Bench**	EX	2.24	3.26		**Roger Bresnahan**	DB	1.07	1.19
3	Joe Torre	EX	2.14	2.99	18	**Ernie Lombardi**	LB	1.05	1.93
4	**Bill Dickey**	LB	2.04	2.56	19	Elston Howard	EX	0.95	1.49
5	**Carlton Fisk**	FA	1.93	3.28		Tim McCarver	EX	0.95	1.15
6	#**Buck Ewing**	NC	1.90	1.90		**Ray Schalk**	DB	0.95	0.93
7	**Gabby Hartnett**	LB	1.88	2.43	22	*Deacon McGuire*	NC	0.94	1.28
8	Gary Carter	FA	1.83	2.64	23	*Darrell Porter*	FA	0.90	1.24
9	Ted Simmons	EX	1.74	3.16	24	Thurman Munson	EX	0.84	1.53
10	**Mickey Cochrane**	LB	1.68	2.03	25	**Rick Ferrell**	LB	0.80	1.06
11	**Roy Campanella**	W	1.20	1.47	26	Jim Sundberg	FA	0.76	0.74
12	*Duke Farrell*	NC	1.19	1.33	27	Bob Boone	FA	0.74	1.18
13	Wally Schang	LB	1.12	1.15		Johnny Kling	DB	0.74	0.86
14	Gene Tenace	FA	1.11	0.88		*John Roseboro*	EX	0.74	0.71
15	Bill Freehan	EX	1.09	1.62	30	Walker Cooper	PW	0.73	1.33

Here's a surprise, no doubt the biggest among the positional rankings: for most of three decades, fans have been conditioned by the raves of sportswriters and broadcasters to believe that Johnny Bench was the greatest catcher ever, no contest. Bench's anointment came early in his career, boosted by two MVP awards in his first six seasons, and it's a tribute to him that for all the hoopla about his skill and potential, and unlike poor Clint Hurdle and some other over-hyped kids, he actually reached or exceeded it. But Johnny's glory also obscured appreciation of the fact that, statistically, more great catchers were active during his career than had played in all of baseball's previous eras combined. Along with Bench, Joe Torre, Carlton Fisk, Gary Carter, Ted Simmons, Gene Tenace, Lance Parrish, Bill Freehan, Darrell Porter, Elston Howard, Tim McCarver, Jim Sundberg, Thurman Munson and Bob Boone make up half the top 30 above. All of them played during Johnny's era.

Bench may be the greatest catcher subjectively, but he's not statistically. Statwise, Yogi Berra is the all-time backstop, regardless of which measure you prefer. Berra's Total-Z is one-third of a standard deviation higher than Bench's, and his Core-Z average is a point better.

Offensively, Bench has an edge on Berra, averaging +3.01 for the 21 batting variables in the measure, compared to Yogi's score of +2.60. But Yogi played for 14 pennant winners and 10 World Series champs, the highest totals for both variables among all the players in the survey. Bench's four pennants and two Fall-Classic titles can't compete with either total, Z-wise.

Also, much of Bench's early reputation was based on his defense, so you'd expect him to be among the all-time leaders for the fielding variables. But Berra tops him in that area too, by far. Among all backstops, the career Z-Score leaders for isolated defense are three dead-ballers, Bill Killefer (+1.54), Ossee Schreckengost (+1.52) and Hall of Famer Ray Schalk (+1.50). They are followed by Cooperstown member Gabby Hartnett (+1.48), Gary Carter (+1.42) and Berra (sixth, at +1.38). Others in the top 10 include Jim Sundberg (+1.36), Johnny Edwards (+1.21), Tony Peña (+1.14) and Buck Ewing (+1.09), the first catcher ever elected to the Shrine. Bench's career score for fielding is almost exactly average among the 271 catchers measured (just +0.03), and only good enough to tie with five other men for 112th place, the lowest defensive mean of any HOF backstop, including Roy Campanella, who had a much shorter career. Even Ted Simmons, who always came up second-best or worse to Johnny among NL catchers of their era, scored better for fielding (+0.15, tied for 90th). Granted, few men tried to steal on Bench, his ability to block throws in the dirt can't show up in his fielding stats, and there's no way to quantify his quick release, how well he called pitches or blocked baserunners from the plate. But you can't quantify those things for any other backstop either. Bench, simply, is nowhere near the fielding icon he's been made out to be.

The four most often-cited errors of omission all made the top 30. Among them, the scores above confirm the implication in the periodic rankings that Joe Torre and Wally Schang are better candidates than Thurman Munson and Walker Cooper; and, on average, Torre's career stats are better than every HOF catcher but Berra and Bench.

As noted in the next chapter, relative to the number of eligible players it's produced, catcher is the most under-represented position on the Cooperstown roster. And since both of the most recent historical periods are proportionately short-changed as well, it's logical to expect that the high-ranking backstops from recent eras should make up a substantial portion of the men selected to fill out the 210-player HOF roster proposed in chapter 5. But Torre, Carter, Simmons, *et al.* cannot be inducted based on these scores alone. Their credentials still must withstand the disadvantages the position imposes upon their Z-Score averages among all eligible players as a group.

First Basemen

Unlike catcher, there aren't many surprises among this list, and, predictably, the rankings are dominated by men who put up great numbers at the plate. But given the results of recent BBWAA elections, the rankings do expose one possible Hall-of-Fame injustice in progress.

There are 155 first sackers in the database, or 6.8 percent of all players considered (10.4 percent of the non-pitcher subset). Nineteen are enshrined, accounting for 10.3 percent of players in the Hall (15.0 percent of Cooperstown non-pitchers). They include Cap Anson, Ernie Banks, Jake Beckley, Jim Bottomley, Dan Brouthers, Rod Carew, Orlando Cepeda, Frank Chance, Roger Connor, Jimmy Foxx, Lou Gehrig, Hank Greenberg, George Kelly, Harmon Killebrew, Willie McCovey, Johnny Mize, Tony Perez, George Sisler and Bill Terry; plus Charles Comiskey (elected as an executive). Chance and Kelly have been called unworthy by many. Dick Allen, Dolph Camilli, Jake Daubert, Charlie Grimm, Gil Hodges, Ted Kluszewski, Ed Konetchy, Frank McCormick, and Mickey Vernon have, on the other hand, have been called errors of omission.

From the rankings shown, among first basemen eligible for the BBWAA voting as of 2000, the most-qualified unenshrined player at the position, statistically, was Keith Hernandez, and not Tony Perez (who was elected that year) or Steve Garvey. But you'd never know it from the three men's vote histories. Perez appeared on the ballot in 1992, receiving 2224 votes from the writers through 1999 (averaging 278 votes and 60.2-percent support per ballot). He was elected by the scribes in 2000, with 385 votes and 77.2 percent support. Garvey became eligible in 1993, and he had received 1385 votes through 2000, for averages of 173 votes and 36.7-percent support per ballot. In contrast, Hernandez netted just 206 votes in the five years since he became eligible in 1996, an average of 41 votes and 8.6-percent support per ballot.

As evidenced by the differences in their Core-Z averages, one reason for Hernandez's comparatively poor showing to date is the widespread perception

Table Thirty-One
First Base Z-Score Leaders

Rank	First Baseman		Total Era Z Avg	Core Z Avg	Rank	First Baseman		Total Era Z Avg	Core Z Avg
1	**Lou Gehrig**	LB	1.96	2.66	18	Bill Buckner	FA	0.73	1.01
2	**Jimmie Foxx**	LB	1.58	2.51		*Ed Konetchy*	DB	0.73	0.68
3	*Eddie Murray	FA	1.53	2.29	20	**Harmon Killebrew**	EX	0.72	1.69
4	#**Cap Anson**	NC	1.52	1.59	21	*Don Mattingly	FA	0.68	0.96
5	#**Dan Brouthers**	NC	1.29	1.26	22	**George Sisler**	LB	0.67	0.70
6	#**Roger Connor**	NC	1.25	1.31	23	**Bill Terry**	LB	0.65	0.60
7	Keith Hernandez	FA	1.21	0.89	24	*Chris Chambliss*	FA	0.63	0.66
8	**Ernie Banks**	EX	1.13	1.74	25	**Hank Greenberg**	LB	0.62	1.14
9	#**Jake Beckley**	NC	0.95	1.29		Stuffy McInnis	DB	0.62	0.57
10	**Tony Perez**	EX	0.94	1.43	27	**Orlando Cepeda**	EX	0.61	1.22
	Rod Carew	EX	0.94	0.69		Norm Cash	EX	0.61	0.83
12	Steve Garvey	FA	0.92	1.36	29	Kent Hrbek	FA	0.59	1.02
13	**Willie McCovey**	EX	0.88	1.62	30	Harry Davis	DB	0.58	0.60
	Gil Hodges	PW	0.88	1.22	*31*	*Jake Daubert*	*DB*	*0.55*	*0.64*
15	**Johnny Mize**	LB	0.87	1.21	34	**Jim Bottomley**	LB	0.45	0.92
	Mickey Vernon	PW	0.87	0.92	49	**Frank Chance**	DB	0.19	-0.01
17	*Cecil Cooper*	FA	0.74	1.10	t56	**George Kelly**	LB	0.13	0.07

that Perez and Garvey were better hitters. That may be true for Perez, overall, but Garvey's offensive advantage is a Core-related mirage. Isolating the 21 offensive variables for this measure, Perez has a Z average of +1.17, Hernandez +0.78, and Garvey just +0.74.

Beyond that, the BBWAA of the late 1990s has overlooked the man who, statistically, is the most-qualified defensive first baseman in the history of the game, by a considerable margin. Among first sackers, Hernandez has an isolated defensive-Z average of +1.69, compared to +0.47 for Garvey and +0.17 for Perez. Keith is followed on the list of fielding leaders by Hall of Famers Bill Terry (+1.47), plus Ernie Banks (+1.39, a score influenced by his stats as a shortstop), soon-to-be Cooperstown member Eddie Murray (+1.19), deadballer Ed Konetchy (+1.14), the live-ball era's Frank McCormick (+1.13), Hall of Famer Cap Anson (+1.12), seven-time Gold Glove winner Vic Power (+1.06), Wally Pipp (+1.02), plus Elbie Fletcher and Fred Tenney (tied for 10th at +1.00). Hernandez's isolated fielding stats raise his overall score to a point well above Perez and Garvey, and into the upper echelon of baseball's first sackers.

The result raises curiosity about just how much the fielding variables impact each man's score. With only seven defensive stats among the 30 in the measure, they represent a little over 23 percent of the variables overall. Her-nandez's Z-average for the non-fielding stats (including pennants and World Series won) is +0.76 and his Total-Z average, without periodic adjustment, is +0.98, so his scores in the defensive categories raise his overall average by 22 points, or about 29 percent. But the impact of the fielding variables differs greatly for each man in the data set, dependent upon the relative quality of his career figures for all of the stats, both for offense and defense; and, on average, the fielding scores among all first basemen actually lower their posi-tional Total-Z by about 14 percent per man. So, the average impact of field-ing on each man's overall score does not conflict with the HOF electors' focus on offense, and the only men who will benefit significantly from them are those who truly rank among the best fielders, statistically, at their position. With that in mind, Hernandez's high ranking here is more a tribute to the value of his all-around performance than fielding prowess.

Among first sackers often-cited as errors of omission, four of them — Gil Hodges, Mickey Vernon, Ed Konetchy and Jake Daubert — rank among the top 31. Hodges scores the best above, tied with Willie McCovey at number 13. But only Gil and Vernon rank among the top 10 percent of the 155 first basemen measured.

Second Basemen

There are no big surprises here either, except perhaps for the high rank-ing of Bid McPhee, an almost-forgotten defensive wizard enshrined by the VC in its 2000 voting. Like the first basemen, this list is dominated by offensive stalwarts, and granting the disadvantages imposed by the brevity of Jackie Robinson's career, it partially validates the HOF credentials of all the current Cooperstown second sackers, except for Johnny Evers.

The 165 second basemen in the database make up 7.2 percent of all play-ers considered (11.1 percent of the non-pitcher subset), and HOF the posi-tion's 14 Hall of Famers account for 7.6 percent of all players enshrined (11.0 percent of Cooperstown non-pitchers). They include Eddie Collins, Bobby Doerr, Johnny Evers, Nellie Fox, Frankie Frisch, Charlie Gehringer, Billy Herman, Rogers Hornsby, Nap Lajoie, Tony Lazzeri, Bid McPhee, Joe Mor-gan, Jackie Robinson and Red Schoendienst. Bucky Harris, and Miller Hug-gins both second baseman, were elected as managers. Evers and Schoendienst have been called unworthy by their critics; Larry Doyle, Joe Gordon, Bill Mazeroski and Buddy Myer, on the other hand, have their advocates.

The defensive leaders at second base include five Hall of Famers and one man often cited as being among Cooperstown's most glaring omissions to date. Topping the chart for isolated defense is that possible omission, Bill Mazeroski (+2.32), followed closely by 2000 inductee Bid McPhee (+2.14).

Table Thirty-Two
Second Base Z-Score Leaders

Rank	Second Baseman		Total Era Z Avg	Core Z Avg	Rank	Second Baseman		Total Era Z Avg	Core Z Avg
1	Rogers Hornsby	LB	2.60	3.37	16	Tony Lazzeri	LB	0.88	1.35
2	Eddie Collins	DB	2.19	2.21		Billy Herman	LB	0.88	1.03
3	Nap Lajoie	DB	2.01	2.38	18	R. Schoendienst	PW	0.85	1.21
4	Joe Morgan	EX	2.00	2.52	19	Jackie Robinson	PW	0.78	1.10
5	Charlie Gehringer	LB	1.90	2.59	20	*#Fred Pfeffer*	NC	0.67	0.61
6	Frankie Frisch	LB	1.47	2.02	21	Buddy Myer	LB	0.64	0.93
7	#Bid McPhee	NC	1.24	0.94	22	Frank White	FA	0.60	0.97
8	*Ryne Sandberg	FA	1.17	1.79	23	*Cupid Childs*	NC	0.54	0.65
9	Bobby Doerr	LB	1.13	1.65	24	*Dick McAuliffe*	EX	0.53	0.98
10	*Lou Whitaker	FA	1.10	1.86	25	Dave Lopes	FA	0.50	0.79
11	Bobby Grich	FA	1.07	1.29	26	*Tony Taylor*	EX	0.49	0.84
	Bill Mazeroski	EX	1.07	1.09		George Grantham	LB	0.49	0.71
13	Nellie Fox	PW	1.00	1.15	28	Marty McManus	LB	0.48	1.03
14	Willie Randolph	FA	0.92	0.91		Davy Johnson	EX	0.48	0.55
15	Joe Gordon	LB	0.90	1.10	30	*Del Pratt*	DB	0.47	0.59
					t57	Johnny Evers	DB	0.15	-0.08

Third place entails a substantial drop to McPhee's contemporary Fred Pfeffer (+1.64), followed by Hall of Famers Nap Lajoie (+1.62), Nellie Fox, Bobby Doerr (+1.60 each) and Charlie Gehringer (+1.36), with live-ballers Oscar Melillo (+1.35) and Hughie Critz (+1.26) and free-agent second sacker Glenn Hubbard (+1.15) rounding out the top ten.

Although many baseball fans have never heard of McPhee, his anointment was no error of selection. Bid's career spanned 1882–99, including eight seasons in the American Association and 10 in the National League. He topped his circuit in putouts eight times, chances-per-game on seven occasions, and assists on six — so his range was excellent. He also led his league in double plays 11 times and fielding nine. Bid never came close to leading a circuit in errors at his position, averaging 44 per season over his 18 years. That's a lot by today's standards, but the most fumblesome second sackers of McPhee's era usually had 70 errors or more in a season, and sometimes topped 100 . Although he was no slouch at the plate, Bid's .271 batting average is three points lower than the mean for his era. Overall, his career and HOF credentials are the prototype for Bill Mazeroski.

According to the published reports, Mazeroski just missed election by the Veterans Committee in 2000, getting 10 of a possible 14 votes, which was one shy of the required number — so his candidacy may succeed in 2001. He led the National League in assists and chances-per-game 10 times each, double plays eight times, putouts five, and fielding on three occasions. But, unlike McPhee, he did top the NL in errors once. Mazeroski's supposed lack of offense has hindered his Cooperstown chances, but, while his era included 15 second sackers with higher career batting averages and one Hall of Famer noted for his power at the position (Joe Morgan), he still managed to lead his league's second basemen in RBI on seven occasions.

Six-time All-Stars Bobby Grich and Willie Randolph received 11 and five Hall-of-Fame votes, respectively, in their first years of BBWAA eligibility (1992 and 1998), and both men were then dropped from the ballot for failure to earn 5-percent support. The same fate may await Lou Whitaker, whose multiple skills were overshadowed by the fame of Ryne Sandberg during their careers. But the scores above are evidence that all three men are almost as qualified for the Hall as Sandberg, a possible first-year inductee in 2003.

Joe Gordon won the AL MVP award in 1942 and later received 426 Hall-of-Fame votes spread over fourteen ballots, with a high of 97 (28.4-percent support) in 1969. Although eligible for the VC process since the mid–1970s, Gordon received little attention from the panel before he earned a spot on their final ballot in 2000; and, like several other players from his era (see the Vern Stephens comment in the next chapter), his candidacy apparently has suffered because a significant portion of his success occurred during World War Two, when absences due to military service lowered the overall quality of major-league play. All the same, Gordon hit 253 career home runs, a total surpassed among all second sackers only by HOF members Rogers Hornsby (301) and Joe Morgan (268), plus the not-yet-eligible Sandberg (282); and only 59 of them came during his three wartime seasons (he also served in the military during 1944-45). Gordon's career slugging average (.466) is also sixth-best among all the second basemen measured, and the five men above him on that list are all in the Hall

If treated as a second sacker, the stats of Hall of Famer Rod Carew equate to a Total-Z of +1.46, with a Core-Z average of +2.07. That would be good enough to put him in seventh place on this list, sandwiched between Frankie Frisch and Bid McPhee.

CHAPTER 9

A Question of Balance

Hall of Famer Satchel Paige was famous for his showmanship, which included occasions when, confident of his ability to strike out a certain batter (or the side), he instructed his Negro-League teammates to leave their defensive positions and take a seat on the bench while he finished working the inning with no fielders behind him and only a catcher to handle his pitches. Through the 2000 voting, the way the roster was constituted positionally, you'd think that Paige was the permanent starter for the Cooperstown All-Stars — because, in terms of proportional balance, some positions have been grossly shortchanged in their level of Hall-of-Fame representation.

Based on the proportions of eligible players at each position among the data set as a whole, catchers, pitchers and third basemen are the primary victims of that positional imbalance, with outfielders, first basemen and shortstops the beneficiaries. Table Thirty-Three gives a positional breakdown of Hall-of-Fame membership, including the actual and ideal representational totals for each spot, in the same format used for Table Twenty-Two at the beginning of chapter 7 (Rod Carew and Ernie Banks were counted at their HOF-cited second base and shortstop for this table).

The 12 catchers elected through 2000 represent barely more than half the number that should've been chosen if the position were represented proportional to its number of eligibles. But given its inherent offensive disadvantages from effects of the defensive spectrum — which insure that first-string backstops play less frequently than regulars at other positions, run slower, and (due to their higher risk of injury) often have shortened careers — it's no surprise that catchers are so under-represented at Cooperstown. Although pitchers

Table Thirty-Three
HOF-Eligible Players by Position, Number Elected, and Variation

Position	Elgbl Plyrs	Elgbl Pct	HOF Total	HOF Pct	Ideal Total	Pos Var
Pitcher	813	35.4	58	31.4	65	-7
Catcher	271	11.8	12	6.5	22	-10
First Base	52	6.6	17	9.2	12	+5
Second Base	166	7.2	15	8.1	13	+2
Shortstop	181	7.9	19	10.3	15	+4
Third Base	158	6.9	9	4.9	13	-4
Left Field	197	8.6	18	9.7	16	+2
Center Field	173	7.5	16	8.6	14	+2
Right Field	184	8.0	21	11.4	15	+6
(Outfield)	(554)	(24.1)	(55)	(29.7)	(45)	+10)
TOTALS	*2295*	*99.9*	*185*	*100.1*	*185*	*0*

are next in line among the shortchanged positions, it's probable that their representational shortage has occurred, much as anything else, from random chance, because their statistics are entirely different from those of position players, and are not likely to be seen by the HOF electors as comparable in any way to those of batters. As for third basemen, the apparent reasons for their shortfall are complicated and examined in detail in the positional commentary below.

But, unlike representation by era, the Hall-of-Fame selection process has no built-in regulations that might hinder its voters from assuring positional balance among the Cooperstown roster. Granted, some positions are more difficult to play, defensively, and that might produce some marginal favoritism for the men who play them. But it's obvious from the lack of impact that fielding statistics have on HOF election (recall chapter 5, Table Twelve) and from the fact that first base and left field — the two easiest defensive positions — are over-represented at present, pro-fielding bias (if there is any) has little or nothing to do with the current imbalances. So unless you want to argue that a team can win a pennant without anyone playing catcher and/or third base, there is no justifiable excuse for perpetuating the representational inequities evident in Table Thirty-Three.

With all of that in mind, it's fair to assert that, given the over-representation of outfielders and shortstops to date, there should be compelling reasons why anyone from those positions should be added to the final, 210-man Cooperstown roster proposed in a later chapter, especially if there is a catcher or third baseman with relatively equal statistical credentials available. In that light, one of the goals of the current Veterans Committee should be to correct the representational deficits at those two positions.

Shortstops

The rankings for this position reveal at least one apparent error of omission. But, because he is long-gone and largely forgotten, and with 18 shortstops already in Cooperstown (including several of his contemporaries), the chances of his ever getting in are slim.

Of all the players in the database, 7.8 percent or 180, are shortstops (12.1 percent of the non-pitcher subset). Eighteen have been enshrined, accounting for 9.7 percent of players in the Hall (14.2 percent of Cooperstown non-pitchers). They include Luis Aparicio, Luke Appling, Dave Bancroft, Lou Boudreau, Joe Cronin, George Davis, Travis Jackson, Hughie Jennings, Rabbit Maranville, Pee Wee Reese, Phil Rizzuto, Joe Sewell, Joe Tinker, Arky Vaughan, Honus Wagner, Bobby Wallace, Monte Ward and Robin Yount. Leo Durocher and George Wright were elected as a manager and contributor, respectively. Often-cited errors of selection are Aparicio, Bancroft, Jackson, Jennings, Rizzuto, Tinker and Wallace, often-cited errors of omission, include Dick Bartell, Bill Dahlen, Herman Long, Marty Marion, Johnny Pesky, Vern Stephens and Maury Wills.

Table Thirty-Four
Shortstop Z-Score Leaders

Rank	Shortstop	Era	Total Z Avg	Core Z Avg	Rank	Shortstop	Era	Total Z Avg	Core Z Avg
1	**Honus Wagner**	DB	2.77	2.91	18	**Phil Rizzuto**	PW	0.78	0.38
2	**Robin Yount**	FA	1.63	2.93	19	Maury Wills	EX	0.77	0.97
3	*Cal Ripken, Jr.	FA	1.55	2.42	20	Jim Fregosi	EX	0.75	1.27
4	Luis Aparicio	EX	1.34	1.60	21	Herman Long	NC	0.74	1.00
5	*Ozzie Smith	FA	1.28	0.94	22	**Joe Sewell**	LB	0.73	1.14
6	**George Davis**	NC	1.26	1.55	23	*Julio Franco	FA	0.72	1.44
7	**Joe Cronin**	LB	1.25	1.83	24	Dick Bartell	LB	0.70	0.77
	Bill Dahlen	NC	1.25	1.23		**Lou Boudreau**	LB	0.70	0.60
9	**Luke Appling**	LB	1.11	1.41	26	Leo Cardenas	EX	0.66	1.11
10	**Pee Wee Reese**	PW	1.05	1.34		**Hughie Jennings**	NC	0.66	0.42
11	*Alan Trammell	FA	1.04	1.86	28	Garry Templeton	FA	0.65	0.91
12	**Arky Vaughan**	LB	0.97	1.27		*Tony Fernandez	FA	0.65	0.73
13	Bert Campaneris	EX	0.96	1.24	30	**Dave Bancroft**	LB	0.62	0.37
14	*Vern Stephens*	PW	0.94	1.87	31	*Dick Groat*	PW	0.60	0.73
15	Dave Concepcion	FA	0.89	1.27	35	**Travis Jackson**	LB	0.54	0.91
16	**Rabbit Maranville**	LB	0.85	0.67	38	**Joe Tinker**	DB	0.50	0.40
17	**Bobby Wallace**	DB	0.81	1.03	t50	#Monte Ward	NC	0.34	0.57

These rankings validate the 1998 election of George Davis and suggest that his contemporary, Bill Dahlen, has been unfairly overlooked by the Hall's two elective organs. Dahlen got one vote each from the OTC1 in 1936 and the BBWAA in 1938, two more than Davis ever received prior to his election by the VC. But five of Dahlen's relative contemporaries — Wagner, Davis, Wallace, Jennings and Tinker — are already in Cooperstown, which greatly dims his prospects.

Alan Trammell's high rating confirms that he and second baseman Lou Whitaker were the premier keystone combo of their era. Trammell becomes eligible for Cooperstown in 2002 (Whitaker became eligible in 2001), and Alan may fare better than Lou among the BBWAA voters, thanks to his second-place finish in the 1987 MVP balloting. But Ozzie Smith also joins the ballot in 2002, and it's probable that Trammell will be overshadowed by the Wizard for as long as it takes Smith to gain his inevitable (but, perhaps not first-ballot) election.

The biggest surprise on the shortstop list is probably Bert Campaneris, who received 14 votes (3.1-percent support) in 1989, his first and only time on the ballot. But Campy's score here indicates that he is marginally better-qualified among the men at his position than his relative contemporary Dave Concepcion, who became eligible in 1994 and had averaged 58 votes and 12.1-percent support over seven ballots through 2000. Both men were integral to the Oakland and Cincinnati dynasties of the 1970s; but both teams already have three members in the Hall — so Campy's election might be problematic even if he were eligible for VC consideration.

No doubt, Vern Stephens' HOF candidacy suffered from the perception that he put up great numbers against inferior wartime pitching. But, unlike contemporary second sacker Joe Gordon, Stephens never received a single Cooperstown vote, and his failure to gain even cursory notice from those electors is a signal indictment of the flaws inherent in the BBWAA process. Stephens missed wartime military service because of a gimpy knee, but — contrary to popular belief — his best seasons did not occur against depleted pitching. From 1943 to 1945, Vern averaged 159 hits, 22 home runs and 96 runs batted in, becoming the first AL shortstop to lead the league in RBI (109 in 1944) and the first man ever from that position to top either circuit in homers (24 in 1945). But, despite all that, his postwar stats were even better: he averaged 166 hits, 25 dingers and 117 RBI over the five-year period 1946–50; he set an all-time record for homers by a shortstop in 1949 (39, broken by Ernie Banks in 1955); he set a mark for total bases by a shortstop over a two-season period in 1949-50 (650, also broken by Banks in 1958-59); he drove in 303 ribbies in those two campaigns, the most ever recorded in back-to-back seasons by anyone from his position; and he tallied 159 RBI in 1949, the most by any middle infielder (including second basemen) ever.

When Stephens retired in 1955, his 213 homers as a shortstop were the major-league record for the position (he hit 247 in all), and a total that has been surpassed since only by Banks and Cal Ripken, Jr. Anyone whose records required no less than Banks and Ripken to top them should have, it seems fair to argue, received far more notice from the writers. (Note that Stephens' Core-Z average, +1.87, is the fourth-best on this list, behind only Honus Wagner, Robin Yount and Cal Ripken, Jr., and even ahead of Joe Cronin.)

Three other often-cited errors of omission, Herman Long, Dick Bartell and Maury Wills, also rank among the shortstop leaders. But Long played during the same era as Bill Dahlen, and based on the scores in Table Thirty-Four, should not go in ahead of him. Bartell's chances are diminished by the presence of seven other live-ball shortstops at Cooperstown, and his relative position among these leaders does nothing to verify any error in his omission. Wills's Total-Z of +0.77 is indicative that he would be a marginal Hall of Famer, at best. The presence of a higher-ranked, unenshrined contemporary (Bert Campaneris) doesn't enhance Maury's credentials.

It's no surprise that Ozzie Smith tops the list of fielding leaders at this position. Smith earned an isolated defensive-Z average of +2.12 for his career, almost half a standard deviation better than second-place Rabbit Maranville (+1.70) and — unlike Johnny Bench — justifying his recent reputation as the best glove man ever at his position. Hall of Famers Dave Bancroft (+1.41), Luis Aparicio (+1.34) and Lou Boudreau (+1.31) follow Maranville, in third, fourth and fifth places, respectively. Behind them are Cal Ripken, Jr. (+1.26), Eddie Miller (+1.17), Dick Bartell (+1.16), Roy McMillan (+1.12) and Cooperstown member Luke Appling (+1.10).

As a shortstop, Ernie Banks has a Total-Z average of +1.97, with a Core of +3.54. The former score is good enough to rank in second place on the list above, behind only Honus Wagner; and the latter is easily better than every other Core average posted by the men at this position.

Third Basemen

Just nine third basemen had been elected to Cooperstown through 2000, so — excluding pitchers — the hot corner ranks with catcher as the most under-represented position in the Shrine. But the reasons for the shortage are more subtle than they are for backstops, as there is no obvious offensive disadvantage inherent to the position's spot midway along the defensive spectrum.

For half of major-league history third base was essentially a defensive position at which — much like catcher, shortstop and second base — offense was a bonus rather than a requirement. And, although Hall-of-Fame third sacker Home Run Baker helped glamorize the long ball in the years before

Babe Ruth's shift from pitching, he earned that monicker solely for swatting two circuit clouts in the 1911 World Series, and never had more than 12 home runs in a season. So the batting stats of most early third basemen were much like those of middle infielders, and because the position produced no hitters comparable to Honus Wagner or Nap Lajoie during dead-ball times, or to Joe Cronin and Rogers Hornsby in subsequent decades, it was the last of those three infield spots to get a rep in Cooperstown (Jimmy Collins, the first third sacker chosen, was not inducted until 1945).

Similarly, most of the best-regarded live-ball third sackers were like Pie Traynor and Stan Hack, who hit for average and drove in some runs but rarely, if ever, had double-figure seasonal totals for homers. One man changed all that in the late 1930s, setting a new standard for power at the position that foretold later sluggers like Eddie Mathews and Mike Schmidt. Somehow, the guy who did it never appeared in an All-Star Game, and — like Vern Stephens — never got a Cooperstown vote.

But, the advent of slugging third basemen is likely to make it even more difficult for men from the position to get elected in the future. With Mathews, Schmidt, George Brett and Brooks Robinson having set the modern standards for admission, the recent BBWAA failures of others like Ron Santo, Ken Boyer, Graig Nettles and Darrell Evans — all of whom are clearly more qualified, statistically, than almost every man at the position who came before them — seem to imply, quite unfairly, that a legitimate HOF third sacker now must be someone with either 500 homers, 3000 hits, or an unmatched reputation for defensive genius. And those expectations will be chiseled in stone after the inevitable elections of Paul Molitor and Wade Boggs, two more 3000-hit men.

The 158 third baseman in the database represent 6.9 percent of all players considered (10.6 percent of the non-pitcher subset). Only nine have made it to Cooperstown, accounting for 4.9 percent of players in the Hall (7.1 percent of Cooperstown non-pitchers). They include Frank Baker, George Brett, Jimmy Collins, George Kell, Fred Lindstrom, Eddie Mathews, Brooks Robinson, Mike Schmidt and Pie Traynor. John McGraw and Bill McKechnie were elected as managers. Often-cited errors of selection are Kell and Lindstrom, often-cited errors of omission, Ken Boyer, Harlond Clift, Lave Cross, Stan Hack, Willie Kamm, Ken Keltner, Al Rosen and Ron Santo.

The man who forever altered the stereotype for third basemen was Harlond Clift, whose 12 seasons in the majors were spent with the St. Louis Browns and Washington Senators, perennial American League doormats. Clift's association with those losers explains some of his failure to get any HOF votes. Harlond was actually selected for one All-Star team in 1937, but stayed on the bench while manager Joe McCarthy used his Yankee third sacker Red Rolfe and the rest of the AL's starting lineup (except for one pinch hitter and two pitching

Table Thirty-Five
Third Base Z-Score Leaders

Rank	Third Baseman	Era	Total Z Avg	Core Z Avg		Third Baseman	Era	Total Z Avg	Core Z Avg
1	**Mike Schmidt**	FA	2.13	2.19	19	*Larry Gardner*	DB	0.76	0.90
2	**George Brett**	FA	1.88	2.41	20	Bob Elliott	PW	0.74	1.36
3	**Eddie Mathews**	PW	1.60	2.43	21	#Arlie Latham	NC	0.73	0.70
4	**Brooks Robinson**	EX	1.50	1.85	22	Buddy Bell	FA	0.72	1.16
5	Ron Santo	EX	1.37	1.80		Sal Bando	EX	0.72	0.97
6	*Paul Molitor	FA	1.31	1.56	24	Stan Hack	LB	0.69	0.70
7	Darrell Evans	FA	1.28	1.51	25	*Eddie Yost*	PW	0.68	0.71
8	**Frank Baker**	DB	1.17	1.20	26	**George Kell**	PW	0.59	1.00
9	Lave Cross	NC	1.16	1.71	27	Ron Cey	FA	0.57	0.94
10	*Wade Boggs	FA	1.01	1.23	28	*Heinie Zimmerman*	DB	0.55	0.70
11	Ken Boyer	EX	0.98	1.59	29	Richie Hebner	EX	0.53	0.88
12	Graig Nettles	FA	0.95	1.34	30	#Ned Williamson	NC	0.51	0.18
13	**Jimmy Collins**	DB	0.90	1.19	31	*#Denny Lyons*	NC	0.50	0.72
14	**Pie Traynor**	LB	0.89	1.29	32	Toby Harrah	FA	0.49	0.69
15	Heinie Groh	DB	0.87	0.67	33	*#Bill Shindle*	NC	0.45	0.54
16	Jimmy Dykes	LB	0.85	0.83	34	Don Money	EX	0.43	0.53
17	*#Billy Nash*	NC	0.77	0.85		*Harlond Clift*	LB	0.43	0.50
	John McGraw	NC	0.77	0.80	65	**Fred Lindstrom**	LB	0.07	0.60

changes) for all nine innings. Clift's 29 homers in 1937 broke Ned Williamson's single-season, hot-corner record of 27, set in 1884. Harlond surpassed that mark with 34 the next season. He led AL third sackers in circuit clouts for four straight years (1936–39), and ended his career with 178, to go with 1070 runs scored, 829 RBI and a batting average of .272. A good fielder, Clift had 637 total chances, 405 assists and 50 double plays during his All-Star season. The first total remains the second-best single-season mark for third sackers ever; the last two were records for the position until 1971; and, although surpassed by 17 others since then, Clift's 309 career double plays were the positional record when he retired. Despite all that, the career achievements of the modern third sackers for which he set the mold have eclipsed Harlond's performance so thoroughly that he now ranks no better than 34th at the position, a testament to how easily a trendsetter can get lost in the statistical shuffle.

Despite his fielding prowess, Clift does not rank among the hot corner's Z-Score leaders for career defense. The top man in that category is Darrell Evans (+1.45), whose score is no doubt enhanced by his 856 career games at first base. Behind Evans, and bunched closely together, are Brooks Robinson

(+1.39), Mike Schmidt (+1.34) and Ron Santo (+1.30). Trailing them are the dead-ball era's Lee Tannehill (+1.18), Expansion-era Yankee Clete Boyer (+1.07), live-baller Willie Kamm (+0.99), plus Buddy Bell (+0.91), Jimmy Dykes (+0.90) and Ray Boone (+0.87).

Much like catcher, the third-base rankings are dominated by recent players. Nine of the top 34 are from the free-agent era, five others are expansion players, and two of the four postwar third sackers on the list (Mathews and Eddie Yost) had careers that extended well into the 1960s.

Among the recent, currently eligible, unenshrined players on this list, there is no doubt that Santo, Evans, Ken Boyer and Nettles all have statistical credentials for their position that are more than adequate for the Hall. But Evans and Nettles along with Buddy Bell, Ron Cey and Toby Harrah have become victims of the 5-percent-support curse, so none of those five is eligible for further consideration. Santo's BBWAA eligibility expired in 1998, and Boyer's ended four years earlier, but thanks to grandfathering, both men qualify for VC consideration despite never receiving 60-percent support from the writers.

Lave Cross and Stan Hack, two other oft-cited errors of omission, also made the top 34. Hack, the more recent of the two, is widely celebrated as a Cooperstown oversight, but Cross's overall statistical credentials are more impressive by far. Unless you count Jimmy Collins (whose career, like Cross's overlapped the turn of the century) or John McGraw (cited as a manager), the 1800s have no third sacker at Cooperstown. In that light, Lave's election would be more justifiable than adding Hack from an era that already has one legitimate Hall of Famer (Pie Traynor) and an almost certain error of selection (Fred Lindstrom) at the position.

Left Fielders

As with first base, and unlike the other infield spots, there are no glaring omissions among the upper echelon of left field Z-Score leaders. Rickey Henderson, the only man among the top 12 not yet in the Hall, was still active in 2000, and because of his ownership of the career stolen base record and high rank among the all-time leaders in runs and walks, he is — like Lou Brock in 1985 — an almost certain first-year inductee. But there are some surprises on this list, notably the high ranking of the free-agent era's Tim Raines, and of dead-ballers Jimmy Sheckard and Sherry Magee. Also, just as occurred with the postwar-era measurement in chapter 7, the combined effects of the cumulative variables and Stan Musial's longevity push "The Man's" Total-Z average (as well as that of Carl Yastrzemski) ahead of Ted Williams on this scale.

The database's 197 left fielders account for 8.6 percent of all players considered (13.3 percent of the non-pitcher subset), and the 18 Hall of Famers among them make up 9.7 of all player enshrinees (14.2 percent of Cooperstown non-pitchers). They include Lou Brock, Jesse Burkett, Fred Clarke, Ed Delahanty, Hugh Duffy, Goose Goslin, Chick Hafey, Joe Kelley, Ralph Kiner, Heinie Manush, Joe Medwick, Stan Musial, Al Simmons, Willie Stargell, Zach Wheat, Billy Williams, Ted Williams and Carl Yastrzemski. The only often-cited error of selection is Hafey. Often-cited error of omission are Mike Donlin, Indian Bob Johnson, Minnie Miñoso, Lefty O'Doul, Riggs Stephenson, Harry Stovey and Ken Williams.

As noted earlier, the list of career fielding leaders for this position is suspect and compromised because the scores of several men are greatly enhanced by their service at other, more defensively active posts, especially first base. Those fielding leaders include Carl Yastrzemski (+2.55), Stan Musial (+2.11), John Anderson (+1.51), Howard Shanks (+1.37), Kevin McReynolds (+1.22), Willie Stargell (+1.19), Hector Lopez (+1.13), Harry Stovey (+1.07), Dave Kingman (+1.06) and Warren Cromartie (+1.01). Among them, only McReynolds was an outfielder throughout his career; Shanks and Lopez both spent considerable time

Table Thirty-Six
Left Field Z-Score Leaders

Rank	Left Fielder	Era	Total Z Avg	Core Z Avg	Rank	Left Fielder	Era	Total Z Avg	Core Z Avg
1	**Stan Musial**	PW	2.92	3.21	18	#Harry Stovey	NC	0.86	0.39
2	**Carl Yastrzemski**	EX	2.33	2.67	19	**Joe Medwick**	LB	0.84	1.26
3	**Ted Williams**	PW	2.15	2.96	20	Sherry Magee	DB	0.81	0.83
4	*Rickey Henderson	FA	1.46	1.30	21	Bob L. Johnson	LB	0.79	1.01
5	**Willie Stargell**	EX	1.41	1.81	22	Don Baylor	FA	0.78	1.27
6	**Al Simmons**	LB	1.40	2.08	23	George Foster	FA	0.76	1.18
7	**Ed Delahanty**	NC	1.38	1.64	24	**Hugh Duffy**	NC	0.75	1.26
8	**Goose Goslin**	LB	1.26	1.63		Brian Downing	FA	0.75	1.06
9	**Fred Clarke**	DB	1.20	1.33	26	Jose Cruz	FA	0.67	0.96
10	**Billy Williams**	EX	1.14	2.02	27	Frank Howard	EX	0.64	1.01
	Lou Brock	EX	1.14	1.42	28	**Ralph Kiner**	PW	0.63	0.86
12	**Zach Wheat**	DB	1.00	1.51	29	*Hal McRae*	FA	0.59	0.97
13	Jim Rice	FA	0.98	1.87		Dave Kingman	FA	0.59	0.87
14	**Joe Kelley**	NC	0.93	0.97	31	Minnie Miñoso	PW	0.58	0.92
15	**Jesse Burkett**	NC	0.91	1.40		*Bobby Veach*	DB	0.58	0.83
	*Tim Raines	FA	0.91	0.94	t34	**Heinie Manush**	LB	0.50	1.08
17	Jimmy Sheckard	DB	0.87	0.52	t57	**Chick Hafey**	LB	0.21	0.28

as third basemen; and the other seven all played at least one-third of their defensive games at first (Kingman nearly half). Yaz, Musial and Stovey, at least, may have rated among the top 10 even without their first-base service, thanks to the former pair's longevity and the latter's speed. But a better picture of the true leaders for the position is gained if one carries the list to 15th place, where it also includes Don Buford (+0.98, but much time at second and third base) and four career outfielders: Rickey Henderson (+0.96), Ed Delahanty (+0.93), Jimmy Sheckard (+0.92) and Fred Clarke (+0.86).

After Henderson, Jim Rice is the highest-ranked unenshrined player on this list, at 13th, and his placement, ahead of seven Hall of Famers argues strongly for his election at a position that already has 18 men in Cooperstown. But Rice's BBWAA vote history has been inconsistent: he received just 29.8-percent support in 1995, his first year eligible; he improved steadily to 42.8 percent in 1998; he fell to 29.4 percent support the following year, when first-time eligibles Nolan Ryan, George Brett and Robin Yount were chosen; then he climbed to 257 votes and 51.5-percent support in 2000, placing third behind electees Carlton Fisk and Tony Perez. In six tries through 2000, Rice had averaged 181 votes and 37.8-percent support per ballot. Unless his candidacy gains momentum (an unlikely prospect given all the de facto qualifiers who will join the ballot in the next few years), he will not get the 60-percent-support required for VC consideration.

Three other high-ranked left fielders are forgotten now by almost everyone outside of SABR. In another era, the 19th century's Harry Stovey might've been Babe Ruth and Rickey Henderson, combined. He topped his league in home runs five times, and triples and runs scored four times each. Unusual for a slugger in any time, Stovey also led his circuit in stolen bases twice, ending his career with 509 thefts. Dead-baller Jimmy Sheckard was the left fielder for the great Cubs teams of the century's first decade, and it's plausible that he and right fielder Frank "Wildfire" Schulte both were more deserving of enshrinement than the club's more-renowned double-play trio. But prior to the 1906 World Series, Sheckard boasted that he would bat .400 in the Fall Classic against the crosstown White Sox, then went 0-for-21 in the Series. So his HOF credentials do not include modesty or the common sense to avoid hyper-motivating his opponents. Sherry Magee was a contemporary of Sheckard's whose HOF chances may have been hurt by his innocent, peripheral connections to the Black Sox scandal. In his last season, and no longer a regular, Magee played for Cincinnati in the tainted 1919 Series, going one-for-two as a pinch hitter. That same year, Brooklyn outfielder Lee Magee (no relation) was proven in court to have bet against his own team. After that season Sherry retired and Lee was blacklisted from baseball, so neither man ever appeared in the majors again. It's possible that some HOF electors confused them later on, as Sherry got only 11 votes spread over seven different ballots —

which wasn't much for a man who hit above .300 five times, won three RBI titles, two slugging crowns, and topped his league in batting, hits and runs scored once each.

Indian Bob Johnson's absence from the Shrine is curious. When he retired in 1945 Johnson ranked number eight on the list of career home-run leaders, and he remained among the top 20 as late as 1960, before his BBWAA eligibility had expired. With one exception, Johnson's Core-Z numbers are almost identical to but marginally better than those of Cooperstown's Earl Averill, a center fielder who played in the same league at virtually the same time: Earl had 2019 hits, 238 home runs, 1224 runs scored and 1164 RBI; Indian Bob posted 2051 safeties, 288 homers, 1239 runs and 1283 RBI. So, you'd think that Johnson's career marks for those stats would have earned him election from an era with 62 Hall of Famers. But Averill also batted .318 for his career, while Johnson hit just .296. Earl was elected by the VC in 1976, after receiving 36 BBWAA votes spread over seven ballots; Johnson got just one vote in each of two elections, 1948 and 1956. His omission from the Hall may be signal evidence of the electors' fixation on .300 hitters. In that sense, .300 is a reverse de facto standard, in that failure to reach the figure — especially during Johnson's era — is often cited as sufficient subjective justification for a player's omission.

Center Fielders

The top five players here are no surprise. For those who can't wait to look, their specific order of finish is Mays, Cobb, Speaker, Mantle and DiMaggio — and Mays' Core-Z is easily the best of the lot. More fuel for debate: Duke Snider is just 10th.

With 173 players in the database, center fielders make up 7.6 percent of the men considered (11.7 percent of the non-pitcher subset). Sixteen have made it to the Hall of Fame, equivalent to 8.6 percent all players enshrined (12.6 percent of Cooperstown non-pitchers). They include Richie Ashburn, Earl Averill, Max Carey, Ty Cobb, Earle Combs, Joe DiMaggio, Larry Doby, Billy Hamilton, Mickey Mantle, Willie Mays, Jim O'Rourke, Edd Roush, Duke Snider, Tris Speaker, Lloyd Waner and Hack Wilson. Ned Hanlon was elected as a manager. Often-cited errors of selection include Combs, Waner and Wilson. Often-cited errors of omission are Wally Berger, Pete Browning, Doc Cramer, Dom DiMaggio, Curt Flood, Vada Pinson, Pete Reiser, Jimmy Ryan, Bobby Thomson, George Van Haltren and Cy Williams.

Tris Speaker heads the fielding list (+2.13), followed by Richie Ashburn (+1.97) and Max Carey (+1.96), but some of the men below them spent more than a third of their big-league time at other positions. Tommy Leach is

Table Thirty-Seven
Center Field Z-Score Leaders

Rank	Left Fielder	Era	Total Z Avg	Core Z Avg	Rank	Left Fielder	Era	Total Z Avg	Core Z Avg
1	**Willie Mays**	EX	2.55	3.60	18	*Amos Otis*	EX	0.72	1.00
2	**Ty Cobb**	DB	2.53	3.04	19	*Jimmy Ryan*	NC	0.70	1.13
3	**Tris Speaker**	DB	2.26	2.21	20	*Brett Butler	FA	0.69	0.63
4	**Mickey Mantle**	PW	1.98	2.24	21	**Edd Roush**	LB	0.68	0.97
5	**Joe DiMaggio**	LB	1.62	2.02	22	*Jimmy Wynn*	EX	0.65	0.84
6	Al Oliver	FA	1.26	1.76	23	Tommy Leach	DB	0.62	0.33
7	**Max Carey**	DB	1.05	0.74	24	Geo. Van Haltren	NC	0.60	1.07
8	Dale Murphy	FA	1.01	1.58	25	*George Hendrick*	FA	0.59	1.16
9	Vada Pinson	EX	0.97	1.67		Chet Lemon	FA	0.59	0.85
10	**Duke Snider**	PW	0.90	1.54	27	Cy Williams	LB	0.55	0.94
11	Cesar Cedeño	FA	0.86	1.10	28	**#Jim O'Rourke**	NC	0.52	0.80
12	*Kirby Puckett	FA	0.85	1.32	29	Doc Cramer	LB	0.51	0.84
	Richie Ashburn	PW	0.85	0.60	30	**Hack Wilson**	LB	0.50	0.85
14	*Willie Davis*	EX	0.78	1.25	31	***Earle Combs***	LB	0.49	0.64
15	**Earl Averill**	LB	0.77	1.34	37	**Lloyd Waner**	LB	0.39	0.68
16	Fred Lynn	FA	0.76	1.33	42	**Larry Doby**	PW	0.30	0.56
	Billy Hamilton	NC	0.76	0.98					

fourth (+1.58), for instance, but played a lot at third base, He is followed by Al Oliver (+1.38) and Johnny Hopp (+1.30), both of whom saw considerable duty at first. Solly Hofman and Catfish Metkovich are tied for seventh (+1.19 each), but the latter was also a first sacker. Willie Mays is ninth (+0.99), and Whitey Witt, who also played shortstop, is 10th (+0.90). As with the left fielders, some legitimate flychasers make up the next five: Sammy West (+0.87) is 11th; Dom DiMaggio (+0.85) ranks 12th; Garry Maddox (+0.67) is number 13; and Curt Flood and Jim Hickman (+0.63) are tied for fourteenth.

Subjectively, Al Oliver's high ranking is a mild surprise, but given his Core-Z average — sixth-best among center fielders — so is that fact that he's another casualty of the 5-percent support rule. A seven-time All-Star, he led the NL in batting, hits, doubles and RBI in 1982, and for his career he had 2743 hits, 1189 runs, 1326 and a .303 average.

Many print-media observers assumed — apparently because of his two MVPs and 398 homers — that when Dale Murphy became eligible in 1999, he was as much of a cinch for election as de-facto candidates George Brett, Robin Yount and Nolan Ryan. But the others were elected while Murphy finished 11th in the balloting with only 96 votes and 19.3-percent support.

Dale followed that with 116 votes and 23.2 percent in 2000. Murphy and Kirby Puckett were both credits to the game, and, subjectively, both are better candidates overall than their relative contemporary, Cesar Cedeño, who is sandwiched between them on this list. But given Murphy's weak early showing, he may have a tougher time getting elected than Puckett, and may never be chosen by the scribes.

Like Curt Flood, Vada Pinson played the same position, in the same league, at the same time as Willie Mays, and it's probable that his HOF fortunes might have been happier if he hadn't. He did collect over 500 Hall-of-Fame votes, having led the NL in hits, doubles and triples twice, in runs scored once, and batted above .300 five times. It's hard to fault any of his career stats (2757 hits, 256 homers, 1366 runs and 1170 RBI) except for his .286 batting average, which still was 30 points above the norm for his era. One suspects that more than anything else, and like Bob Johnson, he's another victim of the below-.300, reverse-de facto whammy.

It's hard to figure how all of the Old-Timers Committee voters of 1936 ignored Jimmy Ryan (no HOF votes then, or ever, although he was considered by the Veterans Committee in its 2000 voting). During a career that spanned 1885–1903, Ryan had 2502 hits, 118 home runs, 1642 runs scored and 1093 RBI. At the turn of the century, while still active, he ranked among the all-time top 10 in the first three of those categories, and was 11th in RBI. He remained among the top 10 in homers as late as 1925, and at the time of the first HOF election, he still ranked 26th among the career leaders in hits, 31st in homers, 11th in runs scored, and 33rd in RBI. He also batted .306 for his career.

Center fielder Cy and left fielder Ken Williams are one of three pairs of contemporaries whose similarities of name and statistics may have hurt each man's chances for Cooperstown. The other two combos are third sacker Darrell and right fielder Dwight Evans (both well-qualified for the Shrine), plus first baseman George H. and left fielder George J. Burns (who are less qualified, individually, than the other four). As home-run savants, Cy and Ken (especially the former) were also disadvantaged by the fact that their careers began in the dead-ball period and extended into the next era. Cy got to the bigs with the Cubs in 1912, so almost half of his 19-year major-league tenure occurred before the home-run barrage of the twenties. Ken joined the Reds in 1915, but spent four years as a part-timer before the St. Louis Browns installed him as a regular in 1920. Cy led the NL in homers with a dozen in 1916, the first of four such titles in his career. Ken topped the AL in 1922, with 39 circuit clouts. Both men ranked just below Babe Ruth and Rogers Hornsby as the most potent sluggers of the Live-Ball era's first decade. In fact, through 1920, baseball's career leaders in home runs were Roger Connor 138, Sam Thompson 127, Harry Stovey 122 and Gavvy Cravath 119. A decade later, the top of the list read Ruth 565, Hornsby 279, Cy Williams 251 and Ken Williams 196. Despite all the sluggers of the 1930s, however, Cy remained among the all-time top 10 through 1945. Like Bob Johnson, Cy's major drawback is his career batting average of just .292. Ken batted .319, but his stats aren't as good as a whole. All the same, both men sustained their performance level for a longer period than some live-ball outfielders who made it to Cooperstown (notably, Chuck Klein, Hack Wilson and Ross Youngs) and others who didn't but get more attention (like Lefty O'Doul).

Right Fielders

In this realm, no one comes very close to the Bambino and Hank, not even Shoeless Joe. The biggest challenge with this list is explaining why Joe Jackson and Tony Gwynn rank no better than 28th and 30th, respectively.

The 184 right fielders considered account for 8.0 percent of all players in the database (12.4 percent of the non-pitcher subset). Twenty-one of the men have earned Cooperstown recognition, and right fielders represent 11.4 percent of all players enshrined (16.5 percent of Cooperstown non-pitchers). They include Hank Aaron, Roberto Clemente, Sam Crawford, Kiki Cuyler, Elmer Flick, Harry Heilmann, Harry Hooper, Reggie Jackson, Al Kaline, Willie Keeler, King Kelly, Chuck Klein, Tommy McCarthy, Mel Ott, Sam Rice, Frank Robinson, Babe Ruth, Enos Slaughter, Sam Thompson, Paul Waner and Ross Youngs. Casey Stengel was elected as a manager. Often-cited errors of selection include Flick, Klein, McCarthy, Rice and Youngs, often-cited errors of omission, Rocky Colavito, Gavvy Cravath, Carl Furillo, Tommy Henrich, Babe Herman, Shoeless Joe Jackson, Harvey Kuenn, Roger Maris, Tony Oliva and Pete Rose.

Again, the defensive leaders among right fielders are confused by a lot of part-time first sackers. Pete Rose (+2.21) tops that listing, and although it's obvious he gets a boost from his time at first base, his service at second and third didn't hurt him, either, relative to the stats put up by full-time outfielders (who make fewer plays than infielders). Numbers two and three, Vic Wertz (+1.68) and Jack Clark (+1.63), were also part-time first sackers. Fourth-place Harvey Kuenn (+1.52) was not, but began his career at shortstop. So the most-qualified defensive right fielder of all time was really either Rusty Staub or the 19th century's Pop Corkhill, both tied for fifth (+1.22 each)—unless you also dismiss Staub's credentials because about one-fourth of his games were at first. Beyond them are some real right fielders: Roberto Clemente (+1.09) is seventh; Andre Dawson (+1.08) ranks eighth; and Roy Cullenbine (+1.04) is number nine; followed by Bob Bailor (+1.02), a part-time shortstop. The second 10 includes Sam Rice (+0.94) at 12th and Jesse

Table Thirty-Eight
Right Field Z-Score Leaders

Rank	Right Fielder	Era	Total Z Avg	Core Z Avg	Rank	Right Fielder	Era	Total Z Avg	Core Z Avg
1	**Babe Ruth**	LB	2.66	3.05	18	**#King Kelly**	NC	0.95	0.91
2	**Hank Aaron**	EX	2.09	3.24	19	**Harry Heilmann**	LB	0.91	1.40
3	Pete Rose	EX	1.93	1.94	20	Rusty Staub	EX	0.86	1.10
4	**Frank Robinson**	EX	1.59	2.24	21	Vic Wertz	PW	0.85	0.82
5	**Mel Ott**	LB	1.48	2.08	22	**Willie Keeler**	DB	0.83	1.46
6	**Reggie Jackson**	FA	1.40	1.86	23	**Harry Hooper**	DB	0.80	0.74
7	**Sam Crawford**	DB	1.23	1.48	24	**Sam Rice**	LB	0.78	0.97
8	*Dave Winfield	FA	1.21	2.15	25	Reggie Smith	EX	0.70	0.80
9	**Al Kaline**	EX	1.17	1.78	26	**Chuck Klein**	LB	0.68	1.00
10	**Enos Slaughter**	PW	1.15	1.31		Harvey Kuenn	PW	0.68	0.67
11	*Andre Dawson	FA	1.12	1.66	28	Joe Jackson	DB	0.65	0.88
12	Dwight Evans	FA	1.09	1.44	29	*#Mike Tiernan*	NC	0.61	0.93
13	Dave Parker	FA	1.07	1.55	30	*Tony Gwynn	FA	0.58	0.86
14	Jack Clark	FA	1.03	0.88		*Kiki Cuyler*	LB	0.58	0.80
15	**Roberto Clemente**	EX	1.00	1.46	37	**Elmer Flick**	DB	0.39	0.51
	#Sam Thompson	NC	1.00	1.37	47	**#Tommy McCarthy**	NC	0.27	0.36
17	**Paul Waner**	LB	0.96	1.40	t67	**Ross Youngs**	LB	0.08	-0.02

Barfield (+0.89) in 14th, followed sequentially by Reggie Smith (+0.84), Al Kaline (+0.83) and Hank Aaron (+0.76).

Among modern players not yet enshrined, excluding Pete Rose, Dave Winfield (eligible in 2001) is a certain electee, and Andre Dawson (2002) is almost a lock. Dave Parker had been eligible on four ballots through 2000, drawing a high of 24.5-percent support. But, as the scores above indicate, Parker's stats are not much different from those of Dwight Evans or Jack Clark — yet both of the other two were 5-percent-support casualties.

The most surprising scores on this list are the low rankings of Joe Jackson and Tony Gwynn. Subjectively, one expects them to be higher, and their weak numbers occurred for different reasons.

Jackson ranks only 15th-best among the dead-ball leaders in chapter 6, with a Total-Z average of +0.87. He rates no better than 28th here, at +0.65. Those low scores occurred because a majority of the non-pitcher variables are cumulative, and strongly impacted by longevity. Shoeless Joe played 13 seasons, and was just 31 years old at the time of his banishment. Barring serious injury, he probably had six good years left by 1920, and if you credit him with just two-thirds of his normal yearly production in hits, runs and RBI after that date, that would put him above 2400 hits and 1100 runs and RBI each. In turn, his .356 batting average might have declined some with age, but it's hard to imagine it dropping below .330. There are only a few dead-ball players who compiled similar numbers and are not in Cooperstown. Stuffy McInnis is the only dead baller above 2400 hits, and only Sherry Magee and Bobby Veach are over 1100 RBI. Just seven unenshrined men from the era have at least 1100 runs scored, and, as noted in chapter 6, Mike Donlin is the only dead-baller besides Jackson with a .330 average or better who is not in the Hall. So there's no disputing Shoeless Joe's talent. And it's virtually certain that, absent the Black Sox travesty, he would be on the Cooperstown roster. But whether or not he deserved his fate, the Z-Score sum of his career stats — as is — equates to marginal Hall-of-Famer status, at best.

Finally, there is Gwynn. Through 1999, Gwynn was a 14-time All Star and an eight-time batting champ (only Ty Cobb had more titles). He also had moved up to number 17 among the leaders for career hits (3067), having surpassed the de facto standard at midseason 1999. His career batting average of .339 was the 16th-best ever. All of this puts him among very select company. Except for Pete Rose, every man above him on the hits list is in Cooperstown, or will be as soon as they're eligible; and the only two with higher batting averages who aren't there are Pete Browning, the Louisville Chugger, and the blacklisted Joe Jackson. A recent book by Michael J. Schell even rates Gwynn as the greatest hitter of all time, based on batting average relative to the norms of his era, and accounting for the variations in offensive production caused by different ballparks. So, although Gwynn's scores above are based on performance through 1994 only, why does he rank no better than tied for 30th?

Gwynn's stats are great until you look closely at his run-production numbers. Through his first 18 seasons (1982–99) he had scored 1361 runs and driven in 1104. With 133 homers, that gave him 2332 runs produced (i.e., runs-plus-RBI minus home runs). His ratio of runs batted in to hits (RBI/H) was .360 — so, on average, slightly more than one-third of his safeties had driven in a run. Comparing Gwynn to the men ahead of him on the career-hits and batting-average lists through 1999 (29 in all, with two men — Ty Cobb and Tris Speaker — ranked above him on both), the only ones with lower figures were Rose (.309), Billy Hamilton (.342) and Willie Keeler (.276), the latter two leadoff hitters. The average for both groups as a whole was .499, and the leader was Babe Ruth (.770, more than double Tony's rate). Similar, but worse, Gwynn's ratio of runs produced to hits (RP/H) was .760, and that figure was the lowest from either list (Ruth was the leader for that one, too, at 1.278; the mean was .974). So each of Tony's hits produced roughly three-fourths of a run (including those he had scored or driven in), every one of Ruth's created over one and a quarter, and everyone else on that list did better than Gwynn.

None of this means that Gwynn is an over-rated player. The problem is that, through 1999, 76 percent of his career hits had been singles. The group average was .688, and Ruth's figure, again the best, was .528 (a low score is more impressive for that stat). When you toss in Tony's on-base average of .392 and 325 stolen bases through 1999, what you get is the picture of a guy owning the batting skills of a leadoff hitter with power similar to that of Lou Brock, albeit without his speed. Gwynn, then, has been statistically victimized by the circumstances of his career. Due mostly to the weak offensive talent on many of his San Diego teams, Tony has spent much of his career hitting in the number three slot, with occasional time at number two. Regardless of his high batting average, there's just no way a guy who hits singles three-fourths of the time can produce as many runs from that spot, especially on a team with poor offense, as one who hits for a similar average with more power on higher-scoring ball clubs (like most of the Hall of Famers above him among the leaders for both lists). Many of the right fielders ahead of Gwynn in the rankings above batted third or fourth in the order and had both of those skills. So, compared to men like Ruth, Aaron, Robinson and Ott, and for reasons beyond his control, many of Tony's Z-Score averages are relatively wimpy.

CHAPTER 10

The Pick of the Litter

Previous chapters demonstrated that Hall-of-Fame selection is dependent, in part, upon a man's performance relative to others from his era and to those who played the same position. But in the minds of most people — casual fans and baseball cognoscenti alike — above all else, Cooperstown membership is supposed to signify a man's status among the very best in the history of the game.

When measured against the career statistics of all eligible candidates as a whole, 57 of the 185 players enshrined at Cooperstown through 2000 post Total-Z averages that are insufficient to place them among either the top 127 non-pitchers or 58 hurlers in the overall scale, indicating that nearly one-third of the Hall-of-Fame roster may represent statistical errors of selection. With that in mind, this chapter will focus on whether the lowest-ranked Hall of Famers possess any other credentials that might offset the apparent deficiencies in their statistical performance enough to justify their memberships. Those who don't will be dismissed as errors of selection because their low scores in each of the first three measures are compelling evidence that they do not belong in Cooperstown.

Although there are only two ratings lists in this chapter, space requirements again prohibit their length from being as inclusive as might be desired. But, as before, a more complete list of the leaders among the overall rankings may be found in the Appendix.

First, however, it's important to identify the statistical parameters established by the full set of players in the database. Table Thirty-Nine lists the means and standard deviations for each of the applicable variables among all 1484 non-pitchers and 813 hurlers in the data set. Values for the Core variables are boldfaced.

Table Thirty-Nine
Sample Means and Standard Deviations, All Players and Variables

Batter Variables	Mean	s	Pitcher Variables	Mean	s
Years Played	13.3	3.2	Years Played	13.1	3.1
Games Played	1324.7	523.7	**Games Won**	**117.3**	**67.9**
Hits	**1241.5**	**649.4**	**Winning Percentage**	**.5165**	**.0636**
Doubles	203.4	117.2	Fibonacci Wins	75.5	70.7
Triples	49.5	40.2	**Earned Run Average**	**3.581**	**.5256**
Home Runs	**87.6**	**98.6**	Games Pitched	416.8	151.6
Home-Run Frequency	150.3	251.6	**Innings Pitched**	**1952.1**	**1007.2**
Total Bases	1806.7	1014.4	Opps' Batting Avg	.2573	.0162
Runs Scored	**632.1**	**375.1**	Opps' On-Base Avg	.3224	.0186
Runs Batted In	**563.3**	**356.2**	Hits-per-9 Innings	8.821	0.729
Runs Produced	1107.9	641.1	BB-per-9 Innings	3.095	0.799
Walks	443.3	294.1	Ratio	11.917	0.958
Stolen Bases	107.4	130.3	**Strikeouts**	**979.1**	**589.1**
Batting Average	**.2686**	**.0260**	SO-per-9 Innings	4.647	1.447
Slugging Average	.3867	.0603	SO-to-BB Ratio	1.563	0.540
On-Base Average	.3358	.0334	HR-per-9 Innings	0.613	0.258
On-Base+Is. Power	.4538	.0692	Pitching Runs	48.5	102.2
Runs Created	653.3	413.8	Saves	30.4	49.3
Batter Runs	38.9	166.4	Cy Young Points	41.7	79.6
Babe Ruth Points	157.0	319.3	Led Lg., Pitching	4.0	7.8
Led Lg., Batting	2.4	6.8	Fielding Average	.9527	.0218
Fielding Average	.9669	.0245	Assists-per-Game	.9252	.5387
Assists-per-Game	1.092	1.059	Range Factor	1.188	0.622
DP-per-Game	.2381	.2370	Fielding Runs	1.7	15.5
Range Factor	4.136	2.018	Pennants Won	1.5	1.6
Fielding Runs	7.1	63.8	World Series Won	0.7	1.1
Led Lg., Fielding	5.3	7.0			
Gold-Glove Points	130.3	157.9			
Pennants Won	1.6	1.8			
World Series Won	0.8	1.2			

With two exceptions on the pitchers' side, each of the means for the full set of batters and hurlers is statistically inferior to those for the Hall-of-Fame members provided in chapter 5 (Table Thirteen); and, for some cumulative variables, the means among HOF members are twice as good as those posted by the subset as a whole. Only the mean number of saves (30.4 for the full data set, compared to 26.3 for Hall of Famers) and fielding average by pitchers (.9527 for all moundsmen, versus .9517 for Cooperstown hurlers) exceed the HOF averages. The higher number of saves among the full data set is predictable because only two of the 224 relief pitchers included in this scale are in Cooperstown, and most of the other 222 are from the expansion and free-agent eras during which the number of saves increased dramatically after changes in relief-pitching strategies. So their higher performance level for that statistic was bound to push the mean for the overall scale above the HOF average, to which only two modern relievers contributed. Similarly, the marginal superiority among pitchers' fielding averages as a whole may have resulted because a majority of HOF hurlers (35 out of 58, or about 60 percent) played during the first three of baseball's historical eras, before fielding reached its modern norms. In contrast, 524 of the pitchers measured (64 percent of the overall total) performed during the latter three of baseball's historical periods, when fielding stats were better.

Pitchers

Among the pitchers in Cooperstown through 2000, all but 13 rank among the top 58 hurlers in the overall ratings, reinforcing the relative statistical validity of 45 Hall-of-Fame memberships. The 13 who rank below the 58th ordinal include just one man, Ted Lyons, who was chosen by the BBWAA, with the other dozen being selections of the veterans committees. Six of the 13 are from the dead-ball era, three each are from the 19th-century and live-ball periods, and only one — expansion hurler Jim Bunning — played his entire career after World War Two. Both of the Hall's relief pitchers, Hoyt Wilhelm (31st at +1.06) and Rollie Fingers (tied for 33rd at +1.03), rank among the top 58. So all of the HOF moundsmen below that mark — the possible errors of selection — are starters, facilitating comparison of their credentials.

Table Forty provides the leaders among the rankings for pitchers in the overall scale, adjusted to remove periodic bias. Once again, the names of Hall-of-Fame members are boldfaced, men with no HOF votes at all are listed in italics, asterisks denote players active since 1994, and pound signs indicate hurlers who played the majority of their career before 1893.

The cutoff point for the top fifty-eight pitchers in Table Forty is a Total-Z average of +0.79. Five of the 13 HOF members below that mark — Waite Hoyt (+0.76), Rube Waddell (+0.72), Pud Galvin (+0.70) and Jim Bunning and Charley Bender (tied for 73rd, at +0.69) — have scores that fall within one-tenth of a standard deviation of that minimum. Two of those, Bunning (+1.55) and Galvin (+1.33), also have Core-Z averages that rank among the top 58 for that measure (live-baller Jack Quinn has the 58th-best Core-Z among the 813 pitchers in this scale, at +1.16). At this point, given their proximity to the cutoff and the fact that the numbers in Table Forty do not represent their final scores, it would be premature to label any of them as errors of selection.

Among the remaining eight (Ted Lyons, Vic Willis, Amos Rusie, Joe McGinnity, Jesse Haines, Jack Chesbro, Mickey Welch and Rube Marquard), one of them — Welch — is a de facto qualifier whose credentials merit close

Table Forty
Overall Pitcher Z-Score Leaders

Rank	Pitcher	Pos	Total Z Avg	Core Z Avg	Rank	Pitcher	Pos	Total Z Avg	Core Z Avg
1	Walter Johnson	sp	2.15	2.74	41	Kid Nichols	sp	0.98	1.44
	Cy Young	sp	2.15	2.73	42	Burleigh Grimes	sp	0.97	1.34
3	Christy Mathewson	sp	2.01	2.27	43	Ron Guidry	sp	0.94	1.22
4	Warren Spahn	sp	1.84	2.50	44	Bob Lemon	sp	0.91	1.14
5	Tom Seaver	sp	1.82	2.75	45	Jack Quinn	sp	0.89	1.16
6	Grover Alexander	sp	1.75	2.01	46	Catfish Hunter	sp	0.87	1.29
7	Whitey Ford	sp	1.67	1.92		*Dwight Gooden	sp	0.87	1.23
8	Lefty Grove	sp	1.64	2.19	48	Early Wynn	sp	0.85	1.78
9	Nolan Ryan	sp	1.63	3.25		Red Faber	sp	0.85	1.35
10	Steve Carlton	sp	1.61	2.83		#Hoss Radbourn	sp	0.85	1.22
11	Ed Walsh	sp	1.47	1.06		Stan Coveleski	sp	0.85	1.15
12	Carl Hubbell	sp	1.43	1.64	52	*Bret Saberhagen	sp	0.82	0.76
	Sandy Koufax	sp	1.43	1.46	53	Goose Gossage	rp	0.81	0.62
14	Jim Palmer	sp	1.36	1.93	54	Eppa Rixey	sp	0.80	1.34
15	Don Sutton	sp	1.34	2.58		Addie Joss	sp	0.80	0.58
16	Carl Mays	sp	1.30	1.13	56	Jim Kaat	sp	0.79	1.66
17	Gaylord Perry	sp	1.29	2.41		Jack Morris	sp	0.79	1.52
	Bert Blyleven	sp	1.29	2.35		Dizzy Dean	sp	0.79	0.89
19	Bob Feller	sp	1.28	1.95		*Tom Henke	rp	0.79	-0.10
20	#Tim Keefe	sp	1.24	1.64	60	Vida Blue	sp	0.78	1.39
21	Phil Niekro	sp	1.22	2.40		Dolf Luque	sp	0.78	0.78
22	Juan Marichal	sp	1.18	1.77		#Tommy Bond	sp	0.78	0.40
23	*Roger Clemens	sp	1.17	1.50	63	Billy Pierce	sp	0.76	1.27
24	Don Drysdale	sp	1.15	1.46		Waite Hoyt	sp	0.76	1.05
25	Bob Gibson	sp	1.13	2.01	65	Bob Shawkey	sp	0.75	1.01
	Dazzy Vance	sp	1.13	1.25		Fred Fitzsimmons	sp	0.75	0.90
27	Fergie Jenkins	sp	1.12	1.99		#Jim McCormick	sp	0.75	0.90
28	Robin Roberts	sp	1.10	1.79	68	Rube Waddell	sp	0.72	1.02
29	Tommy John	sp	1.09	1.86		Bucky Walters	sp	0.72	0.84
30	Herb Pennock	sp	1.07	1.12	t70	#Pud Galvin	sp	0.70	1.33
31	Hoyt Wilhelm	rp	1.06	0.85	t73	Jim Bunning	sp	0.69	1.55
32	Hal Newhouser	sp	1.05	1.29		Charley Bender	sp	0.69	0.93
33	Eddie Plank	sp	1.03	1.78	t94	Ted Lyons	sp	0.60	1.01
	*Dennis Eckersley	rp	1.03	1.19	t107	Vic Willis	sp	0.52	0.90
	Rollie Fingers	rp	1.03	0.40	t111	Amos Rusie	sp	0.51	0.67
36	Mordecai Brown	sp	1.01	1.15	t114	Joe McGinnity	sp	0.50	0.84
	Spud Chandler	sp	1.01	0.78	t139	Jesse Haines	sp	0.43	0.78
38	Red Ruffing	sp	1.00	1.40	t183	Jack Chesbro	sp	0.32	0.55
	#John Clarkson	sp	1.00	1.38	t194	#Mickey Welch	sp	0.29	1.20
40	Lefty Gomez	sp	0.99	1.10	t328	Rube Marquard	sp	0.04	0.38

scrutiny for that reason. Welch was the last of the 19th century's 300-game winners elected to the Shrine, tabbed by the VC in 1973. Mickey was the third pitcher ever to accomplish that feat: Pud Galvin did it first, in 1888; Welch and Tim Keefe both reached the milestone in 1890, but Keefe beat him to it (Hoss Radbourn, the first purely 19th-century hurler chosen for the Hall, in 1939, didn't get his 300th win until 1891). Mickey's career record was 307–210 (.594), all of it coming before the mound was moved in 1893.

Welch played in an era when most teams carried two hurlers who started and finished the vast majority of games, with most third or fourth pitchers (sometimes players from other positions) used mainly to provide additional rest. So, typically, the members of those two-man rotations earned most of a club's decisions in a season, and as a result, Welch's high victory and loss totals are as much a function of the way pitchers were used during his time as they are evidence of superior skill — and the same is true for every other hurler of the first couple decades of major-league play.

Welch and Tim Keefe both entered the Show in 1880. The two righthanders were NL rotation mates for eight seasons, with Troy (1880–82) and New York (1885–89). Although Mickey's career began more impressively (he won 69 games, for a .519 winning percentage with Troy, compared to Keefe's 41 wins and .410 ledger), he spent much of his big-league tenure playing Don Drysdale to Keefe's Sandy Koufax. During the five-year span they were teammates in New York, Keefe was 172–77 (.691) while Welch went 152–79 (.658). So, on average, Tim won four more games per season, while losing about the same number as Welch. A clue to the difference in their skills and importance to their team is evident in the club's two pennant-winning seasons, 1888 and 1889, when Keefe was a combined 63–25 (.716) while Welch went 53–31 (.531). New York won the lengthy postseason series against the American Association champions, St. Louis and Brooklyn, in both of those years. Keefe started seven of the 20 games played in both postseason series combined, winning three. Mickey started only three of the contests, losing two; and he was bypassed several times in favor of the less-renowned Cannonball Crane, who started six of the games despite a 72–96 (.429) record in his eight-year career.

Overall, Keefe's career record was 342–225 (.603), and he topped his circuit in a major statistical category 15 times in his career. Welch did it just once, leading the NL in winning percentage in 1885 (when he was 44–11, for a percentage of .800, easily Mickey's best season). But Keefe's statistical superiority should not demean Welch's HOF membership any more than Koufax's should diminish Drysdale's — provided that Mickey is qualified on his own merit. Unfortunately, Welch is the lowest-ranked HOF pitcher among the 19th-century hurlers in all three scales (15th in the era ratings, tied for 109th among starters, and no Total-Z above +0.45). So, while Mickey's career totals rank third among his era's moundsmen for innings pitched, and fourth for strikeouts, his 307 victories are his prime HOF credential. All those wins never bought him a single vote from the OTC1 or the BBWAA; and maybe the electors of the late 1930s knew something significant about his career that was forgotten — or merely overshadowed by the de facto standard — by 1973. Among the de-facto pitchers on the Cooperstown roster, Welch is — by far — the most probable error of selection.

Amos Rusie, whose career record was 246–174 (.586), is a different story. Rusie appeared in one postseason series, 1894, winning both of his starts as his second-place Giants swept the pennant-winning Orioles in four games. After a contract dispute with New York owner Andrew Freedman, Rusie sat out the 1896 season, at age 25, after four straight years in which he'd posted a minimum of 32 victories, a .612 winning percentage overall, and an average per-season record of 34–21—so his career mark might've been around 275–195 if he had played that year. Speculation aside, and despite the missing season, Amos still won 15 statistical titles in his 10-year career, including four leaderships in shutouts, two in earned run average, and one each in games won, games pitched, complete games and innings.

Rusie's awesome fastball also made him a five-time NL strikeout leader. He whiffed over 450 big-league batters before the age of twenty; his 4.62 strikeouts per-nine-innings were the most of any 19th-century hurler (one full K better than the 3.57 averaged by his era's seven other HOF pitchers); and, during 1890–92, Amos became the first moundsman ever to fan 300 or more hitters for three consecutive years (averaging 327 per season). The Nolan Ryan of his age, Rusie had the control problems typical of a power pitcher, which led to a career average of 4.07 walks per-nine-innings, the second-worst figure among his era's hurlers. But, he also posted the second-best hits-per-nine-innings ratio of the period, allowing just 8.08. In an era without batting helmets, the intimidation caused by Rusie's speed and wildness is cited by most authoritative sources as the primary reason why the mound was moved back 10 feet in 1893 — an impact that puts Amos in a class with Babe Ruth as one of the few men whose individual skills forever altered the game. With all that in mind, and given that Amos's score is also limited by the relative brevity of his career, there is ample evidence — both statistical and subjective — to justify Rusie's HOF membership, regardless of his low score in Table Forty.

Joe McGinnity also played in only 10 seasons, and like Rusie, he was very good in each. His worst year was 1908, his last in the majors, when he went 11–7 and (albeit retroactively) captured his third seasonal leadership in saves. Over his first nine seasons Joe never won less than 18 games, and he led his circuit in at least one major statistical category during each campaign (except for 1902, when he split his season evenly between Baltimore of the

AL and the New York Giants). He pitched his way to a 246–142 (.634) career mark, topped his circuit in victories five times, led his team in wins on seven occasions (three while pitching on the same staff with Christy Mathewson) and, in 1903-04, was a combined 66–28 (.702). He also led his league in games pitched six times, innings in four seasons (hence, his nickname, "Iron Man"), winning percentage and complete games twice each, and ERA and shutouts once apiece. In his only Fall Classic, the 1905 World Series made famous because all five games were shutouts (three of them by Mathewson), McGinnity faced fellow Hall of Famer Eddie Plank twice, losing Game Two by a score of 3–0 and then getting the Giants' other shutout in Game Four. His low score in Table Forty results mainly from his lack of longevity, and there is ample statistical evidence of his worthiness for Cooperstown.

As the only BBWAA-elected pitcher among the Hall's bottom eight, Ted Lyons also merits in-depth discussion. Lyons is tied for 94th with a Total-Z of +0.60. He played exclusively for the White Sox, and during his twenty-one seasons Chicago finished third three times, fourth once, and spent the rest of those years in the AL's second division, so he was the quintessential good pitcher for bad teams, with a career ledger of 260–230 (.531). Lyons won 20 games or more three times in his career, and led the circuit in victories twice. He won seven other statistical crowns, including two leaderships in complete games, shutouts and innings pitched, and one ERA title. He topped his club in victories on nine occasions, but, because the Sox were perennially so bad, it required just 10 wins to do that in two of those campaigns and only 14 in a couple others. Overall, he averaged a less-than-awe-inspiring 12–11 won-lost record per season. Lyons was never in a World Series, and in 11 opportunities beginning with 1933, he was chosen for only one All-Star squad (1939) but didn't get into the game, so he never accomplished anything historic in either of baseball's showcase events.

From 1939 to 1942 Chicago manager Jimmy Dykes used the popular hurler almost exclusively as a starter in Sunday games to boost attendance and prolong the aging pitcher's career. Lyons responded with a 52–30 record over those four seasons. His career mark prior to that time, then — during his supposed prime — was just 207–196 (.514), which doesn't merit a Cooperstown plaque any more than his low scores in all three scales. Nevertheless, he was elected by the BBWAA in 1955, with just 12 fewer votes than Dazzy Vance. In fact, the only live-ball hurlers to precede him into Cooperstown, were Lefty Grove, Carl Hubbell, Herb Pennock and Dizzy Dean. In sum, his longevity-driven HOF membership is a good thing only because it proves that the writers also make mistakes.

Statistically, the other four Hall of Famers who rank below Lyons — Jack Chesbro, Vic Willis, Rube Marquard and Jesse Haines — are also errors of selection. Chesbro posted a 196–132 (.600) record in an 11-season career in which he was 21–22 in the first two years, 24–35 over the last three, and 153–75 during the middle six. He is in the Hall mainly because he is the only man except Ed Walsh to win 40 games or more in a season (41–12 in 1904) during the 20th century. Willis won more games (249) during the same era as Chesbro and led his team in victories during seven of his 13 seasons — impressive when you note that he pitched on clubs that included Hall of Famer Kid Nichols, Babe Adams, Howie Camnitz, Bill Dinneen, Chick Fraser, Sam Leever and Deacon Phillipe. All of them received HOF votes at some point, but Willis never did until the VC tabbed him in 1995 — a definite injustice, given that (except for Nichols) none of them scored as high as Willis in any of the three scales, nor won as many as 200 games. But meriting support and deserving election are different things, and Vic's Total-Z doesn't crack the top 100 in Table Forty. Neither do those of Haines and Marquard, who posted average seasonal ledgers of 11–8 and 11–10, respectively, during their careers. Haines won more than 13 games only four times in his career, Marquard just five. Jesse is tied for 154th in the final rankings, with Rube at 336th (and a +0.03 Total-Z that is barely above average for the 813 pitchers measured).

Non-Pitchers

Of the 127 non-pitchers in Cooperstown through 2000, 44 of them post Total-Z averages in the overall scale that rank below the 127th ordinal for that measure. Six of those — Lou Boudreau, Roy Campanella, Mickey Cochrane, Rabbit Maranville, Jackie Robinson and Pie Traynor — were elected by the BBWAA, the other 38 by the veterans committees. The low-ranked Hall of Famers include 12 shortstops, seven catchers, seven center fielders, five second basemen, four third sackers, four right fielders, three left fielders and two first basemen. Twenty-two of them played most of their careers during the live-ball era; eight during the dead-ball period, eight during the postwar era and six during the 19th century. Table Forty-One presents the rankings for the overall scale, with all positional-defensive and periodic biases removed.

The cutoff point for the 127th ordinal in the overall scale for non-pitchers is a Total-Z average of +0.86. But with 1,484 players from eight different positions included among this subset, the non-pitcher portion of the 210-man Hall-of-Fame roster proposed in the next chapter will require a little more numerical leeway than the pitchers' portion to assure that each position and historical era are adequately represented. With that in mind, and given that — due to the effects of the other two scales, the final Z-Score averages may fluctuate considerably from the overall scores posted above — every current Hall

Table Forty-One
Overall Non-Pitcher Z-Score Leaders

Rank	Non-Pitcher	Pos	Total Z Avg	Core Z Avg	Rank	Non-Pitcher	Pos	Total Z Avg	Core Z Avg
1	Babe Ruth	rf	3.24	3.90	41	Roberto Clemente	rf	1.36	2.16
2	Ty Cobb	cf	3.02	3.46	42	Tony Perez	1b	1.34	2.18
3	Stan Musial	lf	2.83	3.49		#Jake Beckley	1b	1.34	1.84
4	Hank Aaron	rf	2.66	3.99	44	Darrell Evans	3b	1.33	1.67
5	Willie Mays	cf	2.60	3.66	45	Willie Stargell	lf	1.32	2.14
6	Tris Speaker	cf	2.57	2.67		Paul Waner	rf	1.32	1.89
7	Lou Gehrig	1b	2.52	3.11		George Davis	ss	1.32	1.52
8	Ted Williams	lf	2.43	3.24	48	#Bid McPhee	2b	1.31	0.85
9	Honus Wagner	ss	2.38	2.50	49	Billy Williams	lf	1.30	2.33
10	Eddie Collins	2b	2.27	2.21		Willie McCovey	1b	1.30	2.16
11	Mickey Mantle	cf	2.26	2.60		Goose Goslin	lf	1.30	2.00
12	Rogers Hornsby	2b	2.18	2.53		Dwight Evans	rf	1.30	1.95
13	Carl Yastrzemski	lf	2.14	2.99	53	Robin Yount	ss	1.29	2.09
14	Pete Rose	rf	2.13	2.68		Ron Santo	3b	1.29	1.69
15	Frank Robinson	rf	2.11	3.17		Frankie Frisch	2b	1.29	1.58
16	Jimmie Foxx	1b	2.10	2.94	56	Duke Snider	cf	1.27	1.90
17	Nap Lajoie	2b	2.07	2.30		Lou Brock	lf	1.27	1.67
18	Mike Schmidt	3b	2.05	2.31		Bill Dahlen	ss	1.27	1.22
19	#Cap Anson	1b	1.95	2.28	59	Dave Parker	rf	1.26	2.03
20	Mel Ott	rf	1.88	2.83	60	Rod Carew	1b	1.25	1.80
21	George Brett	3b	1.75	2.46		Fred Clarke	lf	1.25	1.62
22	#Dan Brouthers	1b	1.71	1.75		Keith Hernandez	1b	1.25	1.24
23	Reggie Jackson	rf	1.69	2.50	63	*Andre Dawson	rf	1.24	2.19
24	#Roger Connor	1b	1.66	1.74	64	*Paul Molitor	3b	1.19	1.67
25	Joe DiMaggio	cf	1.64	2.05		Enos Slaughter	rf	1.19	1.51
26	Charlie Gehringer	2b	1.63	1.99	66	Harmon Killebrew	1b	1.18	2.17
27	*Eddie Murray	1b	1.62	2.57	67	Harry Heilmann	rf	1.16	1.90
	Yogi Berra	c	1.62	1.74		Rusty Staub	rf	1.16	1.85
29	Al Kaline	rf	1.59	2.59		Jesse Burkett	lf	1.16	1.74
30	Joe Morgan	2b	1.56	1.74	70	Joe Kelley	lf	1.15	1.34
31	Ed Delahanty	lf	1.55	2.00	71	Jim Rice	lf	1.13	2.06
32	*Rickey Henderson	lf	1.51	1.46	72	George Sisler	1b	1.12	1.56
33	*Dave Winfield	rf	1.49	2.75		Mickey Vernon	1b	1.12	1.42
34	Sam Crawford	rf	1.48	1.91	74	Graig Nettles	3b	1.11	1.52
35	Al Simmons	lf	1.47	2.45		Gil Hodges	1b	1.11	1.48
36	Ernie Banks	1b	1.46	2.38		Bill Dickey	c	1.11	1.13
37	Eddie Mathews	3b	1.42	2.19	77	Zach Wheat	lf	1.10	1.81
38	Brooks Robinson	3b	1.40	1.71		Hank Greenberg	1b	1.10	1.39
	Max Carey	cf	1.40	1.26		Bill Terry	1b	1.10	1.34
40	Johnny Mize	1b	1.38	1.62	80	*Cal Ripken, Jr.	ss	1.09	1.51

(cont.)

Rank	Non-Pitcher	Pos	Total Z Avg	Core Z Avg	Rank	Non-Pitcher	Pos	Total Z Avg	Core Z Avg
	Billy Hamilton	cf	1.09	1.37	146	Rabbit Maranville	ss	0.79	0.54
	*Wade Boggs	3b	1.09	1.37	t147	Ralph Kiner	lf	0.78	1.16
83	Vada Pinson	cf	1.08	1.77		Mickey Cochrane	c	0.78	0.76
	Hugh Duffy	lf	1.08	1.63	t151	Arky Vaughan	ss	0.77	0.96
	Richie Ashburn	cf	1.08	0.99		Billy Herman	2b	0.77	0.78
86	Steve Garvey	1b	1.06	1.72	t155	Earl Averill	cf	0.76	1.39
87	Willie Keeler	rf	1.05	1.79	t160	Bobby Wallace	ss	0.75	0.87
	Joe Cronin	ss	1.05	1.35	t164	#Jim O'Rourke	cf	0.74	1.19
89	Carlton Fisk	c	1.04	1.75		Jimmy Collins	3b	0.74	0.95
90	Reggie Smith	rf	1.03	1.50		#Buck Ewing	c	0.74	0.73
91	*Ozzie Smith	ss	1.02	0.63	t175	Heinie Manush	lf	0.71	1.42
92	Joe Medwick	lf	1.01	1.61		Jackie Robinson	2b	0.71	0.79
	#Harry Stovey	lf	1.01	0.77	t184	Edd Roush	cf	0.69	1.02
94	Orlando Cepeda	1b	1.00	1.97	t190	Joe Sewell	ss	0.68	0.92
	Al Oliver	cf	1.00	1.76	193	Hughie Jennings	ss	0.67	0.56
	Jim Bottomley	1b	1.00	1.50	t194	Tony Lazzeri	2b	0.66	0.90
	#Sam Thompson	rf	1.00	1.47	t206	Larry Doby	cf	0.62	0.94
98	Sam Rice	rf	0.99	1.41	t209	Phil Rizzuto	ss	0.61	0.18
	Jack Clark	rf	0.99	1.33	t226	Elmer Flick	rf	0.58	0.81
	Gary Carter	c	0.99	1.31		Lou Boudreau	ss	0.58	0.39
	Sherry Magee	lf	0.99	1.16	t233	George Kelly	1b	0.56	0.67
	*Tim Raines	lf	0.99	1.09	t243	Dave Bancroft	ss	0.54	0.25
103	Johnny Bench	c	0.97	1.65	t249	George Kell	3b	0.53	0.83
	Dale Murphy	cf	0.97	1.61	t254	Hack Wilson	cf	0.52	0.90
	Chuck Klein	rf	0.97	1.54		Earle Combs	cf	0.52	0.71
	*Ryne Sandberg	2b	0.97	1.27		Roy Campanella	c	0.52	0.52
	Luke Appling	ss	0.97	1.18	t262	#Monte Ward	ss	0.49	0.71
108	*Jimmy Ryan*	cf	0.96	1.51	t279	Joe Tinker	ss	0.46	0.28
	Frank Baker	3b	0.96	0.98	t285	Travis Jackson	ss	0.45	0.55
	Nellie Fox	2b	0.96	0.96	t327	Lloyd Waner	cf	0.38	0.75
111	Norm Cash	1b	0.95	1.41		Chick Hafey	lf	0.38	0.64
	Harry Hooper	rf	0.95	1.12	t345	Johnny Evers	2b	0.36	0.23
	Luis Aparicio	ss	0.95	0.98	t355	Frank Chance	1b	0.35	0.30
t114	Bobby Doerr	2b	0.92	1.11	t397	Ross Youngs	rf	0.27	0.32
	Gabby Hartnett	c	0.92	1.01	t412	Ernie Lombardi	c	0.25	0.70
t124	Kiki Cuyler	rf	0.87	1.26	t450	#Tommy McCarthy	rf	0.20	0.40
t130	Pie Traynor	3b	0.85	1.20		Ray Schalk	c	0.20	-0.14
t138	Red Schoendienst	2b	0.81	0.96	t474	Fred Lindstrom	3b	0.16	0.58
t143	#King Kelly	rf	0.80	0.98		Roger Bresnahan	c	0.16	0.08
	Pee Wee Reese	ss	0.80	0.93	t485	Rick Ferrell	c	0.15	0.05

of Famer within 0.20 of the 127th ordinal will be given the benefit of a doubt for now (i.e., all of the men listed ahead of Larry Doby in the second half of Table Forty-One).

That leaves twenty-four Hall-of-Fame non-pitchers as potential errors of selection. They include Larry Doby, Phil Rizzuto, Elmer Flick, Lou Boudreau, George Kelly, Dave Bancroft, George Kell, Hack Wilson, Earle Combs, Roy Campanella, Monte Ward, Joe Tinker, Travis Jackson, Lloyd Waner, Chick Hafey, Johnny Evers, Frank Chance, Ross Youngs, Ernie Lombardi, Tommy McCarthy, Ray Schalk, Fred Lindstrom, Roger Bresnahan and Rick Ferrell.

In fairness, the careers of Larry Doby (+0.62) and Roy Campanella (+0.52) involved circumstances which argue against their identification as errors of selection. Because of the timing of their major-league entries, it's impossible to discuss the statistics of either player without considering the effects of baseball's segregation. Neither may have been forced to endure as much as Jackie Robinson, but Doby's role as the American League's first African American unavoidably imposed similar, if less-publicized pressures upon a man who, at 23, was less mature than Robinson (28) when the latter joined the Dodgers. Campanella, who entered the majors within a year of both of their debuts, also suffered his share of racial backlash. Though he did not join the Dodgers until he was 26; the numbers he put up in the decade before his career-ending auto accident were far more impressive than Thurman Munson's, whose tenure behind the plate was one year longer before it also ended in tragedy. There is simply no justification for criticizing Campanella's Cooperstown plaque. Doby's statistical credentials are much more arguable, but the role he played mitigates any criticism of them at this point.

No doubt, Monte Ward (+0.49) would rank higher in Table Forty-One if he hadn't switched from pitching to position play a third of the way through his career, as the change limited his scores in every scale. He went 47–19 as a hurler in 1879; he never had a won-lost record below .500 in six full seasons and part of a seventh as a moundsman; and, although his stats were not included among the pitching data sets, his Total-Z average as a hurler in the overall scale is +0.63, better than his average as a non-pitcher, and good enough to tie Jerry Koosman for 91st place. Given all that, he is the only man in the data set except Babe Ruth who compiled impressive career stats as a hurler and a position player (Ruth's Total-Z for Table Forty would be +0.28). As a result, his HOF election should not be criticized for his low scores in any measurement.

Four catchers — Roger Bresnahan, Ray Schalk, Ernie Lombardi and Rick Ferrell — are among the six Hall of Famers with the lowest scores in Table Forty-One. Their poor numbers, however, are attributable in part to the offensive disadvantages suffered as a result of the defensive spectrum by players at their position. With only a dozen backstops in the Hall through 2000, the position is about 10 men shy of proportional representation, and it seems axiomatic that each historical era should have at least one man from each position on the HOF roster. As live-ballers, Lombardi and Ferrell are from an era that has three other catchers in Cooperstown (Mickey Cochrane, Bill Dickey and Gabby Hartnett). But if both Bresnahan and Schalk are deemed errors of selection, then the dead-ball period has no Hall-of-Fame backstop. So it may be unfair to dismiss all four of their memberships, and—despite their statistical failings—one or two of them may be worthy by default.

As explained in chapter 8, the positional rankings for catchers are probably the best measure of their relative HOF credentials. Bresnahan ranks highest in that scale (+1.07, tied for 16th), just ahead of Lombardi (18th at +1.05, but with a Core average of +1.93 that is the best of the four) and Schalk (+0.95, tied for 19th), with Ferrell trailing (+0.80, 25th).

There is no doubt that, statistically, Ferrell's election was an error. He is often cited as one of the Hall's fielding-based selections but the poor HOF-predictive rates for defensive stats as a whole demonstrate that such selections are nonexsistent. Also, it's hard to defend him as a defensive choice when (as revealed in chapter 8) his fielding numbers fail to rank among the 10 best at his position. Offensively, Rick's career live-ball-era batting average (.281) was only one point better than that of his brother, pitcher Wes Ferrell, and the latter also hit ten more career homers (38-to-28) in just 1176 at-bats than Rick did in 6028.

With regard to the dead-ball backstops, Bresnahan was the best hitter, finishing with 26 career home runs and a .279 batting average, compared to Schalk's 11 homers and .253 (the latter two numbers being the worst among all Cooperstown non-pitchers). But Bresnahan's offensive edge is compromised by the fact he played 29 percent of his defensive games at other positions (primarily the outfield) where his career numbers generate Total-Z averages unworthy of mention in the same sentence as Cooperstown. Also, despite the fact that John McGraw and Connie Mack both rated Bresnahan as the best-fielding backstop they ever saw, Schalk's defensive stats as a whole are among the best ever at his position and, through 1999, he still held the major-league record for career double players by a catcher (226) and was second in career assists (1811, the most by any backstop after 1900). Bresnahan's other credential doesn't hold up, either: he first donned shin guards early in the 1907 season and is properly credited for having popularized their use, but the best available research identifies Mike Kahoe as the first major-leaguer to wear them, in 1902—so rationalizing Roger's HOF status on that basis is especially lame.

In truth, the dead-ball catcher with the best statistical credentials for Cooperstown is Wally Schang, who ranks 13th in chapter 8 (+1.12). Schang's offensive stats are superior to those of Bresnahan and Schalk in almost every category, and, although Wally is rarely mentioned among the best defensive catchers in history, he was a backstop for seven pennant winners with four different AL clubs (three more flags than Bresnahan and Schalk, combined), so he obviously knew how to handle a pitching staff with championship skill. But, although Schang's career spanned a period almost identical to Schalk's (recall chapter 1, Table Three), a majority of Schang's at-bats came in the live-ball era, making it hard to tag him as a true dead-ball player.

Complicating all of this is Lombardi, whose credentials are probably more one-dimensional than anyone else ever elected to the Hall. One of the slowest runners in baseball history, legend has it that many of Ernie's singles would have been doubles for any player of average speed, and he was never regarded as a good fielder. So Ernie's qualifications rest solely on his hitting: his career BA was .306; he topped .300 on ten occasions; and he is the only catcher ever to win two batting championships (the NL titles of 1935 and 1943).

Copping two batting crowns is not that unique: more than forty men have won that many or more since 1876, and 11 of them who were eligible for Cooperstown through 2000 have not been elected. But a hitting title by a catcher is something special. The only other backstop ever to do it was Cincinnati's Bubbles Hargrave in 1926. The uniqueness of the feat is even more evident when you note that, in the 235 separate league seasons played during 1876–1999, only 39 times out of 1185 opportunities did a catcher place among the top five hitters in his league. Eight backstops have done that twice (including Hall of Famers Ewing, Cochrane, Hartnett and Campanella, plus Jack Clements, Chief Meyers, Spud Davis and Ted Simmons), but only Lombardi and Mike Piazza have achieved that distinction four times. With all of that in mind, and given that Bresnahan's numbers are compromised by his outfield duty (and weak for that position), Lombardi and Schalk are the two most defensible selections among the four.

Third base is the other under-represented position at Cooperstown, and two of its denizens — Fred Lindstrom and George Kell — are among the suspect two-dozen in Table Forty-One. As a rookie in the 1924 World Series, Lindstrom achieved his two greatest claims to fame without doing much more than showing up. When Fred came to the plate as New York's leadoff hitter in Game One, he became the youngest man ever to appear in a World Series to date, aged 18 years, 10 months and 13 days. Then, in the 12th inning of Game Seven, Washington's Earl McNeely hit a grounder that struck a pebble in front of Lindstrom, bounced over his head and brought home Muddy Ruel with the Series-winning run. As indicated by Fred's low scores in all three scales, he did almost as little to get into Cooperstown, and it's possible that his election was a payback for a slight he experienced in 1932. When John McGraw retired as Giants skipper that year, Bill Terry was named his successor, although Lindstrom claimed he'd been promised the job. Incensed, Fred demanded to be traded; Terry obliged, shipping him to Pittsburgh. Fred was elected to the Hall by the VC in 1976, the last year that Terry was on the panel — perhaps Bill's ultimate apology.

Kell is often cited as the best player to emerge from the pool of replacement talent used during World War Two, and he and Red Schoendienst are the only Hall of Famers whose careers began during the seasons that marked the height of the wartime player shortage (1943–45). George ranks 26th in the third-base ratings in chapter 9, compared to 65th for Lindstrom, so Kell's credentials are far more solid and varied than Fred's, highlighted by a batting title in 1949 and seven different fielding leaderships (he also was named to 10 All-Star squads, compared to none for Lindstrom). But both men played in eras that already have better-

Fred Lindstrom's Total-Z averages in each of the scales mark him as one of the worst Hall-of-Fame selections ever. It's possible that his election by the Veterans Committee in 1976 was panel member Bill Terry's belated apology for getting the Giants managerial job in 1932, when Lindstrom expected it. (*The Sporting News*).

qualified representatives at their position among the Cooperstown roster (Pie Traynor and Eddie Mathews), and other third sackers ahead of them in the final ratings (eight other live-ball third basemen rank ahead of Lindstrom, and Kell's final score is topped by both Bob Elliott and Eddie Yost). There also are many more recent third sackers with much better credentials, so there's no harm in acknowledging that both men are errors of selection. Lindstrom's final score (+0.14, tied for 490th) is the worst of any HOF non-pitcher, placing him in the company of Jesse Haines and Rube Marquard as Cooperstown's least-qualified members.

Left fielder Chick Hafey, whose scores in all three scales so far offer no evidence of HOF credentials, may have benefitted from circumstances similar to the possible Terry-Lindstrom payback noted earlier. Throughout his big-league tenure, Hafey was plagued by a chronic sinus condition that required several surgeries and diminished his vision in an inconsistent fashion that forced him to switch among three sets of eyeglasses with vary-ing prescriptions. He was also hampered by a nearly as chronic over-estima-tion of his importance to the Cardinals, which prompted him to hold out after both of the 1930 and 1931 seasons and led Branch Rickey to trade Chick to the Reds during the second holdout. Hafey won the senior circuit's bat-ting crown in 1931, leading St. Louis to a pennant, but he finished only fifth in the BBWAA's first-ever MVP voting while teammate Frankie Frisch won the honor (overall, Chick's stats were marginally better that year). After his career was over, Hafey received votes on 12 different Hall-of-Fame ballots, but never more than the 29 — for 12.5-percent support — he got in 1962. In that light, one might conclude that Hafey's election to Cooperstown while Frisch served on the VC was the latter's attempt to make amends for winning the MVP and (no doubt) depriving Hafey of that contract-bargaining lever-age.

Haines, Marquard, Lindstrom and Hafey all were chosen by the VC dur-ing the years 1970–76, as was Mickey Welch, the Hall's most probable de facto error of selection. As noted in chapter 2, several of the panel's other choices during that period — notably Dave Bancroft, George Kelly and Ross Youngs — are also among the men most often cited as evidence of Cooperstown's slide toward mediocrity. All of those latter three are also among the lowest-scor-ing players in Table Forty-One and were chosen while former teammates Frankie Frisch or Bill Terry, or both, were VC members. In that light, the selections from that era deserve special attention.

A total of seven Hall of Famers were Veterans Committee members dur-ing the period 1967–76, spanning the time of Frisch's appointment to the date that Terry stepped down. They included Charlie Gehringer (who served on the VC during 1953–90), Joe Cronin (1961–84), Ted Williams (appointed in 1966), Frisch (1967–72), Terry (1971–76), Waite Hoyt (1971–76) and Stan Musial (1973–). During that decade, the VC chose 23 new Cooperstown members cited as players — Lloyd Waner (1967), Kiki Cuyler and Goose Goslin (1968), Stan Coveleski and Hoyt (1969), Earle Combs and Haines (1970), Jake Beckley, Harry Hooper, Joe Kelley, Bancroft, Hafey and Mar-quard (1971), Lefty Gomez and Ross Youngs (1972), Kelly and Welch (1973), Jim Bottomley and Sam Thompson (1974), Earl Averill and Billy Herman (1975), and Roger Connor and Lindstrom (1976). Based on the scores in the first three scales alone, only pitchers Gomez and Coveleski, plus position players Connor, Beckley, Goslin and Thompson have relatively unassailable statistical credentials. But by the same standard, 10 of the other choices — Waner, Combs, Haines, Bancroft, Hafey, Marquard, Youngs, Kelly, Welch and Lindstrom — are clearcut errors of selection, and they make up half of the men identifiable as such at this point in the ratings.

Two things seem clear from all this: (1) there should probably be a rule preventing any two (or more) former teammates from serving on the Veterans Committee at the same time; and (2) all VC members should definitely be prohibited from voting for anyone they ever played with on the same ball club. If they had existed in the 1967–76 period, such regulations might have prevented the elections of bogus Hall of Famers like Hafey, Haines, Lindstrom *et al.*

Through 2000, 10 sets of brothers had received votes for the Hall: Matty, Felipe and Jesus Alou; Ken and Clete Boyer; Walker and Mort Cooper; Joe and Dom DiMaggio (but not Vince); Rick and Wes Ferrell; Phil and Joe Niekro; Joe and Luke Sewell; Will and Deacon White; George and Harry Wright; plus Paul "Big Poison" and Lloyd "Little Poison" Waner. Three of those men were elected by the scribes (Joe DiMaggio, Phil Niekro and Paul Waner), and five more by the veterans committees (Joe Sewell, Rick Ferrell, Lloyd Waner and the Wright brothers, the latter of whom were cited as contributors), making the two poisons the only siblings enshrined as players.

Lloyd Waner was one of the best defensive center fielders of his time, perhaps ever; and he was no slouch at the plate (a lifetime batting average of .316). He put up Hall-of-Fame numbers for a leadoff hitter during his first six seasons, averaging 196 hits, 100 runs scored and .340 per year. But his production declined considerably over the dozen other full and partial seasons of his career. There's no doubt that his brother belongs in Cooperstown, however, and if there absolutely must be two siblings in the Hall, the Waners may be the best qualified pair. But the younger Waner is still an error of selection.

So are the other three Frisch-Terry cronies, George Kelly, Ross Youngs and Dave Bancroft. John McGraw once claimed that Kelly had made more key hits than any other player he'd ever managed. But George's .297 batting average is unimpressive in the context of his time, and his per-season averages — 99 hits, eight homers, 46 runs scored and 57 RBI — are well below expectations for a Live-Ball first baseman. Youngs had a 10-year career that was contemporary with Kelly's prime but was shortened by his affliction with Bright's disease, a kidney ailment that caused his death in 1927, at age 30. Ross hit .322 for his career and reached base in almost 40-percent of his plate appearances. He also had one of the National League's best right-field arms of his era, leading the circuit in outfield assists on three occasions and throwing out 20 or more baserunners six times. On the whole, Youngs was probably a better all-around player than Kelly, but — crediting the tragedy of his shortened career — none of that compensates for his low scores in all three scales, which are in no way comparable to those of Addie Joss. There is no doubt that Bancroft possessed a Hall-of-Fame glove: his Z-average for isolated defense (+1.41) is the third-best among all shortstops in the data set, and through 1999, he still ranked among the top ten men at his position in more than a dozen of the career- and seasonal-high fielding leaderships listed in *Total Baseball*. But Dave was a much weaker hitter than Kelly or Youngs, and his credentials are plausible only if you believe that the Hall should make allowances to include weak-hitting but exceptional fielding players from key spots along the defensive spectrum. If not, he's another error of selection whose presence at Cooperstown opens the doors for many candidates whose all-around skills are no better than above-average.

In addition to Bancroft, there are four other shortstops among the low-rated two-dozen in Table Forty-One. One of them, Travis Jackson, could have been a Frisch-Terry crony too (because he also played for the Giants during the 1920s, after Bancroft was traded to Boston) but wasn't elected by the VC until 1982 — after Frankie and Bill were no longer on the panel. Jackson had more power than Bancroft (135 career homers to Dave's 32), hit for higher average (.291) and was regarded as one of the consummate bunters of his time. Because most men's credentials are judged mainly on their hitting, Jackson's election is not criticized as often as Bancroft's. But Dave's scores exceed those of Travis in all three scales, and Bancroft (+0.56, 227th) ranks above Jackson (+0.47, 271st) in the final ratings. Like his Giants predecessor, then, Jackson is an error of selection, though relative to all other shortstops, Bancroft's fielding was far more superior than Jackson's above-average offense.

Shortstops Lou Boudreau and Phil Rizzuto won American League MVPs, Boudreau in 1948, Rizzuto two years later. After their playing days, they also had substantial careers as color commentators. Although a majority of Boudreau's at-bats came before the end of World War Two, imposing his identification as a live-ball player (a very marginal call), the two were essentially contemporaries — Lou's career spanned 1938–52, Phil's 1941–56 — at a time when the AL featured a third HOF shortstop (Luke Appling, 1930–50) and two others (Vern Stephens, 1941–55, and Johnny Pesky, 1942–54) with arguable credentials. Appling (1964) and Boudreau (1970) were elected by the scribes; Rizzuto (1994), by the VC. Pesky got only one HOF vote (1960); and, as noted in the previous chapter, Stephens didn't even get that many.

During the 1940s, Boudreau never got as much attention for his fielding as did National Leaguer Marty Marion. But as the chapter 9 numbers indicate, on the whole Boudreau's defensive stats rank as fourth-best among all the shortstops measured, and better than Marion's. Boudreau also won a batting title in 1944 (.327) and topped .300 on three other occasions. But the sum of all of his numbers indicates he's a clearcut error of selection. Rizzuto hit .300 or better only twice in his career, but his relative scores are consistently better than Boudreau's in each of the first three scales, and his final tally (+0.69, tied for 184th) is also better than Boudreau's (+0.61, t204th).

It's instructive, however, that Rizzuto failed to make an All-Star team between the end of World War Two and 1950, during his presumed prime. He was chosen for the 1942 squad, but Boudreau played the entire game, and Rizzuto was not even used by his Yankee manager Joe McCarthy as a pinch hitter. In the military during 1943–45, Rizzuto never made another All-Star squad until 1950, despite the fact that he was runner-up for the MVP in 1949. Rizzuto's four straight All-Star appearances during 1950–53 (including his only two starts) all came — essentially — after Appling had retired, Boudreau had passed his prime, and Stephens and Pesky were hobbled by chronic injuries. And Stephens (+0.74, tied for 163rd) tops Rizzuto in the final standings. In all, 25 other Hall of Famers rank below the Yankee favorite in the final ratings, so he's not the worst player in Cooperstown. But holy cow, he's still an error of selection.

Joe Tinker, the fourth low-rated shortstop, is really part of a Cooperstown trifecta that also includes his double-play mates Johnny Evers and Frank Chance. Tinker apparently was fixated on money. As a Cub, he sat out part of the 1909 season while seeking a 67 percent raise, and later on, when Cincinnati tried to sell him to the Dodgers for $25,000, he demanded 40 percent of the sale price for himself, then jumped to the Federal League's Chicago Whales when it wasn't forthcoming. Evers was a smart player, but had several on-field fist fights with teammates, earned the nickname "Crab" early in his career (along, no doubt, with other monikers less fit to print), and was one of the most combative personalities in major-league history — a dead-ball Billy Martin, sans the marshmallow salesman and booze. All of that probably explains why, although they were the Cubs' keystone combo for 12 seasons beginning in 1902, a dispute over failure to share a taxi ride in 1905 prompted them not speak to each other for 33 years. If not for Monte Ward, whose low score as a shortstop derives in part from his seven-year stint as a pitcher, Evers and Tinker would be the lowest-ranked Hall of Famers at their respective positions in the chapter 8–9 ratings. Their scores on all three scales are ample evidence that neither belongs in Cooperstown.

As noted in chapter 6, several dead-ball first sackers are better qualified for Cooperstown than Frank Chance, and his HOF status can be justified — if at all — only by combining his service as player and manager. As a player, Chance batted .296, with four seasons above .300, but his most distinctive stats — at least for his position — are his 401 career stolen bases and two seasonal theft titles, which are atypical for first basemen. As a skipper, Chance posted a 946–648 ledger for a .593 winning percentage, won four pennants in 11 seasons, was the victor in two World Series, and set the single-season record for games won (116 in 1906). In a helmetless era, Chance took one on the noggin' for his team more than once too often, as his frequent beanings led to headaches, blood clots that required surgery, a loss of hearing and — somehow — caused his voice to acquire a high-pitched whine that grated on the nerves of many of his players during his service as a manager. So, given Evers' personality, Chance's voice probably bothered the second baseman too; but it's safe to assume that Johnny never communicated his irritation to Tinker — not after 1905, anyway. All the same, Chance's citation as a first baseman is another HOF error.

The low-rated Hall of Famers in Table Forty-One include two regulars from the 1927 Yankees, center fielder Earle Combs and second baseman Tony Lazzeri; and their scores give reason to doubt that either man would be in Cooperstown without his connection with that team. Combs spent all 12 of his seasons with New York (1924–35), Lazzeri also a dozen years (1926–37, before moving to the NL for three seasons). A leadoff hitter, Combs scored no fewer than 113 runs for eight consecutive seasons (1925–32), and it's easy to dismiss him as the beneficiary of Murderers' Row (Babe Ruth, Lou Gehrig, Bob Meusel and Lazzeri). But, Earle's career marks for batting (.325) and on-base average (.397) also offer ample evidence that those sluggers' stats benefitted just as much from his setting the table.

Lazzeri preceded Frank Crosetti and Joe DiMaggio on the Yankee roster, becoming the first Italian-American to gain wide popularity in New York. Tony wasn't much as a second baseman: he led the AL in errors at his position three times and his only other fielding title was a leadership in double plays in 1929. His isolated score for defense (-0.15) ranks 99th among the 165 second basemen measured, the worst of any Hall of Famer at his position. Lazzeri's .292 batting average wasn't impressive for his era, either; and he never drove in more than 121 runs in a season (Ruth and Gehrig both topped that total 10 times, Meusel twice). But Lazzeri topped 100 RBI seven times in his career, a total matched by only one other Hall of Famer at his position (Charlie Gehringer), and it's obvious that Ruth and Gehrig's runs-scored totals benefitted from having Tony bat behind them.

Combs didn't get tabbed by the VC until 1970, and Lazzeri wasn't elected by the panel until 1991, facts which — given the '27 Bronx Bombers' reputation as the greatest team ever — contradict those who argue that the BBWAA has a pro–Yankee bias. Their scores in all three scales indicate that Combs and Lazzeri are errors of selection, but — if that's true — it's only by a slim margin.

In his debut season with Boston's Union Association franchise of 1884, Tommy McCarthy batted .215, with a slugging average of .244 and an on-base percentage of .237; and to prove that was no fluke, he also lost all seven of his pitching decisions. Over the next three years, McCarthy was a model of consistency, averaging .184 for those seasons combined, with a high of .186 in 1887 and a low of .182 in 1885, giving every indication that he was the neolithic prototype for John Vukovich. At that point, most players' careers would be over, for cause. But manager Charlie Comiskey saw something in

Tommy, and signed him for St. Louis, where he nabbed his only statistical title in 13 seasons, leading the AA in stolen bases in 1890. From there McCarthy went to Boston for four years, joining fellow Hall of Famer Hugh Duffy in an outfield duo dubbed "The Heavenly Twins." Over Tommy's last nine seasons he batted .301, giving him a career average of .292 on 1496 hits. McCarthy's HOF membership has been rationalized on the basis of his supposed innovations, as he is said to have popularized sign stealing, runner-to-batter signals, the hit-and-run play, fake bunts and intentionally juggling or trapping fly balls to lure baserunners into a force out or possible double play. But his final ranking is 427th, and there are more than four-dozen non-pitchers from his era ahead of him. He is, by far, the worst 19th-century selection on the HOF roster.

Elmer Flick's career spanned 1898–1910, during which he posted batting (.313), slugging (.445) and on-base averages (.389) that were very good for the dead-ball era and might have been higher absent a stomach ailment that impaired his play over his last three seasons. Elmer topped his circuit in batting, slugging, runs scored and RBI once apiece, led his league in doubles three times, and twice in stolen bases. Flick is little remembered now (and often lightly regarded when he is), but the Tigers thought enough of him after the 1907 season (his last good year) to offer 20-year-old, first-time batting champ Ty Cobb for the 31-year-old Flick in a straight-up trade which might have put Cobb and Joe Jackson in the same outfield during 1911–15. But Cleveland owner Charles Somers nixed the deal, and Elmer quickly faded. Flick was added to the HOF roster by the VC in 1963. But there are a half-dozen unenshrined outfielders from his era with equal or better statistical credentials, and that confirms the error of his selection.

Finally, there is Hack Wilson, a creature from the *X Files*, if there ever was one. At five-foot-six, Wilson carried a playing weight that is variously reported as 190–210 pounds. Because of some genetic malfeasance or another, Hack somehow combined an 18-inch collar with size-six shoes. In the few full-body photos we seej187

, his torso looks like a sequoia stump, his arms appear too short, and his hands are tiny. In some photos, his large head and bloated cheeks make him resemble the pumpkin that was left in the patch on Halloween morning because no one had a truck big enough to haul it away.

Wilson spent three seasons with John McGraw's Giants, batting a combined .276, with 16 homers and 87 RBI. When New York omitted his name from its reserve list in 1925, Hack was claimed by the Cubs. The acquisition brought together Wilson and manager Joe McCarthy, who, like Hack, enjoyed his distilled spirits. Over the next five years, with little or no sleep, Hack batted .331 on 914 hits, with 177 homers, 586 runs scored and 707 RBI, for averages of 183 safeties, 35 dingers, 117 runs scored and 141 RBI per season. In

Hack Wilson's short-lived stardom, highlighted by the majors' single-season RBI record, got him elected to Cooperstown by the VC in 1979 — a choice that offends many Hall-of-Fame purists (*The Sporting News*).

the last of those years, 1930, when the ball was at its all-time liveliest and the National League batted .303 as a circuit (including pitchers), Wilson set a still-existent major-league record with 190 RBI and an NL mark of 56 homers that stood until Mark McGwire and Sammy Sosa came along.

But McCarthy then jumped to the Yankees, replaced as Cubs skipper by Rogers Hornsby. The latter refused to attend movies for fear of weakening his batting eye (which one it was, ot why he couldn't watch Wallace Beery with the other is uncertain). Neither would Hornsby tolerate Wilson's drinking. Hack's numbers declined, and he was traded to Brooklyn after a dismal 1931. Wilson rebounded in 1932, hitting 23 home runs, driving in 123 runners and batting .297. But, although McCarthy was just across town, Hack was never happy after he left Chicago, and his 12-year career ended with two more subpar years in which he hit a combined .259, with only 15 homers and 84 RBI.

Wilson received 550 Hall-of-Fame votes spread over 16 ballots from 1937 to 1962, an average of 34 per try. He topped out at 94 votes in 1958, but his best support-percentage was 38.3 on 74 votes in 1956. Shortly after Hack became eligible for the VC process, Frankie Frisch was added to the panel, and when Frisch wasn't campaigning for his cronies, he spent much of his energy blocking Wilson's candidacy. Frisch died in 1973, but Hack wasn't elected to Cooperstown until 1979, after Bill Terry and Waite Hoyt had also left and the panel included Stan Musial, Roy Campanella, Ted Williams, Birdie Tebbetts, Burleigh Grimes and Al Lopez (Wilson's teammate at Brooklyn during his worst seasons, 1932–34). Among all HOF non-pitchers, there is no one whose peak performance was as brief and, apparently, as manager- and park-dependent.

Wilson's credentials are much like those of Roger Maris, except that Hack never won the MVP: there was no official award in 1930, when the Cardinals won the pennant; and, although the Cubs finished second, two games back, *The Sporting News'* version went — ironically — to Bill Terry, who batted .401. So if Maris belongs in Cooperstown, Wilson would seem to, as well. Based on his career numbers, Wilson is an error of selection, but his membership does not and cannot demean a Hall-of-Fame roster that also includes Fred Lindstrom, Chick Hafey, Rube Marquard and Jesse Haines.

CHAPTER 11

The Cooperstown Baseline

The previous three chapters presented rankings based on comparisons of individual career performance to the means established by contemporaries, by men at a given position and by pitchers and non-pitchers as a whole. Some men's scores were relatively consistent in each of those scales, but others fluctuated considerably, and they all change some, depending on their variance from the different averages for each group and the effects of normalization to remove positional and periodic biases.

It remains to put all of those scores in context, providing an ordered ranking that estimates the overall value of each player's complete career performance relative to every other man eligible for Hall-of-Fame election through the 2000 voting. The Total-Z Scores reported here reflect each man's *cumulative* average for all three scales — that is, not just the mean value for each of the three scores reported earlier, but the average Z score for each of the 90 non-pitcher variables in all three scales combined, or the mean for all of the 82 statistics applied to hurlers (and those final scores also reflect the cumulative effects of normalization to remove bias from the previous scales). In turn, the Core-Z averages given are the cumulative means for a total of 15 variables, including the same five from all three measurements of pitchers and non-pitchers. As a whole, the final scores represent the most accurate estimate possible of the relative value of each player's career statistics, without subjective weighting applied to the separate variables.

Table Forty-Two lists the leaders for the final rankings. As in previous chapters, the scores for pitchers are listed separate from those for position players to facilitate comparison with the rankings that preceded them. But the scores for both subsets can also be perceived as a single continuum listing the players among the entire data set possessing the best relative statistical credentials for Cooperstown.

As with the previous ratings, Table Forty-Two also includes cutoff lines, below which are listed Hall of Famers whose scores failed to rank among the leaders of each subset. Unlike all of the preceding tables, these lines have added meaning, as they also represent the Cooperstown Baseline for the entire data set, the demarcation above which resides the 210-man Hall-of-Fame roster proposed at the end of chapter 5.

The composition of that roster is based on the dual premise that each member must have been eligible for Hall of Fame election by 2000 and have posted one of the 210 best Total-Z averages in the final rankings for pitchers and non-pitchers combined. But identification of the cutoff point was complicated by the presence among the Total-Z leaders of 20 players who had met the 10-year service requirement by the end of the 1994 season and were therefore qualified for the data set but who — because they were active after that season — were not yet eligible by 2000 (as in previous chapters, they are identified in Table Forty-Two by asterisks). Their presence among the leaders effectively lowered the final Cooperstown Baseline by 0.03, allowing 20 more men (including six current Hall of Famers) to qualify. As a result, the 210-man cutoff point, or true Cooperstown Baseline through 2000, is a Total-Z average of +0.75, a score equaled or exceeded by 230, or 10 percent of the players in the full data set, including 68 pitchers and 162 position players.

The roster includes 143, or 77.3 percent of the 185 men elected to Cooperstown in a player capacity through 2000. In turn, it also includes 67 other players who were eligible but had not been elected through that date, and — by their omission — identifies 42 Hall of Famers as statistical errors of selection (i.e., every HOF member listed below the cutoff lines). Some of those latter men were chosen for Cooperstown in the distant past, however, when the body of statistics produced by all HOF eligibles to that point was different from the one used here. So a few of them near the cutoff point may not have been statistical errors at the time of their elections, and may have become so only as a result of the weight of changes in modern performance norms — a likelihood emphasized by the fact that, among the 42 identified as errors of selection, 19 of them are from the 19th-century or dead-ball eras.

Among the errors of selection, only three were elected by the BBWAA (pitcher Ted Lyons, outfielder Ralph Kiner and shortstop Lou Boudreau), with 39 being choices by the veterans committees. That result seems to confirm the superiority of the front-door selection process. But the ratings also validate 53 (or, about 58 percent) of the 92 players elected by veterans committees through 2000. The existence of 53 justifiable back-door members says as much or more to support the legitimate need for those panels over the years as their 39 apparent mistakes may imply about their fallibility. The bottom line is that — due to BBWAA omissions — both elective organs are about equally culpable for the errors among the Cooperstown roster.

But the composition of the Cooperstown Baseline roster does expose the dubiousness of the veterans panels' predilection for electing the living over the dead, and testifies that the VC's crony selections have lowered the Hall of Fame's standards for induction. Among the 92 selections by all of the veterans committees combined, 26, or about 62 percent of the 42 inductees who were deceased at the time of their elections, qualified for this roster. In comparison, only 54 percent of the panels' living inductees (27 of 50) made the final cut. Since its inception in 1953, the Veterans Committee has elected 26 players who were former teammates of one or more of its panelists at the time of their selection. Of that group, whose names are preceded by a dagger (†) on the lists, 14 rank as errors of selection, including all six of the Frankie Frisch-Bill Terry cronies (Dave Bancroft, Chick Hafey, Jesse Haines, George Kelly, Fred Lindstrom and Ross Youngs).

No doubt, the composition of the final roster will provoke some disagreement from every reader regarding the inclusion or omission of various players. The current Hall of Famers listed as errors of selection are more than double the number identified as such in the previous chapter, and the 67, higher-scoring "replacements" include several players whose qualifications will be subjectively suspect to many. But beyond the choice of the variables used, there is no subjective weighting in any of the scales which produced the roster, so within the format of the measurement itself, the numbers do not lie. Any disagreement with the result is actually a reflection of the degree to which those results contradict one's subjective preconceptions.

But, with the possible exceptions of Monte Ward and Amos Rusie, the list of Hall of Famers omitted from the roster includes most of the men whose HOF selections have ever been criticized or debated on subjective grounds by anyone relatively knowledgeable about the history of the game. Their presence among the non-qualifiers enhances the probability that many of them are true errors of selection, and that the criticism of their elections over time has been justified. In turn, their exclusion from the final list also argues strongly for the validity of the Cooperstown-Baseline system. As a result, the roster is presented with little commentary to justify its composition.

Among current Hall of Famers who failed to qualify for this roster, five may not be errors of selection, statistically, despite their low scores. They include pitchers Pud Galvin, Charley Bender and Jim Bunning, plus outfielder Ralph Kiner and second baseman Tony Lazzeri, each of whom just missed the cutoff, and whose final Total-Z averages are within the data's margin of error (5 percent, or a Z-Score equivalent of 0.037).

With respect to representation by era and position, the Cooperstown Baseline roster is more proportional than the current Hall-of-Fame membership to the

Table Forty-Two
Cumulative Z-Score Leaders

Rank	Pitcher	Pos	Total Z Avg	Core Z Avg	Rank	Pitcher	Pos	Total Z Avg	Core Z Avg
1	Walter Johnson	sp	2.16	2.79	41	Ron Guidry	sp	0.97	1.14
2	Cy Young	sp	2.11	2.58	42	Goose Gossage	rp	0.96	1.07
3	Christy Mathewson	sp	1.98	2.30	43	†Lefty Gomez	sp	0.95	1.12
4	Tom Seaver	sp	1.93	2.67	44	#John Clarkson	sp	0.94	1.32
5	Warren Spahn	sp	1.89	2.60	45	Bob Lemon	sp	0.93	1.14
6	Grover Alexander	sp	1.71	2.03	46	Jack Quinn	sp	0.92	1.20
7	Steve Carlton	sp	1.70	2.73	47	Early Wynn	sp	0.91	1.83
8	Nolan Ryan	sp	1.69	3.10		Catfish Hunter	sp	0.91	1.27
9	Lefty Grove	sp	1.68	2.29	49	Stan Coveleski	sp	0.90	1.16
10	Whitey Ford	sp	1.65	1.98	50	Red Faber	sp	0.88	1.41
11	Sandy Koufax	sp	1.50	1.46	51	Eppa Rixey	sp	0.87	1.40
12	Ed Walsh	sp	1.48	1.09		*Dwight Gooden	sp	0.87	1.15
13	Carl Hubbell	sp	1.47	1.70	53	*Tom Henke	rp	0.85	0.05
14	Jim Palmer	sp	1.45	1.97	54	Addie Joss	sp	0.84	0.60
15	Gaylord Perry	sp	1.41	2.43	55	Jack Morris	sp	0.83	1.42
16	Don Sutton	sp	1.40	2.48		Firpo Marberry	rp	0.83	0.95
17	Hoyt Wilhelm	rp	1.38	1.40	57	Vida Blue	sp	0.82	1.30
18	Bert Blyleven	sp	1.37	2.24		Dizzy Dean	sp	0.82	0.88
19	Bob Feller	sp	1.31	2.00	59	Jim Kaat	sp	0.81	1.66
	*Dennis Eckersley	rp	1.31	1.92		*Bret Saberhagen	sp	0.81	0.68
	Juan Marichal	sp	1.31	1.79	61	#Hoss Radbourn	sp	0.79	1.15
22	Carl Mays	sp	1.30	1.13	62	Billy Pierce	sp	0.78	1.29
23	Phil Niekro	sp	1.27	2.31		Bob Shawkey	sp	0.78	1.03
24	Bob Gibson	sp	1.24	2.03		Dolf Luque	sp	0.78	0.79
	Don Drysdale	sp	1.24	1.46	65	Bucky Walters	sp	0.77	0.85
26	Rollie Fingers	rp	1.23	0.81	66	Waite Hoyt	sp	0.76	1.08
27	Ferguson Jenkins	sp	1.22	1.99		Bruce Sutter	rp	0.76	0.23
28	*Roger Clemens	sp	1.20	1.42	68	Rube Waddell	sp	0.75	1.05
29	#Tim Keefe	sp	1.18	1.56	t69	#Pud Galvin	sp	0.74	1.24
	Dazzy Vance	sp	1.18	1.31		Charley Bender	sp	0.74	0.94
31	Robin Roberts	sp	1.14	1.84	t72	†Jim Bunning	sp	0.73	1.53
32	Tommy John	sp	1.13	1.79	t94	Ted Lyons	sp	0.64	1.04
33	Eddie Plank	sp	1.12	1.81	t112	Vic Willis	sp	0.55	0.92
34	†Hal Newhouser	sp	1.07	1.31	t123	Amos Rusie	sp	0.50	0.64
35	Herb Pennock	sp	1.06	1.15	t133	Joe McGinnity	sp	0.47	0.85
36	Mordecai Brown	sp	1.05	1.17	t154	†Jesse Haines	sp	0.41	0.78
37	Red Ruffing	sp	1.04	1.48	t188	Mickey Welch	sp	0.33	1.13
38	Burleigh Grimes	sp	1.02	1.40		Jack Chesbro	sp	0.33	0.55
39	Spud Chandler	sp	0.99	0.73	t336	Rube Marquard	sp	0.03	0.38
40	Kid Nichols	sp	0.98	1.37					*(cont.)*

Rank	Non-Pitcher	Pos	Total Z Avg	Core Z Avg	Rank	Non-Pitcher	Pos	Total Z Avg	Core Z Avg
1	Babe Ruth	rf	2.97	3.63		Willie Stargell	lf	1.38	1.96
	Stan Musial	lf	2.97	3.52	42	Carlton Fisk	c	1.37	2.28
3	Ty Cobb	cf	2.75	3.48		Frankie Frisch	2b	1.37	1.72
4	Willie Mays	cf	2.60	3.53		Darrell Evans	3b	1.37	1.62
5	Hank Aaron	rf	2.47	3.82	45	Sam Crawford	rf	1.36	1.90
6	Honus Wagner	ss	2.43	2.77	46	Keith Hernandez	1b	1.35	1.17
7	Tris Speaker	cf	2.42	2.67	47	*Cal Ripken, Jr.	ss	1.34	1.84
8	Ted Williams	lf	2.35	3.26		Gary Carter	c	1.34	1.77
9	Rogers Hornsby	2b	2.27	2.81		*Paul Molitor	3b	1.34	1.70
10	Lou Gehrig	1b	2.26	2.97	50	Joe Torre	c	1.32	1.99
11	Carl Yastrzemski	lf	2.25	2.79		Ron Santo	3b	1.32	1.68
12	Mike Schmidt	3b	2.20	2.29	52	Dwight Evans	rf	1.30	1.81
13	Mickey Mantle	cf	2.19	2.55	53	George Davis	ss	1.29	1.58
14	Pete Rose	rf	2.18	2.39	54	†Goose Goslin	lf	1.28	1.88
	Eddie Collins	2b	2.18	2.24	55	Dave Parker	rf	1.26	1.92
16	Nap Lajoie	2b	2.00	2.43	56	*Andre Dawson	rf	1.25	2.05
17	Frank Robinson	rf	1.94	2.76		Bill Dahlen	ss	1.25	1.30
	Yogi Berra	c	1.94	2.30		#Bid McPhee	2b	1.25	0.90
19	George Brett	3b	1.92	2.51	59	Billy Williams	lf	1.24	2.16
20	Jimmie Foxx	1b	1.88	2.81		Gabby Hartnett	c	1.24	1.48
21	#Cap Anson	1b	1.80	2.13	61	Al Oliver	cf	1.23	1.82
22	Joe Morgan	2b	1.75	1.96		Max Carey	cf	1.23	1.15
23	Mel Ott	rf	1.72	2.58	63	Roberto Clemente	rf	1.22	1.89
	Charlie Gehringer	2b	1.72	2.18		Lou Brock	lf	1.22	1.56
25	*Eddie Murray	1b	1.69	2.52	65	Tony Perez	1b	1.21	1.86
26	Reggie Jackson	rf	1.68	2.31		†Enos Slaughter	rf	1.21	1.50
27	Joe DiMaggio	cf	1.59	2.05	67	#Jake Beckley	1b	1.20	1.73
28	#Dan Brouthers	1b	1.58	1.67	68	Paul Waner	rf	1.19	1.73
29	*Rickey Henderson	lf	1.57	1.45	69	Fred Clarke	lf	1.18	1.59
30	#Roger Connor	1b	1.54	1.74		Rod Carew	1b	1.18	1.42
31	Eddie Mathews	3b	1.50	2.32		*Ozzie Smith	ss	1.18	0.75
	Ed Delahanty	lf	1.50	1.96	72	Ted Simmons	c	1.16	2.10
33	*Dave Winfield	rf	1.45	2.60		Duke Snider	cf	1.16	1.83
	Robin Yount	ss	1.45	2.42		†Johnny Mize	1b	1.16	1.49
	Brooks Robinson	3b	1.45	1.71	75	Jim Rice	lf	1.15	2.05
36	Al Kaline	rf	1.44	2.25		Willie McCovey	1b	1.15	1.90
37	Al Simmons	lf	1.43	2.33	77	*Wade Boggs	3b	1.14	1.41
38	Bill Dickey	c	1.40	1.61	78	Luis Aparicio	ss	1.13	1.17
39	Johnny Bench	c	1.39	2.13	79	#Buck Ewing	c	1.12	1.17
40	Ernie Banks	1b	1.38	2.08	80	Joe Cronin	ss	1.10	1.51

(cont.)

Rank	Non-Pitcher	Pos	Total Z Avg	Core Z Avg	Rank	Non-Pitcher	Pos	Total Z Avg	Core Z Avg
	Mickey Vernon	1b	1.10	1.31	121	*Jimmy Ryan*	cf	0.90	1.50
	Jack Clark	rf	1.10	1.19		†**Harry Hooper**	rf	0.90	1.08
83	Steve Garvey	1b	1.09	1.64	123	Don Baylor	lf	0.89	1.42
	*Ryne Sandberg	2b	1.09	1.48		Willie Randolph	2b	0.89	0.81
85	**Jesse Burkett**	lf	1.08	1.66	125	Jimmy Sheckard	lf	0.88	0.78
	Graig Nettles	3b	1.08	1.46	126	George Foster	lf	0.87	1.34
	Joe Kelley	lf	1.08	1.25		Cesar Cedeño	cf	0.87	1.15
	Mickey Cochrane	c	1.08	1.19	128	†**Orlando Cepeda**	1b	0.86	1.67
89	**Harry Heilmann**	rf	1.07	1.73		*Cecil Cooper*	1b	0.86	1.34
90	Rusty Staub	rf	1.06	1.55		Buddy Bell	3b	0.86	1.30
	Gil Hodges	1b	1.06	1.43		**Pie Traynor**	3b	0.86	1.23
92	**Zach Wheat**	lf	1.05	1.89		Norm Cash	1b	0.86	1.17
	Dale Murphy	cf	1.05	1.61		#**King Kelly**	rf	0.86	1.00
	Richie Ashburn	cf	1.05	0.92	134	**Chuck Klein**	rf	0.85	1.36
95	Vada Pinson	cf	1.04	1.70		Willie Davis	cf	0.85	1.30
	Frank Baker	3b	1.04	1.17		†**Red Schoendienst**	2b	0.85	1.09
97	#**Sam Thompson**	rf	1.02	1.56	137	*Alan Trammell	ss	0.84	1.46
	Nellie Fox	2b	1.02	1.07	138	**Rabbit Maranville**	ss	0.83	0.58
99	**Luke Appling**	ss	1.01	1.25	139	Bill Buckner	1b	0.82	1.33
	*Tim Raines	lf	1.01	1.09	140	Fred Lynn	cf	0.81	1.38
101	*Lou Whitaker	2b	1.00	1.56		Bob L. Johnson	lf	0.81	1.28
	†**Bobby Doerr**	2b	1.00	1.29		†**Arky Vaughan**	ss	0.81	1.07
	Bobby Grich	2b	1.00	1.02		**Billy Herman**	2b	0.81	0.86
104	**Harmon Killebrew**	1b	0.99	1.92	144	*Amos Otis*	cf	0.80	1.05
105	Bill Mazeroski	2b	0.98	0.75		Vic Wertz	rf	0.80	1.00
106	**Hugh Duffy**	lf	0.97	1.59	146	*Don Mattingly	1b	0.79	1.23
	George Sisler	1b	0.97	1.27		**Kiki Cuyler**	rf	0.79	1.10
	#**Harry Stovey**	lf	0.97	0.77	148	Geo. Van Haltren	cf	0.78	1.36
109	**Billy Hamilton**	cf	0.96	1.21		Dick Allen	1b	0.78	1.34
110	**Joe Medwick**	lf	0.94	1.50		**Jim Bottomley**	1b	0.78	1.31
	Lave Cross	3b	0.94	1.44		**Jimmy Collins**	3b	0.78	1.10
	Sam Rice	rf	0.94	1.26		Joe Jackson	rf	0.78	1.08
	†**Pee Wee Reese**	ss	0.94	1.11	153	Brian Downing	lf	0.77	1.21
114	**Bill Terry**	1b	0.93	1.10		**Roy Campanella**	c	0.77	0.84
115	**Willie Keeler**	rf	0.92	1.68		*Brett Butler	cf	0.77	0.70
	Ken Boyer	3b	0.92	1.49	156	Minnie Miñoso	lf	0.76	1.15
	*Kirby Puckett	cf	0.92	1.38		**Jackie Robinson**	2b	0.76	0.93
	Reggie Smith	rf	0.92	1.23		Jimmy Dykes	3b	0.76	0.80
	Sherry Magee	lf	0.92	1.15		Joe Gordon	2b	0.76	0.78
120	**Hank Greenberg**	1b	0.91	1.31	160	†**Earl Averill**	cf	0.75	1.38

(cont.)

Rank Non-Pitcher	Pos	Total Z Avg	Core Z Avg	Rank Non-Pitcher	Pos	Total Z Avg	Core Z Avg
Herman Long	ss	0.75	1.08	**Earle Combs**	cf	0.51	0.69
Tommy Leach	cf	0.75	0.75	t259 †**Hack Wilson**	cf	0.50	0.89
t163 **Ralph Kiner**	lf	0.74	1.08	t271 †**Travis Jackson**	ss	0.47	0.67
t172 **Tony Lazzeri**	2b	0.73	1.05	**Joe Tinker**	ss	0.47	0.33
t178 **Edd Roush**	cf	0.70	1.00	t290 **Monte Ward**	ss	0.43	0.65
t184 **Jim O'Rourke**	cf	0.69	1.07	**Ray Schalk**	c	0.43	0.19
Joe Sewell	ss	0.69	0.99	t312 †**George Kelly**	1b	0.40	0.47
†**Phil Rizzuto**	ss	0.69	0.26	**Roger Bresnahan**	c	0.40	0.44
189 †**Bobby Wallace**	ss	0.68	0.94	t320 **Lloyd Waner**	cf	0.39	0.73
t195 †**Heinie Manush**	lf	0.65	1.31	t332 **Rick Ferrell**	c	0.37	0.38
t198 **Hughie Jennings**	ss	0.64	0.47	t373 †**Chick Hafey**	lf	0.31	0.52
t204 **Lou Boudreau**	ss	0.61	0.48	t403 **Johnny Evers**	2b	0.27	0.09
t219 †**George Kell**	3b	0.58	0.93	t408 **Frank Chance**	1b	0.26	-0.10
t227 †**Dave Bancroft**	ss	0.56	0.29	t427 **Tommy McCarthy**	rf	0.23	0.39
t244 **Elmer Flick**	rf	0.52	0.74	t446 †**Ross Youngs**	rf	0.20	0.20
t252 †**Ernie Lombardi**	c	0.51	1.11	t490 †**Fred Lindstrom**	3b	0.14	0.59
Larry Doby	cf	0.51	0.84				

periodic quotas dictated by the composition of the data set, but less equable with regard to position. Table Forty-Three provides a breakdown of roster membership by both variables and compares its totals for each to those among the current Cooperstown members. The first six columns provide the Cooperstown Baseline roster's total for each position and historical era. The next three columns give the roster's overall total for each position (Ros Tot), the number at that position required for representation proportional to its share of the full data set (Ros Prop), and the plus-or-minus differential between the two (Ros Dif). The last three columns give the positional totals among the Hall of Fame's 185-player roster through 2000 (HOF Tot), the number required for proportionality among that group (HOF Prop), and the difference between both (HOF Dif). The numbers below the line for right fielders identify similar totals and differentials appropriate to proportionality by era. Note that both sets of proportional data by position (Ros Prop and HOF Prop) include separate totals for starting and relief pitchers, and differ from those given in chapter 9 (Table Thirty-Three).

Comparing the absolute scores for both sets of differentials (i.e., without their plus or minus values, and with a score of zero indicative of perfect proportionality), the Cooperstown Baseline's roster has an aggregate differential of 40 for the era score, compared to 94 for the current Hall-of-Fame membership. In contrast, the Table Forty-Two roster scores at 70 for position, compared to 56 for the actual membership. The differences derive from

Table Forty-Three
Roster Qualifiers, by Position and Era

Position	NC	DB	LB	PW	EX	FA	Ros Tot	Ros Prop	Ros Dif	HOF Tot	HOF Prop	HOF Dif
Starting Pitcher	5	8	18	8	9	10	58	54	+4	56	49	+7
Relief Pitcher	0	0	1	0	1	3	5	21	-16	2	16	-14
Catcher	1	0	3	2	3	2	11	25	-14	12	22	-10
First Base	4	0	7	2	8	4	25	14	+11	19	12	+7
Second Base	1	2	6	3	2	2	16	15	+1	14	13	+1
Shortstop	3	1	4	1	1	1	11	16	-5	18	15	+3
Third Base	1	2	2	1	3	5	14	14	0	9	13	-4
Left Field	5	4	4	3	4	4	24	18	+6	18	16	+2
Center Field	3	4	2	3	4	4	20	16	+4	16	14	+2
Right Field	2	4	7	2	7	4	26	17	+9	21	15	+6
Roster Total	25	25	54	25	42	39	210					
Roster Proportion	18	24	42	28	42	56		210				
Roster Differential	+7	+1	+12	-3	0	-17			0			
Hall-of-Fame Total	26	33	62	24	29	11				185		
HOF Proportion	16	21	37	24	37	50					185	
HOF Differential	+10	+12	+25	0	-8	-39						0

the Baseline system's approach toward removing bias from the scales: the statistical advantages related to periodic norms was removed from each of the appropriate measures, but, with regard to position, the only normalization of data involved the defensive variables, which make up less than one-fourth of the stats in each scale. As noted in previous chapters, there is no equitable way to remove the offensive advantages imposed by the defensive spectrum without making weak-hitting catchers and shortstops appear, unfairly, as better-qualified for the Hall of Fame than first basemen and outfielders who were much better hitters. The decision to avoid such normalization left those offensive advantages intact, reducing any prospect that the roster could reflect proportionality by position — especially compared to a Hall-of-Fame membership whose selection process has no similar statistical restraints. As a result, the Cooperstown Baseline roster is dramatically impacted by those offensive advantages, as reflected by the fact it contains more first basemen and outfielders than the actual HOF membership.

But, when the differentials for both rosters are combined, the one proposed in Table Forty-Two scores at 110, while the current Hall-of-Fame membership totals 150. So, overall, the Cooperstown Baseline system is more equitable than the Hall's current composition.

Regardless, as noted in chapter 5, neither the Hall-of-Fame trustees nor their chosen electors are likely to renege the memberships of Cooperstown's statistically unqualified players at any future date. The 185-player HOF roster as constituted through 2000 must be accepted as *fait accompli*. So, with that in mind, the 210-man roster proposed in chapter 5 actually has 25 vacancies, and it remains to identify which of the eligible, but unenshrined players are best-qualified to fill them, within the goals of statistical justice and proportional representation by era and position.

As with the roster in Table Forty-Two, each of the 25 Hall-of-Fame additions proposed below was eligible for election to the Hall by 2000. Beyond that, the selections were made using the guidelines and assumptions below.

• Except for the 19th century and dead-ball eras, when relief pitching had no real meaning, each historical era should be represented in the Hall by at least one man from each position. The lengths of each period are sufficient to encompass, at minimum, one full generation of players eligible under the Hall's 10-year service requirement, any man who ranks as the top player, statistically, from his position in a given era is the most-qualified man at that post for his generation. As a result, he deserves a spot in Cooperstown, regardless of his rank in the final scores. This guideline acknowledges that the Cooperstown Baseline's equivalent score has changed over time, as the statistics of men from succeeding eras cause the data-set norms for each statistic to fluctuate.

• But because the delay of justice is no justice at all, emphasis was placed on choosing the longest-standing statistical errors of omission, regardless of their final Total-Z, concerns about proportional equity, or whether they were alive to attend their mock induction at the author's home.

• Given that the Hall's eligibility restrictions are and always have been subject to change, the absence of proportional representation by era has a marginally better chance of being rectified in the future than the Shrine's imbalanced representation by position, some of which is caused by the negative effects of the defensive spectrum on offensive production. As a result, emphasis was placed on filling the shortages at catcher, third base and pitcher, the most under-represented positions on the HOF roster, regardless of the selections' impact on proportionality by era.

• For these purposes, the free-agent period is defined as the years 1976–94, which—given the five-year wait before players are placed on the BBWAA ballot and the 15-year window of eligibility for the writers' voting, extends the length of time that free-agent players will be on the ballot to about 2014. Given their scores in the final rankings, the de facto standards that rule the selection process or the reputations earned during their careers to date, it's assumed that the new free-agent Hall of Famers elected by 2014 will include, at minimum, Dave Winfield, Eddie Murray, Paul Molitor, Wade Boggs, Tony Gwynn, Cal Ripken, Jr. and Mark McGwire, all de facto qualifiers by the end of the 2000 season; Ozzie Smith, Ryne Sandberg, Dennis Eckersley and Andre Dawson, each of whom retired after 1994 and is not eligible by 2000; plus Barry Bonds, Roger Clemens, Ken Griffey, Jr., Rickey Henderson and Greg Maddux, all still active in 2000. Coupled with the free-agent members elected to date, their inductions will eventually provide a representative from that era for each position.

• Other free-agent-era candidates with 100 votes or more in either the 1999 or 2000 balloting (Gary Carter, Steve Garvey, Goose Gossage, Tommy John, Jack Morris, Dale Murphy, Dave Parker, Jim Rice and Bruce Sutter) are also omitted from consideration because they still have outside shots at election by the scribes. So any players from the era who are proposed for the roster are those most likely to be unjustly overlooked by the current selection process.

• Finally, it's also assumed that Bill Mazeroski, whose 10 votes from the Veterans Committee in 2000 were one shy of the number required for election, will be chosen by that panel in its 2001 voting, before this book reaches print. Absent that assumption, he would definitely be among the twenty-five players listed below.

But, as should be evident from the decisions made in the previous chapter regarding the statistical merits of current Hall of Famers, it's virtually impossible — beyond a systematic method like the one applied for the roster above — to select a Cooperstown membership in any manner that is totally objective. So no matter what criteria are adopted, there is no way to avoid some personal bias in the selections that follow.

Only one person in history ever knew for certain whether Joe Jackson helped throw the 1919 World Series or merely intended to pocket the gambler's money and let his teammates do all the dirty work. That man died in Greenville, South Carolina, on 5 December 1951, taking his knowledge and his .356 batting average with him. Anyone alive who knows for sure whether Pete Rose bet on baseball games, and whether he bet against his own team, isn't talking now — at least not convincingly — and probably never will. Jackson's final Total-Z (+0.78) is above the Cooperstown Baseline, and there's no doubt his score would've been higher if he'd played a full career. Rose's Total-Z is the 14th-best among all non-pitchers. If you haven't already, you can reach your own conclusions regarding both men's moral qualifications for the Hall, and whether morality should have any relevance at all to Cooperstown selection. But, regardless of their possible crimes, no Hall of Fame based on statistics can justifiably omit either of them and possess any credibility.

As of 2000, and discounting the free-agent era, there were four vacancies on the Hall-of-Fame roster for players from a specific historical period and position. They include a third baseman from the 19th century (Jimmy Collins had more at-bats during the dead-ball era, and John McGraw was cited as a manager), a first baseman from the postwar period (Stan Musial's

1016 games at the position do not negate his true status as a left fielder), and a relief pitcher for both the live-ball and postwar/expansion eras (the choice of the latter depending upon whether you count Hoyt Wilhelm, who appeared in 597 of his 1070 games after 1960, as a postwar- or expansion-era pitcher).

With regard to the 19th-century vacancy at third base, the scores in Table Forty-Two offer just one viable candidate, Lave Cross (the next-best score at Lave's position from the same era belongs to Billy Nash, whose final Total-Z of +0.61 is tied for 204th place among non-pitchers). Cross, whose career spanned 1887–1907, was a contemporary of Collins (1895–1908) and McGraw (1891–1906), but his earlier appearance in the majors meant that 5681 of his 9072 at-bats occurred before the turn of the century. Lave is the only man ever to play for four different major-league teams in the same city, having donned the uniforms of Philadelphia clubs in the National and American Leagues, plus the AA and Players circuits — an interesting, if irrelevant, note. The downside to his candidacy is that during his 21 seasons he never once led any of those leagues in a single offensive category, and as a result, his high score in Table Forty-Two is attributable in part to longevity. But Cross also played most of his first five seasons as a platoon catcher, which limited his batting numbers. Despite that disadvantage, his final Total-Z of +0.94 is better than Collins' (+0.78), and second only to Frank Baker's (+1.04) among all third basemen whose careers ended before the beginning of the expansion era in 1961. His career total of 2645 hits is the fifth-best ever among third sackers, trailing only Hall of Famers George Brett and Brooks Robinson, plus 3000-hit men Paul Molitor and Wade Boggs. More impressive, Lave's 2657 runs produced ranks second among all third basemen behind Brett's 2861.

Choosing a postwar first baseman is complicated by two candidates of almost equal statistical merit: Mickey Vernon (+1.10) and Gil Hodges (+1.06). Vernon, who spent most of his career with the dismal Senators of his era, is mostly forgotten now, while everyone remembers Hodges from his long association with the Brooklyn teams of the 1950s and as pilot of the 1969 Mets. Subjectively, Vernon's edge in the ratings seems to be a longevity mirage, but the two men had careers of almost equal length (Mickey played 20 seasons, Gil 19). Vernon won two AL batting titles and led the circuit in doubles three times, while Hodges never topped his league in any offensive category. Vernon also amassed 2495 hits, 1196 runs scored and 1311 RBI to go with a .286 career batting average that was eighteen points above the norm for postwar qualifiers. Each of those numbers is also better than the 1921 hits, 1105 runs, 1274 ribbies and .273 BA Hodges compiled; and, although Gil hit 370 homers, Mickey's total of 172 wasn't shabby in the context of their time. Beyond all that, Vernon's score for isolated defense (+0.87) is also better than Gil's (+0.80).

But Hodges was chosen for the All-Star squad more often than Vernon (eight times to seven), and, while Mickey was his league's starting first sacker in more of the games (four to one), Gil's All-Star performance was better. Vernon went 2-for-14 in all-star play (.143), scoring two runs, with one RBI. Hodges was 4-for-12 (.333), with three runs scored, two RBI, and a solo home run in 1951. Vernon's lengthy service in Washington prevented his appearance in a World Series. Hodges played in seven of them, batting .267 overall, with five homers, 15 runs scored and 21 RBI. Mickey received 539 Hall-of-Fame votes in all, his best showing being 96 votes, for 24.9-percent support, in 1980, his final year on the ballot. In contrast, Gil topped 200 votes nine times, with highs of 242 in 1979 and 63.4-percent support in 1983, his last year eligible; and, as noted in a previous chapter, his 3,010 votes overall are the most ever by a player not elected. So Hodges gets the nod, in a very close call, because his edge in the balloting was much greater than the difference in the two men's performances on the field.

Firpo Marberry is tied for 55th at +0.83, a score that places him within the ordinal equivalent of the number of pitchers in Cooperstown through 2000 (58). There is no real dispute that Marberry was baseball's first closer of true significance and success, so his addition at Cooperstown could be justified on that subjective standard alone. Marberry acquired his groundbreaking relief role because several of the Senators starters during the mid–1920s — notably Walter Johnson, Stan Coveleski and Sad Sam Jones — were long-of-tooth and needed frequent late-inning help. The result was "Marberry Time," the twilight in which his fastball proved most effective in late-inning situations, rather like Goose Gossage pitching just after sunset, without lights. Marberry was 53–37 as a reliever, for a .589 percentage, and he was the first man ever to record 100 career saves (although no one knew it until much later). He was also 94–52 as a starting pitcher, and his .644 percentage in that role would have been the 18th-best among the all-time leaders through 1999, if he had enough decisions to qualify for the list. Marberry also led AL pitchers in appearances on six occasions and topped the circuit in saves five times. There may be too many live-ball players in the Hall already, but Firpo's credentials merit at least one more.

Like Hoyt Wilhelm, Elroy Face's career (1953–69) spanned the postwar and expansion eras, and Face could be assigned to either: 765 of his 1375 innings came before expansion; he appeared in 456 of his 848 games after 1960. Although Face's 18–1 record out of the bullpen in 1959 produced the best league-leading winning percentage in big-league history (.947), its luster is tarnished for some observers because he gave up the tying or go-ahead run before winning 10 of his decisions. But, whether or not Elroy's performance was equal to his won-lost ledger that year, his season helped popularize relief pitching and led to creation of the stat that is now most associated with Face's craft — as Chicago scribe Jerome Holtzman invented the "save," in part, as a means to prove that other relievers were more effective in 1959.

Carl Mays' surly personality and the misfortune of having killed Cleveland's Ray Chapman with a pitch in 1920 probably doomed his chances for election. All the same, his final Total-Z of +1.30 ranks better than those of 39 Cooperstown hurlers (*The Sporting News*).

Face topped the senior circuit in saves three times, led in appearances twice and pitched in no fewer than 55 games in each of the 1956–64 seasons. And Face's 671 Hall-of-Fame votes are the most received to date by any relief pitcher except Hoyt Wilhelm and Bruce Sutter. As (next to Wilhelm) the highest-ranked reliever of his eras, Face merits inclusion, despite the fact that his final Total-Z (+0.68) is 0.07 below the Cooperstown Baseline.

As indicated in Table Forty-Three, the 58 pitchers in the Hall through 2000 were seven less than proportionality required, so the additions of Face and Marberry do not fill that gap. Four starting hurlers' high scores in each of the scales merit their inclusions, however, and their presence on the roster would almost eliminate that deficit.

By most accounts, Carl Mays was one of the surliest players in major-league history, detested by teammates and foes alike long before his fatal beaning of Ray Chapman in 1920. So after the popular Cleveland shortstop died, there were calls for the pitcher's banishment. But Carl was exonerated after witnesses agreed that Chapman had crowded the plate and the pitch that killed him was in, or very near, the strike zone. Mays has never received rightful credit, but his divisive personality also helped create the Yankee dynasty of the 1920s. Pitching for the Red Sox in July 1919, Carl stormed off the mound and demanded to be traded because of a perceived lack of support from his world-champion teammates. Boston owner Harry Frazee obliged Mays, shipping him to New York for two players and $40,000 (this first of his fire-sale donations to the Yanks came six months before Babe Ruth's infamous sale to New York). So maybe "The Curse of the Bambino" should really be called "The Curse of the Nasty Submariner."

Mays posted a 208–126 record and .623 percentage in his 15-year career, winning 20 or more games on five occasions, with three different clubs. He won eight major statistical titles, topping the AL with 27 wins and a .750 percentage in 1921 and leading the circuit in complete games and shutouts on two occasions. Although Carl was eligible for HOF election from the beginning of the balloting in 1936, he got only six votes, all of them in 1958 — from a generation of scribes who may have lacked first-hand experience with his disposition. But Mays posted the best score of any unenshrined hurler in the overall ratings for chapter 10, his Total-Z ranks 23rd in the scale for starting pitchers, and his periodic score is bested only by Lefty Grove and Carl Hubbell for his era. Carl's Total-Z of +1.30 is the 22nd best in the final ratings, second only to Bert Blyleven among unenshrined hurlers, and the highest for any live-ball player not in Cooperstown. His omission is a long-standing error that should be corrected.

The major raps against Spud Chandler's candidacy are that his career was too short and that he only led the Yankees in victories twice in his 11-year career with the club (1937–47). But Addie Joss played just nine seasons, so point number one is moot. In his first six years with the Yanks, Chandler was on the same staff with Hall of Famers Red Ruffing and Lefty Gomez — so arguing that he should have topped the club in wins anytime during 1937–42 is much like criticizing Johnny Podres or John Smoltz for not winning as often as Koufax-Drysdale or Maddux-Glavine. After Ruffing and Gomez had departed, Chandler led New York with 20 wins in 1943; he missed most of 1944–45 to military duty; he topped the team with 20 wins again in 1946; he then won only nine games in 1947, on a pennant-winning staff that included Allie Reynolds, Vic Raschi and Bobo Newsom. Chandler's five statistical titles all came in 1943, when he topped the AL in wins, percentage (.833), complete games (20), shutouts (five) and ERA (1.64), en route to the league's MVP Award against wartime competition. In 1946 Chandler nearly matched his 1943 performance, boasting a .714 winning percentage, 20 complete games again, six shutouts (one more than '43) and an ERA of 2.10, against the "real" major leaguers. He posted a career record of 109–43, for a winning percentage of .717, the highest of any pitcher in history with a minimum of 100 career wins. Except for Babe Ruth, Chandler is also the only hurler with at least ten years in the majors and a winning record in every season he pitched. Despite the brevity of his career, Chandler's final Total-Z of +0.99 is the 39th best among the 813 pitchers in the data set. That ought to be sufficient evidence to silence his critics.

A native of Zeist, Holland, Bert Blyleven would join Luis Aparicio (Venezuela), Rod Carew (Canal Zone), Ferguson Jenkins (Canada), Juan Marichal (Dominican Republic), Tony Perez (Cuba) and Orlando Cepeda and Roberto Clemente (Puerto Rico) as the eighth Hall-of-Fame player born outside the United States, and the first from outside the western hemisphere. He was on the BBWAA ballot in 1998–2000, but his candidacy appears stalled.

Blyleven's lack of support stems from his lackluster winning percentage (.534, from a 287–250 career record that is reminiscent of 19th-century hurlers) and his penchant for allowing home runs (his 430 homers surrendered are the seventh-highest total in history). But, to paraphrase the adage, you can't lose that many games, or give up that many home runs without having something going for you. Five of the men ahead of Bert on the dingers-allowed list, in fact, are Hall of Famers Robin Roberts, Fergie Jenkins, Phil Niekro, Don Sutton and Warren Spahn. Blyleven won 20 games only once in his career, never led his league in victories, never won a Cy Young trophy and was chosen for only two All-Star squads. But, he won seven major statistical titles, topped his club in victories on nine occasions and possessed the premier curveball of his era, regarded by many as one of the best ever. Through 1999, Blyleven's 3701 strikeouts were the third-most ever, behind Nolan Ryan and Steve Carlton; his sixty shutouts ranked ninth on the all-time list; and he had started more games than all but six pitchers in history. Bert's Total-Z of +1.37 is the 18th-best score in Table Forty-Two, and his high ordinal rankings in the other scales reinforce that credential. Finally, because Blyleven's Total-Z is the best among all unenshrined pitchers, his longevity-driven candidacy deserves the benefit of a doubt.

Many Yankee fans think Ron Guidry got shafted when he lost the American League's 1978 MVP Award to Boston's Jim Rice after posting a 25–3 won-lost record and leading the circuit with an .893 winning percentage (the all-time best for a pitcher with 20 or more wins), nine shutouts (tying the league record for a lefty) and 1.74 ERA. It was the first of three 20-win campaigns in Guidry's 14-year career. He posted a 170–91 career record, for a .651 winning percentage that ranked 14th-best on the all-time list through 1999. He was also tough in postseason play, going 5–2 overall, with a 3–1 record and 1.69 ERA in three World Series. Guidry's Hall-of-Fame candidacy has gone nowhere, averaging only 33 votes and about 7-percent support in seven years on the ballot (1994–2000). But he ranks ninth among the free-agent pitchers, and, like Spud Chandler, his final Total-Z of +0.97 places him among the top 50 pitchers in the data set. Those scores indicate there should be room for some "Louisiana Lightning" at Cooperstown.

Catcher Wally Schang is one of baseball's true forgotten men and, as previously argued, a more-deserving choice for the Hall than Ray Schalk among the backstops of their relative era. Beyond being a much better hitter and playing for far more pennant winners than Schalk, Schang also handled more Hall-of-Fame pitchers. Schalk caught three during his career: Ed Walsh, Red Faber and Ted Lyons. Schang handled six, including Eddie Plank, Chief Bender, Herb Pennock, Waite Hoyt, Lefty Grove and Babe Ruth — and the list of the other hurlers he gave signs to includes most of the great or near-great AL moundsmen of his era (Bullet Joe Bush, Bob Shawkey, Jack Coombs, Carl Mays, Sad Sam Jones, Dutch Leonard, Jack Quinn, Urban Shocker, General Crowder, George Earnshaw and Eddie Rommel, to name a few). Maybe Schang was just lucky, but that list is too long to think that Schang's skills behind the plate had no impact on those pitchers' success. Mainly because of his seven seasons as a dead-ball backstop, he fares no better than a tie for 204th in the final rankings (a Total-Z of only +0.61, 13 points below the Baseline). But Schang is 13th among the catcher ratings in chapter 8, ahead of four Hall of Famers. Also, of the 15 catchers ahead of Wally in the final ratings, only 19th-century backstops Buck Ewing and Duke Farrell preceded him. So, when Schang hung up his chest protector in 1931, he was the third-best retired catcher, statistically, in the history of the game. Schang's final score is also 18 points better than Schalk's, and his addition would not tarnish the Shrine a bit.

Every eligible manager with at least three World Series victories had been chosen for the Hall by 2000, so — after his third Fall-Classic win in 1999 —

Joe Torre's selection as a skipper may be a lock. But based on Torre's scores in each of the scales, he should have been elected as a player. He never got more than the 105 BBWAA votes he earned in 1997, his last year on the ballot, but he ranks third in the chapter 8 ratings for catchers, ahead of every Hall-of-Fame backstop except Yogi Berra and Johnny Bench. And his final Total-Z is the fifth-best among men at his position. Torre's .297 career batting average, 2342 hits, 252 home runs and 1185 RBI made him an All-Star at three different positions: he played 903 games as a catcher, where he made five All-Star squads (four as a starter); he played 515 games at third base, where he started two All-Star contests (1971-72) and won the MVP in the first of those seasons; and he played 787 games at first base, where he was an All-Star reserve one year. That versatility probably hurt Torre in the Cooperstown voting, as the writers may have had difficulty defining him. Because the VC's 60-percent rule, Joe is not eligible for future consideration as a player. But, given Torre's Z-Score at his primary position and the Hall's shortage of backstops, there's no logic to denying him a plaque simply because he was capable of playing one-third of the positions on a diamond with All-Star skill.

A lot of men spent their careers in the shadow of another, but few good players were obscured by someone else as much as Ted Simmons by Johnny Bench. For example, NL center fielders Duke Snider, Richie Ashburn, Curt Flood and Vada Pinson all took turns playing second-fiddle to Willie Mays during their careers, (although Snider got to be first chair on occasion during the 1950s). But Snider and Ashburn still made it to the Hall, and Flood and Pinson got 542 and 515 BBWAA votes, respectively, although few of their career numbers match those put up by Mays. In contrast, Simmons topped Bench in more than half of the 30 variables measured here — notably, hits, total bases, RBI, runs produced, batting and on-base averages, plus five of the seven fielding stats — but got only 17 votes and 3.5-percent support in his lone chance on the ballot. The 438 scribes who didn't vote for Simmons in 1994, condemning him to the Hall's 5-and 60-percent-failure oblivion, merely overlooked the man with the most career hits and doubles of any catcher in the data set, and who at the time also ranked second among backstops in total bases, RBI and Runs Created, third in runs produced, fifth in runs scored, sixth in walks and seventh in home runs.

Some might argue that Simmons benefited from his move to the AL in 1981, after which he spent the last five seasons of his 21-year career primarily as a first baseman-DH. But, after three seasons (and two All-Star appearances) as their catcher, the Brewers didn't move him to DH until 1984. And he batted only .248, with 26 homers and 194 RBI over his last five years combined, so his numbers got no real boost after he discarded the tools of ignorance. An eight-time All-Star, Simmons's only shot at a championship came in 1982, when — although he batted only .174 in the World Series — he still socked homers in his first two Fall-Classic contests. His final Total-Z of +1.16 is the eighth-best score among the catchers in the data set with only four Hall-of-Fame backstops ranking above him (Yogi Berra, Bill Dickey, Bench and Gabby Hartnett). His Core-Z average of +2.10 is topped only by Berra and Bench, and he ranks ninth in the positional ratings in chapter 8, with Mickey Cochrane, Roy Campanella, Roger Bresnahan, Ernie Lombardi, Ray Schalk and Rick Ferrell all below him. Simmons wasn't as good as Bench; but he wasn't so much worse as to deserve the thoughtless response he got from the BBWAA. His dismal fate in HOF voting is evidence that the selection process needs a major overhaul.

Because the Cubs blew the 1969 NL-East flag, no one will know whether Ron Santo would've played the same brilliant defense in a World Series that made Brooks Robinson far more famous at the hot corner. Santo's +1.30 career Z-average for isolated defense is only 0.09 behind Robinson's, he won five Gold Gloves, and he ranks fifth behind Brooksie among the career leaders for assists at the position. Santo's career numbers for the Core-Z variables — 2254 hits, 342 home runs, 1138 runs scored, 1331 RBI and a .277 batting average — are also close enough to Robinson's (2848 hits, 268 homers, 1232 runs, 1357 ribbies and a .267 BA) that his final Core average for all three scales is only 0.03 behind the Orioles' third sacker. Santo was a nine-time All-Star in a league that included much stiffer competition for the hot-corner honor — Eddie Mathews and Ken Boyer early on, Dick Allen and Tony Perez for a time in the middle, and Joe Torre, Ron Cey, Mike Schmidt and Darrell Evans toward the end of his career — than Robinson ever faced from the likes of Frank Malzone, Rich Rollins, Max Alvis, Don Wert, Sal Bando or (only occasionally) Harmon Killebrew for any of his 15 consecutive All-Star assignments. None of that diminishes Robinson or his foes, but simply says that Santo was almost as good — close enough to have deserved a better fate from the BBWAA at a position which has only nine Hall of Famers, the fewest of any spot on the diamond. His final Total-Z of +1.32 puts him among the 50-best non-pitchers in the data set. Santo is qualified for the VC ballot beginning in 2002, and hopefully the panel will correct the injustice of his omission by the scribes.

It seems one reason Ken Boyer wasn't elected to Cooperstown is that his brother Clete had a better reputation as a fielder. Ken was a third-base regular from the beginning of his rookie season in 1955. The younger Clete came up with the A's that same year, but didn't become a hot-corner regular until 1960, after he was traded to the Yankees with Bobby Shantz and Art Ditmar in one of KC's pre–Roger Maris gift sets. Clete led his league in total chances five times, assists on three occasions, double plays and fielding average twice each, and putouts once. His only Gold Glove came with the Braves in 1969, after he'd escaped Brooks Robinson's junior-circuit stranglehold on the award.

But Ken's fielding was comparable: he topped the NL in double plays five times, assists and total chances-per-game twice each, and putouts once; and he won five Gold Gloves competing against Mathews, Santo, *et al.* As an outfielder, Ken also led the senior circuit in fielding in 1957. Later, Clete got four Hall-of-Fame votes, while Ken received a total of 838, topped by 25.6-percent support and 109 votes in 1988, sufficient to earn him VC eligibility under the 100-vote exception for postwar players.

Boyer's failure to hit as many homers (282) as his hot-corner contemporary, Eddie Mathews (512) also hurt. Except for batting average, the Braves third baseman had better career stats: Mathews hit .271, with 2315 hits, 1509 runs and 1453 RBI in a 17-year career; Boyer batted .287, with 2143 safeties, 1104 runs and 1141 RBI in 15 seasons, the last five of which he was hampered by a bad back. But Mathews had more power to begin with, and hit in the middle of a better offense as the Braves of 1955–64 outscored St. Louis in eight of those 10 seasons by an average margin of almost 60 runs per year. Mathews also spent most of that time batting just ahead of Hank Aaron, so he saw more good pitches than Boyer, who hit cleanup ahead of an aging Stan Musial and (later) Dick Groat or Mike Shannon. Nonetheless, in that same decade Boyer was named to 11 All-Star squads, and he started the game on six occasions, compared to 10 squads and six starts for Mathews (there were two contests each from 1959 to 1962). Both third sackers hit two homers in All-Star play, but they were Mathews' only hits in 22 at-bats, while Boyer had six others and batted .364. Mathews got into two World Series during that decade (1957–58), getting nine hits in 47 at-bats (.191), with a game-winning home run and seven RBI. In his lone Series (1964), Ken went 6-for-27 (.222), with two dingers and six ribbies. But both homers meant a lot: his grand slam won Game Four, by a score of 4–3, and his solo shot in the seventh inning of the finale sealed the Cards' 7–5 victory. Boyer also won the MVP trophy in 1964, something Mathews never accomplished. In truth, Ken wasn't quite as good as Eddie, but he was good enough — with a final Total-Z of +0.92 and an 11th-best ranking in the positional scores — to merit a Cooperstown plaque.

Here's a quick quiz: Who is the only man with more than 2000 career hits, 400 home runs, 1400 runs scored, 1300 RBI and 1600 walks who, as things stand now, can never, ever become a Hall of Famer? The man in question is also the only player before Mark McGwire to hit as many as 40 homers in a season in both leagues, the oldest player ever to hit that many in a campaign, and the oldest ever to lead his circuit in home runs as well. If all of that is not enough, he's also the only major leaguer on record ever to claim having witnessed a UFO landing (unless Dock Ellis also saw one when he pitched his LSD-enhanced no hitter). Except for that last item, those achievements should have had Darrell Evans elected to the Hall within three or four years — at most — after he joined the ballot in 1995. Instead, they brought a whopping eight votes, for 1.7-percent support, and immediate placement on the list of statistically qualified candidates most unfairly ignored by the BBWAA.

Granted, Evans' Z-Score of +1.45 for isolated defense, the best among all third sackers in the data set, is a mirage created by the 6515 putouts he recorded at first base. All the same, in his 10 seasons as a regular third baseman he topped his league in putouts four times, assists three times, double plays once, and chances-per-game on six occasions — so there were no complaints about his hot-corner glove work. In 1985 Evans led the AL with 40 homers at age 38, and his 1605 career walks are the ninth-best total ever. Darrell was chosen for only two All-Star squads, a decade apart. But Evans spent much of his career competing for fan recognition against Santo, Schmidt, Torre and Cey, some of whom played in cities with bigger populations and more ballot-stuffing potential and, given Darrell's career totals, his omissions from the midsummer classic only reinforce the notion that he was one of the most underappreciated players among the game's all-time best. Among all third sackers in the data set, his career numbers rank among the top five for games played, home runs, RBI, walks and Runs Created; and he's among the top 10 in 10 of the other stats measured. Evans ranks seventh in his positional ratings, and at +1.37, his final Total-Z is better than every third sacker's but Schmidt, Brett, Mathews and Robinson. Can someone please explain why he's unworthy of future consideration by the Veterans Committee?

Although Brooks Robinson had retired in 1977, the Dodgers must have thought he was making a comeback when Graig Nettles made four Brooks-like plays in Game Three of the 1978 World Series. They were not the first or last times that his defense was likened to Robinson's. In his 22-year career, Nettles led his circuit in third-base assists five times, double plays and chances-per-game on three occasions, putouts twice and fielding once. He was also a six-time All-Star, and, although he batted only .225 in postseason play, he had five homers and 27 RBI in his eight league playoffs and five World Series, combined. Beyond that, Nettles was one of the premier power-hitting third basemen ever, belting 390 career homers, with 2225 hits, 1193 runs scored and 1314 RBI to compensate for his weak .248 batting average. Among the data-set third basemen, Nettles ranks third in games played, fourth in home runs, seventh in total bases, ninth in RBI and 10th in Runs Created. Nettles received 125 HOF votes during 1994–97, before being dropped from the ballot when his support fell below five percent. Many will argue that his low batting average disqualifies him for Cooperstown, and that his election would pave the way for other low-average sluggers like Dave Kingman, who hit 442 home runs. But Kingman was a one-dimensional player; Nettles was much more. Even the easily fooled BBWAA voters recognized that, because Kingman received only three HOF votes. Despite his low average, Nettles ranks

12th — just below Ken Boyer — in the third-base ratings. His final Total-Z of +1.08 is tied with three Hall of Famers for the 85th-best score in Table Forty-Two, well above several of the Hall's .300 hitters. That's sufficient proof that he belongs in the Shrine at his under-represented position.

It's probable that Keith Hernandez's poor support in his first four years on the ballot is linked to many scribes' moralizing about his role in the cocaine scandal that rocked baseball in 1985, and to others' hypocritical disrespect for his less-than-secret identity as the "anonymous club source" for newsprint-quoted critical analysis of his team's play during his tenure with the Mets (1983–89). But, Hernandez shared the MVP Award in 1979 and led two different teams to World Series titles, and his on-field leadership was integral to the Mets' rise from the NL-East cellar in 1982–83 to world champs in 1986. Keith's eleven Gold Gloves, a record for first basemen, were won consecutively (1978–88), and he was one of the few first sackers in the history of the game whose range and awareness on the diamond were significant enough to improve his entire team's defensive play.

Some sabermetricians doubt the validity of "clutch" hitting, and several studies have been published which attempt to prove it's a mirage governed by the whims of statistical probability. But if clutch hitters do exist, then Hernandez was a consummate one. During the brief period that the ineptly defined Game-Winning RBI was used as an official statistic, Keith set the all-time records for the most in a season (24) and career (129). His bases-loaded, two-run single tied the seventh game of the 1982 World Series and put the Series-winning run on third base; Hernandez repeated that performance in the decisive game of 1986, hitting another two-run single to tie the game with two outs in the sixth inning and contributing a run-scoring sacrifice fly during the Mets' Series-winning rally in their next time at bat.

It's clear that Hernandez will never come close to election by the writers, or to getting the 60-percent support required to make him eligible for later consideration by the VC. But statistically, Keith was the best-fielding first sacker of all time and a definite gamer. And in the four decades since the beginning of the expansion era, there have been few players, if any, who displayed as much situational intelligence. His final Total-Z of +1.35 is the 46th best score posted by a non-pitcher and the eighth-best among all first sackers in the data set. With a minimum of 16 first basemen in the Hall already (18, if you count Banks and Carew), that ranking means Hernandez clearly belongs in Cooperstown too, regardless of how the writers vote.

Cooperstown is overstocked with shortstops from the 1890s and the dead-ball era (George Davis, Hughie Jennings, Bobby Wallace, Honus Wagner and Joe Tinker), but statistically, except for Wagner and Davis, they're all the wrong men. So although it seems absurd to propose adding another one, it wouldn't be right to ignore Bill Dahlen's scores. Dahlen's final Total-Z of

+1.25 is only 0.04 behind Davis, easily making him the third-most-qualified shortstop of that era (none of those other Hall of Famers scored above the Cooperstown Baseline, and Herman Long also topped the rest of them at +0.75). Dahlen had 2457 hits, 84 home runs, 1589 runs scored, 1233 RBI and a .272 BA. None of those totals is in Wagner's class, but Dahlen had more career runs and homers than Davis, more of everything but batting average than Jennings, and topped both Tinker and Wallace in all five Core variables. With 18 shortstops now, the Hall doesn't need another one all that badly; but Dahlen's omission has persisted too long and ought to be corrected.

The same is true for Vern Stephens. His final score (+0.74, with a Core-Z average of +1.46) failed to make the cut in Table Forty-One, but it was the very best of all among the 1,322 non-pitchers who didn't. And it's true that his great RBI seasons (1948–50) were accomplished in a lineup whose first three hitters (Dom DiMaggio, Johnny Pesky and Ted Williams, plus Billy Goodman for the part of 1950 that Williams was hurt) got on base ahead of him about 800 times per year, batted a combined .319 with an on-base average of .430 over those three campaigns, and that the man hitting behind him (Bobby Doerr) slugged a composite .507 during that period, guaranteeing that Stephens got some good pitches to hit. Granted all of that, Vern still drove them home 440 times in those three years, averaging 147 RBI per season.

So what? Of all shortstops in history, the next-best three-year RBI total ever was only 389 by Ernie Banks in 1958–60. Only two other shortstops (Hughie Jennings and Joe Cronin) ever had as many as 350 over a three-year stretch, and just eight other men who played the position ever posted as many as 300 RBI over an equal period. Including Banks, a total of 66 shortstops had received Hall-of-Fame votes through 2000, and the average single-season, high among that group was just 77 RBI. Vern Stephens just about doubled that figure in each of the 1948–50 seasons. He had 77 or more RBI in nine of his 15 major-league campaigns. Of those 66 shortstops with HOF votes, the only ones who had 77 or more ribbies in more seasons at that position were Joe Cronin and Honus Wagner. Four Hall-of-Fame shortstops never achieved that total even once (Cal Ripken, Jr., had done it 13 times through 1999, but he had yet to receive a Cooperstown vote). As noted in chapter 9, Stephens still has the third-best career-home-run total among all shortstops in history. Stephens, then, rates with Wagner, Cronin, Banks and Ripken as the best all-around run producers ever at the position. That should have been enough to buy him at least one Hall-of-Fame vote. In fact, it should've been enough to get him in the Shrine.

Harry Stovey's power and speed, the highmarks of his statistical credentials, were noted in chapter 9. Given post–dead-ball playing conditions, Stovey might have been baseball's first 30–30 or 40–40 man in homers and stolen bases. In addition to his home-run, triples, runs-scored and stolen-base leaderships, he also topped his circuit in slugging average on three occasions, and doubles and RBI once each, winning 20 statistical titles in all during a 14-year career. In 1890 Stovey became the first major leaguer ever to reach 100 career homers. Except for his weaker batting average (.289 to .341), Stovey's career numbers for the Core variables are better than those of Pete Browning, the most-often mentioned HOF omission from the American Association: Stovey amassed 1771 hits, 122 home runs (third-best total for the 19th century), 1492 runs scored and 908 RBI; Browning had 1646 hits, 46 dingers, 954 runs and 659 ribbies (with two seasons of missing data for the latter). Stovey is also said to have been one of the earliest players to slide into bases feet first, and the first man to wear a sliding pad on his hip — so, for what little it's worth, he was just as much an innovator as Roger Bresnahan or Tommy McCarthy. Stovey's final Total-Z of +0.97 is tied with that of Hugh Duffy and only 0.09 behind Jesse Burkett and Joe Kelley, three Hall-of-Fame left fielders from the same era. Given all that, it's difficult to understand how he was virtually overlooked by the original Old-Timers Committee in 1936 (just six votes) and completely ignored by its innovation-fixated successor of the 1940s. Having lasted 10 seasons, the AA certainly deserves at least two representatives in the Hall. Along with Bid McPhee, Stovey is the best candidate.

In 1980 Al Oliver collected 209 hits and 117 RBI for the Texas Rangers. Two years later, with Montreal, Oliver won the National League batting title, and led the circuit with 204 hits and 109 RBI. As a result, he became the first man to achieve that 200-hits-100-ribbie feat in both leagues. Although he was a batting champ and seven-time All-Star, with the possible exception of Darrell Evans, he had the most invisible career of any good player from the free-agent era. He spent ten of his 18 seasons with Pittsburgh, where he was overshadowed by Willie Stargell and Dave Parker; and the best of his other years were on clubs like the Rangers and Expos, with whom broad media attention is hard to come by. That lack of notice was evident in 1991, when Oliver got just 19 votes, for 4.3-percent support, in his first and only year on the BBWAA ballot. Nonetheless, Al ended his career with a .303 batting average, 2743 hits, 219 homers, 1189 runs scored and 1326 RBI. Oliver's stats rank 13th for his era, just ahead of almost-certain Hall of Famer Andre Dawson. Oliver is sixth among the center-fielders, above every HOF member except the position's big five — Mays, Cobb, Speaker, Mantle and DiMaggio (although Oliver's best years came as a first baseman or DH, two-thirds of his defensive games were as an outfielder, most of them spent playing in center, next to Parker at Pittsburgh). Oliver's final Total-Z is tied with Max Carey for the 61st ordinal in the non-pitcher rankings. Even if he was invisible, anyone who ranks that high should be in Cooperstown.

It's doubtful anyone would've predicted in 1975 that, among Boston's three young outfielders, Dwight Evans would enjoy the longest career and compile the best all-around statistics. Evans became the Red Sox right fielder a season and a half before center fielder Fred Lynn won the unprecedented combination of Rookie of the Year and MVP honors in 1975, with left fielder and fellow-freshman Jim Rice finishing as runner-up for the first award, and third in the balloting for the other. But, while Lynn and Rice both enjoyed substantial careers, Evans' overall statistical achievements surpassed both. His final Total-Z of +1.30 ranks fifty-second in Table Forty-Two; Rice is tied for seventy-fifth place (+1.15), and Lynn (+0.81) is deadlocked for 140th. In addition to his statistical credentials, Evans possessed one of the strongest, most accurate right-field throwing arms of his era, and his all-around defensive prowess is evidenced by eight Gold Glove awards. Among the trio, only Rice — who is clearly qualified, statistically — still has a chance for enshrinement, as Evans and Lynn were casualties of the 5-percent rule. Lynn was dropped from the ballot after getting only 22 votes in 1997, his second year eligible and Evans was removed after 1999, when his support fell to only 18 votes in his third try for the Hall. But the final scores leave no room for doubt that Evans merits Cooperstown election.

Although they may stir some disagreement, it's clear that, within the bounds of their final, era and/or positional scores, a plausible case can be made for each of the HOF additions proposed thus far. But the final two choices are more problematic, statistically; and both reflect an unavoidable urge to vote from the heart.

Minnie Miñoso's last year on the BBWAA ballot was 1999, when he received 73 votes for 14.7-percent support. He does not meet the VC requirements for postwar eligibility. It's rumored that Miñoso was older than the record books indicate when he entered the majors with Bill Veeck's Cleveland Indians in 1949. Miñoso and Veeck had a symbiotic relationship akin to that of George Steinbrenner and Billy Martin, but one that was warm and fuzzy instead of emotionally erratic and boorish. As owner of the White Sox, Veeck traded Miñoso to Cleveland in 1957 for pitcher Early Wynn and outfielder Al Smith, who in 1959 helped Chicago win its first pennant since the Black Sox. After that season, Veeck dealt to get Miñoso back, and awarded the left fielder with a championship ring even though he hadn't been part of the club. The outfielder promptly repaid the gesture with two homers in Chicago's home opener of 1960, allowing Veeck his first use of the $350,000 exploding scoreboard he'd installed during the offseason to celebrate the team's infrequent dingers. Even if the encyclopedias are correct about Miñoso's 1922 birth date, he was still 53 when he went 1-for-6 as a DH in 1976 as part of a publicity gimmick during Veeck's second tenure as owner of the Sox. He was four years older when he went hitless in two more at-bats for the same club and owner in 1980, becoming the only man besides Nick Altrock to play in five different decades.

Miñoso led the American League in triples and stolen bases three times each, topped the circuit in doubles once, won its slugging crown in 1954, and his 184 hits were the best in the league in 1960 (at age 37, or older). His scores in each scale indicate that, absent the subjective value of Larry Doby's historic role as the AL's first African American, Miñoso is a better statistical choice for the Hall than Doby from the postwar era. Miñoso rates ahead of Doby in the periodic measurement; his ranking among left fielders is higher than Doby's for center field; he is 55 ordinals above Doby in the overall scale (although he didn't make the cutoff for the appropriate table in chapter 10); and his final Total-Z of +0.76 is a point above the Cooperstown Baseline, while Doby's fell 25 points short. There are several other unenshrined outfielders ahead of Miñoso in the final rankings, but his addition to Cooperstown would move the postwar subset closer to its appropriate level of representation and give the Hall an extra dose of class.

The roster proposed thus far includes only four relief pitchers (Wilhelm, Fingers, Marberry and Face), a position where a half-dozen members are proportionally justifiable. The selection of Dan Quisenberry requires dipping below the Cooperstown Baseline (his final score is +0.65), and ignoring another free-agent reliever with marginally better stats (Kent Tekulve, at +0.69). Quisenberry never won MVP or Cy Young honors, but his team (even with George Brett) was a perennial playoff loser before he took over as its closer. He was also the first five-time winner of the Fireman of the Year trophy and, along with Bruce Sutter, the only man to lead his circuit in saves for four consecutive seasons. As noted in chapter 2, his great control — easily the best of any career reliever in the data set — fulfilled the primary need at his position (keeping runners off base), and his opponents' on-base average (.297) was twelve points better than Tekulve's (.309), and comparable to those of Wilhelm (.290), Fingers (.295), Sutter (.289) and Dennis Eckersley (.291). Beyond all that, no one in the history of baseball gave better award-acceptance speeches, and none but Lou Gehrig showed as much dignity and good humor while confronting the illness which took his life. Like several of the other selections, Quiz was dropped from the ballot after his first appearance garnered only 18 votes and less than five-percent support. He should have gotten more.

The Hall-of-Fame additions proposed above include three men still on the BBWAA ballot in 2000 (Blyleven, Guidry and Hernandez). But the voting evidence to date suggests that each man's candidacy is certain to fail. The other additions feature 11 men who are, or soon will be, eligible for Veterans Committee consideration (Boyer, Chandler, Cross, Dahlen, Hodges, Marberry, Mays, Santo, Schang, Stephens and Stovey) and eleven others who are no longer eligible for the Hall for various reasons, most of them spurious (Darrell and Dwight Evans, Face, Jackson, Miñoso, Nettles, Oliver, Quisenberry, Rose, Simmons and — as a player only — Torre).

The selections also include four starting pitchers (Blyleven, Chandler, Guidry and Mays), three relievers (Face, Marberry and Quisenberry), three catchers (Schang, Simmons and Torre), two first basemen (Hernandez and Hodges), two shortstops (Dahlen and Stephens), five third basemen (Boyer, Cross, Darrell Evans, Nettles and Santo), and six outfielders (left fielders Miñoso and Stovey, center fielder Oliver, and right fielders Dwight Evans, Jackson and Rose). In terms of proportionality, along with the 185 players already in Cooperstown, the additions of those players would give the Hall of Fame a total of 60 starting pitchers (six more than required for proportional equity) and five relievers (16 pitchers shy of the proper total), plus 15 catchers (also ten below the position's appropriate share), 19 first basemen (five more than the position's quota), 15 second sackers (equal to its proportional requirement), 21 shortstops (five more than needed), 14 third basemen (exactly the amount required), 20 left fielders (two over the number necessary), 17 center fielders (an excess of one) and 24 right fielders (seven more than needed). The totals produce an aggregate score of 52, an 18-point improvement on the Cooperstown Baseline roster, and four points better than that accrued by the Hall-of-Fame membership through 2000.

The choices also include three players from the 19th century (Cross, Dahlen and Stovey), one from the dead-ball era (Jackson), four from the live-ball period (Chandler, Marberry, Mays and Schang), four from the postwar era (Face, Hodges, Miñoso and Stephens), five from the expansion group (Boyer, Rose, Santo, Simmons and Torre), and eight from the era of free agency (Darrell and Dwight Evans, plus Blyleven, Guidry, Hernandez, Nettles, Oliver and Quisenberry). When added to the current HOF totals, they would give Cooperstown 29 players from the 19th century (11 more than needed), 34 from the dead-ball era (an excess of one), 66 from the live-ball period (24 above the proportional requirement), 28 from the postwar era (equal to its appropriate share), 34 from the expansion period (eight below its quota) and 19 from the free-agent era (for a deficit of 37). The aggregate score for periodic representation is 81, 41 points worse than the Cooperstown Baseline roster but still 13 points better than the real HOF membership.

So, all things considered, the 210-man membership proposed here is more equitable by position and era than the current Cooperstown membership. The 25 additions suggested would also correct many of the Shrine's most notable errors of omission.

CHAPTER 12

Dugout Geniuses

Being a major-league manager is a high-stress job. When a team wins, the players usually get the credit; when it loses, the manager often gets the blame; and, whatever the outcome, a skipper's decisions are always second-guessed by media and fans. Many fans will forget a bad call by an umpire, or a game-losing error by a player quicker than they forgive a perceived managerial blunder. On the road, they are sure to get booed every time they leave the dugout. At home, their reception depends almost entirely on the club's record and position in the standings.

The stress of the job is indicated by relative managerial longevity. Through 1998, a total of 591 men had managed in the majors since 1876, and their mean career length was 4.6 years. Only 186 (or 31.5 percent) had exceeded that average, and just 77 of them (13.0 percent) had managed for 10 seasons or more. The toll that managing takes on a man, and the lack of job security inherent in the role, is even more evident from the fact that 203 of those 591 (34.3 percent) had managerial careers that lasted for one season or less, and that among the men with 10 seasons or more, only seven of them had served their entire careers as a skipper with just one franchise. Surprisingly, although Connie Mack and John McGraw had the longest careers among all managers (53 and 33 years, respectively) and are usually associated with only one team (the Philadelphia A's and New York Giants, respectively), both of them began their careers with other clubs, and are not among the seven — Walter Alston and Tommy Lasorda (Dodgers), Tom Kelly (Twins), Bill Terry (Giants), Danny Murtaugh (Pirates), Red Schoendienst (Cardinals) and Earl Weaver (Orioles), the latter three of which had two separate tenures with their teams.

But, some men must thrive on managerial stress. Among all the skippers in history, 204 of them (34.5 percent) piloted two different clubs. Perhaps many of them tried again, elsewhere, because they felt they got a raw deal from their first dismissal (e.g., the team had little talent to work with, or they were fired too quickly to show their ability). But 84 of them also managed three clubs or more, including 17 who piloted five or more teams. The all-time record is seven different clubs, by 19th-century skipper Frank Bancroft, and the twentieth-century leaders were Rogers Hornsby, John McNamara and Dick Williams, who managed six teams each. No doubt, a few of those 204 men were egomaniacs, masochists, or both; or perhaps, like skydivers and bungie-jumping adrenalin junkies, they were simply addicted to the rush they got giving their third-base coach those tension-packed signals for the batter to take a pitch on a 3–0 count, or the boos received while strolling to the mound to change pitchers.

All managers chosen for Cooperstown have been elected by the veterans committees. Through 2000, 16 men had been added to the Shrine's roster for their roles as skippers — Walter Alston, Sparky Anderson, Leo Durocher, Ned Hanlon, Bucky Harris, Miller Huggins, Tom Lasorda, Al Lopez, Connie Mack, Joe McCarthy, John McGraw, Bill McKechnie, Wilbert Robinson, Frank Selee, Casey Stengel and Earl Weaver. But, 65 of the Hall's other members had also served as managers, including 57 of the men elected as players. In some instances — notably, Lou Boudreau, Frank Chance and Hughie Jennings — their memberships would be more justifiable if they had been formally cited for both capacities.

All the same, superior playing skills are no guarantee of managerial success. The 57 Hall-of-Fame players who served as skippers have a composite winning percentage of only .516, claiming only 37 pennants and 13 World Series in 330 full or partial seasons as pilots. Thirty-two of them had losing records. In contrast, Joe McCarthy, Frank Selee and Earl Weaver never appeared as players in a major-league game, but they have a combined winning percentage of .600, with 18 pennants and nine World Series victories in 57 seasons between them.

No objective standards exist for election as a manager, except the Hall's 10-year minimum-service requirement. Beyond Cooperstown's abhorrence of formal statistical criteria, the absence of any standards is predictable given the wide variety of philosophies and personal styles applied by practitioners of the craft. Some good managers have been rigid tacticians, like Gene Mauch, whose situational decisions consistently followed the old-school wisdom of "inside" baseball. And along those lines, many recent skippers like Tony LaRussa and Buck Showalter have relied on computer printouts of player's situational performances to determine specific tactical decisions. Some, like Joe Torre, have appeared content to send their men onto the field and let them play the game relatively unfettered by tactical intrusions; others, like Earl Weaver, have used intricate platoon and pitching systems but disdained one-run tactics in favor of the big inning; and a few, like Whitey Herzog, have seemed to micro-manage every possible aspect of the game on virtually every pitch.

Almost all skippers are psychologists by necessity, but even their motivational styles may vary. Tom Lasorda and Sparky Anderson always seemed upbeat, using *rah-rahs* and *atta-boys* to keep their men motivated. Dick Williams never shirked a perceived need to lead by verbal intimidation. And Billy Martin, perhaps compulsively, often took confrontational motivation to its darkest extremes. Each of these men had lengthy careers, so there is no evidence that a single tactical approach or personal style is the only method to assure managerial success.

Absent any formal standards, it's predictable that — as with player selections — precedent has established de facto standards for the election of managers. And like the de facto criteria for players, they are never acknowledged by the trustees or Veterans Committee. All the same, through 2000, every HOF-eligible skipper in major-league history with at least 2000 regular-season wins, six pennants or three World Series titles had been enshrined for their managerial careers .

As a result of all these factors, the records of Cooperstown's 16 managers evidence much inconsistency. Only seven of them ended their careers with winning a percentage of .555 or better (the equivalent of 90 wins over a 162-game season), two with more losses than wins (Mack and Harris), two more with a record seven World Series apiece (McCarthy and Stengel) and two others with no championships at all (Lopez and Robinson). The career victory totals among all 16 men range between Mack's 3731 and Selee's 1284, for a huge spread of 2447 wins that is larger than the individual victory totals for all but two of the managers in history (Mack and McGraw).

One reason for that inconsistency is the fact that the number of statistics applicable to managers is very small in comparison to those for players. For most of baseball history, the only stats relevant to managerial performance have been length of service, won-lost record, winning percentage, and the number of pennants and World Series won (plus division titles, after 1968). Since the 1970s, most sabermetricians have concentrated on developing new ways to measure player performance, and the discipline has developed only one real innovation by which to assess managerial achievement. The stat in question, usually called Actual-Minus-Expected Wins (A-E, for short), purports to measure a pilot's skill, but its validity is debatable because there are many other factors besides a skipper's ability — all of them unmeasureable — that can impact its numerical result.

So, until now, anyone hoping to rate the performance of managers has generally been forced to rely on the traditional statistics. As a result, most people habitually cite Connie Mack's 53 seasons as a skipper, Casey Stengel's 10 pennants won, and Joe McCarthy's all-time-best .615 winning percentage as evidence of their dugout genius, without much discussion of the degree to which Mack's ownership of the Philadelphia A's assured his long-term job security (he was 38 when he took over the club in 1901, 87 when he quit in 1950), the fact that Stengel's record as a skipper was mediocre before the Yankees brought him into their winning tradition, or whether anyone could have managed the Gehrig-DiMaggio-Dickey Bronx Bombers to as many wins as McCarthy did.

But use of the Z-Score system can solve that problem in the same manner that it does for player performance. In the process, it removes any subjective bias that attends the evaluation of managers by comparing each skipper's career achievement to the average performance among all the pilots eligible for HOF consideration.

Compared to the data set for players, the measurement of relative managerial performance is simplified by the limited number of statistics available. Only 10 variables were used, including the six major traditional statistics (years managed, games managed, games won, winning percentage and, separately, pennants and World Series won), plus four sabermetric measures (the Average Yearly Standing of the manager's teams, Fibonacci Wins, and two versions of Actual-Minus-Expected Wins, one for career performance and one that was normalized to the yardstick of a 162-game season). As with the player statistics, no subjective weighting was given to any of the variables, so each stat counts equally in the manager's Z-Score. And although the skippers were identified with a specific historical era, there was no separate periodic measurement, because the number of eligible pilots with 10-year experience or more (77) was insufficient to produce separate era subsets large enough to possess statistical significance of their own. As a result, with no separate positional scale as well, the manager's scores are all based on just one measurement.

The variables used provide a balance between measures of longevity, absolute success, relative success and apparent managerial skill. Years and games managed are both clear measures of longevity, while games won is a combination of longevity and absolute success (because in theory, anyway, the length of a skipper's career is linked to how often he wins). Absolute success is also evident in winning percentage and the number of pennants and World Series won, while Average Yearly Standing and Fibonacci Wins are measures of relative success. Finally, as noted earlier, the two variables for Absolute-Minus-Expected Wins purport to measure skill.

Among the six traditional variables, all but winning percentage merely count career totals; and, along with the data for Actual-Minus-Expected

Wins-Career (Career A-E), the values for all six were taken from the individual stats provided in the Manager Register of *Total Baseball*. But, additional calculation beyond that data was necessary to derive career numbers for Average Yearly Standing, Fibonacci Wins and the Actual-Minus-Expected Wins-per-162 Games (or, Normalized A-E). Some technical points regarding the selection and form of the variables follow.

• The six traditional variables were used in their most common forms. Years managed was not normalized for the effect of partial seasons because significant differences arise between the lengths of 19th-and 20th-century seasons. Totals used for games managed, games won and winning percentage did not include postseason play. For managers in the years 1969–98, the number of division championships or wild-card playoff berths won was ignored because it has no application to the careers of men who managed only prior to 1969.

• Average Yearly Standing was the most difficult variable to define and handle fairly, and the method used is not the only one viable. For each full or partial season managed, each man was credited with the ordinal standing (first-place, second, third, etc.) of his team in its league (from 1876 to 1968) or division (from 1969 to 1998) at the end of his term as skipper for that season. The career number was derived by dividing the ordinal total for all seasons by the number of years managed, so low numerical results represent better scores than high ones and 1.00 is the best possible score. Managers fired at midseason were credited with their team's ordinal standing at the time of their dismissal, and skippers at the helm through the end a partial season were credited with the team's standing at year's end. Men managing more than one club in a season were credited for that season with the average ordinal standing for those teams at the close of their separate terms as skipper. As a result, some pilots hired at midseason are penalized for poor finishes that may have been more directly attributable to their predecessors, but these instances tend to balance out over the course of hirings and firings in a manager's career. For the split-season formats used in the National League of 1892 and in both major circuits in strike-shortened 1981, managers were credited with their team's ordinal standing in its league or division for the season as a whole (e.g., John McNamara was credited with a first-place finish with the 1981 Reds, although the split-season playoff format deprived Cincinnati of a divisional title that year). By limiting the lowest possible ordinal ranking to seventh place, the advent of divisional play in 1969 appears to provide a slight numerical advantage to skippers active since then (compared to men who managed when eighth-through twelfth-place finishes were possible), but that is offset by the fact that the Average Yearly Standing's value increases with proximity to the highest ordinal number (one), rather than the largest cardinal number.

• Fibonacci Wins were derived by the same formula used for pitchers — that is, FW = (Games won × Winning percentage) + Games over .500. Its application is just as valid for managers as it is for pitchers, because the data is identical to that of pitching records. And its effect is the same — it puts a skipper's wins into a context relative to his winning percentage.

• The Career Actual-Minus-Expected Wins (A-E) data measures, to one decimal place (e.g., ±2.3), the number of games won above or below the number of victories predictable from the relationship between a team's totals of runs scored and runs allowed, under the hypothesis that a team which scores the same number of runs that it allows should play exactly .500 base-ball. A more thorough explanation can be found in *Total Baseball's* Manager Register and Glossary of Statistical Terms. It is used in *Total Baseball* as an estimate of a manager's apparent skill (i.e., the number of games, plus or minus, that his ability alone has decided in his career), with the caveat that as longevity increases, the impact of chance declines. Note, however, that A-E's validity as a measure of managerial skill is unproven. The statistical relationship between a team's actual won-lost record and its runs scored–v.–runs allowed has been demonstrated mathematically by numerous sabermetric studies, but the portion of the variation between actual and expected wins that can be attributed directly to a manager has never been identified. The degree to which a team plays at, above, or below its runs scored–v.–runs allowed totals for a season may also be attributable to factors such as injuries, player chemistry, scheduling, travel fatigue, weather, luck, voodoo curses or free-agent athletic supporters like Margot Adams. But any error inherent in its use as a measure of managerial performance applies equally to all managers, with no bias, and therefore favors no one.

• Normalized A-E was calculated by the formula Norm A-E = Career A-E/Career 162-game units. It changes the Career A-E into a per-season format to counter any cumulative advantage that might result from longevity and — if the statistic as a whole is a true measure of managerial skill — guages a pilot's average seasonal impact on his team's won-lost performance. The values used were calculated to two decimal places (e.g., +1.69).

It should be noted that the Veterans Committee's current eligibility rules for managers do not require the same 23-year waiting period applied to players. Instead, managers can be eligible for VC consideration if they have been retired for five seasons or are retired and have reached the age of 65 at the time of their election. As a result, the data set measurements include all career totals through the 1998 season (i.e., the data supplied by the most recent edition of *Total Baseball*), rather than the 1994 cutoff used for the player scales. This was done to assure that the data for all qualified skippers was as up-to-date as possible.

The variables in the managerial data set also include a Core measurement similar to the one used in the player scales. Those variables include five traditional statistics — games managed, games won, winning percentage, and pennants and World Series won — which have been available to the Veterans Committee and its precursors since Connie Mack and John McGraw became the first skippers enshrined for that capacity in 1937.

Finally, although the Z-Score averages produce an ordered ranking of the pilots who qualified for the data set, the predominance of "counting" variables used (years, games managed, games won, pennants and World Series won, and Career A-E) imposes that the numerical result obtained is a measurement of overall career significance, and not a direct measure of a manager's skill. A high ranking implies only that a skipper's overall career performance is statistically superior in a cumulative sense. It should not be interpreted as any evaluation of his tactical or leadership ability.

The 77 managers who met the Hall's 10-year minimum-service requirement through 1998 include the 16 men elected to Cooperstown as skippers, plus 11 chosen as players (Cap Anson, Lou Boudreau, Frank Chance, Fred Clarke, Joe Cronin, Frankie Frisch, Rogers Hornsby, Hughie Jennings, Frank Robinson, Red Schoendienst and Bill Terry) and four men elected in other capacities (Charles Comiskey, Clark Griffith, Branch Rickey and Harry Wright). Overall, the group includes 10 men each who managed a majority of their games during the 19th-century and postwar eras, 17 from the live-ball period, nine from the dead-ball era, eight from the Expansion period and 23 from the free-agent era. Table Forty-Four provides the basic descriptive statistics for the sample as a whole, including the means, standard deviations, maximum and minimum career figures, Hall-of-Fame predictive rates and the names of the statistical leaders for each. The managerial Core-Z variables are indicated by boldface type.

Table Forty-Four
Statistics, Career Leaders and Predictive Rates, Managerial Variables

Variable	Mean	SDev	Max	Min	Rate	Leader(s)
Years Managed	16.2	6.6	53	10	.588	Mack
Games Managed	2278	1052	7755	682	.625	Mack
Games Won	1179	558	3731	299	.625	Mack
Winning Percentage	.517	.044	.615	.411	.438	McCarthy
Pennants Won	2.2	2.4	10	0	.667	McGraw/Stengel
World Series Won	1.0	1.4	7	0	.611	McCarthy/Stengel
Avg Yearly Standing	4.06	1.07	2.00	7.36	.563	Johnson
Fibonacci Wins	715	455	2434	7	.813	McGraw
Career A-E	4.4	15.4	37.3	-32.5	.250	McKechnie
Normalized A-E	0.33	1.11	2.24	-2.05	.250	McKeon

One or more Hall-of-Fame managers own the career leadership in eight of the 10 statistics. Connie Mack leads in years (53) and games managed (7755), plus games won (3731). John McGraw tops the list for Fibonacci Wins (2434) and is tied with Casey Stengel for most pennants won (10). Joe McCarthy has the best winning percentage (.615) and is deadlocked with Stengel for the most World Series victories (seven). Bill McKechnie is the leader for Career A-E (+37.3). Non–Hall of Famers Dave Johnson and Jack McKeon, both active in 2000, have the best Average Yearly Standing (2.00) and Normalized A-E (+2.24), respectively, through 1998.

Adopting the current total of 16 managers in the Hall of Fame as a standard of measurement, and including ties that carry beyond the 16th ordinal, Fibonacci Wins proves to be the best predictor of Cooperstown election among the ten variables used in the scale. Thirteen HOF skippers rank among the top sixteen career scores for Fibonacci Wins, for a success rate of .813. Pennants won is second-best, with 12 Hall of Famers among the leaders and a predictive rate of .667 (eight men are tied for eleventh place). Games managed and games won both score at a .625 clip (10 of 16), with years served at .588 (10 of 17; four men tied for 14th). Average yearly standing has a predictive rate of .563 (nine of 16). Winning percentage scores at only .438 (seven of 16), and the two A-E variables have a rate of .250 (four of 16).

Overall, the traditional variables have a combined predictive rate of .594 (60 out of 101), compared to just .469 for the sabermetric tools (30 of 64). The relative success of the traditional statistics is no surprise. To whatever degree career stats impact the election of managers to Cooperstown, that process is (and has been) prisoner to the type of statistics available at any given time; and, as with player data, the traditional variables have been around much longer and more readily available to influence the electors. The data for Career A-E was not easily available to anyone until the second edition of *Total Baseball* (1991), and, even now, there is no published source for Normalized A-E, Average Yearly Standing or Fibonacci Wins.

With that in mind, the most striking aspect of the variables' predictive values is the fact that the traditional statistics which measure longevity are better predictors of Hall-of-Fame membership by managers than those which measure absolute success. Among the six traditional variables, the three that evidence longevity (years, games and, to some extent, games won) have a composite predictive rate of .612, compared to .577 for those that only measure success (winning percentage, pennants and World Series won). Although the difference in those scores is not large, it helps explain some of the inconsistencies among the 16 HOF skippers' career statistics. Table Forty-Five provides the career records of the 16 Hall-of-Fame managers, including the year they were inducted (Ind), the era in which they piloted the most games (Era), the number of years (Yrs) and games (G) they managed, their career won-lost

Table Forty-Five
Career Records, Hall-of-Fame Managers Chosen through 2000

Manager	Ind	Era	Yrs	G	W	L	Pct	PW	WSW
Connie Mack	1937	LB	53	7755	3731	3948	.486	9	5
John McGraw	1937	DB	33	4769	2763	1948	.586	10	3
Bucky Harris	1975	LB	29	4408	2157	2218	.493	3	2
Sparky Anderson	2000	FA	26	4030	2194	1834	.545	5	3
Casey Stengel	1966	PW	25	3766	1905	1842	.508	10	7
Bill McKechnie	1962	LB	25	3647	1896	1723	.524	4	2
Leo Durocher	1994	PW	24	3739	2008	1709	.540	3	1
Joe McCarthy	1957	LB	24	3487	2125	1333	.615	9	7
Walter Alston	1983	EX	23	3658	2040	1613	.558	7	4
Tommy Lasorda	1997	FA	21	3050	1599	1439	.526	4	2
Wilbert Robinson	1945	LB	19	2819	1399	1398	.500	2	0
Ned Hanlon	1996	NC	19	2530	1313	1164	.530	5	1
Miller Huggins	1964	LB	17	2570	1413	1134	.555	6	3
Earl Weaver	1996	FA	17	2541	1480	1060	.583	4	1
Al Lopez	1977	PW	17	2425	1410	1004	.584	2	0
Frank Selee	1999	NC	16	2180	1284	862	.598	5	1
Averages			24	3586	1920	1639	.546	6	3

records (W and L), winning percentages (Pct), and the number of pennants (PW) and World Series (WSW) they won, along with the mean values among all 16 skippers for each traditional variable.

Table Forty-Five reveals the primacy of longevity in the selection process for managers. The mean career length for HOF skippers is 24.3 years, with a standard deviation of 9.0 seasons. Through 2000, the veterans committees have tended to enshrine men with service that equaled or exceeded that average — regardless of their won-lost ledgers — as, among the nine managers in history with 24 years of service or more, eight of them (89 percent) had been inducted at Cooperstown (all but Gene Mauch, with 26 years as a skipper). The rate is much higher than the 10 of 17 (59 percent) enshrined among men with careers of 20 years or more, and the 16 of 38 (42 percent) among those whose service equals or exceeds 15 seasons, the career length that is one standard deviation below the HOF average.

The weight of longevity in the election process also helps to demonstrate why winning percentage is a poor predictor of Hall-of-Fame membership by managers. The skippers listed in Table Forty-Five with 24 years service or more posted a combined winning percentage of .531. In comparison, those with shorter careers had a group winning percentage of .552. The effect is even more striking when you isolate the six men who exceeded the HOF career-length average from those with 24-year service or less — the former group has a winning percentage of only .520, compared to .558 for the latter.

Note also that three of the five men with the longest careers — Mack, Harris and Stengel — are among the four HOF skippers with the lowest winning percentages

The absence of any strong correlation between longevity and winning percentage in the selection of Hall-of-Fame managers can be explained, largely, by what is known as the Law of Competitive Balance, which dictates that the extremes among any set of statistical events must tend to even out over time. With regard to managerial careers, the axiom imposes that, on average, a pilot's career winning percentage should approach .500 as his longevity increases, reducing his chances of posting a high (or low) career mark for that variable.

But, although winning percentage has relatively little influence on Hall-of-Fame election for managers, the other two traditional measures of absolute success have considerably greater impact. The 16 managers in Cooperstown through 2000 owned 88 of the 173 pennants won (50.9 percent) and 43 of the 77 World Series victories (55.8 percent) posted among all of the 77 HOF-eligible skippers, combined. In comparison, the same group averaged no more than 34 percent of the total years managed, games managed or games won among the data set as a whole. So, predictably, a given skipper's chances for career longevity in general, and Hall-of-Fame election in particular, climb steadily as his number of pennant and World Series victories increase. Table Forty-Six compares the separate impacts of pennant and World Series success on a pilot's career length and chances for induction, including the number of pennants (Pen Won) or World Series won (WS Won), the number of HOF-eligible managers with each total (Tot Mgrs), the average longevity for each group (Avg Long), the number from each subset elected to Cooperstown through 2000 (HOF Tot) and the probability of election for members of each group (Elect Prob). Note that, on both sides, the probability factors increase as either total climbs, and that — with one exception at four pennants won — so does the average longevity.

Table Forty-Six
Effects of Pennants and World Series
Won on HOF Election and Longevity

Pen Won	Tot Mgrs	Avg Long	HOF Tot	Elect Prob	WS Won	Tot Mgrs	Avg Long	HOF Tot	Elect Prob
5–10	10	25.6	9	.900	4–7	4	31.3	4	1.000
4	8	16.9	3	.375	3	3	25.3	3	1.000
3	7	21.1	2	.286	2	11	18.5	4	.364
2	15	14.9	2	.133	1	23	14.7	3	.130
0–1	37	13.0	0	.000	0	36	13.8	2	.056

The sharpest delineations in Table Forty-Six occur at the points where the number of pennant or World Series victories exceeds one standard deviation above the norm for the sample. The sum of the sample mean (2.2) and standard deviation (2.4) for pennants won is 4.6, and the sum of the average (1.0) and s value (1.4) for World Series victories is 2.4. Commensurately, 90 percent of the skippers with five or more pennants are in the Hall of Fame, compared to only 10 percent of those with less than the average for that variable; and every pilot with three or more World Series victories is in Cooperstown, compared to just 13 percent of those below that mark. Similarly, the managers with five or more pennants have an average career length of 25.6 years, compared to 14.7 for those with less. The skippers with three or more World Series wins have a mean longevity of 28.7 years, while those with fewer Fall-Classic victories average 15.5 seasons.

So, historically, a combination of longevity and postseason success are vital to a manager's chances for election to Cooperstown, but a high winning percentage for regular-season games is relatively incidental to his prospects. In rare instances, however, a substantial winning percentage may substitute for postseason success sufficiently to let a skipper slide into the Hall — witness Al Lopez, with only two pennants and no World Series victories, but the seventh-best winning percentage among all HOF-eligible pilots. At the same time, managers with great longevity alone, but whose careers include no postseason triumphs, are likely to be overlooked — as demonstrated by the cases of Bucky Harris and Gene Mauch. Both men rank among the top five for years managed (Harris managed for 29 seasons, Mauch for 26), and both of their career winning percentages are below .500 and comparable (Harris at .493, Mauch with .483). But Harris won three pennants and two Fall Classics, and was elected to the Shrine in 1975. Mauch never guided a team to the World Series and, to date, has been passed over by the VC.

The 16 managers in the Hall through 2000 account for about 2.7 percent of the 591 skippers in big-league history. If the same representational standard were applied to the 14,000 players who appeared in the majors during 1876–1994, there would now be 378 players enshrined at Cooperstown, twice the number through 2000. So, statistically, the HOF standard of excellence for players is almost twice as stringent as the one in force for managers.

That representational imbalance is very recent. From 1937 through 1993, only 10 managers were enshrined, an average of about one every 5.7 years, producing a ratio (1.7 percent) more in line with the current 1.3 percent of all major-league players through 1994 that are now on the HOF roster. But since 1994 the Veterans Committee has expanded the number of skippers on the roster by 60 percent, adding six new inductees — Durocher (1994), Hanlon and Weaver (both 1996), Lasorda (1997), Selee (1999) and Anderson (2000) — for an average of almost one per year. In the panel's defense,

Durocher and Anderson's elections were dictated by de facto precedent, and the choices of Hanlon and Selee were obviously intended to correct long-standing oversights which had precluded the inductions of either of the 19th century's two best skippers.

But, whether one believes that Cooperstown is already overstocked with mediocrity or that many deserving candidates remain excluded from its roster, the existence of inconsistent standards that favor managers over players is logically indefensible. With few exceptions, people do not fork over their hard-earned money to attend ball games simply for the privilege of watching Earl Weaver kick dirt on umpires during one of his expectorating tirades, Tom Lasorda waddle to the mound to make a pitching change, or Yogi Berra scratch the lower extremities of his torso while leaning on the dugout steps (the latter of which could be seen much better on television anyway). And while each of those events may have had its own perverse appeal, none of them ever prompted the same roar from any crowd that attended a Babe Ruth homer, a great catch by Curt Flood, or even the sight of Mark McGwire swinging doughnut-weighted lumber on deck.

All the same, the Hall-of-Fame trustees and their electors are not about to throw out eight of the roster's current managers to redress excess representation. So if 16 managers is accepted as an appropriate standard at this time, then the Z-Score measurements compared to the means among all HOF-eligible managers validate the credentials of 10 of the skippers now enshrined at Cooperstown. Table Forty-Seven provides the final scores for all of the 77 pilots measured.

Given a 16-manager standard, the Cooperstown Baseline for skippers, indicated by the line in Table Forty-Seven, is located at a Total-Z average of +0.51. The score is 24 points lower than the baseline reported for players in chapter 11, demonstrating that — relative to the one applied for players — the Hall's current standard for managers is too low. But, the bottom line for player inclusion was based on a 1.5-percent standard instead of the 2.7 percent dictated by the Hall's current roster of pilots, and if the player standard is applied to the list above, the baseline would include only the top nine skippers and lie at a score of +0.73 almost identical to the one applied in chapter 11 — reaffirming the statistical consistency of the Cooperstown Baseline system.

Connie Mack and John McGraw, the first two managers chosen for Cooperstown in 1937, earn the top two scores in the final ratings, with Mack the only skipper to post a Total-Z average above plus two. Mack's high score is mainly attributable to his longevity: his Z Scores for years, games managed and games won (+5.58, +5.21 and +4.58, respectively) are all outliers. He posted negative scores for winning percentage, average standing and the two A-E variables. Seven other Hall-of-Fame skippers — Alston, McCarthy,

Table Forty-Seven
Rankings for Managers

Rank	Manager	Era	Total Z Avg	Core Z Avg	Rank	Manager	Era	Total Z Avg	Core Z Avg
1	Connie Mack	LB	2.19	2.94	40	Don Zimmer	FA	-0.11	-0.58
2	John McGraw	DB	1.73	2.29	41	Ned Hanlon	NC	-0.13	0.53
3	Walter Alston	EX	1.52	1.58		*Tom Kelly	FA	-0.13	-0.19
4	Joe McCarthy	LB	1.51	2.43	43	Fred Hutchinson	PW	-0.14	-0.56
5	Sparky Anderson	FA	1.30	1.34	44	Chuck Tanner	FA	-0.16	-0.06
6	Casey Stengel	PW	1.05	2.00	45	Bill Terry	LB	-0.17	-0.35
7	Bill McKechnie	LB	0.99	0.88	46	Alvin Dark	EX	-0.21	-0.18
8	Earl Weaver	FA	0.92	0.61	47	Harry Wright	NC	-0.22	-0.17
9	Miller Huggins	LB	0.73	0.91	48	*Jim Leyland	FA	-0.24	-0.34
10	*Bobby Cox	FA	0.68	0.45	49	Paul Richards	PW	-0.26	-0.56
11	Al Lopez	PW	0.63	0.26	50	*Bobby Valentine	FA	-0.29	-0.70
12	Billy Southworth	LB	0.58	0.51	51	*Lou Piniella	FA	-0.31	-0.27
	Ralph Houk	EX	0.58	0.51		*Jack McKeon	FA	-0.31	-0.83
14	Billy Martin	FA	0.54	0.17	53	Bill Virdon	FA	-0.34	-0.46
15	Leo Durocher	PW	0.51	0.74	54	Lou Boudreau	PW	-0.38	-0.23
	*Tony LaRussa	FA	0.51	0.36	55	Bill Rigney	EX	-0.39	-0.41
17	Frank Chance	DB	0.50	0.43	56	John McNamara	FA	-0.40	-0.38
18	Whitey Herzog	FA	0.47	0.19	57	Rogers Hornsby	LB	-0.43	-0.67
19	Frank Selee	NC	0.45	0.62	58	Buck Rodgers	FA	-0.44	-0.67
20	Dick Williams	FA	0.44	0.50	59	Fielder Jones	DB	-0.46	-0.36
21	Hughie Jennings	DB	0.43	0.03	60	Patsy Tebeau	NC	-0.57	-0.27
22	Tom Lasorda	FA	0.37	0.63		George Stallings	DB	-0.57	-0.40
23	Fred Clarke	DB	0.36	0.67	62	Burt Shotton	LB	-0.59	-0.67
24	*Dave Johnson	FA	0.33	-0.02	63	Birdie Tebbetts	PW	-0.63	-0.65
25	Clark Griffith	DB	0.32	0.01	64	Frank Robinson	FA	-0.66	-0.86
26	Steve O'Neill	PW	0.30	-0.04	65	Roger Craig	FA	-0.70	-0.63
27	Cap Anson	NC	0.26	0.41		Fred Haney	PW	-0.70	-0.68
28	Bucky Harris	LB	0.24	0.85	67	*Jim Fregosi	FA	-0.71	-0.62
29	Charlie Grimm	LB	0.11	0.03	68	Patsy Donovan	DB	-0.77	-0.83
30	Danny Murtaugh	EX	0.07	0.16	69	Lee Fohl	LB	-0.81	-0.84
	Wilbert Robinson	LB	0.07	-0.06	70	Dave Bristol	EX	-0.82	-0.93
32	Charles Comiskey	NC	0.04	0.28	71	Luke Sewell	LB	-0.92	-0.79
33	Joe Cronin	LB	0.01	-0.03	72	Billy Barnie	NC	-0.96	-1.04
34	Gene Mauch	EX	-0.04	0.09	73	Jack Chapman	NC	-0.98	-1.30
	Red Schoendienst	EX	-0.04	-0.10	74	Bob Ferguson	NC	-1.02	-1.28
36	Chuck Dressen	PW	-0.06	-0.31	75	Jimmy McAleer	DB	-1.07	-0.90
37	Frankie Frisch	LB	-0.09	-0.14	76	Branch Rickey	LB	-1.10	-0.93
38	*Joe Torre	FA	-0.10	0.08	77	Gus Schmelz	NC	-1.25	-0.92
	Jimmy Dykes	LB	-0.10	-0.30					

Anderson, Stengel, McKechnie, Weaver and Huggins — also rank in the top 10. Among them, Anderson and Weaver are the only ones added to the roster since 1994. Just two other HOF managers — Lopez and Durocher — rank among the top 16 ordinals.

The scores of the other five Hall-of-Fame managers — Frank Selee, Tom Lasorda, Bucky Harris, Wilbert Robinson and Ned Hanlon — all indicate that, based on the body of statistics compiled among HOF-eligible pilots through 1998, they are probable errors of selection. But the relative validity of their Cooperstown membership as managers depends in part on their historical and statistical significance at the times of their inductions and can fairly be judged only on a case-by-case basis.

Wilbert Robinson managed for 19 seasons and was elected by the OTC2 in 1945, the first skipper enshrined after Mack and McGraw. Except for a partial season at Baltimore in 1902, the former catcher's career as a pilot spanned 1914–31, with the Dodgers. As a manager, Wilbert had a good reputation for handling pitchers. His Dodger teams won pennants in 1916 and 1920, but lost both World Series. Overall, his teams won exactly one more regular-season contest than they lost, with an average yearly standing of 4.84 (or, about fifth place) in an eight-team league. His Career A-E is +16.4, for an average of +0.94 per 162 games, indicating that his apparent managerial skill was good enough to win about one extra game per season more than his clubs would've done on the merit of their run totals, alone. Both of those marks are well above the +4.4 and +0.33 scores averaged by the 77-man data set. So if Actual-Minus-Expected Wins has any validity as a measure of managerial skill, Robinson's abilities were substantial. At the time Wilbert retired, he ranked fifth among the all-time leaders in games managed and games won, and his career length was tied for the same ordinal. His scores for the other three traditional variables were not among the all-time top ten to that date.

Although Robinson is tied for the 30th ordinal in the final rankings, he has the 10th-best score among all eligible managers whose careers ended before his did or who had managed for at least 10 seasons prior to 1931 (those above him include Mack, McGraw, Huggins, Chance, Selee, Jennings, Clarke, Griffith and Anson). By the time he was enshrined, Robinson had dropped to eighth among the leaders for games managed and ninth for career length and games won. Joe McCarthy, Bill McKechnie and Bucky Harris had also completed at least 10 seasons as skippers by 1945, and, because they rank ahead of Robinson in the final ratings, Robinson was no worse than the 13th-best pilot in history, statistically, when inducted. None of that, however, makes a compelling case for Robinson's election, especially as the very first skipper enshrined after Mack and McGraw.

But most of the men ahead of Robinson in the final rankings and who preceded him historically were either already in the Hall as players (Anson was elected in 1939) or were chosen for Cooperstown in a non-managerial capacity at about the same time that Wilbert was inducted (Clarke and Jennings were enshrined in 1945, as players; Chance and Griffith went in the following year, as a player and executive, respectively). That left only three other men — Frank Selee and Ned Hanlon from the 19th century, and Miller Huggins — who were viable choices at the time. Given his career record and success with the Yankees of the 1920s, Huggins clearly would have been a better statistical choice in 1945. He won more games in less time than Robinson, could boast a higher winning percentage and had more pennants and World Series victories. Also, both men were dead — Huggins died in 1929, Robinson five years later — so the impulse to reward someone living was not a factor.

Subjectively, however, there were many things that Robinson had done which Huggins and Wilbert's other predecessors had not. None of them had managed players who read newspapers on the bench. They had not allowed Babe Herman to stand on third with two other baserunners, an incident that helped Brooklyn become known as the Daffy Dodgers during Robinson's tenure. They had not instituted a "Bonehead Club" to cut down on mental errors and then become its first and only member after submitting the wrong lineup card at the pre-game meeting with umpires. And none of them had believed themselves dead after catching an exploding grapefruit dropped from an airplane by Casey Stengel. Obviously, Huggins and the others were bypassed in 1945 because of the Daffy Factor. Robinson clearly earned his place in managerial lore, and, although unjustifiable statistically, he no doubt got his Cooperstown plaque — much as anything else — for doing all the wrong things much better than anyone else who came before him, and possibly since. In that light, it's difficult to criticize Wilbert's election on a subjective basis, because his presence in the Hall secures a future place for the game's most-deserving flakes.

Although Bucky Harris was younger and his career lasted a decade longer, he was a contemporary of Robinson during the years 1924–31. As implied earlier, if Harris had never won a pennant, he might now be viewed as the live-ball version of Gene Mauch. As players, Harris and Mauch both were second basemen who acquired early reputations as serious students of the game. Harris was only 27 when he was named as player-manager of the Senators in 1924; Mauch took over the Phillies in 1960, not much older at age 34. Both men piloted a lot of mediocre teams. Bucky's clubs finished in the second division in 19 of his 29 seasons as a skipper, and his average yearly standing was only 4.79. Mauch's teams were in the second division in five or his first nine seasons as a manager; they finished in fourth place or worse in thirteen of his seventeen years of divisional play; and Gene's average yearly standing was 4.67. And, as noted earlier, the two men's career winning percentages are nearly identical. Despite all that, through 1998 both men also ranked among the top five, all-time, in years and games managed. Harris was fourth in career games won, and Mauch was ninth in that category.

Harris and Mauch both had three chances at postseason glory. Mauch missed the brass ring on all three tries, watching his 1964 Phillies define "choke" for many baseball fans after they blew a 6.5-game lead in the last two weeks of that season. And two of his Angels teams of the 1980s couldn't get over the hump of winning the AL playoffs, despite being one pitch away from the World Series in 1986. In Harris' first two seasons as a manager, the Senators parlayed Walter Johnson's swan song as an effective pitcher into consecutive American League pennants and a World Series victory in 1924. Given the impact of postseason play on managerial longevity, Harris' immediate success may have assured his 29-year career. As a result, more than two decades later, Harris also was blessed to pilot the postwar Yankees during 1947-48, sandwiched between fellow Hall of Famers Joe McCarthy and Casey Stengel. The club won a pennant and World Series his first year, before Harris was fired after a third-place finish in the latter one. So, his better postseason fortune is the substantive difference in the two men's careers.

Bucky's A-E numbers indicate he wasn't much of a skipper. His career total is -32.5, with a seasonal average of -1.19, indicating that he may have cost his team more than one additional loss per season. But Harris ranked third in all three of the longevity variables and sixth in World Series victories when he retired in 1956. By 1975, the year of his election, he still held third place in years, games and games won and had dropped only one ordinal position in the other category. Also, among the 27 skippers who rank ahead of Harris in Table Forty-Seven, 10 of them were active as managers in 1975, or had not yet begun their careers as pilots. So although Bucky rates as an error of selection now, he didn't 25 years ago.

Given the presence of Mack, McCarthy, McKechnie and Huggins, the exclusion of Robinson and Harris from the Cooperstown roster would not deprive their era of managerial representation in the Shrine. But the same is not true of Frank Selee and Ned Hanlon, the only 19th-century skippers in the Hall. Selee misses the Cooperstown Baseline for managers by only six points and four ordinals, while Hanlon's Total-Z average is 64 points and 26 ordinals beneath the cutoff line. Beyond Selee, the other two 19th-century skippers above Hanlon (Anson and Comiskey) have been enshrined for other capacities, so if one believes the era should be represented by at least one manager, then Selee and Hanlon are the only viable options.

As skippers, Hanlon (who managed from 1889 to 1907) and Selee (from 1890 to 1905) were immediate contemporaries. Ned managed five different clubs, but only two of them were special. After a rough start in Baltimore (a 103–155 record for 1892–93), Hanlon's Orioles won three straight National League flags, followed by two second-place finishes. Hanlon and several of his players moved to Brooklyn in 1899, also winning pennants in his first two seasons at their new locale. In contrast, Selee managed for only two franchises, but both tenures were historically significant. During 12 seasons at Boston (1890–1901), Selee's teams won five NL flags and finished second once. He moved to the Cubs for 1902, and the club never placed higher than second during his four seasons as its skipper. But, by the time tuberculosis forced his retirement during the 1905 season, Selee had put together the Chicago roster that became another NL dynasty under his successor, Frank Chance. That team claimed four pennants in the five-year period 1906–10, setting the majors' regular-season record for games won (116) in 1906.

As noted earlier, Hanlon was not chosen by the VC until 1996, but that was still three years earlier than Selee's election. Although Selee's Z-Score average indicates he is better qualified, it's easy to trace why Hanlon was tabbed first.

The data set of HOF-eligible managers includes ten 19th-century skippers. Among them, Hanlon ranks first in career games, games won and for victories in his era's version of World Series play. He is also tied for first in pennants won, ranks second in years managed, and sixth in winning percentage among the pilots of his era. In comparison, Selee's only periodic leadership among those traditional variables is a first-place tie with Hanlon for pennants won. He is second in winning percentage and tied for that ordinal with Hanlon for World Series victories, and he ranks no higher than third in the other three categories.

The sequence of Hanlon and Selee's elections can also be understood from their separate impacts on managerial posterity. No fewer than 18 of Selee's players later became big-league skippers, and six of them — Chance, Jimmy Collins, Hugh Duffy, Johnny Evers, Kid Nichols and Joe Tinker — have been elected to Cooperstown as players. Hanlon's list of future managers includes only 13 men, two of which (Hughie Jennings and Joe Kelley) are also in the Hall for their playing achievements. But Hanlon's list also includes three Hall-of-Fame managers — Connie Mack, who played for Hanlon at Pittsburgh in 1891, plus John McGraw and Wilbert Robinson, from his clubs at Baltimore. All three, plus Hughie Jennings, rank among the top 30 skippers in Table Forty-Seven. In comparison, Selee had only two of his proteges — Chance and Patsy Donovan — qualify among the 77 men eligible for Cooperstown election as skippers, and only Chance (tied for 15th) ranks as high as any of Hanlon's pupils. Mack, McGraw, Robinson and Jennings managed in the majors for 121 years, combined, and begat a huge group of third-generation pilots to continue Hanlon's legacy, while Chance and Donovan were managers for a total 22 years and had much less impact on posterity. The proliferation and longevity of Hanlon's dugout proteges do far more than either man's managerial statistics to explain why Hanlon preceded Selee at Cooperstown.

Tom Lasorda's Total-Z of +0.37 ranks above three other Hall-of-Fame managers. But it is only good enough for 22nd place in Table Forty-Seven and is only the eighth-best score among the skippers of his era, making his election in 1997 more difficult to justify within the context of his time than the other apparent errors. Lasorda's induction apparently was rationalized on the basis of his ordinal scores among his era for the six traditional variables: he ranks second among free-agent era managers in games and games won; he is tied for second in years managed, pennants and World Series victories; he stands sixth in winning percentage; and only Sparky Anderson, who ranks first among the era in five of the categories, has a higher average ordinal rank (1.5, compared to Lasorda's 2.7).

But much of Lasorda's ordinal average derives from his rankings among the longevity variables, where his career numbers benefitted greatly from the O'Malley/Dodgers tradition of managerial stability (the club had only two skippers from the time Walter Alston was hired in 1954 until Lasorda left in 1996). Lasorda had six seasons in which his team played .488 baseball or worse, and in four of them his club's winning percentage declined by huge margins over the previous year: In 1979 the Dodgers fell from .586 and first place the year before to .488 and third; in 1984 they dropped from .562 and first to .488 and fourth; in 1986 they went from .586 and first to .451 and fifth; and in 1992 they declined from .574 and second by a one-game margin to .389 and last. Granted, that happens to almost every skipper, but it usually gets them fired after the first or second occurrence. With the O'Malley Dodgers, these nosedives were overlooked because Lasorda's longevity was institutionally guaranteed. His job-security advantage also allowed him to win at least one pennant and World Series (1988) after other clubs of his era might have canned him (e.g., the George Steinbrenner Yankees); and boosted his ordinal scores for two of the other traditional variables as well.

The real issue regarding Lasorda's merit as a Hall of Famer involves his poor scores for Actual-Minus-Expected Wins, and the doubt they create about whether he was a good manager at all. If the A-E data is removed from the measurement process, Lasorda's Total-Z average for the other eight variables is +0.76, second only to Sparky Anderson (+1.39) among his free-agent contemporaries. But, his total of -15.5 for Career A-E ranks 23rd — or dead-last — among the data-set managers of his era and is 72nd — or fifth from the bottom — among the 77 skippers measured overall. Among the eight highest-ranked free-agent era pilots in Table Forty-Seven (Anderson, Earl Weaver, Bobby Cox, Billy Martin, Tony LaRussa, Whitey Herzog, Dick Williams and Lasorda), Tommy is the only one to compile a negative career mark for either of the A-E statistics. And, except for Williams, Lasorda's total for the career variable ranges between 35.6 and 45.4 games worse than any of those better-scoring contemporaries. His score is also 37.8 games worse than the average Career A-E among the other seven men.

Lasorda's Normalized A-E is -0.82, indicating that his managerial approach may have cost his teams almost one full loss per season. The yearly total may actually be higher, because the other twenty-two free-agent era pilots in the data set average +0.61 for the same variable. That's a variation of 1.43 games per season versus many of Lasorda's contemporaries, clearly enough to make the difference in a close pennant race. In fact, Lasorda's managing may have cost the Dodgers at least three divisional titles during his tenure with the team — in 1980, 1982 and 1991. The Dodgers finished second by one game in each of those races (the first of which was decided by a playoff), and in each instance, the difference between Lasorda's A-E for the season and that of the first-place manager was greater than that one-game margin: in 1980 Tommy (+2.7) was 3.5 games worse than Houston's Bill Virdon (+6.2); in 1982 Lasorda (-1.4) trailed Atlanta's Joe Torre (+4.3) by 5.7 games; and in 1991 his score (1.1) was 1.2 games behind Atlanta's Bobby Cox (+2.3).

Beyond even that, Lasorda's seasonal A-E scores also indicate that his managing may have almost cost the Dodgers two other divisional crowns. In 1978, when Los Angeles won the NL West by 2.5 games over Cincinnati, Lasorda's A-E was -2.3 compared to Reds manager Sparky Anderson's +9.3, so the combination of the two men's relative skills as pilots that season gave the Reds an 11.6-game advantage that may have created a much closer race than would've occurred in the context of player performance alone. Similarly, the Dodgers won the World Series in 1981 after qualifying for the playoffs by leading the NL West during the first half of that strike-interrupted season. But overall, Cincinnati had the division's best record that year and missed the playoffs only because it didn't win either portion of the split-season format. Lasorda posted an A-E of -2.4 that season, while the Reds' John McNamara scored at +9.5; and, because the Reds' overall record was four games better than the Dodgers' for the season as a whole, Lasorda's leadership might have cost the team another flag in a normally formatted pennant race. With all of that in mind, and given the higher Total-Z averages posted by several of his contemporaries, Lasorda can be tentatively identified as the Fred Lindstrom of HOF managers, and the error of his election is far more clear-cut than those of Robinson, Harris, Selee or Hanlon.

The seasonal variations in Actual-Minus-Expected Wins by Lasorda and every other skipper are evidence that managers have good and bad seasons, just like players. In that light, seasonal A-E is analogous to the ERA posted by a pitcher or the batting average of a position player, both of which change from year to year depending on the player's physical health, relative consistency of performance, and ability to adapt to changing playing conditions. In his 21 years as a pilot, Lasorda had nine seasons with positive scores for A-E and 12 with negative ones, ranging between a high of +5.1 when the Dodgers won the pennant in 1983 (and he was named NL Manager of the Year) to a low of -8.2 in 1992, when Los Angeles finished last in its division. Presumably, in any skipper's better years, and regardless of the relative performance by the men on his roster, the balance of offense and defense is better-suited to his particular tactical style, or perhaps he does a better job of adapting that style to those changing conditions. But the scores of individual managers might be influenced just as much by their own psychological reactions to changes in the team's roster chemistry from one season to the next, or to his perception of the club's innate ability to contend for first place.

The Hall of Fame's current roster of managers already reflects a level of representation that is unjustifiably higher than the standard applied for players. As a result, it's dubious to argue that there are any errors of omission at the present time.

But, although his era is already overstocked with skippers, it's possible that the omission of Billy Southworth represents a long-standing error by the Veterans Committee. Southworth managed the Cardinals for part of the 1929 season, was replaced, and came back to pilot the same club during the years 1940–45 before moving to the Boston Braves for 1946–51. A majority of his games as a major-league skipper occurred during the live-ball period. He is tied with the expansion era's Ralph Houk for 12th place in the pilots' rankings, with a Total-Z of +0.58 that is seven points above the Cooperstown Baseline for managers — better than six of the skippers already enshrined. Beyond that, Southworth has the fifth-best average yearly standing (2.69) among the 77 skippers in the data set and occupies the 14th ordinal for Normalized A-E (+1.56). More impressively, he is fourth-best among all the measured pilots in winning percentage; and, because two of the men above him are 19th-century skippers Charlie Comiskey and Ned Hanlon, his career mark of .597 is second only to Joe McCarthy among all of the HOF-eligible managers from the 20th century. Southworth ranks just 18th in Fibonacci Wins, but his career total of 963 was compiled in only 13 seasons, and everyone above him on that list managed for 16 years or more. When normalized for 162-games, his average of 88.1 Fibonacci Wins per season is the fourth-best figure among all the skippers measured. Southworth also won four pennants for his two National League clubs (three with St. Louis and one with the Boston) and two World Series (for the Cardinals, in 1942 and 1944), tying him for 11th and eighth place, respectively, in those variables.

Southworth's failure to gain election clearly has resulted from the emphasis placed on longevity by the Veterans Committee electors. His 13-year career was three seasons shorter than the mean among the 77-man data set, and barely half the 24 years averaged by the 16 skippers enshrined at Cooperstown through 2000. In turn, the relative brevity of his career implies that his prospects for future election are dim, unless the current VC — which includes several men from his era, and one that played for him (Stan Musial) — decides to honor one of their own.

CHAPTER 13

The Token Few

On 14 July 1887, the defending National League champion Chicago White Stockings were scheduled to play an exhibition at Newark, whose International League Giants were part of a circuit which — as it does today — represented the highest rung of the minors. The Newark team included two African Americans, catcher Moses Fleetwood Walker (who had played in the major-league American Association for Toledo in 1884) and pitcher George Stovey (who would set a still-existent league record of 35 wins that season). When Chicago's player-manager, Hall of Famer Cap Anson, insisted that his club would refuse to take the field unless Walker and Stovey were barred from the game, Newark management folded to the demand rather than lose the exhibition's substantial gate. That same day, at a league meeting in Buffalo, a clique comprised of six of the circuit's 10 owners approved a resolution to deny future contracts to men of color.

The International League's action set a precedent which, at the insistence of men like Anson, the majors and all of organized baseball — i.e., members of its umbrella administration, the National Association of Professional Baseball Leagues — soon agreed to follow. In the aftermath, Stovey was released by Newark after the season; two other IL blacks, Toronto hurler Robert Higgins and Buffalo second sacker Frank Grant, were out of the circuit by the end of 1888; and, although Walker managed to hang on in the league the longest, he also was gone by the middle of the 1889 season, becoming the last African American to appear in organized baseball until Jackie Robinson joined the Montreal Royals in 1946 (in the same league in which the color barrier had been established).

In the six-decade interval that was ruled by that color barrier, there were

234

many independent teams and several organized circuits made up of African Americans and other "men of color," notably Cubans. Some of them preceded the racial barrier: the first known club of all-black professionals was formed as the Babylon, Long Island-Argyle Hotel Athletics in 1885; and the first African American professional league — with teams in Baltimore, Boston, Cincinnati, Louisville, New York, Philadelphia, Pittsburgh and Washington, D. C. — operated in 1887, the year of the IL's resolution, but folded because of financial problems before the end of that season. As a result, and because much of American life was segregated during those decades, it's inaccurate to claim that these leagues and franchises resulted because of organized baseball's racial restriction.

But it's also true that the teams and circuits that eventually became known under the umbrella designation "Negro Leagues" acquired that social identity — in large part — because of the disgraceful barrier that prevented men of color from performing in the whites-only country club of organized baseball. And there's no doubt that the color barrier was a tragedy for players of every race, because the exclusion also prevented several generations of the world's greatest players from competing against the very best talent available, thereby demeaning for posterity the performance of men in every professional league, regardless of their race.

Beyond that, the hypocrisy of the racial barrier is also evident from the fact that, during the years 1911–35, almost a dozen men of "color" — all of them light-skinned enough to appear passably white — played in the majors anyway, despite performing for Negro-League teams before or after their careers in the Show. The best-known of these were pitcher Dolf Luque, who posted a 194–179 record in a 20-season career with four National League clubs, and catcher Mike Gonzalez, who hit .253 in his 17-year tenure in the senior circuit. Both men also received Hall-of-Fame votes after they retired: Gonzalez got eight spread over five elections during 1950–60; Luque netted 26 on nine ballots during 1937–60, and — as his Z-Scores in previous chapters indicate — he deserved more.

At the peak of their existence, the Negro Leagues included seven different circuits which operated at various times, beginning with formation of the Negro National League in 1920. The first incarnation of the NNL folded in 1931, at the height of the Great Depression, and was succeeded by an offspring of the same name that existed from 1933 to 1947. The five other circuits included the Eastern Colored League (ECL, which operated during 1923–27), the American Negro League (ANL, 1929), the East-West (EWL) and Negro Southern Leagues (NSL, both of which existed as majors only in 1932), and the Negro American League (NAL, 1937–60).

The Negro Leagues produced at least three generations of players, the best of whose skills were undoubtedly equal to those of many Hall of Famers who performed in the white majors during the same era. But, while Jackie Robinson was enshrined at Cooperstown in 1962, in his first year of eligibility, Hall-of-Fame recognition was denied to Negro-League players until 1971, almost a decade after Robinson's induction.

There was much initial resistance to the enshrinement of Negro leaguers at Cooperstown, and their inclusion was agreed to only after ardent, and mostly secret, lobbying by Bowie Kuhn, the baseball commissioner at the time. The fruit of that effort ripened in 1971, when pitcher Satchel Paige was named as the first Negro-League inductee, chosen by a special committee formed to weigh the credentials of candidates and mandated to elect a series of Negro-League representatives annually through 1977.

After the special panel's mandate had ended, it was difficult to avoid the conclusion that the enshrinement of Negro Leaguers accomplished through 1977 had been anything more than tokenism. The nine men chosen were exactly enough — no more, no less — to make up a solitary lineup of players from the Negro circuits, and, but for the absence of a second baseman and the inclusion of an extra outfielder-pitcher, their positional citations represented just one man for each of the spots on a baseball diamond. This token all-star team included pitcher Paige (inducted in 1971); catcher Josh Gibson and first baseman Walter "Buck" Leonard (1972); outfielder Monte Irvin, (1973); outfielder James "Cool Papa" Bell (1974); third baseman William "Judy" Johnson (1975); and outfielder Oscar Charleston (1976); along with shortstop John Henry "Pop" Lloyd and outfielder-pitcher Martin Dihigo (1977).

Predictable criticism followed and led to approval of further selections. Former pitcher, team owner and NNL founder Rube Foster was elected in 1981 (the token executive, perhaps), and third baseman Ray Dandridge was added six years later. When they also proved insufficient to silence critics, the Veterans Committee was temporarily empowered to select one more man per year. Sequentially, those most recent choices included pitchers Leon Day (1995) and Bill Foster (Rube's brother, 1996), shortstop Willie Wells (1997), hurlers, "Bullet" Joe Rogan (1998) and "Smokey" Joe Williams (1999), and outfielder Norman "Turkey" Stearnes (2000), bringing the total of Negro Leaguers enshrined at Cooperstown to 17. But the clamor for further VC selections has quieted, and the prospect for additional selections may have been diminished by establishment, in the late 1990s, of a Negro League Hall of Fame located in Kansas City, as the new museum's existence seems likely to quell any sense of urgency to add more choices at Cooperstown.

All the same, the most thorough register of Negro-League players published to date, *The Negro Leagues Book*, (SABR, 1994), lists 4,385 men who were active in African American baseball in some capacity during the years 1862–1960, about one-fourth of which were team or league officials rather than players. Given Cooperstown's current representational standards (1.3 percent for players, and 2.7 percent for managers), justice would seem to require somewhere between 43 (or, 1.3 percent of about 3,300 players) and 118 (2.7 percent of 4,385) Negro-League representatives in the Hall. So the Shrine was, at minimum, 26 men short of equal treatment for those circuits through the 2000 voting.

But the issue of appropriate representation is muddled by the unavoidable fact that, although the Negro leagues were the highest level of play available to men of color during their time, the minimum skill level in each of those circuits was never equal to that which existed in the white majors during the years 1920–50, the black circuits' heyday. That conclusion, which might be interpreted incorrectly as racism by some, is the inescapable result of statistical analysis comparing the populations from which both environments drew their personnel.

Until after 1950, few of the players who appeared in the major leagues were born outside of the United States, and except for extremely rare instances of men in their late forties, all of them ranged between 15 and 44 years of age. In comparison, during the three decades before their talent level was depleted by integration of the majors, the Negro Leagues drew most of their players from the African American population in the United States and from men born in Cuba. With slightly more frequent exceptions, these players also came from the same age group as the whites. The available census data for that age group of males in the U.S. and Cuba during that period makes plain that, on average, the number of men on Negro-League rosters during each of the decennial years between 1920 and 1950 represented a proportion of their available population base that was never less than four times larger than the corresponding one for the white majors — undeniable evidence that the overall level of talent in the Negro circuits at each interval was more diluted than in the Show.

Because there is no objective method by which to measure what percentage of players on Negro-League rosters possessed a level of skill equal to or better than the worst major leaguer at the time, any attempt at estimation of that dilution would be spurious. But it seems fair to argue that on average, the overall level of talent in the Negro leagues at any given time was more analogous to that of the highest rung of the minors than to that of the major leagues.

All of this could be used to argue for the adequacy of the current level of Negro-League representation at Cooperstown. But despite the implications of the population data, and unless one adopts an overtly racist presumption that the very best athletes among one race are innately more talented than the best among another, it remains an inescapable statistical fact that — given adequate coaching — the talent level among the top 1 or 2 percent of

Negro leaguers must have been comparable to the Hall-of-Fame proportion of the whites on major-league rosters at any given time. So at the level of skill implied by HOF membership, there is no acceptable way to rationalize any proportion of Negro Leaguers included at Cooperstown which is significantly less than that of their major-league counterparts.

But the identification of qualified Negro-League candidates is hampered by the absence of complete statistical records for any Negro circuit. At present, there is not one man who played for 10 seasons or more in the Negro Leagues prior to 1950 for whom the available career batting or pitching data is in any manner complete. Currently, there are two major sources for such data among widely published works: the 1994 SABR volume noted above contains statistical records for 176 batters and 85 pitchers, and the ninth edition of the Macmillan *Baseball Encyclopedia* includes statistical registers for 129 non-pitchers and 65 hurlers. But the statistics in the SABR publication focus mainly on the records for former Negro Leaguers in organized baseball, including their performances in the major leagues, the high minors, and the Mexican and winter circuits. In contrast, the Macmillan registers do concentrate on Negro-League performance, but the season-by-season data and career totals provided are unavoidably incomplete for each, and limited in the number of statistical categories included (games, at-bats, hits, doubles, triples, home runs, stolen bases and batting average for batters; and wins, losses, winning percentage, games, games started, complete games, innings pitched, hits allowed, walks allowed, strikeouts, shutouts and saves for pitchers). As a result, the use of Z Scores to measure those career totals in their published form is inappropriate and statistically meaningless.

There is a method, however, by which the Z-Score format can be applied to the available Negro-League data to create a rough estimate of the Hall-of-Fame credentials of each of the players listed in Macmillan. The statistics provided by the *Baseball Encyclopedia* include partial totals for almost every year of each of the players' careers. Although the availability of these statistics is certainly haphazard in one sense (i.e., they come from disparate sources and times), they do not represent a random sample in purely statistical terms, because there is no way to be certain that they reflect performance against all possible teams and talent, under all possible conditions. Nonetheless, they do constitute a cross section of each man's batting or pitching performance at virtually every stage of his career. As a result, they can be treated very tenuously as a random sample of each player's achievements over time.

Because the available data for some of the men listed in Macmillan is too scarce to make their career totals useful, each man's stats must be converted to a form that possesses statistical significance and equity. The most viable method, given the shape of the data, is to normalize each man's career statistics by placing them into the context of a single season's performance.

Among several possible methods, the one selected for this measurement involved normalizations based on either a 502-at-bat or 162-inning season, standards chosen because they are the current minimums required to qualify for a major-league batting or earned-run-average leadership (at-bats had to be substituted for 502 plate appearances, because the available Negro-League data does not include walks by batters).

Unfortunately, the level of statistical confidence applied to each man's normalized data varies greatly, depending on the size of the career sampling for each player. Among the batters listed in Macmillan, the most significant sample is the data for Hall of Famer Cool Papa Bell, whose available stats include 3876 Negro-League at-bats. The least useful sample is the offensive data for pitcher Hilton Smith, whose batting totals include only 32 times at the plate. Among the pitching data, Hall of Famer Bill Foster has statistics for 1764 of his career innings, while Sam Bankhead's numbers represent only 16 of his career innings pitched.

The Macmillan registers include only 109 batters and 46 pitchers who appeared in at least 10 Negro-League seasons. The mean number of at-bats among the 109 batters is 1531, with a standard deviation of 655. The average career innings among the 46 hurlers is 817, with s equal to 390. Overall, the confidence level for each man's Z-Score measurement depends on the size of his career sample: those whose total of at-bats or innings is equal to or exceeds the mean for the appropriate group can be given relatively high confidence; those whose total ranges between the mean and one standard deviation below it merit only moderate confidence; and those whose total falls more than one s below the average deserve little confidence at all.

Owing to the operative dates of the circuits' existences, a large majority of the 10-year men played most of their careers during the live-ball era. As a result, no separate periodic or positional measurements were taken (all of the pitchers were starters, per se; and, except for outfielders as a group, none of the other positions would have produced a large enough sample to be statistically significant on their own). So, like the ratings for managers presented in chapter 12, the Z Scores reported below involve only one scale.

The measurement for batters was severely limited in scope. Because the scale was normalized to a 502-at-bat season, the value for that statistic is the same for each player measured and has no Z-Score relevance. The other stats available — games, at-bats, hits, doubles, triples, home runs, stolen bases and batting average — allow for only limited calculation of other variables not included. So the non-pitcher scale was restricted to those eight variables, plus home-run frequency and slugging average, a total of ten statistics in all. For pitchers, innings pitched was also normalized and had no application. The 10 useful variables provided by Macmillan — wins, percentage, games, games started, complete games, hits, walks, strikeouts, shutouts and saves — offered considerably greater opportunity for extrapolation. As a result, the pitcher scale included all of those statistics plus 11 others that could be calculated or estimated from that data (innings pitched per game, complete-game percent, hits- and walks-per nine innings, Ratio, opponents' batting and on-base averages, strikeouts-to-walks ratio, strikeouts-per-nine innings, plus shutout and saves percentages). Because the absence of all of the appropriate data, no Core measurements comparable to those for major leaguers were taken for either scale.

Table Forty-Eight provides the Z-Score rankings of the 46 Negro-League pitchers measured. As usual, the names of current Hall of Famers are bold-faced. Men who also played in the major leagues are noted in italics. In the column where previous tables have provided the Core-Z averages, a figure is given denoting the relative confidence of the player's Total-Z measurement (Conf Level). This number represents the ratio of the innings pitched reported by Macmillan for that player to the mean among the 46-man data set (817 innings). Numbers equal or greater than one have a high level of confidence, those between 0.99 and 0.47 (representing one *s* below the mean) have moderate confidence, and those below 0.47 possess little meaning at all. Just as the Core-Z averages were used in earlier measurements, the confidence level has been used as a tie breaker, but the number itself is in no way analogous to the Core-Z averages presented in earlier chapters.

The scores in Table Forty-Eight must be interpreted with extreme caution. Within the limitations of the data available, those for players with a confidence level of 1.00 or higher represent the most accurate estimates of career value among the pitchers measured. But, all the same, it remains probable that the statistics used to derive these scores represent no more than one-third of the full career performance by any hurler in the group, and often reflect a much smaller portion of a given man's career. Also, the range of Total Z Scores reported is not analogous to those established among the major-league pitchers listed in chapters 6 through 11. This sample, however, represents only 46 of the thousand or so hurlers included in SABR's 1994 Negro-League register, which itself is incomplete. As a result, the failure of any pitcher to post a Total-Z of more than +0.67 says far more about the shape and limitations of the database than it does about their quality of performance relative to any big-leaguers. Given the number of 10-year Negro-League pitchers whose stats are not available, it's possible that many of the men shown in Table Forty-Eight — including several with a negative Total-Z — would post scores above +1.00 when measured against a full data set of the circuits' HOF-eligible hurlers. So, at best, the scores provide only a loose, ballpark estimate of the relative career value of men eligible for future consideration by the Veterans Committee, and in no way reflect any final, statistical truth.

Table Forty-Eight
Negro League Pitcher Z Scores

Rank	Pitcher	Pos	Total Z Avg	Conf Level	Rank	Pitcher	Pos	Total Z Avg	Conf Level
1	Bernardo Baro	LB	0.67	0.03	24	Bill Holland	LB	0.00	1.67
2	*Satchel Paige*	LB	0.57	1.95	25	Bill Byrd	LB	-0.01	1.68
3	**Bill Foster**	LB	0.53	2.16	26	Ted Trent	LB	-0.02	1.45
4	**Bullet Joe Rogan**	LB	0.52	1.76		Crist. Torriente	LB	-0.02	0.07
5	Frank Wickware	DB	0.42	0.47	28	Jesse Winters	LB	-0.03	1.30
6	Dave Barnhill	LB	0.33	0.72	29	Willie Powell	LB	-0.05	1.04
7	**Leon Day**	LB	0.30	0.89	30	Chet Brewer	LB	-0.06	1.38
8	Dick Redding	LB	0.27	1.01	31	Webster McDonald	LB	-0.10	1.39
	Connie Johnson	LB	0.27	0.13	32	Rube Currie	LB	-0.13	1.52
10	Ray Brown	LB	0.25	1.35		Sam Streeter	LB	-0.13	1.30
11	Rats Henderson	LB	0.24	0.82	34	Luther Farrell	LB	-0.16	0.70
12	**Rube Foster**	DB	0.19	0.26	35	Terris McDuffie	LB	-0.18	0.75
13	**Joe Williams**	DB	0.18	1.14	36	Ed Rile	LB	-0.22	0.93
14	Hilton Smith	LB	0.16	0.92	37	Verdell Mathis	LB	-0.25	1.15
15	Max Manning	LB	0.10	0.80	38	Plunk Drake	LB	-0.26	1.39
	Leroy Matlock	LB	0.10	0.72		Phil Cockrell	LB	-0.26	1.28
	Luis Tiant, Sr.	LB	0.10	0.66		Ben Taylor	LB	-0.26	0.06
18	Harry Salmon	LB	0.07	1.29	41	Roosevelt Davis	LB	-0.29	1.08
19	William Bell	LB	0.06	1.36		Dizzy Dismukes	LB	-0.29	1.02
20	Ted Radcliffe	LB	0.06	0.71	43	Sam Bankhead	LB	-0.31	0.02
21	Andy Cooper	LB	0.02	1.82	44	Connie Rector	LB	-0.35	0.93
	Gene Bremmer	LB	0.02	0.66	45	Logan Hensley	LB	-0.37	1.03
	Martin Dihigo	LB	0.02	0.37	46	Sug Cornelius	LB	-0.39	0.90

To whatever degree they may have statistical significance, the scores appear to validate the credentials of several men chosen for the Hall to date, notably Satchel Paige, Bill Foster, Bullet Joe Rogan and Leon Day, each of whom ranks high among the leaders of the 46 pitchers measured and whose scores possess relatively good confidence levels. In turn, the reliability of the lower scores posted by Smokey Joe Williams, Rube Foster and Martin Dihigio is compromised by the absence of complete career data for all three, and — especially for the latter two — by the low confidence levels of their available data.

Table Forty-Nine provides a listing for the full, 109-man data set of Macmillan's Negro-League batters and, with one exception, uses the same

Table Forty-Nine
Negro League Non-Pitcher Z Scores

Rank	Batter	Era Pos	Total Z Avg	Conf Level	Rank	Batter	Era Pos	Total Z Avg	Conf Level
1	**Turkey Stearnes**	L-O	1.72	2.21	41	Neil Robinson	L-O	0.26	1.06
2	**Josh Gibson**	L-C	1.69	1.23	42	Odem Dials	L-O	0.24	0.18
3	Heavy Johnson	L-O	1.55	0.90	43	Biz Mackey	L-C	0.21	1.97
4	**Oscar Charleston**	L-O	1.42	2.17	44	Dick Lundy	L-S	0.18	1.37
5	John Beckwith	L-S	1.33	1.08	45	Lazaro Salazar	L-O	0.16	0.29
6	Mule Suttles	L-1	1.20	2.07	46	Louis Santop	D-C	0.15	0.51
7	Ed Rile	L-1	1.10	0.84	47	Nat Rogers	L-O	0.14	0.85
8	Luther Farrell	L-O	1.06	0.16	48	Valentin Dreke	L-O	0.10	1.00
9	Steel Arm Davis	L-1	1.03	0.16	49	Robt. Hudspeth	L-1	0.05	0.85
10	Chas. Blackwell	L-O	0.93	1.17	50	Bill Byrd	L-P	0.03	0.18
11	**Willie Wells**	L-S	0.82	2.35	51	Rev Cannady	L-S	0.00	1.01
12	Edgar Wesley	L-1	0.81	1.08	52	How. Easterling	L-3	-0.02	0.66
	Monte Irvin	L-O	0.81	0.59	53	Lenny Pearson	L-1	-0.03	1.06
14	Cris. Torriente	L-O	0.79	1.54	54	Newt Joseph	L-3	-0.04	1.43
15	*Willard Brown*	P-O	0.76	1.20	55	Dewey Creacy	L-3	-0.07	1.91
16	**Bullet Joe Rogan**	L-P	0.72	1.19	56	Terris McDuffie	L-P	-0.07	0.20
17	**Cool Papa Bell**	L-O	0.65	2.53	57	Ben Taylor	L-1	-0.09	1.42
	Jud Wilson	L-3	0.65	1.85	58	Sammy Hughes	L-2	-0.12	0.75
19	**Buck Leonard**	L-1	0.63	1.15	59	**Judy Johnson**	L-3	-0.13	1.79
20	John Russell	L-2	0.63	1.60		Clarence Jenkins	L-O	-0.13	1.23
	Buck O'Neil	P-1	0.63	0.92		Pete Hill	D-O	-0.13	0.73
22	**Martin Dihigo**	L-OP	0.59	0.91	62	Red Parnell	L-O	-0.14	1.27
23	Tom Young	L-C	0.56	0.62	63	Ray Brown	L-P	-0.15	0.34
24	Burnis Wright	L-O	0.55	0.63	64	George Giles	L-1	-0.16	0.86
25	Tubby Scales	L-2	0.54	1.35	65	Bernardo Baro	L-O	-0.22	0.62
26	Frog Redus	L-O	0.53	1.43	66	Lester Lockett	L-S	-0.23	0.87
27	Spoony Palm	L-C	0.52	0.61	67	Chaney White	L-O	-0.24	1.40
28	Branch Russell	L-O	0.51	1.53		Ed Stone	L-O	-0.24	0.71
29	Hilton Smith	L-P	0.50	0.02	69	Vic Harris	L-O	-0.25	1.24
30	Tank Carr	L-1	0.48	1.24	70	Lyman Bostock	L-1	-0.26	0.11
31	*Quincy Trouppe*	L-C	0.45	0.13	71	Alex Radcliff	L-3	-0.27	1.05
32	**Pop Lloyd**	D-S	0.42	1.51		Oliver Marcelle	L-3	-0.27	1.00
	Jimmy Lyons	L-O	0.42	0.63	73	Newt Allen	L-2	-0.28	2.23
34	Hurley McNair	L-O	0.39	1.59	74	Rabbit Shively	D-O	-0.32	0.74
35	Candy Jim Taylor	D-3	0.38	0.59		**Ray Dandridge**	L-3	-0.32	0.58
	Rube Foster	D-P	0.38	0.07	76	Crush Holloway	L-O	-0.33	1.88
37	Clint Thomas	L-O	0.35	1.64	77	Ted Radcliffe	L-C	-0.34	0.75
	Rap Dixon	L-O	0.35	1.37	78	Cy Perkins	L-C	-0.38	0.73
39	Orville Riggins	L-S	0.32	1.52		Alejandro Oms	L-O	-0.38	0.60
40	Barney Serrell	P-2	0.27	0.16		Julio Rojo	L-C	-0.39	0.57

Rank	Batter	Era Pos	Total Z Avg	Conf Level	Rank	Batter	Era Pos	Total Z Avg	Conf Level
81	Jim West	L-1	-0.40	1.30	96	Spottswood Poles	D-O	-0.81	0.18
	Cherokee Davis	L-O	-0.40	0.93	97	Larry Brown	L-C	-0.84	1.59
	Lick Carlisle	L-2	-0.40	0.38	98	Ted Page	L-O	-0.92	0.22
	Tetelo Vargas	L-O	-0.40	0.30	99	Showboat Thomas	L-1	-0.96	0.67
85	Jim Brown	L-C	-0.43	1.26		Bruce Petway	D-C	-0.96	0.59
86	Jelly Gardner	L-O	-0.45	1.40	101	Frank Duncan	L-C	-1.00	1.51
87	Jumbo Kimbro	L-O	-0.46	1.56		Jim Crutchfield	L-O	-1.00	0.66
88	Parnell Woods	L-3	-0.50	0.32	103	Dave Malarcher	L-3	-1.18	1.39
89	Sam Bankhead	L-S	-0.55	1.09	104	Morty Clark	D-S	-1.33	0.69
90	Gene Benson	L-O	-0.57	1.24	105	Bingo DeMoss	D-2	-1.34	1.26
91	**Leon Day**	L-P	-0.59	0.40	106	Sol White	D-2	-1.35	0.03
92	Pelayo Chacon	L-S	-0.67	0.53	107	Pee Wee Butts	P-S	-1.40	1.18
93	Leroy Morney	L-S	-0.70	0.38	108	Dick Seay	L-2	-1.76	0.79
94	Frank Warfield	L-2	-0.73	1.86	109	Paul Stephens	L-S	-1.77	1.08
95	Jerry Benjamin	L-O	-0.77	1.04					

conventions established in Table Forty-Eight. Because many of the men listed are unfamiliar to some readers, their historical era and positions are both given in abbreviated form in the column labeled "Era Pos." The first character in that column designates the player's era (D for dead-ball, L for live, and P for postwar). The second notation indicates his primary position (C for catchers, O for outfielders, S for shortstops, and 1-2-3 for either first, second or third basemen). The confidence level for this table was derived from the 1531-at-bat mean for the non-pitcher data set.

Because the Macmillan data for batters is extremely limited in scope, the scores for Table Forty-Nine are even less reliable, (relative to those presented in earlier chapters for major-league batters) than the pitching scores reported in Table Forty-Eight. Nonetheless, counting Martin Dihigo as an outfielder, eight of the 10 Negro-League non-pitchers currently enshrined at Cooperstown rank among the top one-third of the 109 batters measured. Of the three who rank lower, one of them (Leon Day) was enshrined as a pitcher, so his low score for batting has little HOF relevance. That leaves only Judy Johnson (a Total-Z of -0.13) and Ray Dandridge (-0.32) as possible errors of selection. But like the errors among the major-league Hall of Famers, neither man is about to be expelled from Cooperstown, and certainly should not be on the basis of the incomplete statistics available to date.

Applying the 1.5-percent representational standard used for the final selection of Hall-of-Fame players in chapter 11 implies that a minimum of 50 (i.e., 1.5 percent of 3,300) of the men in Tables Forty-Eight and Forty-Nine should be enshrined to give the Negro Leagues the same proportional treatment proposed in that chapter for major leaguers. As a result, the Cooperstown Baseline for both tables should reflect the top fifty players with confidence levels above the 0.47 minimum for the moderate range, less any current Hall of Famers who score below that mark.

Within those guidelines, the top 50 scores in both tables (combined) extend to a Total-Z average of +0.15; and, as indicated by the lines drawn in both tables, that is the Cooperstown Baseline for the Negro-League data. Above that point, a total of 12 men — four pitchers (including Hall of Famer Rube Foster) and eight batters — have confidence levels insufficient to validate their scores. But on the whole, the Cooperstown Baseline verifies the credentials of every other current Negro-League Hall of Famer except Johnson and Dandridge (note that, although Leon Day and Martin Dihigo also post scores below +0.15 on one scale, they qualify on the other).

The bottom line for both Negro-League scales is that they can only be used as a loose guideline to aid in the evaluation of any candidates that might receive the Veterans Committee's future consideration. Although the data from which the scores were derived is incomplete, the Total-Z averages reported are nonetheless accurate within their limited context and provide a better frame of reference for the relative merits of each man's available statistics than mere subjective analysis.

Clearly, equal treatment of the Negro Leaguers requires many more HOF selections than the token few made to date. Granted that the VC is unlikely to induct a couple dozen of them *en masse*, and despite the limitations of the statistics currently available, the scores in this chapter do offer a framework for the advocacy of several candidates who have clearly been overlooked by the selection process to date. So the 10 Hall-of-Fame additions proposed below are presented only as suggestions for a minimal head start toward Negro-League equity at Cooperstown. Some of the individual statistics discussed include unofficial data from sources other than Macmillan that may involve performance against non-league competition, and the advocacy of these candidates is far more subjective than any which appear elsewhere in this text.

Although Hall of Famer Josh Gibson is considered the premier power hitter in Negro-League history and reputedly hit 800–900 home runs overall, the largest total among the official data collected to date (190) belongs to first baseman George "Mule" Suttles, who compiled the sixth-best Total-Z in Table Forty-Nine. Suttles's available data for 3077 at-bats shows a total of 1011 hits and a .329 batting average. His normalized figures are 164 hits, 27 doubles, 11 triples, 31 homers, 306 total bases, seven base swipes, and a .610 slugging average per 162-game season. Among the 18 big-league first sackers in Cooperstown, only six posted higher normalized scores for hits, five for home runs and batting average, and two for slugging percentage. Mule's known career home-run frequency (16.2) is identical to Lou Gehrig's. Suttles may have won a triple crown in 1926, too, as he is credited with the NNL leadership in home runs and batting average for that season (RBI data is not available for any Negro league). He won two other home-run titles, batted .389 in five all-star games (1933–35, 1937 and 1939), and set the official record for most home runs in a Negro-League season (27).

The Macmillan data credits "Cannonball" Dick Redding with a record of only 69–54 (.561) spread over 21 seasons (1911–31), but it's clear from unofficial statistics that his skills as a pitcher were far greater than that ledger implies. Redding teamed with current Hall of Famer Smokey Joe Williams on several different clubs to form one of the Negro Leagues' most potent pitching duos during the last decade of the dead-ball era. Including all competition, Redding is credited with a total of 30 no-hitters in his career, a 17-game winning streak in his rookie season, and a 43–12 record in 1912. He is also reputed to have won 20 consecutive games in 1915. Among the official stats, the nearest to a full-season ledger is his 17–12 record while serving as player-manager with the AC Bacharach Giants for 1921.

Louis Santop earns a Total-Z of only +0.15, but the available evidence indicates that he was a statistical rarity — a dead-ball catcher who batted over .300. Santop's career spanned 1909–26, almost identical to the period in which Hall of Famer Ray Schalk was hitting a feeble .253. The Macmillan data, which includes only 735 at-bats (for a confidence level of just 0.51), shows Santop at .321, and some sources claim the six-foot-four-inch, 240-pound backstop actually batted over .400 in his career against all competition. Whether true or not, it is known that Santop hit .316 in all of his exhibitions against big-league pitching. By reputation, Louis was the Negro Leagues' first great power hitter, preceding Josh Gibson, Mule Suttles and Turkey Stearnes by a decade or more. By the World War One years he was nicknamed "Big Bertha" for the presumed similarity between his long home runs and the trajectories of shells fired by Germany's most famous cannon. Santop also had a great arm, often staging pre-game exhibitions in which for 15 minutes he would sit in a catcher's squat and fire strikes to each infielder. Legend has it he was capable of throwing a ball from home plate over the center-field fence.

The Negro circuits' best backstop in the decade between Santop's prime and the early years of Josh Gibson's career was probably Raleigh "Biz" Mackey, whose tenure spanned three decades (1918–47). In the 2925 at-bats recorded in Macmillan, Mackey batted .322 with 60 home runs, the fifteenth best homer total among the men listed. Mackey reputedly batted .423, with 20 homers and a .698 slugging percentage for the Hilldales in the Eastern Colored League's inaugural season of 1923, and had back-to-back years of .400 and .376 in 1930-31. He also led the ECL in homers in 1926. Although his best years were behind him, he did appear in four all-star games (1933/35-36/38), going 3 for 14. Mackey also had a strong, accurate throwing arm, was a great student of opposing hitters' weaknesses, and many Negro-league historians consider him the best all-around catcher in the circuits' history — better even than Gibson.

Willard Brown has the 15th-best Total-Z in Table Forty-Nine, based on a confidence level of 1.20. His Negro-League career spanned 1934–52, and he also had a brief stint as a 36-year-old "rookie" with the St. Louis Browns in 1947 (he batted only .179 in 21 games, but his lone home run was the first ever hit by a black player in the American League). The Macmillan data, based on 1773 at-bats, shows Brown batted .352, and SABR has credited him with consecutive NAL batting titles with the Kansas City Monarchs of 1937-38 (.371 and .356), another one in 1941, and as a seven-time home-run champ. Brown also appeared in six all-star games.

In the 2763 at-bats recorded by Macmillan Jud "Boojum" Wilson is credited with 63 home runs and a .347 batting average. The left-handed-hitting third sacker is tied with Hall of Famer Cool Papa Bell for 16th place in Table Forty-Nine, with a Total-Z of +0.65 and a confidence level of 1.85. The SABR data credits Wilson with ECL batting titles for 1923 (.373) and 1927 (.469), and he never hit below .315 in the period 1923–37. Wilson was a starting third baseman in the first three Negro all-star games, going 5-for-11 (.455). His full career spanned 1922–45, and (born in 1899) he is one of many Negro-League stars simply too old for a shot at the majors by the time Jackie Robinson debuted in 1947. Stocky (five-foot-eight, 185 pounds) and quick-tempered, Wilson frequently brawled with opponents. He was known to have manhandled an umpire or two; and even his teammates learned to fear his short fuse. But there is no doubt that Wilson was one of the premier hitters in Negro-League history.

Although Pop Lloyd and Willie Wells have already been enshrined, there are still several Negro-League shortstops with solid credentials who have been overlooked by Cooperstown. Among them, the greatest offensive force was John Beckwith, who split most of his career (1916–35) between short and third base. Beckwith posted the fifth-best Total-Z in Table Forty-Nine (+1.33) on a confidence level of 1.08. In the 1638 at-bats recorded in Macmillan, Beckwith slugged 91 home runs and batted .356. In 1927, while Babe Ruth was clouting 60 homers for the Yankees, Beckwith was credited with hitting 72 against all levels of competition, and he followed the performance with 44 the next season. In 1930, although there was no formal eastern circuit in competition with the west-based NNL, John is credited with having led all eastern teams with a .480 batting average; and he also topped the eastern clubs in circuit clouts in 1930-31.

Another shortstop, Dick Lundy, was almost as good as Beckwith at the plate. Although Lundy's Total-Z (+0.18) is only good enough for forty-fourth place in Table Forty-Nine, his Macmillan data shows him batting .324, with 47 home runs in 2017 at-bats. He also tied Hall of Famer Oscar Charleston for the ECL lead in homers for 1924. Lundy is credited with two seasons above .400 (.484 in 1921 and .409 in 1928), as well, and hit below .310 only once during the 1920s. He is generally regarded as the Negro Leagues' best defensive shortstop in the period between the careers of Hall of Famers Lloyd and Wells.

The Negro circuits produced numerous players who acquired fame as both hitters and pitchers, the most notable being Hall of Famer Martin Dihigo. Another man just about as good was Cristobal Torriente, a native Cuban who clearly would have played in the majors during the era of Dolf Luque and Mike Gonzalez had he appeared passably white. John McGraw coveted the light-skinned Torriente, but never signed him because the tightly curled texture of his hair gave away his ancestry. Torriente began his career with the New York Cubans in 1913 and played through the early 1930s. Macmillan gives him 53 homers and a .335 batting average in 2311 at-bats, along with a 19–11 pitching record and .633 winning percentage. He won two NNL batting crowns, leading the circuit with a .411 mark in its inaugural season (1920) and hitting .412 in 1923. He backed up those stats by hitting .352 in 13 seasons of Cuban winter-league play, and he was among the first group of players elected to the Cuban Baseball Hall of Fame.

For much of his career Hilton Smith was known as Satchel Paige's "relief." Smith spent 12 of his 17 Negro-League seasons (1932–48) with the Kansas City Monarchs, including eight years with Paige on the roster. Paige would often start a game, pitch three or four innings, and then be replaced by Smith, who proved just as tough to hit. His stats in Macmillan include a 69–33 record, for a .676 winning percentage. He led the NAL in victories five times. Over one six-year stretch he reportedly compiled a 129–28 (.822) record against all opposition, including seasons of 25–2, 21–3, 25–1 and 22–5 during 1939–42. Smith played in five all-star games (1937–40 and 1942), splitting two pitching decisions.

Beyond these men the Negro Leagues produced a host of other candidates with viable Cooperstown credentials. Justice requires their admission in numbers adequate to redress the tokenism of the past.

CHAPTER 14

The Z-Score Solution

In one sense, resistance to the application of any purely objective criteria for Hall-of-Fame membership is well-founded. Baseball is a game of nuance, and many of its most-telling moments occur in events for which there can be no meaningful statistics — the timing and smooth swing of a batter as he lines an outside fastball to the opposite field for a single, the fluid twist of a second baseman as he pivots to make the relay throw in the middle of a double play, or the combative determination on a pitcher's face as he stares past the hitter for the catcher's sign on a 3–1 count. Those moments and others like them are just as integral as a batting, fielding or earned run average to the methods by which we judge a player's relative skills. No one who truly loves baseball wants them removed from the process to evaluate greatness.

The removal of subjectivity from the election process would also destroy a significant part of Cooperstown's charm. Any system of selection whose rigid reliance upon objective, statistical facts prevented the enshrinement of unique candidates like pitcher Dizzy Dean (whose flamboyant personality enhanced the aura of his achievements, but whose period of brilliance on the mound was almost too short to merit Hall of Fame recognition) or manager Wilbert Robinson (whose own daffiness set the tone for his colorful teams) would deprive the game of its inherent right to honor some of its most revered characters for the quality of their legends, alone.

Also, the criteria for the game's highest honor should never be reduced to the kind of automatic-qualification standards used for admission to the Ladies Professional Golf Association's Hall of Fame. Eighteen tournament victories — or whatever the current total might be — may be enough to satisfy the LPGA, but every career .300 hitter does not belong in Cooperstown.

Neither, perhaps, does every man with 500 home runs. The long-ball barrage of the late 1990s helped Jose Canseco move to within striking distance of that career total, and with 446 homers through the 2000 season, he seemed certain, given freedom from injury, to achieve that de facto standard. Canseco's career began with great promise — in 1988 he became the first major leaguer ever to hit forty homers and steal as many bases in a single season, en route to a well-deserved MVP Award. But later, his penchant for parties, fast cars and pop-music divas apparently reduced his ability or desire to fully utilize his talents; and his long-term performance has proven him little more than a circuit-clout savant, like Dave Kingman. As a result, even with the requisite home-run total, Canseco, whose final Total-Z through 1994 was +0.34 — tied for 352nd place among the data set's non-pitchers — would not meet most people's subjective definition of a Hall of Famer.

But as evidenced by the BBWAA voting of 1999, when first-year de facto qualifiers Nolan Ryan, George Brett and Robin Yount were the only candidates elected, a 75-percent majority (or more) of the voting scribes has obviously become captive of the rigid, one-dimensional thinking that accompanies application of the Hall's current de facto standards for admission. Within that perverse logic (which probably cannot be reversed), Canseco's likely achievement of the home-run standard augurs the near-future enshrinement of Cooperstown's first de facto error of selection since 300-win pitcher Mickey Welch.

It's also evident that the Hall's institutional resistance to the use of formal objective criteria has exacted its own price on the overall quality of its membership. The Z-Score method of evaluation applied in chapters 6 through 12 identified 46 — or 22.9 percent — of the 201 players and managers chosen for Cooperstown through 2000 as statistical errors of selection, and an equal or larger number of other, better-qualified men as errors of omission. So it's clear that, except for de facto standards, to whatever degree statistics are used as a voting guideline by HOF electors, their application has never been consistent over time, or on a case-by-case basis.

As a result, the only solution to the dilemma is some alteration of the selection process which assures that errors of selection and omission are at least minimized, if not eliminated. Realistically, there is no way to do that without some objective system that helps to counterbalance the subjective biases operative among the BBWAA voters. Such a solution should take all relevant aspects of performance into account, apply them on a relative — rather than absolute — basis, and be easily adaptable to the current Hall-of-Fame voting process.

The Z-Score method presented in this book meets all of those criteria, yet both of the Z-Score averages devised for this book are probably inappropriate for adaptation to the current selection procedure. Although the Core-Z average (including hits, home runs, runs scored, RBI and batting average for non-pitchers, and wins, winning percentage, ERA, innings pitched and strike-outs for hurlers) includes those statistics which are — and traditionally have been — given high priority by the HOF electors and fans alike, it clearly involves too few variables to be a thorough measure of either type of perfor-mance, and its five pitching stats severely disadvantage relievers. In turn, the Total-Z used as the basis for each of the scales in chapters 6 through 11, whose scope was intended to include virtually every stat which might be relevant to Cooperstown election, probably encompasses too large a field of statistics to be practical. As a result, the Z-Score averages applied to HOF voting might work best with around 15 or 20 different variables for each data set.

One suggestion for a more workable set of non-pitcher variables would include career games played, hits, home runs, total bases, runs scored, RBI, runs produced, stolen bases, batting average, slugging average, on-base aver-age, Babe Ruth and Gold-Glove Points (or a comprehensive facsimile of each), Runs Created, fielding average, range factor, pennants won, World Series won, as well as times led league in batting and fielding (combined as one vari-able) and Batting and Fielding Runs (also combined) — a total of 20 statis-tics that reflect a broad scope of on-field, postseason and award-voting performance, and which retains a semblance of the relative proportion of offense to defense used in the Total-Z calculations provided here.

For pitchers, an equal number of relatively balanced variables might include wins, winning percentage, earned run average, Fibonacci Wins, games pitched, innings pitched, opponents' batting average, opponents' on-base aver-age, the baserunners-per-nine-innings Ratio, strikeouts, strikeouts-per-nine innings, the strikeouts-to-walks ratio, saves, Pitching Runs, Cy Young Points (or a facsimile), times led league in pitching, fielding average, range factor, pennants won and World Series won — a group which retains the most impor-tant statistics, keeps measures of fielding prowess at a ratio similar to that of the Total-Z scale and would still allow relief pitchers to be competitive ver-sus starters (within the scope of modern relief strategies, complete games and shutouts by starters are becoming increasingly irrelevant to HOF creden-tials — although those stats may remain important to the BBWAA voters).

Although it was not done for this study, the variables listed above — or any alternative groupings — could also be weighted according to the relative Hall-of-Fame significance of each statistic. But any method of weighting applied should be based on objective criteria of some kind, not merely on the relative importance given within the BBWAA electors' subjective biases; oth-erwise, the elective impact of that bias is doubled.

Whatever variables and weighting are used, the Z Scores derived from both new scales should be applied in the form of era, positional and overall measurements, with each man receiving a cumulative average as calculated herein — because each scale is vital to any fair assessment of a man's relative career achievement, and the cumulative averages provide the most accurate method to combine each measure. The resulting Total-Z averages would once again reflect each player's combined career performance, representing an objective measurement of the quality of his overall statistical achievement.

These averages would need to be updated on an annual basis to include any and all new players who become eligible for Hall-of-Fame consideration. So the composition of the data sets, the resultant scores for men already in the system, and the Cooperstown Baseline itself would change very marginally, year to year. Nonetheless, the scope of this averaging process is easily within the abilities of the Elias Sports Bureau, which handles all of baseball's official statistics.

Each man's final Total-Z would then be converted — by a simple movement of the decimal — to a percentage equivalent applied to augment his performance on the BBWAA ballot. A man with a Total-Z of +1.28 would therefore have whatever support percentage he receives from the voting scribes increased by 12.8 percent, and one with a Total-Z of +2.32 would get a 23.2-percent boost.

But there is one catch to all of this. Without another adjustment, men whose Total-Z averages are below average (0.00) would actually have their support percentages reduced by this method — a result which complicates the system's subsequent applicability to the Veterans Committee procedure.

To avoid that outcome, each man who passes the Screening Committee process would also have his Total-Z average augmented by a longevity bonus of +1.00. The enhancement is justifiable within the argument presented in chapter 3 that, in a theoretical sense, players with 10 years of major-league service are roughly one standard deviation above the big-league norm by virtue of their longevity alone. As a result, by moving the decimal for that bonus to the right again, each man on the ballot would actually have his support percentage increased by a minimum of 10 percent (i.e., the +1.00 longevity bonus) plus the percentage equivalent of his Total-Z. So a man with a Total-Z of +1.28 would have his score increased by 22.8 percent, one with a final average of +2.32 would receive a 33.2-percent boost, and a man with a Total-Z of -0.62 would have his percentage increased by only 3.8 percent (i.e., 10.0 percent added to negative 6.2). As a result, and fittingly, players with negative Total-Z averages will have an extremely difficult time getting elected. (It's likely that very few of them would ever pass the Screening Committee process anyway, especially those with Total-Z averages worse than -1.00.)

There is no need for any other adjustment to the current BBWAA voting procedure. The qualified scribes may continue to cast their annual ballots, applying their subjective biases in whatever fashion they deem fit; and the system can and should retain its current requirement of 75-percent support for election.

But to safeguard the integrity of the process, the final adjustment value for each player should never be made available to voters before the ballots are collected. Each player should receive his Total-Z adjustment only after the ballots have been turned in and counted. And his final score for that ballot — the one announced publicly — would reflect the combined result of the voting itself and whatever augmentation the player's career statistics merited. The BBWAA electors could conceivably, record each man's adjustment from the previous year's voting and cast ballots intended to counter specific individual adjustments, but their only motive for doing so would be to derail the candidacy of a player they do not want enshrined and probably wouldn't vote for anyway. Because the adjustment would fluctuate slightly each year, however, they would not know the exact change in advance. So the tactic could have no meaningful impact.

Finally, the application of the Z-Score system to Hall-of-Fame voting requires two simple alterations in the current BBWAA election regulations. First, although the candidate Screening Committee should be retained, the number of men allowed on each ballot should be increased. The current limitation of 40 candidates or less is insufficient given the increased number of men with 10-year major-league service produced by baseball's multiple expansions since 1961. Assuming that the need for balanced league and divisional sizes will eventually require another tier of expansion to 32 teams, a loose, 50-man guideline would be more appropriate to the number of viable candidates likely to ensue from that and other recent expansions. Second, the current rule by which players who receive less than 5-percent support in a given year are dropped from the ballot should and must be abandoned. Given the existence of the Screening Committee, the 5-percent-support rule is both unnecessary and redundant. Historically, many worthy candidates who received little support in their early years on the ballot have been elected later, after their individual credentials acquired increased luster over time; and modern players should be afforded an equal opportunity to achieve that result as were their earlier counterparts.

At first, this plan sounds as if it would produce an inordinate number of new Hall of Famers every year. But it would not and never could work that way. To begin with, expansion of the ballot to accommodate about fifty candidates and the elimination of the 5-percent-support rule would lead to a gradual increase in the number of names on each ballot, an effect which will spread the voters' support among a larger group of candidates, reducing the probability that more than one or two men might be elected in a given year.

The maximum upward adjustment in this system is 49.9 percent (10 percent for the longevity bonus, plus the 39.9 percent increase commensurate to the maximum possible average Total-Z of +3.99). So under this system, and

given the optimum enhancement in his vote percentage, a man could theoretically get elected to Coopertown with only 25.1-percent support from the
writers (the 75-percent support required for election minus 49.9 percent).

But no player would ever receive a 49.9-percent boost, because the rules
of bell-curve/Z-Score theory assure that it could never happen. In order for
a player to receive the maximum adjustment, his career performance would
have to register as an outlier (i.e., at a Z Score of +3.99 or higher) for well
over half of the variables measured in each of the three scales, simply to counterbalance the lowering effects of any statistics in which his career performance
was not above the normal range. That is extremely unlikely, as evidenced by
the scores of Babe Ruth and Stan Musial, who are tied in chapter 11 for the
highest Total-Z average posted by any player in either data set (+2.97). Among
the 90 variables for which their performance was measured (30 in each of the
three scales), Ruth's career statistics included a total of 34 Z Scores at +3.99
or above, and Musial had 22 — so 62 percent of Babe's scores were in the normal range, as were 76 percent of Stan's. Under this system, both men would
earn a 39.7-percent adjustment in their BBWAA support percentage, or about
10 percent below the possible maximum. Given Ruth's exceptional batting performance and Musial's longevity, it's extremely unlikely that any player would
ever exceed their Total-Z averages; and, even if one did, it's absolutely certain that he would merit Cooperstown induction even without the upward
adjustment to his score — as any player with better career stats than Babe
Ruth is certain to be perceived by virtually everyone as a legitimate Hall of
Famer.

Among the 2295 players who qualified for this book's two data sets, only
141 of them — or 6.1 percent — earned a final Total-Z of +1.00 or higher. A
total of 101 of those 141 players (71.6 percent) have been elected to the Hall
of Fame already, and 11 of the others (Wade Boggs, Roger Clemens, Andre
Dawson, Tony Gwynn, Rickey Henderson, Paul Molitor, Eddie Murray, Cal
Ripken, Jr., Ryne Sandberg, Ozzie Smith and Dave Winfield) are virtually
certain of future enshrinement. Given that the Hall included only 185 players through 2000, and that the Cooperstown Baseline for a 210-man HOF
roster was +0.75 in this study, it is easily arguable that anyone with a final
Total-Z of +1.00 or better is, beyond question, a legitimate Hall of Famer.
None of these players could possibly be statistical errors of selection. So historical precedent indicates that almost 94 percent of all eligible players will
earn an adjustment of less than 20 percent and that more than three-fourths
of the players who receive larger adjustments would be likely for election anyway, even without the enhancement of their support percentages.

On a practical level, the only men who might slide into Cooperstown
as a result of this system are those whose actual support percentages in a given
election are already within striking distance of the 75-percent required for

election — hypothetically, men who receive 50-percent support or more from the writers. To be elected, they would still require an upward adjustment of up to 25 percent. Among all the men in both data sets, only 43 earned Total-Z averages that, when added to the proposed longevity bonus, are sufficient to merit that large of a boost. Forty of them have been elected to Cooperstown already (all but four — Cap Anson, Dan Brouthers, Roger Connor and Ed Delahanty — by the BBWAA), and barring one man's eligibility problem, the three who have not — Pete Rose, Eddie Murray and Rickey Henderson — are also indisputable Hall of Famers.

What's more, in the entire history of Hall-of-Fame voting during 1936–2000, there were 279 occasions when a candidate received 50-percent support or more on a BBWAA ballot, and among the 110 men who had earned that total through 2000, only two of them — Gil Hodges and Jim Rice — had not yet been chosen for Cooperstown by one of its elective organs. Whether or not you think that either man belongs in the Shrine, there's no dispute that, at some point, a majority of the BBWAA voters have perceived their credentials as formidable Their final Z-Score credentials indicate that both men are statistically qualified.

Hodges became eligible for election in 1969 and received 50-percent support or greater on 11 different BBWAA ballots. He also posted a final Total-Z of +1.06 in chapter 11, indicating that his upward adjustment in this system, including the longevity bonus, would be 20.6 percent. Even with that enhancement, Hodges would not have been elected until his fifth year on the ballot (1973), when his 57.4-percent support was finally sufficient, in conjunction with the 20.6-percent enhancement, to put him over the required 75 percent.

Rice joined the ballot in 1995, but did not top 50-percent support until the 2000 election, and then just barely (he netted 257 votes, for 51.5-percent support). His Total-Z in chapter 11 is +1.15, so his stats merit a 21.5-percent boost — an amount that, when added to his support in the 2000 voting, would've left him two percent shy of election that year.

A better sense of how the Total-Z enhancements would work can be gained from the 1999 BBWAA voting. Overall, there were 27 men on the ballot that year, and all but four of them — Mike Boddicker, Charlie Leibrandt, Frank Tanana and Mike Witt — received votes (Pete Rose got some write-in support but wasn't on the ballot). As noted above, Nolan Ryan, George Brett and Robin Yount were elected, with Carlton Fisk and Tony Perez finishing fourth and fifth, respectively, each with more than 60-percent support. Table Fifty demonstrates how the Z-Score-adjustment system would have altered the outcome of 1999 voting as a whole. On the left, it gives the name of each player, his primary position (Pos), along with the number of votes (Tot Vote) and support percentage (Sup Pct) each man actually received.

Table Fifty
Hall-of-Fame Voting Results, 1999;
and Projected Effect of Z-Score Bonus
(497 Votes Possible, 373 Needed to Elect)

Player	Pos	Tot Vote	Sup Pct	Long Bonus		Tot-Z Bonus	Final Bonus	Pct Bonus	Adj Pct
Nolan Ryan	sp	491	98.8	1.00	+	1.69 =	2.69	26.9	125.7
George Brett	3b	488	98.2	1.00	+	1.92 =	2.92	29.2	127.4
Robin Yount	ss	385	77.5	1.00	+	1.45 =	2.45	24.5	102.0
Carlton Fisk	c	330	66.4	1.00	+	1.37 =	2.37	23.7	90.1
Tony Perez	1b	302	60.8	1.00	+	1.21 =	2.21	22.1	82.9
Gary Carter	c	168	33.8	1.00	+	1.34 =	2.34	23.4	57.2
Jim Rice	lf	146	29.4	1.00	+	1.15 =	2.15	21.5	50.9
Bruce Sutter	rp	121	24.3	1.00	+	0.76 =	1.76	17.6	41.9
Jim Kaat	sp	100	20.1	1.00	+	0.81 =	1.81	18.1	38.2
Dale Murphy	cf	96	19.3	1.00	+	1.05 =	2.05	20.5	39.8
Tommy John	sp	93	18.7	1.00	+	1.13 =	2.13	21.3	40.0
Dave Parker	rf	80	16.1	1.00	+	1.26 =	2.26	22.6	38.7
Minnie Miñoso	lf	73	14.7	1.00	+	0.76 =	1.76	17.6	32.3
Bert Blyleven	sp	70	14.1	1.00	+	1.37 =	2.37	23.7	37.8
Dave Concepcion	ss	59	11.9	1.00	+	0.74 =	1.74	17.4	29.3
Luis Tiant	sp	53	10.7	1.00	+	0.68 =	1.68	16.8	27.5
Keith Hernandez	1b	34	6.8	1.00	+	1.35 =	2.35	23.5	30.3
Ron Guidry	sp	31	6.2	1.00	+	0.97 =	1.97	19.7	25.9
Bob Boone	c	27	5.4	1.00	+	0.46 =	1.46	14.6	20.0
Mickey Lolich	sp	26	5.2	1.00	+	0.54 =	1.54	15.4	20.6
Dwight Evans	rf	18	3.6	1.00	+	1.30 =	2.30	23.0	26.6
Pete Rose	rf	16	3.2	1.00	+	2.18 =	3.18	31.8	35.0
George Bell	lf	6	1.2	1.00	+	0.22 =	1.22	12.2	13.4
John Candelaria	sp	1	0.2	1.00	+	0.59 =	1.59	15.9	16.1
Mike Boddicker	sp	0	0.0	1.00	+	0.24 =	1.24	12.4	12.4
Charlie Leibrandt	sp	0	0.0	1.00	+	0.21 =	1.21	12.1	12.1
Frank Tanana	sp	0	0.0	1.00	+	0.71 =	1.71	17.1	17.1
Mike Witt	sp	0	0.0	1.00	+	-0.05 =	0.95	9.5	9.5

To the right of that data are calculations of the system's adjustments to each man's score, including those for longevity (Long Bonus), Total-Z average (Tot-Z Bonus) and their combined value (Final Bonus), plus their conversion to a percentage (Pct Bonus) and the adjusted percentage each candidate would've received as a result of that enhancement (Adj Pct). Men whose Total-Z in chapter 11 ranked among the 210-best final scores are listed in italics. The names of those who would have been elected under the Z-Score system are noted in boldface.

The Z-Score-adjustment system would have expanded the number of BBWAA inductees for 1999 by two, allowing Fisk and Perez to join Ryan, Brett and Yount at Cooperstown that year. Both men's career statistics clearly merited Hall-of-Fame honors. As evidence of that, both were elected by the scribes the following year.

But beyond that result, and within the scope of the current guidelines governing eligibility for the BBWAA and Veterans Committee ballots, the system's most important effect is the upward enhancement of scores for men who received 1999 support percentages lower than that of Perez. Discounting Pete Rose, there were a dozen other men on that ballot whose Total-Z averages indicate they are statistically qualified for Cooperstown. But, among them, their actual support percentages ranged between a high of only 33.8 percent for Gary Carter (who received 168 votes) and a low of just 3.6 percent for Dwight Evans (18 votes, and dropped from future ballots for failure to achieve a minimum of 5-percent support). Given the BBWAA's voting trends over the past decade, none of those totals offers much likelihood that any of those men will ever be elected by the writers or, perhaps more important, that they might someday receive as much as the 60-percent support currently required for subsequent eligibility for the Veterans Committee process.

But the scores in chapter 11 indicate that Carter and Evans are both well-qualified for the Hall, as are at least 10 of the men whose 1999 support percentages rank somewhere between them. Also, the slight difference between Carter's final Total-Z (+1.34, at the 47th ordinal) and Evans' (+1.30, ranked 52nd) offers no adequate justification, beyond the effects of subjective bias, for the large variation in their support from the scribes. And, except for the top four vote-getters, the real support levels in Table Fifty are thoroughly inconsistent with the relative quality of the other candidates' statistical performances (as reflected by their Total-Z values in chapter 11). With all of that in mind, and especially given the low support percentages earned by many Veterans Committee inductees from the past (19 from the pre–1946 era had a maximum support from the BBWAA of less than 10 percent), none of the italicized men in Table Fifty should ever be denied future consideration by the VC.

Given all that, one other change in the selection process is required for the Z-Score method to work as intended. The Veterans Committee's current eligibility requirement of 60-percent support from the BBWAA must be abandoned because, regardless of the writers' feelings on this issue, the current support requirement accomplishes little beyond assuring that the injustices prevalent among the current Hall-of-Fame roster are perpetuated. If some minimum requirement is absolutely necessary, then it should represent a number that strikes a reasonable balance between preventing the future election of mediocre players and denying adequate consideration and ultimate justice to those who were not.

One suggestion would be to lower the VC's minimum eligibility requirement to 25 percent, a figure that is equal to the average highest-ever support

Keith Hernandez is one of a dozen as-yet-unelected players on the 1999 BBWAA ballot whose Total-Z is clearly good enough for Cooperstown. But his prospects in the writers' voting are poor. (*The Sporting News.*)

percentage among the veterans committees' 92 player selections through 2000, and one that is exceeded in the history of Hall-of-Fame voting by only nine men from before 1946 who have not been elected to date (Hodges, plus Phil Caverretta, Joe Gordon, Hank Gowdy, Mel Harder, Marty Marion, Allie Reynolds, Johnny Sain and Johnny Vander Meer). If the Z-Score enhancements were then applied to all past and subsequent balloting, they would assure that only the "best-qualified rejects" could ever be eligible for VC consideration. Among the unelected men in Table Fifty, that would include everyone from Carlton Fisk through Dwight Evans, except for catcher Bob Boone, who — given a Z-Score adjustment — might have exceeded 25 percent on some future ballot (Boone got only 4.2-percent support in the 2000 voting and was dropped from further consideration). A couple of those men may be less-qualified for Cooperstown than Joe Gordon or Marty Marion, but most of them are much better candidates, statistically, than Cavarretta, Gowdy or Vander Meer. So, barring their election by the writers, and given some of the riff-raff chosen by the VC in the past, there is no doubt that Gary Carter, Jim Rice, Bruce Sutter, Jim Kaat, Dale Murphy, Tommy John, Dave Parker, Minnie Miñoso, Bert Blyleven, Dave Concepcion, Luis Tiant, Keith Hernandez, Ron Guidry, Mickey Lolich and Dwight Evans are each deserving of the same HOF consideration currently available to those nine men from before 1946.

Because it gives appropriate weight to the relative value of career performance and allows for retention of the subjective foundation of the voting, the adoption of the Z-Score method and its attendant adjustment to the BBWAA vote totals would — in conjunction with a lowering of the Veterans Committee eligibility requirement to 25 percent — go a long way toward assuring statistical justice among future Hall-of-Fame elections. The continued insistence on purely subjective criteria can only compound both the frequency and degree of injustices of the current election process, leading to ever more errors of selection and omission. In the long run, fairness demands the implementation of some kind of change; and failure to take appropriate action must inevitably damage the credibility of both the Hall of Fame and the game itself. The beginning of a new millennium, with its inherent promise of new possibilities, is a perfect time for those changes.

Appendix

The pitcher and non-pitcher lists that follow include all men elected to the Hall of Fame through the 2000 voting, plus everyone else among the 2,295-man data set whose final Total-Z was +0.35 or higher, a total of 542 players. They comprise the top 533 scores in the final rankings (almost one-fourth of the candidates measured), plus nine Hall of Famers who failed to score at or above that Total-Z minimum. Among them are also included every player whose final Core-Z average was +1.00 or better.

Both lists follow the same identification conventions used for the rankings in Chapters Six through Eleven. The lines for each player include his final Total-and Core-Z scores, plus his Total-Z average for the era, positional and overall ratings.

Pitchers

Rank	Player	Pos	Era	Final Tot Z	Final Core Z	Era Tot Z	Pos Tot Z	Overall Tot Z
1	**Walter Johnson**	sp	DB	2.16	2.79	2.02	2.29	2.15
2	**Cy Young**	sp	NC	2.11	2.58	1.91	2.26	2.15
3	**Christy Mathewson**	sp	DB	1.98	2.30	1.89	2.03	2.01
4	**Tom Seaver**	sp	FA	1.93	2.67	2.18	1.80	1.82
5	**Warren Spahn**	sp	PW	1.89	2.60	2.01	1.84	1.84
6	**Grover Alexander**	sp	DB	1.71	2.03	1.54	1.83	1.75
7	**Steve Carlton**	sp	FA	1.70	2.73	1.91	1.61	1.61
8	**Nolan Ryan**	sp	FA	1.69	3.10	1.81	1.63	1.63
9	**Lefty Grove**	sp	LB	1.68	2.29	1.96	1.47	1.64
10	**Whitey Ford**	sp	PW	1.65	1.98	1.80	1.51	1.67
11	**Sandy Koufax**	sp	EX	1.50	1.46	1.80	1.30	1.43
12	**Ed Walsh**	sp	DB	1.48	1.09	1.53	1.45	1.47
13	**Carl Hubbell**	sp	LB	1.47	1.70	1.69	1.31	1.43
14	**Jim Palmer**	sp	EX	1.45	1.97	1.68	1.33	1.36
15	**Gaylord Perry**	sp	EX	1.41	2.43	1.60	1.35	1.29
16	**Don Sutton**	sp	FA	1.40	2.48	1.50	1.38	1.34
17	**Hoyt Wilhelm**	rp	EX	1.38	1.40	1.22	1.81	1.06
18	Bert Blyleven	sp	FA	1.37	2.24	1.48	1.36	1.29
19	**Bob Feller**	sp	PW	1.31	2.00	1.43	1.23	1.28
	*Dennis Eckersley	rp	FA	1.31	1.92	1.06	1.77	1.03
	Juan Marichal	sp	EX	1.31	1.79	1.53	1.23	1.18
22	Carl Mays	sp	LB	1.30	1.13	1.45	1.18	1.30
23	**Phil Niekro**	sp	FA	1.27	2.31	1.38	1.22	1.22
24	**Bob Gibson**	sp	EX	1.24	2.03	1.41	1.20	1.13
	Don Drysdale	sp	EX	1.24	1.46	1.46	1.13	1.15
26	**Rollie Fingers**	rp	FA	1.23	0.81	1.03	1.58	1.03
27	**Ferguson Jenkins**	sp	EX	1.22	1.99	1.39	1.16	1.12
28	*Roger Clemens	sp	FA	1.20	1.42	1.40	1.05	1.17
29	#Tim Keefe	sp	NC	1.18	1.56	1.05	1.24	1.24
	Dazzy Vance	sp	LB	1.18	1.31	1.41	1.01	1.13
31	**Robin Roberts**	sp	PW	1.14	1.84	1.22	1.11	1.10
32	Tommy John	sp	FA	1.13	1.79	1.24	1.08	1.09
33	**Eddie Plank**	sp	DB	1.12	1.81	1.15	1.17	1.03
34	**Hal Newhouser**	sp	PW	1.07	1.31	1.22	0.95	1.05
35	**Herb Pennock**	sp	LB	1.06	1.15	1.12	0.99	1.07
36	**Mordecai Brown**	sp	DB	1.05	1.17	1.12	1.03	1.01
37	**Red Ruffing**	sp	LB	1.04	1.48	1.07	1.04	1.00
38	**Burleigh Grimes**	sp	LB	1.02	1.40	1.13	0.96	0.97
39	Spud Chandler	sp	LB	0.99	0.73	1.06	0.91	1.01
40	**Kid Nichols**	sp	NC	0.98	1.37	0.88	1.06	0.98

Rank	Player	Pos	Era	Final Tot Z	Final Core Z	Era Tot Z	Pos Tot Z	Overall Tot Z
41	Ron Guidry	sp	FA	0.97	1.14	1.18	0.80	0.94
42	Goose Gossage	rp	FA	0.96	1.07	0.73	1.30	0.81
43	**Lefty Gomez**	sp	LB	0.95	1.12	1.04	0.85	0.99
44	**#John Clarkson**	sp	NC	0.94	1.32	0.80	1.00	1.00
45	**Bob Lemon**	sp	PW	0.93	1.14	1.08	0.81	0.91
46	Jack Quinn	sp	LB	0.92	1.20	1.09	0.80	0.89
47	**Early Wynn**	sp	PW	0.91	1.83	0.96	0.91	0.85
	Catfish Hunter	sp	EX	0.91	1.27	1.01	0.86	0.87
49	**Stan Coveleski**	sp	LB	0.90	1.16	1.03	0.84	0.85
50	**Red Faber**	sp	LB	0.88	1.41	1.02	0.80	0.85
51	**Eppa Rixey**	sp	LB	0.87	1.40	0.98	0.83	0.80
	*Dwight Gooden	sp	FA	0.87	1.15	1.04	0.71	0.87
53	*Tom Henke	rp	FA	0.85	0.05	0.78	0.96	0.79
54	**Addie Joss**	sp	DB	0.84	0.60	0.85	0.88	0.80
55	Jack Morris	sp	FA	0.83	1.42	0.98	0.74	0.79
	Firpo Marberry	rp	LB	0.83	0.95	0.58	1.39	0.43
57	Vida Blue	sp	FA	0.82	1.30	0.92	0.75	0.78
	Dizzy Dean	sp	LB	0.82	0.88	0.99	0.69	0.79
59	Jim Kaat	sp	EX	0.81	1.66	0.91	0.75	0.79
	*Bret Saberhagen	sp	FA	0.81	0.68	1.02	0.63	0.82
61	**#Hoss Radbourn**	sp	NC	0.79	1.15	0.65	0.88	0.85
62	Billy Pierce	sp	PW	0.78	1.29	0.87	0.72	0.76
	Bob Shawkey	sp	LB	0.78	1.03	0.87	0.71	0.75
	Dolf Luque	sp	LB	0.78	0.79	0.89	0.68	0.78
65	Bucky Walters	sp	LB	0.77	0.85	0.82	0.76	0.72
66	**Waite Hoyt**	sp	LB	0.76	1.08	0.87	0.67	0.76
	Bruce Sutter	rp	FA	0.76	0.23	0.61	0.99	0.65
68	**Rube Waddell**	sp	DB	0.75	1.05	0.74	0.77	0.72
69	**#Pud Galvin**	sp	NC	0.74	1.24	0.54	0.94	0.70
	Charley Bender	sp	DB	0.74	0.94	0.85	0.68	0.69
	Fred Fitzsimmons	sp	LB	0.74	0.90	0.80	0.68	0.75
72	**Jim Bunning**	sp	EX	0.73	1.53	0.82	0.68	0.69
	Paul Derringer	sp	LB	0.73	1.01	0.86	0.67	0.69
	*Lee Smith	rp	FA	0.73	0.24	0.51	0.97	0.67
75	*Frank Tanana*	sp	FA	0.71	1.40	0.77	0.67	0.68
	*Dennis Martinez	sp	FA	0.71	1.14	0.83	0.61	0.70
	#Jim McCormick	sp	NC	0.71	0.83	0.58	0.78	0.75
78	*Dave Stieb	sp	FA	0.70	0.87	0.83	0.60	0.68
	#Tommy Bond	sp	NC	0.70	0.38	0.58	0.75	0.78
80	*F. Valenzuela	sp	FA	0.69	0.70	0.83	0.59	0.65

Rank	Player	Pos	Era	Final Tot Z	Final Core Z	Era Tot Z	Pos Tot Z	Overall Tot Z
	Kent Tekulve	rp	FA	0.69	0.49	0.47	0.99	0.56
	Smoky Joe Wood	sp	DB	0.69	0.40	0.80	0.62	0.67
83	Luis Tiant	sp	EX	0.68	1.40	0.74	0.69	0.62
	Bob Welch	sp	FA	0.68	1.20	0.82	0.56	0.68
	Rick Reuschel	sp	FA	0.68	1.15	0.76	0.60	0.69
	Urban Shocker	sp	LB	0.68	0.92	0.78	0.61	0.66
	Art Nehf	sp	LB	0.68	0.82	0.75	0.63	0.68
88	Elroy Face	rp	PW	0.67	0.30	0.54	0.98	0.43
89	Lon Warneke	sp	LB	0.66	1.01	0.74	0.60	0.64
	Harry Brecheen	sp	PW	0.66	0.62	0.78	0.56	0.66
91	Lindy McDaniel	rp	EX	0.65	0.83	0.48	0.96	0.46
	*Orel Hershiser	sp	FA	0.65	0.72	0.80	0.52	0.66
	Dan Quisenberry	rp	FA	0.65	0.19	0.47	0.93	0.50
94	Jerry Koosman	sp	FA	0.64	1.36	0.69	0.60	0.63
	Charlie Hough	sp	FA	0.64	1.07	0.75	0.50	0.70
	Ted Lyons	sp	LB	0.64	1.04	0.69	0.63	0.60
	Tommy Bridges	sp	LB	0.64	0.99	0.71	0.59	0.62
98	Allie Reynolds	sp	PW	0.63	1.05	0.67	0.57	0.64
	Stu Miller	rp	EX	0.63	0.42	0.48	0.94	0.43
100	*Mike Cuellar*	sp	EX	0.62	0.98	0.72	0.57	0.57
101	Emil Leonard	sp	LB	0.61	0.77	0.73	0.52	0.58
	Andy Messersmith	sp	EX	0.61	0.74	0.78	0.49	0.59
	Johnny Murphy	rp	LB	0.61	0.24	0.39	1.00	0.40
104	Wilbur Cooper	sp	LB	0.60	1.19	0.70	0.59	0.53
	Lew Burdette	sp	PW	0.60	0.82	0.66	0.55	0.60
	Don McMahon	rp	EX	0.60	0.49	0.53	0.75	0.51
107	John Candelaria	sp	FA	0.59	0.94	0.72	0.43	0.64
108	*Jesse Orosco	rp	FA	0.58	0.26	0.52	0.68	0.52
109	Eddie Lopat	sp	PW	0.57	0.72	0.61	0.53	0.58
110	Bullet Joe Bush	sp	LB	0.56	0.72	0.62	0.55	0.53
	Mort Cooper	sp	LB	0.56	0.66	0.62	0.52	0.54
112	**Vic Willis**	sp	DB	0.55	0.92	0.49	0.64	0.52
	Mel Stottlemyre	sp	EX	0.55	0.68	0.69	0.52	0.47
	Sparky Lyle	rp	EX	0.55	0.52	0.42	0.78	0.42
	Jeff Reardon	rp	FA	0.55	0.14	0.40	0.73	0.48
116	Mickey Lolich	sp	EX	0.54	1.35	0.58	0.55	0.50
117	*Jimmy Key	sp	FA	0.53	0.72	0.73	0.34	0.56
	Ed Reulbach	sp	DB	0.53	0.67	0.55	0.51	0.52
119	Dave McNally	sp	EX	0.52	0.94	0.61	0.47	0.50
	Eddie Cicotte	sp	DB	0.52	0.76	0.56	0.48	0.52

Rank	Player	Pos	Era	Final Tot Z	Final Core Z	Era Tot Z	Pos Tot Z	Overall Tot Z
	Bobby Shantz	sp	PW	0.52	0.31	0.67	0.36	0.55
	Dick Hall	rp	EX	0.52	0.16	0.48	0.62	0.44
123	Virgil Trucks	sp	PW	0.50	0.88	0.58	0.43	0.49
	Steve Rogers	sp	FA	0.50	0.73	0.53	0.49	0.48
	Dizzy Trout	sp	LB	0.50	0.65	0.60	0.41	0.49
	Amos Rusie	sp	NC	0.50	0.64	0.48	0.49	0.51
	Doc White	sp	DB	0.50	0.55	0.51	0.53	0.47
128	#Bob Caruthers	sp	NC	0.49	0.46	0.48	0.47	0.54
	McGraw, Tug	rp	EX	0.49	0.36	0.39	0.67	0.39
130	Sad Sam Jones	sp	LB	0.48	0.82	0.50	0.48	0.45
	Vic Raschi	sp	PW	0.48	0.52	0.50	0.42	0.51
	*Rick Aguilera	rp	FA	0.48	-0.06	0.30	0.68	0.43
133	**Joe McGinnity**	sp	DB	0.47	0.85	0.42	0.49	0.50
	John Tudor	sp	FA	0.47	0.56	0.63	0.32	0.48
	Gene Garber	rp	FA	0.47	0.22	0.27	0.72	0.37
136	Charlie Root	sp	LB	0.46	0.92	0.60	0.36	0.45
	Claude Osteen	sp	EX	0.46	0.80	0.53	0.44	0.41
	Larry Jackson	sp	EX	0.46	0.78	0.54	0.43	0.41
	#Tony Mullane	sp	NC	0.46	0.78	0.42	0.49	0.45
	Camilo Pascual	sp	EX	0.46	0.67	0.52	0.42	0.43
	Don Newcombe	sp	PW	0.46	0.64	0.51	0.40	0.47
142	Ken Holtzman	sp	EX	0.45	0.63	0.51	0.41	0.44
143	Jerry Reuss	sp	FA	0.44	1.07	0.43	0.45	0.43
	Joe Niekro	sp	FA	0.44	0.97	0.47	0.41	0.45
	Bob Friend	sp	PW	0.44	0.79	0.50	0.42	0.42
	Clay Carroll	rp	EX	0.44	0.39	0.32	0.66	0.29
147	Milt Pappas	sp	EX	0.43	0.97	0.47	0.43	0.38
	Gerry Staley	rp	PW	0.43	0.53	0.21	0.82	0.19
	Wilbur Wood	sp	EX	0.43	0.53	0.55	0.33	0.44
	*Sid Fernandez	sp	FA	0.43	0.39	0.58	0.25	0.48
	Jesse Barnes	sp	LB	0.43	0.29	0.49	0.39	0.41
152	J. R. Richard	sp	FA	0.42	0.58	0.49	0.34	0.44
	Gary Nolan	sp	EX	0.42	0.41	0.57	0.26	0.45
154	**Jesse Haines**	sp	LB	0.41	0.78	0.42	0.39	0.43
	#Will White	sp	NC	0.41	0.52	0.26	0.50	0.44
	Babe Adams	sp	DB	0.41	0.39	0.43	0.41	0.40
	Willie Hernandez	rp	FA	0.41	0.10	0.32	0.55	0.34
158	Sam McDowell	sp	EX	0.40	0.79	0.52	0.29	0.39
	Dean Chance	sp	EX	0.40	0.52	0.52	0.32	0.36
160	Mike Garcia	sp	PW	0.39	0.65	0.47	0.32	0.39

Rank	Player	Pos	Era	Final Tot Z	Final Core Z	Era Tot Z	Pos Tot Z	Overall Tot Z
	Burt Hooton	sp	FA	0.39	0.59	0.44	0.35	0.40
	#Charlie Buffinton	sp	NC	0.39	0.57	0.37	0.40	0.39
	Hal Schumacher	sp	LB	0.39	0.53	0.44	0.34	0.40
	Eddie Rommel	sp	LB	0.39	0.47	0.44	0.32	0.43
165	Curt Simmons	sp	PW	0.38	0.89	0.42	0.37	0.35
166	Sal Maglie	sp	PW	0.37	0.64	0.43	0.31	0.38
	*Dave Stewart	sp	FA	0.37	0.64	0.54	0.19	0.41
	Claude Passeau	sp	LB	0.37	0.54	0.46	0.31	0.33
	Harvey Haddix	sp	PW	0.37	0.50	0.47	0.27	0.39
	Deacon Phillippe	sp	DB	0.37	0.49	0.40	0.35	0.37
	Murry Dickson	sp	PW	0.37	0.48	0.43	0.32	0.37
	*Jose Rijo	sp	FA	0.37	0.48	0.53	0.17	0.44
	Bob Locker	rp	EX	0.37	0.18	0.36	0.44	0.29
	Mike Marshall	rp	EX	0.37	0.07	0.22	0.64	0.20
175	*John Franco	rp	FA	0.36	0.28	0.16	0.61	0.28
	*Mark Eichorn	rp	FA	0.36	0.08	0.32	0.43	0.32
177	Larry French	sp	LB	0.35	0.78	0.37	0.37	0.31
	Johnny Allen	sp	LB	0.35	0.56	0.45	0.24	0.37
	Denny McLain	sp	EX	0.35	0.40	0.43	0.31	0.33
	Mike Scott	sp	FA	0.35	0.34	0.45	0.25	0.37
	*Dave Righetti	rp	FA	0.35	0.27	0.13	0.61	0.26
	*Alejandro Peña	rp	FA	0.35	0.12	0.29	0.48	0.27
	Clem Labine	rp	PW	0.35	0.04	0.19	0.60	0.21
t188	#Mickey Welch	sp	NC	0.33	1.13	0.22	0.45	0.29
	Jack Chesbro	sp	DB	0.33	0.55	0.30	0.35	0.32
t336	Rube Marquard	sp	DB	0.03	0.38	0.04	0.01	0.04

Non-Pitchers

Rank	Player	Pos	Era	Final Tot Z	Final Core Z	Era Tot Z	Pos Tot Z	Overall Tot Z
1	Babe Ruth	rf	LB	2.97	3.63	3.02	2.66	3.24
	Stan Musial	lf	PW	2.97	3.52	3.17	2.92	2.83
3	Ty Cobb	cf	DB	2.75	3.48	2.69	2.53	3.02
4	Willie Mays	cf	EX	2.60	3.53	2.66	2.55	2.60
5	Hank Aaron	rf	EX	2.47	3.82	2.65	2.09	2.66
6	Honus Wagner	ss	DB	2.43	2.77	2.15	2.77	2.38
7	Tris Speaker	cf	DB	2.42	2.67	2.41	2.26	2.57
8	Ted Williams	lf	PW	2.35	3.26	2.48	2.15	2.43
9	Rogers Hornsby	2b	LB	2.27	2.81	2.03	2.60	2.18
10	Lou Gehrig	1b	LB	2.26	2.97	2.31	1.96	2.52
11	Carl Yastrzemski	lf	EX	2.25	2.79	2.27	2.33	2.14
12	Mike Schmidt	3b	FA	2.20	2.29	2.41	2.13	2.05
13	Mickey Mantle	cf	PW	2.19	2.55	2.33	1.98	2.26
14	Pete Rose	rf	EX	2.18	2.39	2.47	1.93	2.13
	Eddie Collins	2b	DB	2.18	2.24	2.08	2.19	2.27
16	Nap Lajoie	2b	DB	2.00	2.43	1.92	2.01	2.07
17	Frank Robinson	rf	EX	1.94	2.76	2.12	1.59	2.11
	Yogi Berra	c	PW	1.94	2.30	1.63	2.58	1.62
19	George Brett	3b	FA	1.92	2.51	2.14	1.88	1.75
20	Jimmie Foxx	1b	LB	1.88	2.81	1.96	1.58	2.10
21	#Cap Anson	1b	NC	1.80	2.13	1.93	1.52	1.95
22	Joe Morgan	2b	EX	1.75	1.96	1.70	2.00	1.56
23	Mel Ott	rf	LB	1.72	2.58	1.80	1.48	1.88
	Charlie Gehringer	2b	LB	1.72	2.18	1.62	1.90	1.63
25	*Eddie Murray	1b	FA	1.69	2.52	1.91	1.53	1.62
26	Reggie Jackson	rf	FA	1.68	2.31	1.95	1.40	1.69
27	Joe DiMaggio	cf	LB	2.05	1.59	1.51	1.62	1.64
28	#Dan Brouthers	1b	NC	1.58	1.67	1.73	1.29	1.71
29	*Rickey Henderson	lf	FA	1.57	1.45	1.75	1.46	1.51
30	#Roger Connor	1b	NC	1.54	1.74	1.70	1.25	1.66
31	Eddie Mathews	3b	PW	1.50	2.32	1.48	1.60	1.42
	Ed Delahanty	lf	NC	1.50	1.96	1.56	1.38	1.55
33	*Dave Winfield	rf	FA	1.45	2.60	1.65	1.21	1.49
	Robin Yount	ss	FA	1.45	2.42	1.43	1.63	1.29
	Brooks Robinson	3b	EX	1.45	1.71	1.44	1.50	1.40
36	Al Kaline	rf	EX	1.44	2.25	1.56	1.17	1.59
37	Al Simmons	lf	LB	1.43	2.33	1.43	1.40	1.47
38	Bill Dickey	c	LB	1.40	1.61	1.05	2.04	1.11
39	Johnny Bench	c	EX	1.39	2.13	0.96	2.24	0.97
40	Ernie Banks	1b	EX	1.38	2.08	1.56	1.13	1.46

Rank	Player	Pos	Era	Final Tot Z	Final Core Z	Era Tot Z	Pos Tot Z	Overall Tot Z
	Willie Stargell	lf	EX	1.38	1.96	1.43	1.41	1.32
42	**Carlton Fisk**	c	FA	1.37	2.28	1.14	1.93	1.04
	Frankie Frisch	2b	LB	1.37	1.72	1.35	1.47	1.29
	Darrell Evans	3b	FA	1.37	1.62	1.50	1.28	1.33
45	**Sam Crawford**	rf	DB	1.36	1.90	1.37	1.23	1.48
46	Keith Hernandez	1b	FA	1.35	1.17	1.58	1.21	1.25
47	*Cal Ripken, Jr.	ss	FA	1.34	1.84	1.37	1.55	1.09
	Gary Carter	c	FA	1.34	1.77	1.20	1.83	0.99
	*Paul Molitor	3b	FA	1.34	1.70	1.51	1.31	1.19
50	Joe Torre	c	EX	1.32	1.99	1.00	2.14	0.81
	Ron Santo	3b	EX	1.32	1.68	1.30	1.37	1.29
52	Dwight Evans	rf	FA	1.30	1.81	1.51	1.09	1.30
53	**George Davis**	ss	NC	1.29	1.58	1.29	1.26	1.32
54	**Goose Goslin**	lf	LB	1.28	1.88	1.29	1.26	1.30
55	Dave Parker	rf	FA	1.26	1.92	1.45	1.07	1.26
56	*Andre Dawson	rf	FA	1.25	2.05	1.39	1.12	1.24
	Bill Dahlen	ss	NC	1.25	1.30	1.24	1.25	1.27
	#Bid McPhee	2b	NC	1.25	0.90	1.20	1.24	1.31
59	**Billy Williams**	lf	EX	1.24	2.16	1.27	1.14	1.30
	Gabby Hartnett	c	LB	1.24	1.48	0.92	1.88	0.92
61	Al Oliver	cf	FA	1.23	1.82	1.42	1.26	1.00
	Max Carey	cf	DB	1.23	1.15	1.24	1.05	1.40
63	**Roberto Clemente**	rf	EX	1.22	1.89	1.31	1.00	1.36
	Lou Brock	lf	EX	1.22	1.56	1.26	1.14	1.27
65	**Tony Perez**	1b	EX	1.21	1.86	1.34	0.94	1.34
	Enos Slaughter	rf	PW	1.21	1.50	1.28	1.15	1.19
67	#Jake Beckley	1b	NC	1.20	1.73	1.32	0.95	1.34
68	**Paul Waner**	rf	LB	1.19	1.73	1.30	0.96	1.32
69	**Fred Clarke**	lf	DB	1.18	1.59	1.09	1.20	1.25
	Rod Carew	1b	EX	1.18	1.42	1.34	0.94	1.25
	*Ozzie Smith	ss	FA	1.18	0.75	1.26	1.28	1.02
72	Ted Simmons	c	EX	1.16	2.10	0.85	1.74	0.88
	Duke Snider	cf	PW	1.16	1.83	1.30	0.90	1.27
	Johnny Mize	1b	LB	1.16	1.49	1.23	0.87	1.38
75	Jim Rice	lf	FA	1.15	2.05	1.33	0.98	1.13
	Willie McCovey	1b	EX	1.15	1.90	1.27	0.88	1.30
77	*Wade Boggs	3b	FA	1.14	1.41	1.30	1.01	1.09
78	**Luis Aparicio**	ss	EX	1.13	1.17	1.11	1.34	0.95
79	#Buck Ewing	c	NC	1.12	1.17	0.71	1.90	0.74
80	**Joe Cronin**	ss	LB	1.10	1.51	1.01	1.25	1.05

Rank	Player	Pos	Era	Final Tot Z	Final Core Z	Era Tot Z	Pos Tot Z	Overall Tot Z
	Mickey Vernon	1b	PW	1.10	1.31	1.30	0.87	1.12
	Jack Clark	rf	FA	1.10	1.19	1.29	1.03	0.99
83	Steve Garvey	1b	FA	1.09	1.64	1.29	0.92	1.06
	*Ryne Sandberg	2b	FA	1.09	1.48	1.13	1.17	0.97
85	**Jesse Burkett**	lf	NC	1.08	1.66	1.17	0.91	1.16
	Graig Nettles	3b	FA	1.08	1.46	1.19	0.95	1.11
	Joe Kelley	lf	NC	1.08	1.25	1.15	0.93	1.15
	Mickey Cochrane	c	LB	1.08	1.19	0.76	1.68	0.78
89	**Harry Heilmann**	rf	LB	1.07	1.73	1.13	0.91	1.16
90	Rusty Staub	rf	EX	1.05	1.55	1.16	0.86	1.16
	Gil Hodges	1b	PW	1.05	1.43	1.18	0.88	1.11
92	**Zach Wheat**	lf	DB	1.05	1.89	1.06	1.00	1.10
	Dale Murphy	cf	FA	1.05	1.61	1.17	1.01	0.97
	Richie Ashburn	cf	PW	1.05	0.92	1.23	0.85	1.08
95	Vada Pinson	cf	EX	1.04	1.70	1.06	0.97	1.08
	Frank Baker	3b	DB	1.04	1.17	0.98	1.17	0.96
97	#**Sam Thompson**	rf	NC	1.02	1.56	1.06	1.00	1.00
	Nellie Fox	2b	PW	1.02	1.07	1.10	1.00	0.96
99	**Luke Appling**	ss	LB	1.01	1.25	0.96	1.11	0.97
	*Tim Raines	lf	FA	1.01	1.09	1.13	0.91	0.99
101	*Lou Whitaker	2b	FA	1.00	1.56	1.02	1.10	0.87
	Bobby Doerr	2b	LB	1.00	1.29	0.93	1.13	0.92
	Bobby Grich	2b	FA	1.00	1.02	1.06	1.07	0.88
104	**Harmon Killebrew**	1b	EX	0.99	1.92	1.06	0.72	1.18
105	Bill Mazeroski	2b	EX	0.98	0.75	1.00	1.07	0.86
106	**Hugh Duffy**	lf	NC	0.97	1.59	1.10	0.75	1.08
	George Sisler	1b	LB	0.97	1.27	1.13	0.67	1.12
	#Harry Stovey	lf	NC	0.97	0.77	1.05	0.86	1.01
109	**Billy Hamilton**	cf	NC	0.96	1.21	1.04	0.76	1.09
110	**Joe Medwick**	lf	LB	0.94	1.50	0.97	0.84	1.01
	Lave Cross	3b	NC	0.94	1.44	0.82	1.16	0.83
	Sam Rice	rf	LB	0.94	1.26	1.05	0.78	0.99
	Pee Wee Reese	ss	PW	0.94	1.11	0.98	1.05	0.80
114	**Bill Terry**	1b	LB	0.93	1.10	1.03	0.65	1.10
115	**Willie Keeler**	rf	DB	0.92	1.68	0.88	0.83	1.05
	Ken Boyer	3b	EX	0.92	1.49	0.89	0.98	0.90
	*Kirby Puckett	cf	FA	0.92	1.38	1.07	0.85	0.85
	Reggie Smith	rf	EX	0.92	1.23	1.03	0.70	1.03
	Sherry Magee	lf	DB	0.92	1.15	0.97	0.81	0.99
120	**Hank Greenberg**	1b	LB	0.91	1.31	1.00	0.62	1.10

Rank	Player	Pos	Era	Final Tot Z	Final Core Z	Era Tot Z	Pos Tot Z	Overall Tot Z
121	*Jimmy Ryan*	cf	NC	0.90	1.50	1.03	0.70	0.96
	Harry Hooper	rf	DB	0.90	1.08	0.96	0.80	0.95
123	Don Baylor	lf	FA	0.89	1.42	1.02	0.78	0.87
	Willie Randolph	2b	FA	0.89	0.81	0.98	0.92	0.77
125	Jimmy Sheckard	lf	DB	0.88	0.78	0.86	0.87	0.92
126	George Foster	lf	FA	0.87	1.34	1.01	0.76	0.86
	Cesar Cedeño	cf	FA	0.87	1.15	0.96	0.86	0.81
128	**Orlando Cepeda**	1b	EX	0.86	1.67	0.99	0.61	1.00
	Cecil Cooper	1b	FA	0.86	1.34	1.00	0.74	0.82
	Buddy Bell	3b	FA	0.86	1.30	0.93	0.72	0.91
	Pie Traynor	3b	LB	0.86	1.23	0.85	0.89	0.85
	Norm Cash	1b	EX	0.86	1.17	1.02	0.61	0.95
	#Mike 'King' Kelly	rf	NC	0.86	1.00	0.84	0.95	0.80
134	**Chuck Klein**	rf	LB	0.85	1.36	0.92	0.68	0.97
	Willie Davis	cf	EX	0.85	1.30	0.89	0.78	0.89
	Red Schoendienst	2b	PW	0.85	1.09	0.91	0.85	0.81
137	*Alan Trammell	ss	FA	0.84	1.46	0.81	1.04	0.65
138	**Rabbit Maranville**	ss	LB	0.83	0.58	0.84	0.85	0.79
139	Bill Buckner	1b	FA	0.82	1.33	0.93	0.73	0.80
140	Fred Lynn	cf	FA	0.81	1.38	0.88	0.76	0.78
	Bob L. Johnson	lf	LB	0.81	1.28	0.82	0.79	0.82
	Arky Vaughan	ss	LB	0.81	1.07	0.71	0.97	0.77
	Billy Herman	2b	LB	0.81	0.86	0.76	0.88	0.77
144	*Amos Otis*	cf	EX	0.80	1.05	0.86	0.72	0.81
	Vic Wertz	rf	PW	0.80	1.00	0.91	0.85	0.64
146	*Don Mattingly	1b	FA	0.79	1.23	0.95	0.68	0.75
	Kiki Cuyler	rf	LB	0.79	1.10	0.92	0.58	0.87
148	G. Van Haltren	cf	NC	0.78	1.36	0.88	0.60	0.86
	Dick Allen	1b	EX	0.78	1.34	0.88	0.53	0.92
	Jim Bottomley	1b	LB	0.78	1.31	0.89	0.45	1.00
	Jimmy Collins	3b	DB	0.78	1.10	0.71	0.90	0.74
	Joe Jackson	rf	DB	0.78	1.08	0.87	0.65	0.83
153	Brian Downing	lf	FA	0.77	1.21	0.83	0.75	0.73
	Roy Campanella	c	PW	0.77	0.84	0.59	1.20	0.52
	*Brett Butler	cf	FA	0.77	0.70	0.88	0.69	0.72
156	Minnie Minoso	lf	PW	0.76	1.15	0.94	0.58	0.77
	Jackie Robinson	2b	PW	0.76	0.93	0.81	0.78	0.71
	Jimmy Dykes	3b	LB	0.76	0.80	0.72	0.85	0.71
	Joe Gordon	2b	LB	0.76	0.78	0.66	0.90	0.70
160	**Earl Averill**	cf	LB	0.75	1.38	0.74	0.77	0.76

Rank	Player	Pos	Era	Final Tot Z	Final Core Z	Era Tot Z	Pos Tot Z	Overall Tot Z
	Herman Long	ss	NC	0.75	1.08	0.77	0.74	0.76
	Tommy Leach	cf	DB	0.75	0.75	0.81	0.62	0.81
163	*Vern Stephens*	ss	PW	0.74	1.46	0.68	0.94	0.60
	Jose Cruz	lf	FA	0.74	1.11	0.78	0.67	0.76
	*Tony Gwynn	rf	FA	0.74	1.09	0.91	0.58	0.74
	Ralph Kiner	lf	PW	0.74	1.08	0.79	0.63	0.78
	Dave Concepcion	ss	FA	0.74	0.98	0.74	0.89	0.60
	Chris Chambliss	1b	FA	0.74	0.89	0.87	0.63	0.71
	Bert Campaneris	ss	EX	0.74	0.84	0.66	0.96	0.59
	Ed Konetchy	1b	DB	0.74	0.62	0.90	0.73	0.88
	Heinie Groh	3b	DB	0.74	0.54	0.68	0.87	0.66
172	**Tony Lazzeri**	2b	LB	0.73	1.05	0.63	0.88	0.66
	Gene Tenace	c	FA	0.73	0.32	0.68	1.11	0.39
174	*Lance Parrish	c	FA	0.72	1.32	0.59	1.07	0.48
	Bob Elliott	3b	PW	0.72	1.28	0.71	0.74	0.72
176	Frank Howard	lf	EX	0.71	1.18	0.75	0.64	0.75
	#*Fred Pfeffer*	2b	NC	0.71	0.62	0.71	0.67	0.74
178	*Hal McRae*	lf	FA	0.70	1.12	0.79	0.59	0.72
	Ron Cey	3b	FA	0.70	1.08	0.79	0.57	0.75
	#*Mike Tiernan*	rf	NC	0.70	1.08	0.79	0.61	0.70
	Edd Roush	cf	LB	0.70	1.00	0.73	0.68	0.69
	Jimmy Wynn	cf	EX	0.70	0.89	0.70	0.65	0.74
	Bill Freehan	c	EX	0.70	0.88	0.55	1.09	0.45
184	Kent Hrbek	1b	FA	0.69	1.13	0.80	0.59	0.66
	#**Jim O'Rourke**	cf	NC	0.69	1.07	0.80	0.52	0.74
	Joe Sewell	ss	LB	0.69	0.99	0.65	0.73	0.68
	Stan Hack	3b	LB	0.69	0.67	0.70	0.69	0.68
	Phil Rizzuto	ss	PW	0.69	0.26	0.68	0.78	0.61
189	**Bobby Wallace**	ss	DB	0.68	0.94	0.48	0.81	0.75
190	Bobby Bonds	rf	EX	0.67	1.10	0.76	0.40	0.83
	Ken Griffey, Sr.	rf	FA	0.67	1.03	0.82	0.50	0.69
192	Bobby Veach	lf	DB	0.66	1.11	0.70	0.58	0.71
	Sal Bando	3b	EX	0.66	0.90	0.63	0.72	0.63
	Duke Farrell	c	NC	0.66	0.68	0.38	1.19	0.41
195	**Heinie Manush**	lf	LB	0.65	1.31	0.72	0.50	0.71
	Eddie Yost	3b	PW	0.65	0.63	0.63	0.68	0.63
	Stuffy McInnis	1b	DB	0.65	0.59	0.77	0.62	0.84
198	Dick Bartell	ss	LB	0.64	0.62	0.61	0.70	0.61
	Hughie Jennings	ss	NC	0.64	0.47	0.60	0.66	0.67
200	*George Hendrick*	cf	FA	0.63	1.19	0.70	0.59	0.58

Rank	Player	Pos	Era	Final Tot Z	Final Core Z	Era Tot Z	Pos Tot Z	Overall Tot Z
	Bill Skowron	1b	EX	0.63	0.52	0.83	0.36	0.70
202	*Larry Gardner*	3b	DB	0.62	0.76	0.52	0.76	0.59
	Willie Wilson	lf	FA	0.62	0.66	0.75	0.49	0.62
204	Dusty Baker	lf	FA	0.61	1.04	0.66	0.55	0.61
	Boog Powell	1b	EX	0.61	0.99	0.73	0.35	0.74
	Chet Lemon	cf	FA	0.61	0.90	0.65	0.59	0.60
	Elston Howard	c	EX	0.61	0.81	0.47	0.95	0.42
	Del Pratt	2b	DB	0.61	0.75	0.72	0.47	0.63
	#Billy Nash	3b	NC	0.61	0.66	0.54	0.77	0.53
	Lou Boudreau	ss	LB	0.61	0.46	0.56	0.70	0.58
	Wally Schang	c	LB	0.61	0.45	0.34	1.12	0.36
212	*Ken Singleton*	rf	FA	0.60	1.08	0.70	0.43	0.66
	Dave Kingman	lf	FA	0.60	1.01	0.70	0.59	0.51
	Joe Judge	1b	LB	0.60	0.67	0.76	0.29	0.76
	George J. Burns	lf	DB	0.60	0.65	0.64	0.47	0.69
216	Carl Furillo	rf	PW	0.59	1.07	0.62	0.56	0.60
	Rocky Colavito	rf	EX	0.59	1.03	0.67	0.33	0.76
	#Jack Glassock	ss	NC	0.59	0.59	0.57	0.56	0.64
219	**George Kell**	3b	PW	0.58	0.93	0.62	0.59	0.53
	George Scott	1b	EX	0.58	0.88	0.74	0.32	0.69
	Roy White	lf	EX	0.58	0.62	0.64	0.49	0.62
	Tim McCarver	c	EX	0.58	0.54	0.41	0.95	0.37
223	Lee May	1b	EX	0.57	1.16	0.71	0.31	0.68
	Greg Luzinski	lf	FA	0.57	1.11	0.64	0.48	0.61
	Toby Harrah	3b	FA	0.57	0.84	0.67	0.49	0.54
	Harvey Kuenn	rf	PW	0.57	0.78	0.61	0.68	0.43
227	*Gary Matthews*	lf	FA	0.56	1.11	0.59	0.49	0.60
	Cy Williams	cf	LB	0.56	0.99	0.57	0.55	0.56
	Jake Daubert	1b	DB	0.56	0.64	0.71	0.55	0.70
	John McGraw	3b	NC	0.56	0.51	0.45	0.77	0.46
	Dave Bancroft	ss	LB	0.56	0.29	0.53	0.62	0.54
232	Del Ennis	lf	PW	0.55	1.32	0.63	0.43	0.58
	Ben Chapman	lf	LB	0.55	0.68	0.60	0.50	0.55
	Maury Wills	ss	EX	0.55	0.67	0.46	0.77	0.42
	Harry Davis	1b	DB	0.55	0.51	0.58	0.58	0.78
236	#Arlie Latham	3b	NC	0.54	0.46	0.42	0.73	0.46
237	Doc Cramer	cf	LB	0.53	0.88	0.53	0.51	0.53
	Buddy Myer	2b	LB	0.53	0.77	0.48	0.64	0.47
	Frank White	2b	FA	0.53	0.76	0.53	0.60	0.47
	Deacon McGuire	c	NC	0.53	0.63	0.30	0.94	0.35

Rank	Player	Pos	Era	Final Tot Z	Final Core Z	Era Tot Z	Pos Tot Z	Overall Tot Z
	Cupid Childs	2b	NC	0.53	0.57	0.49	0.54	0.56
	Gene Woodling	lf	PW	0.53	0.55	0.55	0.44	0.59
	Jim Sundberg	c	FA	0.53	0.24	0.47	0.76	0.34
244	*Harold Baines	rf	FA	0.52	1.29	0.61	0.35	0.60
	*Julio Franco	ss	FA	0.52	1.13	0.47	0.72	0.36
	Tony Oliva	rf	EX	0.52	0.97	0.63	0.24	0.69
	*Joe Carter	rf	FA	0.52	0.86	0.66	0.38	0.53
	Elmer Flick	rf	DB	0.52	0.74	0.58	0.39	0.58
	Rick Monday	cf	EX	0.52	0.71	0.54	0.46	0.56
	*Tony Fernandez	ss	FA	0.52	0.51	0.54	0.65	0.38
	Fred Tenney	1b	DB	0.52	0.45	0.63	0.51	0.69
252	**Ernie Lombardi**	c	LB	0.51	1.11	0.23	1.05	0.25
	Ted Kluszewski	1b	PW	0.51	1.08	0.63	0.33	0.57
	Bobby Murcer	rf	EX	0.51	0.89	0.59	0.28	0.65
	Larry Doby	cf	PW	0.51	0.84	0.60	0.30	0.62
	Earle Combs	cf	LB	0.51	0.69	0.51	0.49	0.52
	Darrell Porter	c	FA	0.51	0.63	0.33	0.90	0.31
	Dick Groat	ss	PW	0.51	0.61	0.51	0.60	0.42
259	*Joe Adcock*	1b	PW	0.50	1.11	0.61	0.32	0.57
	Hack Wilson	cf	LB	0.50	0.89	0.47	0.50	0.52
	Richie Hebner	3b	EX	0.50	0.83	0.52	0.53	0.43
	John Anderson	lf	DB	0.50	0.67	0.61	0.47	0.42
	Garry Templeton	ss	FA	0.50	0.67	0.48	0.65	0.37
	*Andy Van Slyke	cf	FA	0.50	0.53	0.58	0.47	0.45
	Tommy Henrich	rf	LB	0.50	0.25	0.54	0.36	0.59
266	Jim Fregosi	ss	EX	0.49	0.77	0.38	0.75	0.33
	Jackie Jensen	rf	PW	0.49	0.65	0.53	0.46	0.47
	#*Mike Griffin*	cf	NC	0.49	0.52	0.55	0.34	0.58
269	*Kirk Gibson	lf	FA	0.48	0.70	0.53	0.39	0.50
	Bill White	1b	EX	0.48	0.64	0.65	0.22	0.56
271	Alvin Dark	ss	PW	0.47	1.02	0.43	0.59	0.38
	Thurman Munson	c	EX	0.47	0.87	0.29	0.84	0.29
	Rudy York	1b	LB	0.47	0.70	0.58	0.18	0.66
	*Gary Gaetti	3b	FA	0.47	0.67	0.55	0.34	0.53
	Travis Jackson	ss	LB	0.47	0.67	0.42	0.54	0.45
	Garry Maddox	cf	FA	0.47	0.60	0.51	0.45	0.46
	Lonnie Smith	lf	FA	0.47	0.40	0.53	0.41	0.48
	Joe Tinker	ss	DB	0.47	0.33	0.45	0.50	0.46
	Charlie Keller	lf	LB	0.47	0.14	0.49	0.37	0.54
280	*Tim Wallach	3b	FA	0.46	0.79	0.52	0.32	0.54

Rank	Player	Pos	Era	Final Tot Z	Final Core Z	Era Tot Z	Pos Tot Z	Overall Tot Z
	Bob Boone	c	FA	0.46	0.60	0.35	0.74	0.31
	Curt Flood	cf	EX	0.46	0.59	0.51	0.40	0.48
283	Willie Horton	lf	EX	0.45	1.16	0.45	0.35	0.54
284	Joe Kuhel	1b	LB	0.44	0.65	0.60	0.13	0.61
	Dummy Hoy	cf	NC	0.44	0.61	0.53	0.25	0.54
	Dave Lopes	2b	FA	0.44	0.61	0.46	0.50	0.37
	Harlond Clift	3b	LB	0.44	0.50	0.44	0.43	0.44
	Wally Pipp	1b	LB	0.44	0.34	0.58	0.13	0.61
	John Roseboro	c	EX	0.44	0.17	0.33	0.74	0.26
290	*Chili Davis	rf	FA	0.43	0.86	0.48	0.30	0.49
	Babe Herman	rf	LB	0.43	0.84	0.50	0.29	0.50
	#**Monte Ward**	ss	NC	0.43	0.65	0.47	0.34	0.49
	Johnny Callison	rf	EX	0.43	0.57	0.53	0.20	0.55
	#*Paul Hines*	cf	NC	0.43	0.55	0.53	0.29	0.47
	Dolph Camilli	1b	LB	0.43	0.53	0.54	0.14	0.60
	Ray Schalk	c	DB	0.43	0.19	0.13	0.95	0.20
297	Tommy Davis	lf	EX	0.42	0.96	0.44	0.32	0.48
	Felipe Alou	rf	EX	0.42	0.86	0.58	0.15	0.51
	Marty McManus	2b	LB	0.42	0.80	0.40	0.48	0.37
	Leo Cardenas	ss	EX	0.42	0.66	0.34	0.66	0.27
	*Willie McGee	cf	FA	0.42	0.64	0.49	0.36	0.42
	Heinie Zimmerman	3b	DB	0.42	0.63	0.38	0.55	0.32
	Roger Peckinpaugh	ss	DB	0.42	0.54	0.42	0.45	0.38
	*Tony Pena	c	FA	0.42	0.42	0.34	0.69	0.23
	Clete Boyer	3b	EX	0.42	0.13	0.45	0.41	0.38
306	Larry Doyle	2b	DB	0.41	0.77	0.50	0.31	0.43
	Dixie Walker	rf	LB	0.41	0.71	0.50	0.21	0.50
	Ron Fairly	1b	EX	0.41	0.69	0.52	0.14	0.56
	Dom DiMaggio	cf	PW	0.41	0.53	0.52	0.23	0.49
	Sammy West	cf	LB	0.41	0.49	0.41	0.45	0.38
	Jim Gilliam	2b	PW	0.41	0.48	0.42	0.39	0.41
312	Bill Madlock	3b	FA	0.40	1.01	0.48	0.29	0.42
	Ken Williams	lf	LB	0.40	0.72	0.46	0.28	0.45
	Sherm Lollar	c	PW	0.40	0.59	0.28	0.70	0.23
	Don Money	3b	EX	0.40	0.51	0.46	0.43	0.32
	George Kelly	1b	LB	0.40	0.47	0.51	0.13	0.56
	Roger Bresnahan	c	DB	0.40	0.44	-0.04	1.07	0.16
	#*Tom Brown*	cf	NC	0.40	0.43	0.50	0.20	0.49
	Frank Crosetti	ss	LB	0.40	0.06	0.33	0.46	0.40
320	Andy Pafko	cf	PW	0.39	0.81	0.52	0.19	0.47

Rank	Player	Pos	Era	Final Tot Z	Final Core Z	Era Tot Z	Pos Tot Z	Overall Tot Z
	Lloyd Waner	cf	LB	0.39	0.73	0.41	0.39	0.38
	Bob Meusel	lf	LB	0.39	0.66	0.42	0.31	0.44
	*Darryl Strawberry	rf	FA	0.39	0.52	0.48	0.23	0.45
	Roger Maris	rf	EX	0.39	0.46	0.52	0.10	0.55
	George H. Burns	1b	LB	0.39	0.43	0.52	0.08	0.56
	John Mayberry	1b	EX	0.39	0.38	0.55	0.13	0.49
327	#Hardy Richardson	2b	NC	0.38	0.77	0.41	0.31	0.43
	Walker Cooper	c	PW	0.38	0.76	0.18	0.73	0.23
	Steve Sax	2b	FA	0.38	0.51	0.42	0.42	0.30
	Hank Bauer	rf	PW	0.38	0.44	0.36	0.33	0.44
	Paul Blair	cf	EX	0.38	0.16	0.43	0.28	0.41
332	Roy Sievers	1b	PW	0.37	1.05	0.45	0.20	0.47
	#Ed McKean	ss	NC	0.37	1.04	0.39	0.36	0.36
	Rico Carty	lf	EX	0.37	0.83	0.40	0.28	0.43
	Jose Cardenal	cf	EX	0.37	0.69	0.39	0.31	0.42
	Roy Smalley, Jr.	ss	FA	0.37	0.49	0.30	0.56	0.24
	#George Gore	cf	NC	0.37	0.48	0.51	0.15	0.46
	Rick Ferrell	c	LB	0.37	0.38	0.18	0.80	0.15
	Phil Garner	2b	FA	0.37	0.38	0.38	0.38	0.34
	Augie Galan	lf	LB	0.37	0.35	0.43	0.27	0.41
341	Bobby Lowe	2b	NC	0.36	0.75	0.38	0.31	0.39
	George Grantham	2b	LB	0.36	0.51	0.29	0.49	0.29
	Kip Selbach	lf	NC	0.36	0.44	0.43	0.21	0.45
	Eddie Joost	ss	PW	0.36	0.17	0.33	0.49	0.26
	Willie Kamm	3b	LB	0.36	0.14	0.41	0.31	0.37
346	Pedro Guerrero	1b	FA	0.35	0.85	0.41	0.26	0.39
	Wally Berger	cf	LB	0.35	0.73	0.34	0.36	0.35
	#Denny Lyons	3b	NC	0.35	0.53	0.28	0.50	0.27
	Willie Jones	3b	PW	0.35	0.48	0.35	0.34	0.36
	#Ned Williamson	3b	NC	0.35	0.06	0.28	0.51	0.25
	Johnny Hopp	cf	PW	0.35	0.00	0.51	0.25	0.29
t373	**Chick Hafey**	lf	LB	0.31	0.52	0.36	0.21	0.38
t403	**Johnny Evers**	2b	DB	0.27	0.09	0.30	0.15	0.36
t408	**Frank Chance**	1b	DB	0.26	-0.10	0.23	0.19	0.35
t427	**Tommy McCarthy**	rf	NC	0.23	0.39	0.22	0.27	0.20
t446	**Ross Youngs**	rf	LB	0.20	0.20	0.26	0.08	0.27
t490	**Fred Lindstrom**	3b	LB	0.14	0.59	0.19	0.07	0.16

Index